Sex as a Pathway to the Divine

Tantra maintains that sex is a sacred rite and that the same glorious power that produced your body can be invoked and directed to take control of your destiny. All you need is an open mind, attention to the teachings, and a loving partner. To aid you in this virtual shortcut to spiritual evolution, Nik Douglas, who has studied under Indian physicians and Tantric adepts, has compiled this brilliant study of Tantra— the most authoritative and comprehensive volume available to the layperson.

SPIRITUAL SEX reveals everything about Tantra, from its manifestations in the past to the details of its current practices. All of Tantra's techniques for prolonged sexual excitement and heightened consciousness, for both men and women, are fully discussed, along with their most controversial aspects. Also included:

- A manual for Tantric sex—five principal love positions and five evolved ones, and secrets of breath, scent, sound, touch, gaze and sexual expression
- Oral pleasure as a path to enlightenment
- Sacred sex in the Near East, Egypt, Europe, and America
- A Jewish Kama Sutra and other Judeo-Christian sources
- The science of sexology from Havelock Ellis to Margaret Mead
- Tantric sex information on the Internet and the future of sexual enlightenment in the twenty-first century

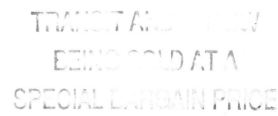

Other Books by Nik Douglas

Sexual Secrets: The Alchemy of Ecstasy (*with Penny Slinger*)

The Pillow Book

The Erotic Sentiment in the Paintings of China and Japan

The Erotic Sentiment in the Paintings of India and Nepal

The Book of Matan

Tantra Yoga

Tibetan Tantric Charms and Amulets

Karmapa: The Black Hat Lama of Tibet

SPIRITUAL SEX

SECRETS OF TANTRA
FROM THE ICE AGE TO
THE NEW MILLENNIUM

Nik Douglas

POCKET BOOKS

New York   London   Toronto   Sydney   Tokyo   Singapore

An *Original* Publication of POCKET BOOKS

POCKET BOOKS, a division of Simon & Schuster Inc.
1230 Avenue of the Americas, New York, NY 10020

Library of Congress Cataloging-in-Publication Data

Douglas, Nik.
    Spiritual sex : secrets of Tantra from the ice age to the new
millennium / Nik Douglas.
        p.   cm.
    Includes bibliographical references.
    ISBN 0-671-53739-3
    1. Sex—Religious aspects—Tantrism. 2. Tantrism. I. Title.
BL1282.842.D68   1997
613.9′6—dc21   97-12494
                                                          CIP

First Pocket Books trade paperback printing September 1997

10 9 8 7 6 5 4 3 2 1

POCKET and colophon are registered trademarks of
Simon & Schuster Inc.

Cover design by Dale Fiorillo
Front cover photos: top, courtesy of the author;
bottom, Arthur Tilley/FPG International
Text design by Stanley S. Drate and Patricia A. Marcinczuk/Folio Graphics Co. Inc.

Printed in the U.S.A.

This book is dedicated to those who give thanks for the spirituality that exists in each new day, in each breath, in each loving glance, in each embrace and each loving action. This book is dedicated to the Goddess in all women who is also in men, and to the God in all men who is also in women. This book is dedicated to spiritual lovers everywhere.

CONTENTS

2 THE ORIGINS OF TANTRA 21

3 THE NATURE OF TANTRA

4 TANTRA AND JUDEO-CHRISTIAN TRADITION

5 TANTRA IN THE WEST

6 TECHNIQUES FOR MASTERING TANTRIC SEX

231

7 THE MAGIC OF SPIRITUAL SEX

8 TANTRA IN THE TWENTY-FIRST CENTURY

9 TANTRA DATABASE

Tantra-Related Web Sites on the Internet   347

Of all we know of life, only in sexual love is there a taste of ecstasy. Nothing else in our life brings us so near to the limits of human possibilities, beyond which begins the unknown.

—P. D. Ouspensky, *A New Model of the Universe*

INTRODUCTION

MORE THAN sixty years ago, the eminent Swiss psychiatrist Carl Jung wrote:

> We are living undeniably in a period of the greatest restlessness, nervous tension, confusion, and disorientation of outlook. Among my patients from many countries, all of them educated persons, there is a considerable number who came to see me not because they were suffering from a neurosis but because they could find no meaning in their lives or were torturing themselves with questions which neither our philosophy nor our religion could answer.

Jung explains further:

> Every one of them has the feeling that our religious truths have somehow become hollow. Either they cannot reconcile the scientific and the religious outlook, or the Christian tenets have lost their authority and their psychological justification. People no longer feel redeemed by the death of Christ; they cannot believe—for although it is a lucky man who can believe, it is not possible to compel belief. Sin has become something quite relative: what is evil for one man is good for another. After all, why should not the Buddha be right too?

Jung wrote this more than half a century ago, yet his observations about people and their spiritual concerns are even more valid today. We need to experience and believe in spiritual reality more than ever before. We need to enjoy spiritual sustenance that relates to today's world. To do so, we need to free ourselves from guilt and superstition, give up judgmental constraints, and explore our authentic spiritual nature.

It has been my good fortune to have been brought up in a loving family, free from feelings of sexual or religious guilt. I had a good education, traveled widely, and immersed myself in different cultures. My own spiritual questioning about the meaning of life caused me to explore the world's different religious traditions:

> Who am I? What do I truly believe in? What is the purpose of my existence? How can I help my spiritual evolution?

These were the main questions to which I tried to find answers and that, over the years, remained relevant. No matter how my life evolved, these questions continued to recur.

I was brought up as a Christian and from an early age was exposed to Western "spiritualism" and occultism. I closely examined Rosicrucian teachings, Masonry, European alchemy, Theosophy, the works of George Gurdjieff and P. D. Ouspensky, as well as hypnotism and modern psychology. During many years of residing in the Middle East, I visited numerous sacred sites and museums, familiarizing myself with the tenets, texts, and esoteric traditions of Christian, Jewish, and Moslem cultures.

I studied Egyptology and archaeology so I could explore the evidence of past spiritual activities in evolved cultures. Convinced about the immortality of the soul, I looked to the East for advanced spiritual instruction. I traveled to India, seeking to experience its spiritual traditions firsthand and was fortunate to meet and be accepted by fine teachers. Over a ten-year period, I made numerous journeys through much of India, Nepal, and Southeast Asia, exploring the sacred sites and learning about the rich spiritual culture of the East. I learned how to do Yoga and how to meditate. I learned to read, write, and chant in Sanskrit and Tibetan; I learned the spiritual songs and secret rites and how to awaken and empower my own spirituality.

I spent much time with Yogis, pundits, Lamas, shamans, and medical doctors. All pointed me toward Tantra as *the* single all-encompassing spiritual tradition suited to the present time, a teaching that, instead of denying the senses, embraces them as potent tools for evolution and liberation. I was fortunate to be initiated into different Tantric traditions by the experienced and the wise. Since I returned to the West, I've been spreading the word about Tantra.

About twenty years ago, I was at dinner in a New York restaurant with an avant-garde group of people, artists, writers, and the like when the topic of discussion turned to the relationship, if any, between sex and spirituality. This was during the era of sexual experimentation, in the mid 1970s, before Acquired Immune Deficiency Syndrome (AIDS) was known.

Over dinner, I presented my views on the relationship between sex and spirituality, citing Oriental tradition and esoteric treatises to get my point across. I mentioned Tantra and this opened up a whole range of discussion.

Some of those present told me they already embraced Tantra as their spiritual authority, believing it to be a philosophy that allows for "total freedom of sexual expression." Others viewed Tantra as unsuited for Westerners, believing its teachings to be culturally alien and largely inaccessible.

I reminded my friends that much of what we think of as Western culture is really a mix of many different influences, many of which originated in the Middle and Far East. I pointed out that since Tantra deals practically with topics such as psychology, sexology, medicine, art, and science, it should not be viewed as inappropriate to modern times. I emphasized that as with any true science, mastery of Tantra can be expected to take both time and discipline. Powerful tools and teachings always need to be protected so they aren't misused.

After dinner, one of those present asked if I would write a book about Tantra and sex. He told me he had been involved with the marketing of the then-current best-seller *The Joy of Sex: A Gourmet Guide to Lovemaking* but was disappointed because the book did not address any of the spiritual or mystical aspects of sex, which were topics that interested him greatly. This dinner conversation led me to a publisher who commissioned a work from me that was published in 1979 as *Sexual Secrets: The Alchemy of Ecstasy*.

Nearly twenty years have passed since then. A whole new generation has emerged. Tantra is now well established on the world-wide New Age map, yet it is often misrepresented and misunderstood. This book is my latest attempt to correct the situation.

We are now approaching the beginning of the twenty-first century. Most of my generation have been through and seen a lot. We don't need to be told that it's okay to enjoy sex, we don't feel guilty when we explore a sexual fantasy, and we know we won't go to Hell on Judgment Day because we had a lustful thought. Nor do we need to be convinced about the existence of the human spirit or the possibility of refining or perfecting it. However, most of us would like to be guided by some signposts on the journey ahead.

We have experienced the sexual revolution, the nuclear arms race, the swinging sixties, drug and pop cultures, psychedelics, the Yuppie era, the wild seventies, the New Age, the selfish eighties, and economic and emotional upheavals. My generation has questioned intensively but has not always found the answers. We've torn down many of the institutions and values that our parents held sacred, but we have not yet found meaningful practical alternatives for all our social and spiritual needs.

Institutions such as worship, marriage, ethics, how to treat our elders, what to say to our children, and the like are no longer clearly defined, understood, or followed. Standards and expectations have changed. If we are to evolve successfully and survive through the twenty-first century, we need to establish new and meaningful paradigms by which to live.

In 1980, Marilyn Ferguson, author of *The Aquarian Conspiracy*, argued that while the "old" paradigm of human evolution saw changes happening "like a steady climb up a ladder," the "new" paradigm is of periodic leaps of evolution by small groups of people. This is in fact what has been happening over the past two hundred years or so, with radical spirituality as the driving force. This book tells as much of the story as I have been able to gather.

Culture is shaped by exceptional people, by charismatic leaders, by visionaries, and by thinkers—by people with the courage of their convictions. Many of my generation have been inspired by radical writings, by the works of authors such as D. H. Lawrence, Havelock Ellis, Margaret Sanger, Margaret Mead, Carl Jung, Aldous Huxley, W. Y. Evans-Wentz, Alan Watts, Heinrich Zimmer, Eric Neumann,

Mircea Eliade, Simone de Beauvoir, Robert Graves, Jack Kerouac, Allen Ginsberg, Henry Miller, Herman Hesse, Khalil Gibran, Richard Wilhelm, Lama Govinda, Timothy Leary, John Lilly, Kate Millett, Germaine Greer, Joseph Campbell, June Singer, Marija Gimbutas, Carlos Castañeda, Marilyn Ferguson, Clarissa Pinkola Estés, and many others who, in the twentieth century, explored and wrote about sexuality, human consciousness and spiritual evolution. We have also been inspired by the wisdom teachers of the past, by the poets, priests, priestesses, and other "spiritual artists." We have followed the lead of the radical, uncompromising, and creative stance of some of our pop-culture heroes.

My purpose in writing this book is to share what I have learned about sex, spirituality, and Tantra with as wide an audience as possible. My purpose is also to help define the new paradigm of spiritual behavior for the twenty-first century. My hope is that the view of sex as a spiritual sacrament presented in this book can become a positive force of hope and healing and liberation.

1 WHAT IS TANTRA?

The Tantras represent a philosophy comprehensive enough to embrace the whole of knowledge, a system of meditation which will produce the power of concentrating the mind upon anything whatsoever, and an art of living which will enable one to utilize each activity of body, speech and mind, as an aid to the path of Liberation.

—JE GAMPOPA

MOST PEOPLE are unclear about what Tantra really is and what it can do for you. Probably the most common view is that Tantra has some connection with Oriental religion, with uninhibited sex, and with the lovemaking positions and techniques outlined in the *Kama Sutra*, Hinduism's oldest sex manual. To some, Tantra is a free-love cult, a survival of the psychedelic sixties; to others, it's New Age spiritual sex therapy, part of the California lifestyle, a slice of 1990s pop culture. Tantra has also been viewed as a radical type of fine art, with erotic, abstract, and fetishist forms of expression. And it has been touted as a secret science and an occult art, a potent form of voodoo or magic involving secret sexual rites.

None of these views of Tantra are wrong outright, but none really explain what Tantra actually is. So what is Tantra? What does it mean? And, most important of all, what is its relevance to us today?

The word *Tantra* is Sanskrit, the sacred language of Hinduism. It derives from the root word *tan*, which translates as "to extend, expand, spread, continue, spin out, weave; to put forth, show, or manifest." Like the universe we inhabit, Tantra is continually expanding, spreading, and manifesting itself like a "cosmic weave,"

1

made up of different energies. We are part of this weave, as are our forefathers and foremothers, all life, and every type of energy and matter. This includes thoughts, actions, and all physical matter.

Tan also evokes concepts of continuity and succession, reminding us of our spiritual "immortality" and the seemingly endless cycle of lifetimes that define existence. It also brings to mind consciousness, which is constantly expanding, evolving from lifetime to lifetime.

Each of us is a living microuniverse or microcosm, inhabiting and intimately linked to the entire macrocosm or greater universe that surrounds us. This link between the microcosm and macrocosm of our existence is exquisitely expressed in the following ancient Hindu sacred text:

> As large and potent as the universe outside,
> Even so large and potent is the universe within our being.
> Within each of us are heaven and earth,
> The sun and moon, lightning and all the myriad of stars.
> Everything in the macrocosm is in this our microcosm.

> —*Chandogya Upanishad*

The outer universe contains traces of every thing and every being that has ever existed. It can be a fine guide on our evolutionary journey, provided we know how to access its data. This universe is naturally wise, vast, unlimited, and interconnected in every way.

Our inner universe also has a natural wisdom, and our cells contain traces of every memory and action in which we and our ancestors have participated. Our inner potential is also unlimited and expansive. Inner and outer, microcosm and macrocosm, spirit and matter, past and present, the heavens and the earth, these are the ingredients that make up the "weave" of Tantric reality.

Some Definitions of Tantra

Because Tantra is a mystical subject, it is nearly impossible to define. Even eminent scholars have had a hard time explaining what Tantra actually is. Mircea Eliade (1907–1986), the eminent Romanian-born professor of religious history, points to Tantra's semantic root for meaning. In his groundbreaking book, *Yoga: Immortality and Freedom* (1954), he wrote:

> It is not easy to define Tantrism. Among the many meanings of the word Tantra (root: tan, "extend," "continue," "multiply"), one concerns us particularly—that of "succession," "unfolding," "continuous process." A definition of Tantra would be *"what extends knowledge."*

Lama Anagarika Govinda's *Fundamentals of Tibetan Mysticism* (1960) deals primarily with Lamaism but includes the following poetic and comprehensive definition of Tantra:

> The word "Tantra" is related to the concept of weaving and its derivatives (thread, web, fabric, etc.) hinting at the interwovenness of things and actions, the independence of all that exists, the continuity in the interaction of cause and effect, as well as in spiritual and traditional development, which like a thread weaves its way through the fabric of history and of individual lives.

The different explanations of what Tantra actually is indicate its multifaceted nature. Tantra is a spiritual science, which means it is also mystical, weblike in its interconnectedness, the holistic wisdom link between ourselves and the universe we inhabit. Tantra is a continually unfolding and balanced interface, made up of both male and female energies. Every aspect of our past or present has been touched by these Tantric energies, which can be used to transform our life.

By embracing Tantra, we become more "real," more "complete." How? By recognizing and stimulating our inherent sensual spirituality, we discover parts of ourselves that have remained "asleep" or have been repressed. With Tantra, an energy is released that is evolutionary and "upwardly motivated." We can learn to use this energy for pleasure, for achieving our worldly goals, and for aiding our spiritual evolution.

Familiarity with Tantra can help a person to enjoy life to the fullest. It can help do away with guilt or fear, break down self-imposed or limiting cultural boundaries, and guide us in our search for solutions. Tantra teaches us to become familiar with our mystical nature, and when we do so, our boundaries expand. We enter into new domains of awareness. We become empowered, more fulfilled, and more perfect.

Traditional dictionary definitions of *Tantra* are revealing. A Sanskrit word, *Tantra* is sometimes translated as "leading principle, essential part, model, system, framework, doctrine, rule, theory, scientific work," also as "order, chief part, rule, authority, science, mystic works, magical formulas, means, expedient, stratagem, medicine." Finally, *a Tantra* is sometimes defined as "a type of mystical teaching set out mostly in the form of dialogs between a cosmic couple." Intimate insightful dialogs, between God and Goddess, Shiva and Shakti, the male and female Tantric adepts, were at times written down and became known as Tantras. Naturally, these dialogs, being intimate, included sexual secrets as well as many other fascinating topics.

Tantra Is Systematic and Scientific

Some Indian medical texts are also known as Tantras. Traditional Indian science, which covers topics ranging from higher mathematics, chemistry, and metallurgy to surgery, astronomy, and astrology, is viewed as Tantric if it is systematized and effective. The same applies to Indian occultism or magic, which is viewed as Tantric if it works in a scientific way, meaning if it is repeatable and reliable.

Tantra has been well tested over thousands of years, not in worldly laboratories but in the laboratories of the human body, by Yogi scientists and Tibetan Lamas who were not driven by commerce but by the earnest desire for spiritual knowledge and liberation. Their observations and insights have been passed down to us.

The sacred Hindu and Buddhist scriptures known as Tantras provide detailed instructions on a wide range of topics, including spiritual knowledge, technology, and science. Their content is often paradoxical. In Tantra, science and mysticism go hand in hand, as do sensuality and asceticism. Just as advanced scientific treatises are difficult for the layperson to comprehend, so traditional Tantras require adequate preparation before they can be properly understood.

Tantrics strive to know the unknowable, to expand and explore.

The systems or doctrines of Tantra, whether Hindu, Buddhist or otherwise, are inherently natural, derived from introspection and from interaction with nature. The magic of nature and the cosmic mysticism of the heavenly powers together form the fabric of Tantra.

Paradoxical, multifaceted, layered, operating on different levels simultaneously—yes, Tantra is all this: double meanings, hidden connections, hypermeanings, inherently unpredictable, surprising, promising, expansive, interwoven, enigmatic, potent, and always entertaining. Such is Tantra at its best.

In Tantra, Each Activity Can Be an Aid to Liberation

The quote at the beginning of this chapter is from Je Gampopa (1079–1135), a great Tibetan spiritual teacher, mystic, writer, and medical doctor whose principal disciples founded major schools of Tantra in the Buddhist tradition.

Je Gampopa, a disciple of the famous Tibetan Yogi and former Tantric sorcerer Milarepa (1052–1135), was renowned for his clarity of mind and deep analytical insight. His straightforward view of Tantras is as valid today as it was more than eight hundred years ago. His comprehensive definition reminds us that each activity "of body, speech, and mind" can be an aid to spiritual liberation. In his definition, sex is unquestionably included as an art of living that can empower spiritual evolution and liberation.

Each of us were born as a direct result of a sexual union and most of us spend our lives seeking sexual satisfaction. Tantra teaches that sex is the most natural of all urges and has the potential to effectively liberate us from the seemingly endless cycle of births and deaths. Tantra shows how sexual energy and the senses can be used as tools to help our spiritual evolution.

Sex as a Sacrament

The core philosophy of Tantra is that sex is a sacrament, a sacred rite, a spiritual act. Most people are unaware that sex was viewed as a sacrament by many early Christians as well as by medieval Jewish mystics, that sacramental sex was once at the core of many other ancient spiritual traditions, and that the sacraments of sex and its secrets, which lead to personal power and spiritual liberation, are accessible to us in the present time.

By viewing every act of sex as a spiritual rite or sacrament, we reconnect with the original source of our existence and empower our life with potent sacredness. Tantra teaches that the same power that brought about our existence, that produced our wondrous human body, can be invoked and directed to take control of our destiny and achieve anything imaginable.

Tantra: The "Mother" of Spiritual Belief

In ancient India, Yogis explored the interconnections between spirit and matter, reviewed the subtle psychology and physiology of mind and body, and brought together their insights into holistic systems that enabled them to shortcut the normally tedious process of spiritual evolution. They took a radical stance, questioned the nature of reality, and experimented on themselves, sometimes denying and other times indulging the senses. Eventually, some of these spiritual pioneers were able to perceive how the fabric of reality was woven and, by trial and error, found how to free themselves from mundane limitations. They discovered the spiritual secrets of the universe and became powerful. Some became mystics, magicians or Tantric sorcerers, spiritual teachers, seers, or saints. They discovered how to use their holistic insight into the nature of the universe as the means to convey spiritual power and liberation. What they had discovered was Tantra.

Basic Tantric practices can be found in the most ancient of spiritual belief systems. Unfortunately, with the advent of Christian missionary activity, many of the places where forms of Tantra were once practiced now have only traces of this knowledge. Africa, the home of humanity, the original motherland, is the best example of this phenomenon. Look closely at traditional African spiritual culture, such as the Orisa of Yoruba Nigeria or the Fang tribes of Gabon, and traces of Tantra become apparent. Belief in reincarnation, in the immortality of the human spirit, the spiritual law of cause and effect, divination, spirit possession, meditation, mystic power phrases, spells and amulets, the power of sacrifice, and the sacrament of sex are some of the Tantric tenets found in many of these mystically focused African cultures.

Hinduism teaches that the human spirit reincarnates until all karmas are resolved and God realization is attained. Like indigenous African spiritual cults, Hinduism teaches that divine beings or powers exist in unseen worlds and can be accessed by spiritual introspection. Among the various esoteric techniques used to achieve spiritual knowledge and liberation, Tantra is, in this materialistic age, said to be the most suitable and the most effective.

Why Tantra?

Why Tantra? Because we are living in a sensual and materialistic era. Because our senses and our desires drive us. And because Tantra is the only evolved spiritual discipline that uses our senses and our desires to achieve the goal of liberation. Most other spiritual traditions preach denial, repression, and sublimation of the senses. In today's world, true spirituality is acquired through wise participation in the gifts that have been given us, not by denying them.

Tantra teaches that the senses can be harnessed and used as a liberating energy, that they can be used as tools to help attain transcendental wisdom and enlightenment in this materialistic era, and that they can be used to shortcut the process of spiritual evolution. Tantra is a "sexual software," a "software of love" that makes use of the senses in the pursuit of spiritual liberation. Tantra's most potent tools are the sense organs: *the mind*, plus the skin, the eyes, ears, tongue, and nose. Our most potent activity is the sexual act.

Tantra is entirely relevant to the present needs of Western or westernized seekers desiring both sensual satisfaction and spiritual liberation. It offers a holistic way of interacting with the universe we inhabit, without denying any of the impulses that drive us. Tantra teaches how we can use sexual energy to take control of and transform consciousness.

Tantra is a radical approach to spiritual liberation, equally relevant to men or women, singles or couples. People from any religious or cultural background can progress their evolution by adopting a Tantric attitude and empowering their natural spirituality with the wisdom of Tantric teachings.

Tantra teaches that *every day* should be viewed as a new life, with new challenges and new potential for both worldly and spiritual fulfillment. By participating fully in the cosmic weave of day-to-day phenomena, we can fulfill our desires, evolve, and clear the way for spiritual liberation in this lifetime.

According to the teachings of Tantra, if we develop our wisdom and participate fully in life's day-to-day dealings *without attachment*, we can live out all our potential "future lifetimes" within a single lifetime and achieve spiritual liberation. To do this, we have to learn some secrets. One of the most important is how to consciously reverse the "normal" outward flow of energies in our physical, emotional, and mental being, how to become master or mistress of our inner universe.

Tantra: The Science and Art of Realization

Westerners first looked closely at Tantra toward the end of the nineteenth century. Those who were not put off by the mysticism, sexuality, and radical ideas found in Tantric texts were rewarded by a wealth of data pertinent to spiritual evolution.

One of the most illustrious Western initiates into Tantra during the early part of this century was John George Woodroffe (1865–1936), an Englishman who read law at Oxford University, became an advocate of the Calcutta High Court, served as legal council to the government of India, and was eventually appointed chief justice and knighted.

An interesting story tells how once, while attending to a case, Justice Woodroffe found it unusually difficult to concentrate and kept losing the thread of argument. On inquiring if anything unusual was happening in the vicinity, he learned that a strange-looking Yogi was seated on the steps outside the courthouse, muttering incantations.

Justice Woodroffe had the Yogi removed and found he was

again able to concentrate and could continue with the case. Fascinated by this incident, he made further inquiries and was told that the Yogi was a Tantric adept. This strange occurrence inspired Justice Woodroffe to study and practice Tantra, even though he remained a Catholic.

Justice Woodroffe published many books on Hindu Tantra, initially under the pen name Arthur Avalon, together with his wife and later in his own name. A scholar of Sanskrit, Bengali, and Hindu philosophy, Woodroffe was instrumental in popularizing Tantric studies during the early part of the twentieth century. In his book *Sadhana for Self Realization*, Woodroffe stated that Tantra is "the science as well as the art of realization," an extremely comprehensive and significant definition of Tantra. It puts Tantra into perspective, encompassing its wide spectrum of activities.

Other Westerners explored Tantra in association with Indian scholars and Tantric Yogis and Lamas, who could add oral tradition and secret meanings to clarify otherwise obscure or difficult references. Pundit Barada Majumdar was one such Indian scholar who taught Tantra to a select group of Westerners around the turn of the century. He described Tantras in the following way:

> The Tantras are an invaluable treasure embracing religion, theology, law, medicine, cosmology, rules regarding the elementals, and all branches of transcendental philosophy.

The fact that among the definitions of Tantra, concepts of continuation or uninterrupted succession are invoked speaks of a tradition of spiritual lineage, the guru–disciple system, whereby esoteric data was conveyed one-on-one.

Many Tantras have parts deliberately concealed and use a secret "twilight" or code language to convey esoteric topics. Such a scenario was especially necessary for conveying essential Tantric truths, which often can be interpreted in more than one way— literally or allegorically.

In the Tantric spiritual "software system," gurus are the "help" icon; they are the toll-free phone number. They can be accessed directly, if one is fortunate enough to connect with a Tantra teacher. They can also be accessed through focused ritual and prayer, communicating their truths through spiritual visions and dreams, and through the body of one's mystical sexual consort. This is discussed in more detail in a later chapter.

Different Manifestations of Tantra

TANTRA: A MYSTICAL YOGA THAT MAKES US MORE COMPLETE

Tantra, in one of its many forms, has evolved as a mystical form of Yoga. In 1939, Theos Bernard (1908–1947), the American scholar, attorney, medical doctor, and Tantric initiate, wrote in his important book *Heaven Lies within Us:*

> The Tantras dealt with every subject, from the doctrine of the origin of the world to the laws which govern society and have always been considered as the repository of esoteric beliefs and practices, particularly those of the Spiritual Science, Yoga, the key to which has always been with the initiate and only passed on by word of mouth.

Tantra or Tantric Yoga is also sometimes referred to as ''the science and mystic art of Kundalini Yoga.'' This reference to Kundalini Yoga connects Tantra with the evolutionary spiritual energy known in Hindu teachings as Kundalini, conceived of as a serpentine inner goddess embodying raw sexual power.

Kundalini, literally meaning ''coiled pool of female energy,'' is normally in a dormant state at the base of the spine but when stimulated, rises up, striving for union with the male consciousness principle, located in the head. Kundalini Yoga is a special Tantric branch of Yoga that aims to bring about such inner union, which in turn leads to spiritual evolution. This is explained in more detail later.

TANTRA AND TIBETAN BUDDHISM

There has been an evolving American interest in Buddhism since the middle of the nineteenth century. Initially, this interest evolved through the American transcendentalist movement, some of whose members organized translations of Buddhist texts. The Theosophical

Society progressed Buddhist studies, but it was not until the 1950s that interest in Buddhism really began to become widespread among radical American thinkers.

Alan Watts (1915–1972) was one of the early Buddhist pioneers in America. He practiced and promoted Zen, an esoteric Tantric form of Buddhism that evolved in Japan. As it emerged, the American beatnik movement of the 1950s also gravitated toward Zen Buddhism, finding its zany philosophy paradoxical yet its highly artistic lifestyle attractive.

When the Dalai Lama escaped Tibet in 1959 and set up his government in exile in northern India, more than a hundred thousand Tibetan refugees followed him. Some were resettled in the West, mostly in Europe, Canada, and America. Once Tibetan refugees reached America, Lamas, monks, nuns, monasteries, temples, and meditation centers soon followed. With encouragement from the Dalai Lama and from Western converts to Tibetan Buddhism, America became the promised land for Buddhist teachings.

Tibetan Buddhism is inherently Tantric, filled with occultism and magic. In Tibetan culture, Buddhas have consorts and are frequently depicted in sexual union. Tibetan Buddhism has peaceful and wrathful icons and is loaded with rituals that seem very exotic to Westerners. It can seem almost Catholic in its outer appearance, filled with pomp and ceremony, creating a spiritually charged atmosphere in which psychic or transcendental experiences can easily be triggered.

Reincarnated lamas; rich silk brocade banners; myriads of images of deities and Buddhist saints; huge bundles of burning incense; high altars laden with extraordinary offerings; thousands of lit butter lamps; sonorous chants; the sound of long horns, oboes, cymbals, gongs, bells, and drums; elaborate rituals; the distribution of sacraments, holy pills, sacred threads—all are very awe inspiring, compelling to many Westerners in search of alternate spiritual disciplines.

Tibetan Buddhist Tantra has both exoteric and esoteric forms. Unlike traditional Hindu Tantric teachings, which are conveyed intimately after required preparation, many Tibetan Tantric initiations are often given en masse in group "spiritual empowerments," known as *wongs*, rather like the Catholic mass.

Chögyam Trungpa (1939–1989), a reincarnate high Lama and teacher of Tantra, was among the first Tibetans to become established in the West. In the early 1960s, he founded a Buddhist monastery in Scotland and subsequently set up centers in Colorado, upstate New York, and elsewhere. Trungpa was the first "modern" Tibetan Lama of his sect, openly promoting Tantric sex as a Buddhist sacramental rite. By his example, he was largely responsible for transforming the Western view of Buddhist Tantra from a purely intellectual meditative exercise into a practical, and at times sexual, experience. Naturally Trungpa's teachings and radical lifestyle have been viewed as worrisome by orthodox Buddhists. However, never bothered by stifling convention, Trungpa lived his life in an authentic Tantric manner.

Many other Tibetan teachers of Tantra have visited the West during the past thirty years or so. They include the leaders of the four main sects of Tibetan Buddhism: the *Nyingmapa* or "old" tradition, which allows its lamas to marry; the *Kargyudpa* or "secret" yogi tradition, which allows its lamas "mystic" consorts; the *Sakyapa* or "hereditary" tradition, in which spiritual lineage passes down to direct genetic offspring, and the *Gelugpa* or "reformed" tradition, which requires celibacy. Dudjom Rinpoche, Gyalwa Karmapa, Sakya Trizin, and the Dalai Lama, the respective leaders of these four main sects of Tibetan Buddhism, have all visited America and given spiritual teachings. All of them, as well as other high Tibetan Lamas representing their spiritual lineages, have imparted Tantric empowerments and initiations to their Western followers. This has led to ever-increasing interest in Tibetan Tantra in the West.

HINDU TANTRA AND THE WEST

Since the early 1960s, a steady stream of Western travelers have made their way to India and the surrounding countries, seekers looking for knowledge or spiritual experiences unavailable in the West. Some have been fortunate enough to connect with genuine spiritual teachers and learn about Hindu Tantra firsthand.

In modern India, though orthodox Hinduism is loaded with Tantric symbolism and ritual, it is rare to come across Hindu Tantrics openly practicing their faith. The influence of prudish Victorian values on the average middle-class English-speaking Hindu is still very strong. Modern Hindus are generally puritanical about sex and feel uncomfortable discussing occult subjects. Tantra is largely a taboo subject to most modern Hindus, a subject to joke or tell anecdotes about, perhaps, but it is rare to find modern Hindus willing to open up about their Tantric leanings or experiences. In India, Tantra is kept in the closet.

Hindu Tantric teachings have traditionally been conveyed only through hard-won initiations in a guru-disciple, teacher-pupil system. Unlike Tibetan Buddhism, in which public mass initiations or spiritual empowerments occur, the secrets of Hindu Tantra are still generally transmitted one-on-one. Hindu Tantric yogis, sometimes known as *Siddhas*, tend to keep their spiritual secrets closely guarded. They usually require disciples to prove their worth by years of service and by putting their spiritual resolve through a series of tests.

NEO-TANTRIC CULTS

Over time, Tantric ideals evolved and were adulterated further. In 1964, Maharishi Mahesh Yogi introduced Westerners to a simple form of Hindu spiritual practice that became known as transcendental meditation (TM). The Beatles became his most famous initiates and TM became linked to pop culture. In this simple meditation technique, mantras or spiritual power words are given to initiates, commonly after payment of a fee. The TM initiate is instructed to repeat these mantras over and over, invoking their transcendental power to protect, purify, transform, and spiritualize consciousness.

TM is essentially a Tantric technique that normally requires the would-be initiate to be adequately prepared. However, even without proper preparation, repetitions of spiritual power words or phrases can effectively focus, reinforce, and refine consciousness, bringing about positive personality changes. Though not a spiritual panacea, TM can produce positive results quite rapidly and can offer a "Tantric shortcut" to the attainment of personal spiritual power.

Since the sixties, transcendental meditation has penetrated deep into Europe and America. The TM movement has its own campus, thousands of trained meditation teachers, and a huge number of practitioners. In recent years, it has branched out into Ayurveda, the indigenous Indian medical system. What is not generally recognized or promoted is transcendental meditation's roots in ancient Tantric meditation techniques.

In the late sixties, Kundalini Yoga began to be popularized in America, largely through the efforts of the Indian Sikh teacher Yogi Bhajan, who founded the 3HO organization and established many spiritual communities. Kundalini Yoga is a Tantric type of discipline that aims to release latent sexual energy within the body, channeling and transforming it into spiritual illumination by physical and mental processes. This type of Tantra Yoga can be disruptive as well as creative; tapping into a normally latent and very potent source of power in the human psyche, without due care and loving guidance, can cause psychological and emotional havoc.

Kundalini Yoga requires considerable preparation, discipline, and supervision to achieve proper results. Correctly practiced, Kundalini Yoga awakens the latent genius within every being, speeds up the natural but normally tedious process of spiritual evolution, and confers divine radiance and illumination.

Siddha Yoga, which is more focused on occult matters, was introduced to America in the late sixties and early seventies by devotees of Swami Muktananda (1908–1982). This charismatic Hindu Siddha teacher acquired spiritual powers (*siddhi*) from Tantric initiation by Nityananda (died 1961) and from prolonged periods of austerity. His highly organized Siddha Yoga Dham of America (SYDA) now has tens of thousands of adherents worldwide. Two of Muktananda's American associates, Albert Rudolph (1928–1973) and Franklin Jones (born 1939), eventually formed their own cults.

Albert Rudolph, who had been a follower of the Indonesian mystic Pak Subud, became known as Swami Rudrananda (''Rudi'' to his closest followers) and Franklin Jones became known as Free John, Bubba Free John, Da Free John, Da Love-Ananda and, most recently, Da Avabhasa. Rudolph and Jones both established extensive spiritual communities.

Both Rudi and Free John developed their cults along Tantric lines while advancing their own spiritual agendas. Rudi started several neo-Tantric ashrams, the principle one in the Catskills, New York, area. He was killed in a plane crash, but his cult lives on. Da

Avabhasa currently has his principle ashrams, known as the Free Daist Communion, in California and Hawaii. His main base is on Naitauba, a private island off Fiji, where he lives with his wives, children, and intimate devotees. He exemplifies the Tantric ideal of "god-man," living in an unconventional style while maintaining close contact with the day-to-day functioning of his ashram.

Bhagwan Sri Rajneesh (1931–1990) opened his ashram in Poona, India, in the early 1970s and offered instant transformation of ordinary persons into renunciate *sannyasi* monks or nuns. His ashram also offered "Tantric" initiations, workshops, and seminars.

Bhagwan promoted the concept of Tantra as a spiritual psychotherapy involving catharsis of the senses and was hugely successful in catching the imagination of many spiritual seekers. For a while, Tantra à la Rajneesh became extremely fashionable.

Rajneesh offered everything Westerners had imagined Tantra to be: a free-love cult with the promise of enlightenment, an exciting radical community, and the opportunity to rise up in the ashram hierarchy and become a spiritual teacher. With Bhagwan in command, the Rajneeshees' practices of spiritual sex seemed to take on a new social relevance for a while. Orthodox Hindus, however, were shocked, and there were many attempts to close down activities at the Poona ashram. Then Bhagwan, later known as Osho, traveled to the West and established a 64,000-acre ashram near Antelope, Oregon.

Rajneesh slipped comfortably into the role of the "Tantric messiah." He published hundreds of volumes, mostly transcriptions of his talks on a wide range of subjects delivered to his ashram audience. His devotees, dressed in their uniform colors, wearing beads and his picture, roamed everywhere, spreading his neo-Tantric philosophy and marketing the numerous ashram products. Largely because of Rajneesh, Tantra reemerged as a New Age cult in the 1970s and 1980s.

Since Rajneesh's death, his following has continued to grow. The Poona ashram has been transformed into the Osho Commune International (OCI), which offers a New Age and neo-Tantric curriculum of activities for paying "spiritual tourists." More than 50,000 visitors passed through OCI last year.

Another neo-Tantric cult leader who has been able to attract a substantial following is Frederick Lenz (born 1950), for a while known as Atmananda, now better known as Zen Master Rama. Originally a recruiter for Sri Chinmoy, a Hindu guru who ran an ashram in Queens, New York, Lenz started his own cult in the early 1980s, initially based in California. Calling his philosophy Tantric mysticism, he focused his students on computer programming. He later formed Vishnu Systems, a computer software development company.

Lenz ran seminars and consultancy sessions with neo-Tantric themes. Rama Seminars, National Personal and Professional Seminars, Advanced Systems, and Infinity Plus Consulting are the names of some of Lenz's ventures. Accusations of mind control, excessive materialism, and his alleged sexual escapades created a spate of negative publicity. He moved his cult to New York and Chicago. His recent successful book, *Surfing the Himalayas*, which has an imaginative support site on the Internet, and his focus on software development are indications of how far neo-Tantra has evolved.

Many Hindu Yogis and Swamis have visited America since the late sixties. Because of bad publicity, usually focused on suspected sexual impropriety and material acquisitiveness, many Westerners have become turned off of both traditional Indian and Western neo-Tantric gurus, finding them too enigmatic and paradoxical to understand.

Many Indian spiritual teachers haven't acted the way their followers *imagine* they should. The common complaint is that they promote asceticism and celibacy as spiritual ideals but follow worldly and sensual lifestyles themselves. In the West, much damage has been done to the public perception of Hinduism and Tantra because of this recurrent phenomena.

The situation has come about mainly because most Westerners have expectations influenced by their Judeo-Christian upbringing, which generally views both sexual activity and material acquisitiveness as nonspiritual. However, in the Tantric tradition, such activities are not incompatible with spiritual life. They are simply viewed as textures. Provided the teacher delivers the teachings authentically and effectively, it is irrelevant whether he or she lives a hedonistic lifestyle.

TANTRA IN THE NEW AGE

During the 1980s and early 1990s, the popularized teachings of traditional Hindu and Buddhist Tantra gradually became merged with those of pagan-inspired Western cults such as Wicca and "Magick," and even with forms of Sufism and the teachings of native American Indians. Tantra was expanded, redefined, and hybridized as an all-encompassing psychedelic, sexomagical, free-form, hedonistic faith.

As the New Age manifested, traditional Tantra was transformed into a Tantra for the masses, a neo-Tantric cult of sensual pleasure with a spiritual flavor. Because of its radical sexual and social stance, Tantra is well on the way to becoming a pop religion. For many people, from the sixties generation onward, Tantra has totally replaced discarded Judeo-Christian beliefs.

Many have jumped on the Tantric bandwagon, some qualified by initiation and years of spiritual practice, others from attending a few seminars. There are now New Age Tantric priests and priestesses, a quarterly publication (*Tantra: The Magazine*), Tantra home pages and Web sites, and proposals for Tantric temples and festivals.

New Age or neo-Tantra is still evolving and will undoubtedly claim its place in the world culture of the twenty-first century. I take this to be a positive phenomenon, requiring input from traditional sources of spiritual knowledge. I am particularly encouraged by the sudden surge of Tantra and Tantra-related topics on the Internet. An address list of some Tantra Web sites and links is included in Chapter 9 (Tantra Database), where I discuss some of the implications and offer suggestions about how to access and learn from Tantric topics on the information superhighway.

TANTRA IN THE DECADENT ERA

More than one thousand years ago, Asian spiritual teachers told of a coming decadent materialistic era, known as the Fourth Age or the *Kali Yuga*. This is the last in a cycle of eras, beginning with the Golden Age of the archaic past. A Buddhist Tantric text defines the *Kali* or Dark Age of Iron as follows:

There is no relief from ever-increasing egoism.
Corrupt and selfish people become leaders.
New and incurable diseases manifest.
Iron birds rule the skies.
Clothing fashions change frequently.
Butchers and murderers rule countries.
Priests and spiritual leaders become robbers.
Yogis become traders and shopkeepers.
Impostors claim psychic powers.
Sacred traditions are forgotten.
Every person must carry a weapon.
Rains are out of season.
Earthquakes, fires, tornadoes, and floods wreak havoc.
Communal unity is lost.

—*Padmasambhava terma*, an esoteric Tibetan Buddhist text

Sound familiar? Esoteric Hindu teachings explain that traditional spiritual disciplines such as denial of the senses, austerities, and Vedic rites, which worked well in a different era, are no longer effective, whereas Tantric practices offer quick and reliable results. An authoritative Hindu text puts the situation very succinctly:

In this Age, Tantric practices are efficacious
And produce immediate fruit.
Success is achieved by Tantric worship alone.
No other path is there to salvation and happiness
Like that shown by the Tantras,
Which give both happiness and liberation.

—*Mahanirvana Tantra*

As the original form of religious expression, Tantra teaches how the senses can be harnessed as a liberating spiritual power. Tantra is uncompromising, antibourgeois, radical. Rather than denying the senses, Tantra teaches how they can be used as tools to help attain spiritual power and enlightenment in this materialistic era.

TANTRA AT THE PRESENT TIME

Perceptions change with time. We are currently living in an era when data flashes across the globe in microseconds, when computer memory rules much of our lives, and when success in business can at times be determined by the operating speed of our central processing unit, our modem, and our band width. We are connected through a myriad of ethereal data pathways that reach throughout our immediate universe. We are all connected, yet most of us are spiritually disconnected.

We've become more and more removed from reality, from our body, from our true emotions, and from our natural spirituality. Communication between men and women is breaking down. Many of us are becoming emotional and spiritual paupers. This is a situation that Tantra can help fix.

Our bodily "hardware" is desperately in need of spiritual "software," of new spiritual programming. Tantra can best be viewed as an extremely well-tested spiritual software designed specifically for this time, software that, when correctly implemented, imparts worldly happiness and spiritual liberation this very lifetime. Happiness and liberation—what more could one really want?

TANTRA: THE OLDEST AND MOST NATURAL RELIGION

In the late nineteenth century, the first Western Tantric initiates viewed Tantra as the oldest and most natural religion, providing a spiritual system that offered the shortest and safest path to mastery of nature's sacred phenomena. Bold statements indeed. At the time, the term *oldest religion* meant animism, paganism, and by extension, phallicism and fertility rites.

In the next chapter, we'll explore the archaic origins of Tantra as the oldest and most natural religion, from the very beginnings of art and human culture through the emerging great civilizations of ancient India, Mesopotamia, Egypt, and Greece. We'll see how the threads of Tantra were woven on the loom of world culture, connecting East with West, south with north. We'll recognize Tantra in traditional African culture as well as in the archaeology of pagan Europe, in the sacred marriage rites of archaic Sumeria, and in the mysticism of ancient Egypt. We'll explore the symbolism and belief systems of Tantra, the oldest and most natural spiritual lifestyle.

We'll check out the first Tantric art, the sexual symbols, the evidence of archaeology. And we'll discover how people of power came to hold that power. We'll explore the evolution and use of magical language, seeing how it can be relevant today in our own spiritual lives.

We'll find out about the first farming communities and how Tantra emerged as a mystical spiritual practice connected to life, death, fertility, rebirth, and generation. We'll encounter the earliest erotic masterpieces, touch on matriarchal cultures, and examine some fascinating magical communities of old Europe. We'll look at and compare these long-lasting great civilizations sharing common spiritual beliefs. We'll explore the high cultures of ancient Egypt and Mesopotamia and trace their interconnecting Tantric threads, leading to the meaning of archaic religious rites and sexual beliefs and practices.

We'll get to know about holy harlots, sacred marriage rites, about Tantra in archaic India, mystic seals, and dancing girls and discover hidden sensual sculptural arts never before seen or published in the West. We'll recover the original ''loom'' of Tantra in archaic Indian tribal society and visit the Temple of the Sacred Vulva, reflecting on how we can apply *her* truths to empower our Tantric awareness as we prepare ourselves for participation in the sacraments of sex.

We'll also explore the meaning of paganism and its relationship to Tantra. We'll even take a look at the Greek philosophers Pythagoras, Plato, and Aristotle, who shared the Tantric view of the natural spirituality of sex. We'll read about Alexander the Great's amazing experiences with a Tantric Yogi and learn about the mysteries of Eleusis, goddess cults, secret initiatory rites, Zarathushtra, the magi, and the interconnections between all these topics and Tantra. And we'll learn how and when the first written Tantras, which fully documented the ancient rites and practices of spiritual sex, came to be.

2 THE ORIGINS OF TANTRA

The Tantra is the oldest religion in the world and is to be found in all sacred scriptures, and in literary records of the earliest denizens of the earth. Instead of fearing, it loves all philosophy, all sciences: it is a natural religion.

—KENNETH SIEBERT LEIGHTON

The Evolutionary Journey

Modern humans are a veritable "rainbow coalition" of different genetic material and behavioral and cultural patterns. Why is this relevant to the orgins of Tantra? Because traces and memories of our most ancient origins still exist within our cells and psyche and can be accessed by our consciousness. Because we need to understand the origins of our feelings about certain symbols and rituals. And because our evolutionary journey is very much a part of our total being and still needs to be completed. Rather than denying or ignoring the clues of the past, we should explore how elements of Tantric practices were developed, passed on, and incorporated by successive civilizations, from the Ice Age to the Golden Age of Egyptian, Greek, and early European cultures.

This journey into the past, to find Tantric origins and understand its evolution, must be made. For too long, we have neglected to look at the evidence of the archaic origins of Tantra in any detail. Though the archaeological record is far from complete, enough has survived of Tantric activities in various ancient societies for us to surmise that Tantra is an archaic teaching once common to all human spiritual cultures.

The threads of Tantra have been intricately interwoven through the worlds of ancient Egypt and Mesopotamia, through the cultures of Africa and the Middle East, across pagan Europe and into archaic India. Tantra has touched and transformed spiritual life in Tibet, China, Japan, and other surrounding countries. Today, Tantra has new relevance, uniting the past with the present, inspiring and guiding. As we shall see in this chapter, the spiritual fabric of Tantra has been present where we might least expect it.

In the Beginning

Neanderthals (*Homo sapiens neanderthalensis*) appeared at least one hundred thousand years ago. They built the first houses—simple circular huts with hearths—wore clothes of animal skins, made sophisticated stone tools, and cared for their dead, apparently believing in an afterlife. Almost fifty thousand years later, Cro-Magnon humans (*Homo sapiens sapiens*) first appeared. Their average brain size was larger than that of most modern humans and they were also taller and more robust. These people made exquisite flint tools, played music, wore tailored animal-skin clothes, lived in cave shelters and large skin-tented huts, made boats, and fished and hunted in groups. They used bows and arrows and created remarkably fine cave paintings and carvings. They also noticed and recorded the cycles of time and performed religious ceremonies.

Traces of observations made by Cro-Magnon people, scratched on rocks, bones, or wood and painted or engraved on cave walls, have survived at sites from France to Siberia. The original intent of many of these marks has now been unraveled; seemingly meaningless scratches have been revealed, in many instances, to be precise notational markings of a calendrical type, linked to the progression of time and the seasons, the onset of specific cultural activities, and, of course, sexual awareness.

The human life cycle, from the sexual act through pregnancy, birth, growing up, maturity, and death, must have been a major topic of thought and communication since the dawning of consciousness. Women's menstrual cycles; seasonal changes of plants; migrations of animals, birds, and fishes; and the patterns of tides and weather were all obvious enough to be noticed and recorded for posterity. Caves and rock shelters were ideal fixed locations for ob-

THE ORIGINS OF TANTRA

serving recurring solar and lunar cycles such as positions of the sun throughout the year, phases of the moon, and awe-inspiring eclipses.

Female Figurines and Sexual Depictions

Much has been written in recent years about Ice Age female figurines and rock carvings, some of which date back at least twenty-five thousand years. Corpulent "mother goddess" sculptures have been recovered from Ice Age sites in Italy, Spain, Germany, Austria, Czechoslovakia, Hungary, Bulgaria, the Ukraine, the Middle East, and Siberia.

These sculptures celebrate the birth-giving function of woman and are probably connected to initiatory rites of fecundity and renewal. It is unclear whether an actual personified goddess is implied by such sculptures.

Probably the best known is the so-called Venus of Laussel, found in the Dordogne, France. Carved in relief on a rock face, this sculpture depicts a heavily built, naked, faceless female with large buttocks and pendulous breasts, her feet together. She holds her left hand on her stomach and her right hand holds up a bull or buffalo horn engraved with thirteen notational marks, interpreted as the thirteen months comprising a lunar year.

The single horn may also represent a container for liquids, most likely of an intoxicating type, as with such ceremonial drinking vessels still used in tribal Africa and elsewhere. The whole figure of the Venus of Laussel was originally colored with red ocher, a Tantric symbol of menstrual blood, and

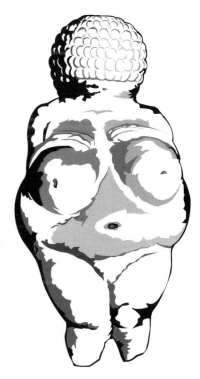

Limestone Venus of Willendorf figurine.
Paleolithic Gravettian culture (Naturhistorisches
Museum, Vienna, Austria)

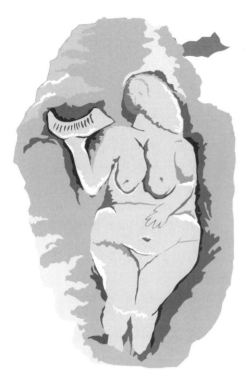

Stone relief carving of Venus of Laussel. Upper Paleolithic period, circa 20,000 B.C.E. (From the Dordogne, South of France; discovered in 1912)

most likely represents a rebirth goddess linked to a calendric myth involving horned animals and the partaking of a liquid sacrament.

At the French Paleolithic site known as Aigle-sûr-l'Anglin, exquisite bas-relief carvings have survived. They depict sensuous female torsos with vaginas as the main focus of the composition. Mystic concepts of rebirth and renewal evolved through such icons of the body or sex of woman, linked to lunar phases, the ''horns'' of the moon, the seasons, and to certain plants and totemic animals.

A relief carving in a cave at Laussel has left us with probably the earliest representation of a couple making love. And at Isturitz in southwestern France, a Paleolithic etching on bone has been recovered that depicts a rather heavyset woman with pendulous breasts seemingly being adored by a man who holds both hands together as if in worship.

Paleolithic etching on bone, depicting a corpulent woman wearing necklace and ankle bracelet being adored by a man with facial hair. He wears a necklace and bracelet. (From Isturitz, Basses-Pyrénées, France; illustration after Marshak)

Sexual Symbols and Magical Language

It was during the Paleolithic era of the Ice Age that the foundations of magic and mysticism were established, with sex as the cornerstone. In this era, sex was undoubtedly a spiritual mystery. The solar orb, with its warm, life-sustaining rays of light and energy, was among the first spiritual symbols, as was the hearth on which meats, roots, and other foods were cooked. Spiritual concepts such as burnt offerings made to ancestors, heroes, gods, and goddesses—by placing a portion of food in the fire—first emerged in such cultural settings. These "pagan" concepts are still part of the living practice of Tantra. Volcanoes must also have been very impressive to early humans and probably led to ideas about the existence of a powerful underworld.

Fire in the sky, fire under earth, the hearth—all were potent early spiritual symbols. The cool mystic light of the full moon and the horn-shaped dark lunar phases were other archaic symbols derived from nature, linked by association of shape to the horns of animals. People undoubtedly made the further connection between the growth of animal horns, animal mating rituals, and the onset of certain seasons.

The rich symbolic sexual content of Ice Age art is evident in the proliferation of early icons depicting both female and male genitalia. Vaginas were stylized as triangles with a slit, ovals with a slash or dot, and especially as seedlike shapes with a central division and a clitoris "sprout." Vagina stylizations were further developed as tri-lines (three parallel lines). All these ancient symbolic representations of female power and potency are still in use in Tantric tradition.

In Ice Age art, the penis was depicted quite realistically, with a slit or mouth at the end, or abstractly as a fingerlike shape or as a type of plant with a head. Examples exist of penile shapes emitting lines or dots, apparently meant to represent sperm. There are also baton-type phallic carvings done in horn or bone, often bearing notational marks.

Some carved phallic batons may have been used as dildos or artificial phalluses, sacred objects used as part of sexual rites. A re-markable double dildo carved from an antler was recovered from the

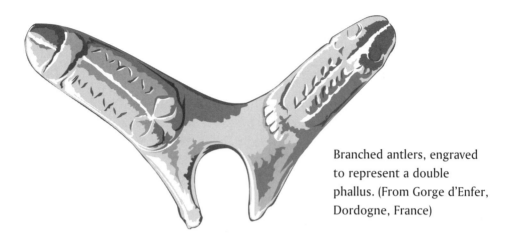

Branched antlers, engraved to represent a double phallus. (From Gorge d'Enfer, Dordogne, France)

Ice Age Gorge d'Enfer site in France. It is likely that such artificial phalluses were used in sexual initiations or magical rites. Such usage has been recorded in some traditions of Indian Tantra, in the Shinto cults of Japan, and in African tribal societies. In these cultures, phalluses and phallic symbols served important roles in ceremonial magic.

Witches in the Batcave: A Neolithic Coven

Signs of ancient ceremonial magic were part of an extraordinary find in the middle of the nineteenth century at a Neolithic cave site in Grenada, Spain, known as the Cave of Bats. Exploration of the entrance area revealed three skeletons, one wearing the remains of a crown and dressed in a woven grass tunic. Deeper into the cave, archaeologists discovered twelve skeletons sitting in a circle around a central skeleton of a woman wearing a leather tunic or dress.

Beside the skeletons were signs of a magical ceremony: bags filled with food remains; containers filled with opium poppy heads, flowers, and amulets; and poppy heads and seeds scattered all over the cave floor.

The evidence suggests that a matriarchal initiatory ceremony had taken place, with an intoxicating brew made of opium poppy heads being shared by all present. Presumably, the central female figure in the center of the circle of twelve celebrants was a priestess or "witch." The crowned woman wearing the straw skirt, at the entrance to the cave, most likely represented the Great Goddess, and the remains of two persons found with her were her spiritual attendants.

The circle of twelve persons plus the central figure found in the Bat Cave may have together symbolized the thirteen lunar months comprising a year, just as the marks on the horn drinking vessel held by the "Venus of Laussel" stone carving have been interpreted.

Clearly, the find at Cave of Bats was the remains of some type of archaic coven, a gathering of pagans involved in a religious rite involving opium, used for its consciousness-altering properties. In this particular instance, the dose of opium tea may have been over-estimated, causing the death of everyone.

Opium poppy heads also figure prominently in sacred art from later periods, such as the Minoan culture of ancient Crete, some thirty-five hundred years ago. Paintings and statuettes from Minoan culture have survived that depict priestesses bearing the ripe pods of opium poppies on their heads.

A potent brew made from the heads of opium poppies mixed with the seeds of datura (jimson weed) and other mind-altering substances is still used today by Tantric Yogis in feasts and rituals to help induce shamanistic trance states. However, the dose is always carefully controlled.

Magical Farming Communities

The first farming communities were established about twelve thousand years ago, with the improvement of the climate at the end of the Ice Age. Small Neolithic farming villages in northern Iraq, around the region of Lake Van in Turkey, in north Iran, Syria, Lebanon, Jordan, and Palestine/Israel, were established near fertile river valleys, where wild edible plants and animals were prolific. With the advent of agricultural technology and the domestication of animals, more time was freed for cultural bonding, religious expression, and the formation of mystical ideologies, as evidenced by the ruins and relics of that era.

Twelve-thousand-year-old sites in Iran and Iraq have revealed

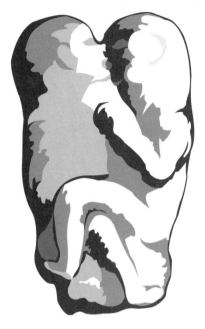

Stone sculpture of a copulating couple. From Ain Sakwi, Natufian culture, circa ninth millennium B.C.E. (In the collection of the British Museum)

the remains of circular houses with hearths. Human sacrifice was practiced in this culture, as were magical rituals involving piled goat-skull altars decorated with the paired wings of white sea eagles. In the Jordan valley, skulls were routinely separated from corpses, their features shaped with plaster or clay and painted with red ocher or bitumen. The eye sockets were filled with shells, especially cowries, thought to be sacred. The shells also resemble the vulva and were associated with spiritual rebirth. Cowry shells are also a feature of African ritual art and are invested with the same sexual symbolism, pointing to the widespread influences of early Tantric mysticism.

The earliest Neolithic representation of a copulating couple from the Middle East comes from the Natufian culture (of which the earliest inhabitants of Jericho were a part) and was found at Ain Sakwi. It dates from around the 9000 B.C.E. Carved from a single small boulder, making use of the natural form of the stone, it depicts a couple making love in a seated Tantric-type posture.

Hearth Triangles and a Vulva Stone

The prehistoric site of Lepenski Vir in northern Yugoslavia, located on the banks of the river Danube, reveals the superimposed remains of eight Neolithic settlements of a preagricultural community dating back more than seventy-five hundred years. This was one of the earliest villages used year-round, with between two hundred and three hundred inhabitants living among the carefully planned structures and organized living quarters at any one time.

The inhabitants of the dramatic Lepenski Vir site built trapezoidal tented houses with square or oblong sunken hearths, much like the Indian Yogic sacred fireplace *(dhuni)*. These fireplaces had stones set in the shape of triangles around them and had altars nearby, from which the burned remains of fish, stags, and dogs have been recovered. All the buildings had areas designated for dwelling and working, with separate areas for magical and religious rites. Apparently, four of the larger buildings may have been exclusively used as temples. Burials at the Lepenski Vir site are most unusual, with many of the corpses set in a seated yogic posture.

More than fifty carved stone boulders, some about twice the size of human heads, have been recovered from the floors in front of the Lepenski Vir hearths. Most are egg-shaped, depicting beings with half-human and half-fish features, ornamented with geometric motifs. One particularly remarkable stone boulder, found at the corner of a hearth, has a vulva prominently carved on it.

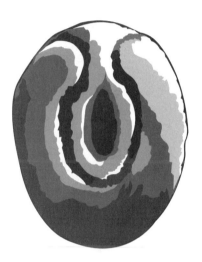

Stone sculpture in the shape of an egg with an engraved vulva motif, early sixth millennium B.C.E.
(From Lepenski Vir, northern Yugoslavia)

An Archaic Matriarchal Tantric Community

The evidence of the existence of an early Tantric-type community at Catal Huyuk, a Neolithic town southeast of Konya, Turkey, is overwhelming. Associations of fertility imagery (rows of breasts, woman in childbirth) with virility imagery (horned animals) clearly suggests the Tantric nature of the religious rites performed by the archaic residents of this fascinating town. Partly excavated in the 1960s by British archaeologist James Mellaart, Catal Huyuk was three to four times the size of the early town of Jericho and must have accommodated between six thousand and ten thousand people.

First settled around eighty-five hundred years ago, Catal Huyuk was continuously inhabited for about two thousand years. Built of mud-brick in at least ten different layers built over each other, nearly a third of the rooms excavated appear to be shrine or cult rooms. But most interesting of all is the fact that a predominantly matriarchal culture flourished here, as evidenced by the wealth of archaeological finds.

Some shrines at Catal Huyuk have wall paintings that depict women giving birth; others have squatting goddesses with uplifted arms, done in high relief. One shrine has two rows of women's breasts, modeled in plaster over a row of pig jaws with huge tusks. Another pair of breasts were modeled over the skulls of vultures. There were special shrines, with floors stained red, where birthing rites took place. A mural at Catal Huyuk depicts a deity presiding over a sexual scenario.

A small stone statuette from Catal Huyuk powerfully portrays a corpulent mother goddess giving birth to a child while seated on a throne flanked by two leopards.

A small stone carving directly links the act of sexual intercourse with the mother-and-child image; a couple make love adjoined to a woman holding a child. This is one of the earliest clear indications of the relationship of the sexual act to the production of children.

Catal Huyuk also has many shrines featuring horned bulls' and rams' heads. There are pillars embellished with bulls' heads and a huge mural of a giant horned animal being hunted by hordes of people. Other murals depict dancers wearing leopard skins and a relief sculpture portrays a huge leopard. In the culture of Catal Huyuk, leopards signified the wild and mystical power of the Great Goddess.

At Catal Huyuk, when a person died, the head was removed and the

Baked clay figure (height, approximately 20 cm) of a mother goddess in the act of giving birth, seated between two leopards, found in a shrine at Catal Huyuk. (Now in the collection of the Ankara Museum, Turkey)

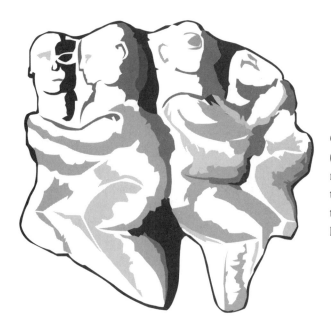

Greenish gray stone carving (height, 12 cm) of a couple making love (on the left) next to a mother with child (on the right). (From Catal Huyuk, shrine level VI)

body was exposed to vultures. A similar tradition still survives in Tibet. Apparently, archaic matriarchal funerary rites at Catal Huyuk were elaborate and involved priestesses dressed up in vulture costumes, as evidenced from one particularly striking mural. This depicts vulture-costumed women (presumably priestesses) shown attacking a headless human corpse. This is Tantric art at its best, reminiscent of similar cremation-ground scenarios depicted in Indian and Tibetan Tantric tradition.

At Catal Huyuk, funerary bones were collected, covered with red ocher, and buried, generally within the clay platform beds of houses. In one remarkable burial, almost certainly of a priestess, the remains were dismembered and placed in a seated position, with the detached head placed on top of the body. Covered in red ocher, carrying a mace, and richly ornamented with necklaces, bracelets, rings, and pendants, the remains of this priestess were wrapped in matting together with the skulls and leg bones of many mice. Nearby was found the cinnabar-stained remains of a small girl adorned with bracelets, necklaces, and pendants, buried in a basket.

Magical Communities in the Neolithic Period

The remains of fascinating Neolithic communities have been revealed in the Balkans and other parts of Europe. The brilliant archaeologist Marija Gimbutas (1921–1994) spent her whole life exploring these finds, which have become significant because of the light they shed on matriarchal culture, feminist symbolism, and the evolution of early language. Her books, especially *The Goddesses and Gods of Old Europe* (1974) and *The Language of the Goddess* (1989), the latter with a foreword by Joseph Campbell, the eminent interpreter of myths, have given us a new perspective on the evolution of spirituality in archaic times.

The many European Neolithic communities were especially evolved in the central and eastern Balkans, where clay images of phalluses have been recovered dating from 6000 B.C.E. Interestingly, male images are less common than female images in all of these European Neolithic cultures.

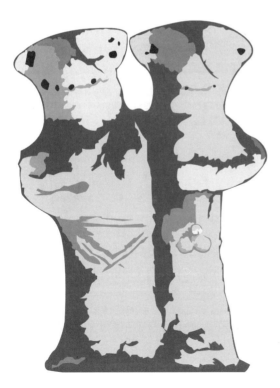

From the late fifth millennium B.C.E., at Cascioarele on the lower Danube, a remarkable clay image has been recovered. Known as the Gumelnita lovers, this small sculpture depicts a conjoined cosmic couple, the woman modeled with her vulva exaggerated, the man with penis erect.

The Gumelnita lovers have their arms around each other in an intimate embrace. This image has been interpreted as the commemoration of a sacred marriage rite. The archaic European cultures,

The Gumelnita lovers (height, approximately 6.8 cm), conjoined man and woman in baked clay, from Cascioarele, east Balkan civilization, circa late fifth millennium B.C.E.

from which this and other related finds have been recovered, involved sexual rites of a magical or Tantric type, in which these lovers could have been taking part. These rituals were certainly influenced by the spread of culture from the direction of the fertile valleys of the Middle East. The culmination of this spread of culture was the birth of advanced civilization.

Three Civilizations, One Common Spiritual Belief

It has been said that civilization began with organized agriculture and recorded history with writing. Over fifty-five hundred years ago, three long-lasting civilizations emerged along fertile river valleys of present-day Egypt, Iraq, and Pakistan/India. Known as the ancient Egyptian, Mesopotamian, and Indus Valley cultures, they each had well-developed agricultural systems, related pictographic methods of writing, and similar spiritual beliefs.

These three great civilizations, which predate those of China, Greece, and Rome, were the foundation on which Western culture was built. Much of modern science, such as the decimal system, basic mathematics, chemistry, physics, metallurgy, astronomy, and medicine, has at its roots discoveries made by inhabitants of Egypt, Mesopotamia, and India.

How these three river-valley cultures evolved and spiritually influenced each other is of great interest. Though the archaeological records are far from complete, there is a mass of evidence showing that contact between these civilizations was profuse. They had similar cultural heroes, common myths, matching overall philosophies of life, and related forms of artistic expression.

People of these three great and long-lasting cultures believed in spiritual immortality and reincarnation and looked forward to an after-life. They also believed in karma and the efficacy of the magical procedures enacted by their priests and priestesses. For them, sex was a spiritual act of great magical potency. Because of this and because their religious rites were founded upon the interwovenness of heavenly and earthly forces, these cultures were, in essence, Tantric.

EGYPT

Interwoven Realms and Sacred Sexual Beings

Religion inspired Egypt's greatest artistic, scientific, and architectural achievements. Its cultural heroes were the god-kings, priests and priestesses, heroes and heroines, later revered as gods and goddesses. According to ancient Egyptian belief, humans, creatures, and all of nature made up the realm of phenomena, while gods, demons, and spirits controlled the realm of ideas and influences. The ancient Egyptians perceived these two realms to be closely interwoven, producing the ever-changing experiences of worldly existence.

They believed that all things, animate and inanimate, possessed souls, including humans, animals, birds, fishes, reptiles, insects, plants, rivers, mountains, stones, and even man-made items. A similar pagan cosmic vision of a totally living and interwoven world is found in the Indian Tantric tradition many thousands of years later.

Sacred sex of a Tantric type was very much a part of ancient Egyptian culture, and explicit images documenting this have survived. For example, an illustration in a papyrus that has survived more than three thousand years shows a bare-breasted woman worshipping the phallus of the pharaoh before he embarks on a spiritual journey. She kneels before the pharaoh, taking his entire organ in her mouth, while a jackal-masked priest stands behind, supporting him.

Some of the sequence of magical sexual positions illustrated in an Egyptian papyrus from the twentieth dynasty. (Now in the Turin Museum)

An ancient Egyptian manuscript, known as the papyrus of Turin, illustrates a sequence of sexual mysteries, with lovemaking positions linked to astrological signs.

In ancient Egypt, as in the Tantric tradition, sex was a sacred rite in which woman was viewed as priestess and initiator into the mysteries of existence.

"The animation of the phallus," a depiction of a sacred sex rite of ancient Egypt. (In the Ani papyrus, eighteenth dynasty)

Sacred Bulls and Transcendental Gods

In Neolithic times, the changing seasons and lunar phases were translated into symbols, such as horns and crescents. This connection was undoubtedly expanded by later civilizations, testament to the far-reaching influences of Tantric symbolism. In ancient Egypt, these notions were manifested as animal worship.

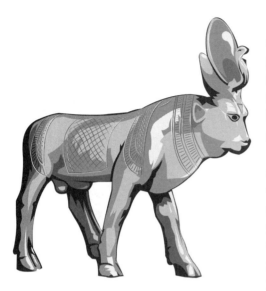

Late period Egyptian bronze casting (height, approximately 9.3 cm) of an Apis sacred bull with a lunar disk between the horns and a central erect serpent. (In the collection of the Hermitage Museum, Leningrad, Russia)

Early Egyptians praised the Apis, a special sacred bull, who symbolized the god-king and, like Neolithic markings, also represented the generative power of nature. Connected to the moon, the Apis bull was said to be the double of Ptah the creator.

The selection of the Apis bull of the ancient Egyptians was difficult. The whole country was searched for the suitable candidate: a specific type of black male calf, supposedly conceived during a thunderclap. This sacred bull was recognized by a triangular white spot on its forehead, a white crescent shape on its right side, the mark of an eagle on its back, and a scarab-shaped nodule under its tongue. Furthermore, its tail had to be half white and half black.

Once there was unanimous agreement that the sacred bull had been found, he was cared for exclusively by women for forty days and was then brought to Memphis in a special boat. The sacred bull was fed the choicest food and drank only water from select fountains. The most perfect cows were sought out and made available for his pleasure. During his lifetime, the Apis bull was enthroned, worshipped, processioned, and consulted as an oracle. But if he reached the age of twenty-five, he was drowned in the Nile, mourned, and mummified.

In later periods, the Apis bull was believed to be the reincarnation of Osiris, the most popular of all the Egyptian gods. Osiris was a vegetation deity, the ultimate symbol of resurrection and immortality, the Lord of Eternity. Evidence suggests that he was an early culture hero from the East who introduced certain mystic teachings to Egypt.

The rich myth of Osiris recounts his dismemberment by the hand of his brother Set. He is resurrected by his faithful wife, the

Image of Osiris, his phallus erect, from an illustrated Egyptian
papyrus manuscript.

goddess Isis, by the muttering of magical words of power given to
her by the god Thot. In ancient Egyptian culture, this momentous
event is connected with the sprouting of barley, wheat, and other
grains.

Many of the events making up the Osiris myth occur in other
cultures and illustrate the mystic concept of life from death, rebirth,
the efficacy of words of power (mantra in the Tantric tradition), and
the eternity of the soul.

The whole process of finding and recognizing the Apis bull and
venerating him as an oracle implies acceptance of the doctrine of
reincarnation at the earliest period of Egyptian history. It is also
somewhat reminiscent of the Tibetan custom by which reincarnate
lamas are located and proven, as was the Dalai Lama.

Other derivations of the Apis tradition are evident in other cultures as well. Priapus, the later Roman male deity of the erect male
organ (Phallus to the Greeks) was derived from the name Apis. In
India, a sacred bull Nandi is associated with Lord Shiva, the ideal of
the Supreme Yogi, whose penis is generally shown erect. The Greeks
worshipped a deity very similar to Shiva known as Dionysius, who
supposedly made a journey to India, and like Shiva, was portrayed
intoxicated and with penis erect. Both were very sexual ideals, filled
with power and potency, yet enigmatic and paradoxical.

MESOPOTAMIA

Fertility Goddesses and Virility Gods

The cradle of civilization has long been held to be in ancient Iraq. No matter from which point one starts to explore the evolution of spiritual sex, all paths converge on the fertile lands known as Mesopotamia, located between or near the Euphrates and Tigris Rivers.

Many different peoples passed through or settled the Mesopotamian region, attracted by the abundant fresh waters, fertile soil, and strategic location. What is now largely desert was, only six thousand years ago, an almost tropical oasis. There were forests and savannas, inhabited by lions, tigers, rhinoceroses, and other exotic creatures.

It was here that the prehistoric people of central Mesopotamia worshipped the power of fertility and the great Mother Goddess in the form of figurines of obviously fertile women, with exaggerated genitalia and breasts, and by venerating bulls' heads with the horns intact. Horned male animals, especially bulls and goats, were revered as embodiments of male virility, transcendental power, and the Father God. In the cradle of civilization, the fertile Mother Goddess, equivalent to Shakti in Tantra tradition, and the transcendental Father God, known to Hindus as Shiva, together exemplify the natural order of the spiritual cosmos.

Sumeria and the Origins of Tantra

The southern part of Mesopotamia, leading into the Persian Gulf, is generally referred to as Sumeria. Archaeologists and historians cannot agree about the homeland of the Sumerians, who were described as "blackheads" or "the dark ones." According to later Mesopotamian priestly traditions, the Sumerians, who were the original civilizing peoples, came from the east. This clue helps to unravel the origins of traditional Indian Tantra, which has rites and spiritual procedures very similar to those found in early Sumerian culture. Shared linguistic traits, common mythological themes, similar social conventions, and matriarchal magical rites of a Tantric type further support the intimate relation between Sumerian and Tantric beliefs.

Archaeological records show that the original dark-skinned Sumerian people migrated from the southern Indus Valley cultural area, due east of the Persian Gulf. These "aboriginal" culture-bearers of a primitive type of Tantric belief system originated in Africa tens of thousands of years previously. Therefore, it is not surprising that, if one compares African spiritual practices with those of Mesopotamia and tribal India, one finds they have so much in common. They were, after all, common links in the chain of spiritual evolution.

Mountains played a major role in Sumerian cosmology. Since there were none in southern Mesopotamia, the Sumerians built "temple mountains," great pyramid-shaped structures of brick, known as ziggurats. Ziggurats were created to commemorate the cosmic mountain, Mount Sumeru, which was believed to exist somewhere in the east and to be the central pivot of the entire world, linking heavenly and earthly forces.

Similarly, according to Hindu and Buddhist myth, a cosmic mountain called Mount Kailash produces, among other marvels, four great rivers and solar and lunar lakes. Mount Kailash is actually located within reach of the Indus Valley region, in the Himalayas to the north. Considered to be the main pilgrimage destination of Hindus and Buddhists, it is referred to as Mount Meru, the center of the universe. This holy mountain is one of the most spiritual ideals to Hindus, Buddhists, and Tantrics.

Vulva-Shaped Temples and a Cult of Cattle

About six thousand years ago, Sumerians erected great oval temples of brick in central and southern Mesopotamia. The layout of these temples, which were thriving centers of goddess cults, resembled the shape of female genitalia. Cattle, as in Egyptian belief, played an important role in religious rites, and were kept in great barns within these huge temple compounds. Surviving mosaics depict priests milking the sacred temple cows, then straining and storing the precious milk, which was the property of the goddess to whom the temple was consecrated. These early temples became great storehouses of wealth—the first banks, repositories of worldly, cultural, and spiritual resources.

Ancient Sumeria is the region where writing was first developed and history first written down. The earliest examples of Sumerian writing consist of several hundred pictographs or ideographic signs cut into clay tablets. They depict objects taken from everyday life: a horned bull's head, a bird, a fish, male and female genitalia, the sun, moon, water, a field, a plow, grain, baskets, nets, weapons, and so forth. Gradually, these pictographs took on conventionalized forms. Many of these ancient Sumerian pictographs are identical to icons found in Tantric magical lexicons, used for esoteric rites.

Mesopotamian Deities and Religious Rites

It has been said that there were as many Mesopotamian deities as there were different tribes. During the earliest period, the Mesopotamians recognized the existence of both celestial and terrestrial spirits. Mesopotamian religious rites included sacrificial offerings of all kinds; the burning of incense; mystic utterings; liturgies; magical gestures; the making of magical diagrams, nets, or traps; singing, dancing, and spiritual sex. Such rites were designed to attract the attention of divine forces and win favors from them.

The Mesopotamians recognized many different malefic spirits, known as the *limnutu*. These spirits could be bound or placated by specific rituals, offerings, incantations, and magical sacrifices, known as "burnings." These procedures usually culminated in the preparation of charms and amulets, worn on the body to help ward off or transform malefic demons. This belief in the power of magical incantations and in the efficacy of amulets and talismans is also an integral part of Tantric tradition.

The Queen of Heaven: A Holy Harlot?

Innana, the queen of Heaven and mother of life, was the Mesopotamian goddess of both love and war. She was referred to as the evening star who "caused the created to reproduce," and was associated with the planet Venus. Her earliest known symbol was an elaborately tied bundle of reeds ending in streamers. Resembling the shepherd's crook, these reed bundles were originally used as doorposts for the reed hut in which her fertility cult first evolved.

Innana's special color was the deep blue of lapis lazuli flecked

The horned goddess Innana in full regalia, from a black stone cylinder seal (height, 4 cm). (In the collection of the Oriental Institute, Chicago)

with gold; in her hands, she held a bow, arrows, a quiver, a scimitar, a staff, weapons of war, or a lion-headed scepter mace. She was also depicted either driving a team of seven harnessed lions, riding atop a lion, or standing with a pet lion on a lead.

The goddess Innana was shown wearing crowns of separate colors at different times, decorated with the crescent moon and an eight-pointed star. According to altering traditions, her father was Anu, ruler of Heaven, or Sin, the lunar deity. The sun god Shamash was said to be her brother.

Innana was also the original archetype of the "holy harlot" of magical tradition. Her rites were celebrated with great sacrifices, liquor, feasts, erotic dancing, bawdy songs, and wild sexual indulgence. The "sacred prostitutes" or *ishtaritu* (also referred to as *quadistu*, meaning "those set apart" or "the holy ones") were dedicated to her cult. The resemblances to the Hindu goddess Kali, which we will later examine in great detail, are not surprising considering the link between ancient Mesopotamian and Tantric belief systems.

Early Sumerian seal of ritual lovemaking with woman on top, third millennium B.C.E. She drinks beer through a tube.

Terra-cotta plaque from ancient Babylon, circa 1800 B.C.E., depicting standing lovemaking with rear entry. The prostitute/ priestess drinks beer through a tube.

Metal plaque of votive lovemaking with a sacred prostitute, Ishtar temple, Assur, Mesopotamia, circa 1000 B.C.E.

Tammuz, the god of vegetation, was Inanna's ever-youthful lover. Originally called Dumuzi, meaning "true son," he represented the male principle in nature, and his symbolic animal was the horned goat.

In the following fragment of an ancient Sumerian text, the goddess Innana praises the erotic ability of her consort Dumuzi, and promises to make love to him:

> He caressed my loins with his fair hands,
> The shepherd Dumuzi poured milk and cream onto me,
> He stroked my pubic hair,
> He irrigated my womb.
> He laid his hands upon my holy vulva,
> He nourished my black boat with his cream,
> He ripened my narrow boat with his milk,
> He caressed me on the bed.
> Now I'll caress my high priest on that bed,
> I'll make love to the faithful shepherd Dumuzi.

Clay plaque, circa 2000 B.C.E., depicting the Mesopotamian sacred marriage rite of Innana and Dumuzi. (Erlenmeyer collection, Basel, Switzerland)

Excavations of the royal tombs at Ur, a Mesopotamian city dedicated to Sin the horned moon god, revealed some remarkable carved seals depicting "sexual banquets." Dated at around 2300 B.C.E., one such seal depicts a priestess of Innana squatting in sexual union upon a recumbent man. A priest stands by her side, holding her left hand. The inscription reads: "This is the king of Ghisgalla."

Sumerian depictions of couples making love on a bed invariably commemorate the annual sacred marriage rite between the human representative of the goddess Innana and the king, by which the prosperity and fertility of the country was empowered. The rite was described by Sir James Frazer as follows:

> On the highest tower (at Babylon), reached by an ascent which wound about all the rest, there stood a spacious temple, and in the temple a great bed, magnificently draped and cushioned, with a golden table beside it. In the temple no image was to be seen, and no human being passed the night there, save a single woman, whom, according to the Chaldean priests, the god chose from among all the women of Babylon. They said that the deity himself came into the temple at night and slept in the great bed; and the woman, as a consort of the god, might have no intercourse with mortal man.

The goddess Innana had seven "principle accouterments." According to Sumerian sacred texts, these were the crown, lapis lazuli

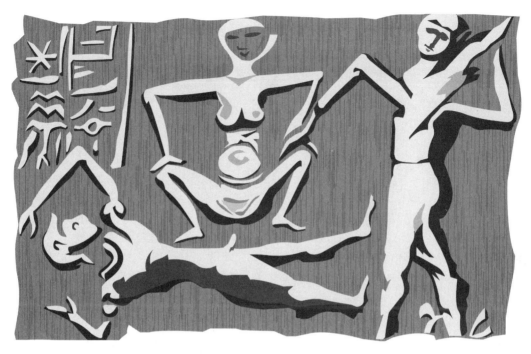

Woman on top. Scene from a Mesopotamian cylinder seal, third millennium B.C.E.

scepter, lapis lazuli necklace, gold bracelets, the precious stones covering her nipples, and her breastplate, known as "Come, man, come" and the "Pala-garment of the ladyship of her body." The following is an ancient Sumerian description of the goddess Innana:

> On her head she wears her special crown;
> Her hair is carefully arranged in dark locks.
> She wears small lapis lazuli beads around her neck.
> Across her breasts she wears the double lapis lazulis.
> Her body is wrapped in the sumptuous Pala robe of heaven.
> Her eyes are colored with the magical ointment called
> "Let him come, let him come."
> She wears her breast-plate called "Come, man, come."
> On her wrist she wears golden rings.
> She carries the lapis scepter like a queen.

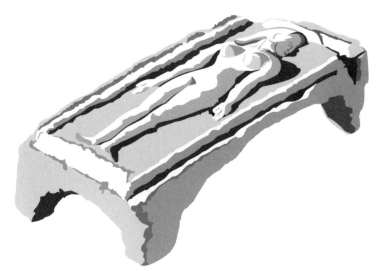

Baked clay model (length, about 12 cm) of a naked woman on a bed, probably associated with the sacred marriage ceremony. From Elan, circa 1750 B.C.E. (In the collection of the Ashmolean Museum, Oxford)

It was said that the goddess Innana liked to be honored with gifts of fine silks, exotic perfumes and exquisite jewelry, including earrings, bracelets, chain necklaces, studded girdles, and anklets. What self-assured woman wouldn't?

Knowledge of the goddess Innana was very ancient. She was worshipped under different names by many different peoples: as Ishtar by the Akkadians, Isis by the Egyptians, Ashtoreth by the Jews, Astarte by the Phoenicians, and Aphrodite by the Greeks.

Much later, Innana reappears in India in the form of the goddesses Durga and Ugra-Tara, venerated by Tantrics. Sumerian sacred marriage rites of the goddess Innana were precursors of similar love feasts that were a form of spiritual communion practiced by some early Christian sects as well as by Hindu and Buddhist Tantrics.

In the New Age, the goddess Innana has been rediscovered. Feminists have adopted her as an ideal of liberated female power and neo-Tantric "priestesses" have identified with her as the epitome of initiatory Goddess wisdom. As we approach the twenty-first century, a new cult of Tantric Innana-Ishtar-Isis is emerging. Her priestesses are even available on the Internet!

THE INDUS VALLEY AND BEYOND

Tantra in Ancient India

The majority of India's indigenous tribal people are Dravidian, a linguistic group that includes Tamil, Telegu, Khond, and Oraon languages, and are related to the aborigines of Australia who first migrated there from India at least 60,000 years ago. The territory controlled by Dravidian tribes once extended from southern Iran to Australia. Originally, in the distant archaic past, these people must have migrated out of Africa.

As in Africa, the culture of ancient India was largely matriarchal. Its people celebrated the spiritual mysteries of birth, the seasons, and lunar cycles, renewal, rebirth, and transcendence. Since the dawn of history, the diverse dark-skinned Indian aboriginal

Vagina-shaped megalithic burial chamber with a mushroom-shaped cap, from south India, circa 1000 B.C.E. or earlier.

tribes worshipped spiritual powers associated with fertility, virility, and the afterlife.

For thousands of years, India's tribal people used anthropomorphic images or idols in their spiritual rites. They used selected herbs, flowers, and trees in their rituals and plant drugs to help induce trance states. Worship was accompanied by mystic phrases, diagrams, and gestures, and by sexual acts. Like most tribal people worldwide, they believed in the efficacy of spells, charms, and amulets.

The Ancient Indus Valley or Harappan Culture

The remains of the ancient Indus Valley culture were discovered in the 1920s, following some initial finds toward the end of the nineteenth-century. The brick-built city of Harappa, located near the Ravi River in Punjab, Pakistan, was the first site to attract attention, followed by Mohenjodaro and Chanhudaro, further south on the river Indus. The close resemblance between objects from the Indus Valley sites and those from ancient Sumeria, in southern Iraq, dateable to between the third and fourth millennium B.C.E., was soon apparent.

Initially, the term *Indo-Sumerian* was used to describe antiquities from the same period in the Indus Valley and southern Iraq.

Since the 1920s, numerous other Indus Valley or Harappan culture sites have come to light, covering an area of more than 1.3 million square kilometers, larger than any other archaic civilization.

People of the Harappan culture, which was well established by the end of the fourth millennium B.C.E., were expert potters and worked with steatite, ivory, and other exotic materials. They used copper, gold, and semiprecious stones and used large ships for trade. Their religion was essentially pagan and animistic and included tree and animal worship as well as the use of sexual symbols such as the penis

Baked clay phallus (Lingam) from Harappa, Indus Valley culture, circa 3000 B.C.E.

and vulva. Symbolic representations of the sexual organs have been recovered from several Indus Valley sites, as have numerous baked-clay triangles that were most likely fertility symbols. A realistic terra-cotta penis from Harappa dates from the end of the third millennium B.C.E.

The Mystery of the Seals and Indian Tantra

Approximately twenty-five hundred small but exquisitely made intaglio seals of the ancient Harappan or Saraswati-Indus river culture are known. The best known Harappan seal is one identified by archaeologist Sir John Marshall as Shiva Pashupati, the yogic Lord of Beasts. This seal is often sited as evidence that people of the Indus Valley culture knew Yoga and practiced Tantra. It is, however, not the only known example of this subject from this culture. A review of the known examples, together with brief analysis of the symbolism and other related art finds, helps firmly establish the archaic Indian origins of Tantra beyond any doubt.

The Marshall Shiva seal, carved in steatite, depicting a seated Yogi with horned headdress and animals about him, a line of pictographic script above. From Mohenjodaro, Indus Valley culture, circa 2500 B.C.E.

The remarkable Marshall Shiva seal depicts a buffalo-horned masked male figure seated on a throne in a verson of the cross-legged lotus posture of Hatha Yoga. The Yogi's penis is erect, with both testicles prominently visible. The precise placement of both heels under the scrotum is an advanced Tantric Yoga technique known as *bandha*, meaning "knot" or "lock." It is normally used to sublimate and redirect sexual energy and can endow the practitioner with spiritual powers.

The Yogi sits on a type of throne or bed that is supported by an object resembling the hourglass-shaped double drum (known in Hindu ritual as the *damaru*) normally associated with Shiva and with shamanistic rituals throughout Asia. The top and bottom of this drum takes the shape of horns, relating directly to the figure's horned mask as well as to later depictions of Shiva, who also wore a similar horned headdress. A large tiger rears upward by the Yogi's right side, facing him. This is the largest animal on the seal, shown as if intimately connected to the Yogi; the stripes on the tiger's body echo those that appear on the Yogi. It looks as if the body of the tiger, like the Yogi's, has a total of thirty stripes, again reinforcing the possible lunar-oriented connection.

Three other smaller animals are depicted on the Marshall Shiva seal. It is most likely that all the animals on this seal are totemic or heraldic symbols, indicating tribes, people, or geographic areas.

Immediately beneath the throne, as if decorating it, are two mountain goats (one mostly missing, due to a break, but enough has survived to enable restoration of the complete composition). These goats are symmetrically placed, mirroring each other. They are separate from and smaller than the other animals shown and are vehicles or magical allies of the seated Yogi, emblems of his authority and of his origin in the wild mountains of the north.

Pictographs or ideograms are supposed to be understood by reading the parts that make up the whole and by the overall composition and impact. The saying that "a picture is worth a thousand words" is particularly true for the intricate and carefully designed Harappan seals, which reveal most of their secrets without the necessity of reading the brief inscriptions.

Other Seals of Shiva

The next best example of a Shiva seal, also from Mohenjodaro, depicts a male figure seated on a throne in another traditional Yoga posture, with the soles of his feet facing each other. The Yogi seems to have either three faces or two faces looking in opposite directions. The central face is masklike but is difficult to make out. A shaft with two horned crescents attached to it is fixed to the top of this third visage. It is surmounted by something resembling branches of a tree with two birds, located precisely in the middle of a line of pictographic script.

Steatite seal of a Yogi with horned headdress. From Mohenjodaro, Indus Valley, circa 2500 B.C.E.

The Yogi's hands rest on his knees. As with the larger, previously described Shiva seal, the arms are marked with stripes, done as if charting some notation. The total number of stripes on the arms is thirty, again indicating a lunar association. It is unclear whether on this depiction the Yogi's penis is erect; he could be wearing a *langoti*, a strip of cotton used by Yogis today to tie and hold the genitals.

The Yogi's posture on this seal is known as *bhagasana*. I once saw this Hatha Yoga posture used by a Tantric Yogi in Bengal as part of a magical rite for controlling flood waters.

A third Shiva seal from Mohenjodaro depicts a seated Yogi in a similar posture, with penis erect, his head turned to the right and

Steatite seal of a Yogi, head turned sideways. From Mohenjodaro, Indus Valley, circa 2500 B.C.E.

shown in profile, revealing a clump of hair falling down his back, like the *jata* of present day Yogi *sadhus*. He wears horns ornamented with branchlike motifs. The right arm is marked with stripes, as with the previously described examples, indicating lunar notation. A snake rises up by the Yogi's right hand.

A fourth related Shiva seal from the Harappan culture, though in poor condition, depicts a single-headed horned Yogi seated upon a high throne in an almost identical posture to the others, with the soles of his feet together. His hands rest above his knees and a human figure kneels at each side, with hands together in obeisance. Hooded cobras uncoil and rise up above the heads of the two devotees. Though this seal is in poor condition, it seems that the devotee to the right side is female and the one on the left side is male. An alternate interpretation is that they represent people of different cultures.

Impression of a steatite seal depicting a Yogi seated on a throne, an attendant at each side. From Mohenjodaro, Indus Valley, circa 2500 B.C.E.

This seal links the classic Yoga posture with the *naga* or snake cult, indicating that the *Kundalini* or serpent power of Tantra was known to the Harappans. Again, the horns are an essential part of what this seal is intended to convey: potent power, virility, spiritual kingship. Terra-cotta statuettes with similar short horns have been recovered from Indus Valley sites.

In this small seal, the horned Yogi is seated in his special posture while he receives obeisance from his two devotees, who themselves are protected or elevated by the uncoiled snakes, probably indicating the right and left psychic channels (*nadis*) of Tantra tradition. The absence of any line of pictographic script confirms that everything we need to know is implied by just the depictions on this seal.

Together, the four different but related representations of seated horned ascetics prove beyond any doubt that people living in the Indus Valley cities venerated a horned shaman deity who, on the strength of the iconographic evidence, must be identified as a form of Shiva, the Supreme Yogi. Above all, this is a very sexual deity, shown with penis erect, horned, and virile.

Virility Rites and the Seal of the Seven Maidens

Representations of horned animals are also commonly found in Harappan art. Bulls were the most popular, followed by a single horned creature that has been interpreted as a unicorn but most likely was a long-horned bull portrayed in profile. These are all symbols of virility and male personal power. In all archaic cultures, the bull has been taken as the ultimate symbol of male potency, and in Hinduism, it is also a symbol of Shiva and of spiritual transcendence.

An enigmatic Harappan seal clearly depicts some kind of religious rite or ceremony. A horned male figure with hair piled up in the *jata* of a Yogi stands within a pipal-tree sanctuary, as if he is the spirit of the tree. In front of him, a male figure kneels in obeisance,

Bronze casting (height, approximately 3.85 cm) of a short-horned bull. From Mohenjodaro, Indus Valley, circa 2500 B.C.E. (In the National Museum, New Delhi, India)

making offerings, with a horned animal behind him. It looks as if the horned animal is about to be offered in sacrifice to the Yogi tree spirit.

Steatite "seal of the seven maidens." From Mohenjodaro, Indus Valley, circa 2500 B.C.E.

Below is a line of seven young women, all identically dressed, wearing their hair down their backs; the top of their heads is ornamented with plumes or feathers. Groups of seven are considered especially auspicious in most archaic cultures and have occult significance. Among the tribal goddesses of south India are the Kannigais, a group of seven sisters or virgins who are deities of the bathing tanks used in religious rites. In modern Hinduism, unmarried maidens are sometimes "married" to the spirits of trees. This seal clearly commemorates an archaic fertility or marriage rite of a Tantric type.

The Mohenjodaro Dancing Girls

The best known artifact from the Indus Valley culture is an approximately four-inch-high copper figure of a dancing girl. Found in Mohenjodaro, close to a fireplace in one of the rooms of a large structure, this exquisite casting depicts a dark-skinned young tribal girl. She is almost naked and her long hair is tied in a bun. Bangles and bracelets entirely cover her left and upper right arms and a cowry-shell necklace is around her neck. She is posed in a dance posture, her right hand on her hip, her left hand clasped in a traditional Indian dance gesture signifying a lotus bud, symbol of spirituality. Though small, this archaic metal sculpture conveys a lot of information.

Front view of a small bronze dancing girl. From Mohenjodaro, Indus Valley, circa 2500 B.C.E.

Several eminent scholars have taken this casting to represent a temple dancer or sacred harlot, perhaps because of her nakedness, the come-hither dance posture with hand on hip, and the expression of self-assurance on her face. Whatever the sculptor intended her to portray, this small figure confirms that the Harappan people were shy about neither nakedness nor explicit sensuality.

A second metal casting of a dancing girl was also found at Mohenjodaro, but it is rarely reproduced in books. Slightly larger than the better-known example, it is unfortunately not in such fine condition. The pose is similar but reversed.

The girl's left arm is covered with bangles, the hand rests on the left hip, and her legs are together. Her upper right arm has an amulet tied on it and her right hand covers her vulva. Interestingly, this metal sculpture seems to have two faces, the second affixed to the back of the head.

Both these metal castings clearly depict a nubile young woman in the role of sacred dancer and effectively convey feelings of sensuality and spirituality. These two ancient figurines of sacred dancers may be the earliest known representations of Dakinis, images of female initiatory power, of paramount importance in Tantric tradition. Together with the several Shiva seals from the same archaic culture, they confirm that the archaic pre-Vedic Indians had Tantric adepts among them.

An Archaic Tantric Matriarchal Figure

Recently, an extraordinary wood sculpture of a large squatting female figure has been proven to be from the Harappan culture. Radiocarbon-dated at approximately 2400 B.C.E., this twenty-eight-inch-high sculpture depicts a matriarch in a birthing posture. Apparently recovered from an archaic tribal culture of Eastern India, this unique sculpture must have been passed down from generation to generation for more than forty-four hundred years.

This matriarch figure is carved in the round from a single tree trunk. She squats and pulls up her dress to reveal her vagina, which is stained from the application of offerings. Her mouth has tattoos painted around it, a custom found in several archaic cultures, signifying that she represents a matriarch, a married woman who has borne children.

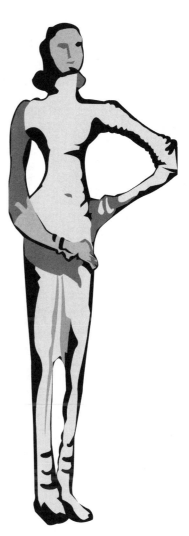

Front view of another small bronze dancing girl, the left hand on her hip. From Mohenjodaro, Indus Valley, circa 2500 B.C.E.

Front view of the large wooden matriarch figure exposing her sex (height, approximately 28 in.). From the Indus Valley culture, radiocarbon-dated at circa 2400 B.C.E.

This large wooden carving of a pre-Vedic matriarch has a shawl over her left shoulder, leaving her right breast bare. She wears her hair pulled back and tied in the same style favored today by the Muria tribeswomen of eastern India. She wears earrings and the upper part of her right arm is tied with an amulet. Such amulets are found on several small Harappan sculptures.

This is the first time a photograph of this extraordinary squatting matriarch sculpture has been published. It is the single most important example of art from the Indus Valley culture, as it is proof of the inherent matriarchal and Tantric nature of this tribal society.

Other Matriarchs in Tribal India

According to Pushpendra Kumar and Bani Kanti Kakati, we must look to eastern India—especially to the region of Assam—as an area where remnants of the ancient matriarchal pre-Vedic religion survive in tribal societies. With reference to Assam, Kumar writes:

> Shaivism (worshippers of Shiva) in some gross form associated with wine and flesh was the prevailing religion of the aboriginal Kiratas. The Aryanised conquerors held this religion in disdain and placed it under a ban. At the same time, to secure easy recognition by aboriginal people, they brought to prominence another local cult, the cult of the mother goddess as worshipped in the *Yoni* symbol as opposed to the cult of Shiva worshipped in the phallic *(Linga)* symbol. This mother cult of Kamakhya must have belonged to certain matriarchal tribes like the Khasis and Garos.

The Khasis of Assam are one of more than a hundred matriarchal tribes that survive in east and southeast India. Among the Khasis, goddesses predominate over gods and priestesses over priests. The Bengali scholar N. N. Bhattacharya writes:

> In the religion of these matriarchal social groups, special importance is attached to the cult of the Mother Goddess, and, in many of the cases, the Mother Goddess is conceived as their tribal ancestress.

Orissa, from where the Indus Valley–period wooden sculpture of the matriarch almost certainly originates, is home to many of India's remaining aboriginal tribes. Supposedly, this region was first inhabited by tribes known as the Shabaras, then the Dravidians, and lastly by the Aryans.

The main festival of the Shabara tribes takes place in the autumn. On this occasion, people traditionally sing loud songs naming the sexual organs. According to anthropologists who have studied them, on such occasions the Shabaras keep company with finely dressed virgins and prostitutes. Apparently, this is a remembrance of an archaic Tantric truth, the potency of virgin and whore, the two poles of female sexuality, seen as magically charged expressions of the Great Goddess's ultimate nature.

In the Hindu Tantric text known as *Kalika Purana*, the *Nava Ratri* festivities on the ninth (and last) day of the autumnal equinox require that "people should be engaged in amorous play, with single women, young girls, prostitutes, and dancers." The text goes on to recommend that participants should "mention aloud the names of the female and male organs, joking and with bawdy play."

One of Orissa's most well-known tribal people are the Muria, another matriarchal society. Murias fall into two main groups: those of the hills and those of the plains. Mostly, they are cultivators; among some of them, a megalithic culture still survives. Muria women leave their breasts exposed and have a simple and natural attitude to sex. Adolescents live together in the *ghotul*, a holy area or temple, where a free-love society prevails.

The role of sexuality in the Muria society was brought to light by the anthropologist Verrier Elwin, an Englishman who was originally sent to India as a Christian missionary, became a follower of Mahatma Gandhi, and then went to live with some of India's matriarchal Dravidian tribal people.

Elwin eventually renounced his Christian faith, married a tribal woman, and started a family. He lived with the Murias for many years, publishing his remarkable book *The Muria and their Ghotul*, in 1947, reissued in 1968 in abridged popular form as *The Kingdom of the Young*. He noted that the Muria have a "natural attitude to sex, strengthened by the absence of any sense of guilt and the general freedom from external interference." Apparently, the Muria seem to regard the sexual organs, whether male or female, as "living things with an independent life of their own." They believe that the penis and vagina are "in a joking relationship to each other," that "sex is great fun."

Muria men wear horns on ceremonial occasions; horns are also used to decorate or empower altars. Murias have no written language but use string figures (cat's cradle) to tell intricate stories that are animated by subtle finger movements and are often sexual in nature. They have a culture rich in symbolism. In their art, they use Tantric symbols that date back to the ancient past.

The Temple of the Sacred Vulva

India's temple of the sacred vulva is known as the temple of Kamakhya, a Hindu goddess. Bani Kanti Kakati describes the object of veneration at the Kamakhya temple as follows:

> The temple is unique from other temples of the Devi (goddess) in different parts of India in that it embodies no image of the goddess. Within the temple there is a cave, in the corner of which stands a block of stone on which the symbol of a Yoni (the vulva) has been sculptured. The stone is kept moist from the oozings of a natural spring within the cave. The offerings of flowers and leaves are made on the Yoni.

The Kamakhya Temple, near Gauhati, Assam, built in the sixteenth century.

The *Kalika Purana*, a Hindu Tantric text, describes the Kama-khya Yoni shrine as follows:

> Within the triangular-shaped Mount Nila is the sacred cave called Manobhava. Within this is the Yoni, the female organ, in the form of a stone, reddish like vermilion, giving all the objects of desire. On this Yoni the amorous Great Goddess (Maha Devi) in her five forms perpetually amuses Herself.

Contemporary painting of the goddess Kamakhya, in her multiheaded and multiarmed form. Under her is Lord Shiva, who is supported by a lion.

কামাক্ষা দেবী

Stone sculpture (circa A.D. sixteenth-century) of the goddess Kamakhya. (Kamakhya temple in Assam, India)

The present Kamakhya Temple of the Yoni was built in the sixteenth century and is of stone. However, its architectural style is derived directly from the traditional tribal temple or temple hut made of wood and woven grass. Though no ancient image of the goddess Kamakhya appears inside the temple, the outer walls are decorated with several stone carvings of goddesses, including a squatting woman exposing her Yoni, a mother suckling an infant, and an Amazon woman holding a drawn bow. The Kamakhya temple is the main pilgrimage place for Shaktas, Tantric followers of the Great Goddess and her various cults.

Interestingly, this is the only Hindu temple in India that specifically declares that any person can worship in it "in whatever manner they are accustomed." One can perform one's own *puja* (or worship) there as one wishes and need not employ the services of a priest or intermediary.

Broken stone sculpture of the goddess embodiment of the Yoni. She is seated in a Yoga posture, the Yoni represented below, being venerated by devotees. From the Bheraghat sixty-four Yogini temple, central India, circa eleventh century C.E.

Detail showing the Yoni being worshipped by two devotees. From the Bheraghat sixty-four-Yogini temple, central India, circa eleventh century C.E.

For Tantrics, the Kamakhya Yoni temple is the ultimate spiritual pilgrimage place. On the sacred hill that houses the cave of the Yoni are Tantric camps of all types. Initiations, Tantric sexual rites, and magical procedures take place on certain nights, driven by the belief that whatever is done in the proximity of the sacred vulva of the Great Goddess will be all the more effective.

The Changing Face of Tantra in Early Europe

PAGANISM AND ITS RELATION TO TANTRA

Paganism remains one of the most misunderstood spiritual developments of Western civilization. Derived from the Latin *pagus*, meaning village, the word *pagan* literally means "villager." Accordingly, paganism was the "old religion," the faith of village or country people, the religion of the majority. Pagans were termed *heathens* by the early Christians, this word meaning "persons who do not acknowledge the deity of the Bible." Throughout pre-Christian Europe, the Middle and Far East, and in Africa, pagans followed many different cults dedicated to the worship of various natural and supernatural powers, spirits, heroes, gods, or goddesses.

It was believed that, like humans, pagan powers were gratified by sensual things, by ritual feasts, offerings, the burning of incense, the lighting of sacred fires, and by sexual intercourse. It was thought that pagan powers had desires but no physical bodies and thus needed humans to help fulfill those desires. Throughout the ancient world, groves of sacred trees were among the main places of pagan worship. The early church leaders saw to it that such groves were cut down; many of the first Western churches were built of wood from those trees.

For village pagan people throughout the ancient world, sex was viewed as a magical act, as a procreative and ecstatic power. People made love in the fields to ensure a good harvest. The sacred groves were places where ritual orgies, which mimicked the lovemaking of the gods and goddesses, were enacted. In pagan life, sex was viewed as a magical act without guilt or inhibition.

Followers of paganism believe in spiritual immortality, reincarnation, a cosmic law of cause and effect, and the efficacy of magical rites. Such rites were ideally performed at special times, with spiritual personalities who required particular offerings at specified times, with priests or priestesses acting as intermediaries. Pagan rites are empowered by sacred utterances, chants and songs, dances, ritual movements and gestures, offerings, and dedicated sexual intercourse. Tantra, which evolved from primitive to sophisticated levels of expression through trial and error over the millennia, refined and codified these traditional pagan rites and offerings.

During the fourth century C.E., Christian rulers managed to overcome much of European paganism by force. The church began to consolidate its hold over the people. Theodosius (346–395 C.E.) came to power, the "pagan" Olympic games were banned, and strict laws were passed prohibiting the lighting of sacred fires at home in honor of the house deity, offerings of food and wine to cult deities, and the burning of incense or the adorning of sacred trees. Those caught contravening Theodosius's draconian laws were prosecuted for high treason and all their property was confiscated.

EXPLORATIONS INTO THE NATURAL SPIRITUALITY OF SEX

More than a hundred years ago, radical European and American Christians seeking to explore the natural spirituality of sex turned to the works of classical philosophers for guidance. Of foremost interest were the writings of the Greek philosophers Pythagoras and Plato. Their open-minded teachings pointed toward a mystical view of reality in which souls were reincarnated, spiritual powers could be attained, and in which sex was viewed as an entirely natural and perfectly respectable act. The writings of these eminent Greek philosophers are true touchstones by which the teachings of Tantra can best be judged, for these scholars' lives and teachings are at the foundation of Western culture. What we seem to have forgotten is that these geniuses of the past embraced and explored science, art, *and* mysticism. They were indeed the first Western Tantrics.

Pythagoras (circa 578–510 B.C.E.), a mathematician and philosopher, traveled widely and was familiar with Hinduism. He studied with Egyptian priests for many years and was eventually initiated into their "mystery teachings." Pythagoras combined rational science with religious mysticism, teaching that the soul transmigrates through many bodies, both human and animal, in successive incarnations, eventually attaining perfection.

Pythagoras was not a dry philosopher. He was very human, falling head over heels in love with Theano, one of his pupils, who herself became a distinguished philosopher. For Pythagoras's time and culture, this was incredible; women had few rights and were generally considered inferior. Likewise, no illustrious Greek philosopher would be expected to fall in love. That this indeed happened—and with Theano, who became the first woman to be recognized as a philosopher in her own right—tells us a lot about Pythagoras's radical and enlightened state of mind.

Plato (427–347 B.C.E.) was particularly interested in the exploration of human consciousness. A student of Socrates and a follower of many of Pythagoras's ideas, Plato believed that reincarnation is necessary for the development of consciousness. He was a well-rounded man who was acquainted with the arts, science, warfare, and was also a sportsman, warrior, successful trader, and an initiate of several mystery cults. Like both Hindu and Buddhist Tantras, most of his writings took the form of dialogs, four of which dealt mainly with questions about love and sexual pleasure.

Plato's writings on love initially focused and commented on the homosexual romanticism of the society of which he was a part. He viewed physical love as inferior to spiritual love, hence the term *Platonic friendship*.

Plato's *Symposium* includes a fascinating dialogue between Diotima and Socrates. Diotima speaks in the role of an instructress in the art of love:

> Love interprets between gods and men, conveying and taking across to the gods the prayers and sacrifices of men, and to men the commands and replies of the gods; he is the mediator who spans the chasm which divides them, and therefore in him all is bound together, and through him the arts of the prophet and the priest, their sacrifices and mysteries and charms, and all prophecy and incantation, find their way.
>
> For god mingles not with man; but through love all the intercourse and converse of god with man, whether awake or asleep, is carried on. The wisdom which understands this is spiritual.

Plato compared the normal human condition to that of slaves held in a cave from which they can see only the shadows of things passing by outside. He pointed out that such cave dwellers generally confuse the shadows with reality, ignoring their source. Plato explained that in such a manner, most people are completely ignorant of spiritual reality.

Aristotle (384–322 B.C.E.) was Plato's greatest student and is generally considered to be the father of Western sexology. He possessed an encyclopedic mind and became a great scientist and philosopher. He rejected Plato's inner spiritual world for one of pure science.

Aristotle saw everything in terms of both matter and form. He attempted to define everything in nature, from inanimate matter to plants, simple life-forms, mollusks, insects, fish, reptiles, birds, and mammals. Aristotle was among the first Westerners to describe the sexual organs and define their functions. He perceived the existence of a vital force or formative element in nature, which he believed "urges beings to achieve self-fulfillment." He argued that the semen of man contains this formative element, which is hot, whereas woman emits a sexual substance, which is cold. He compared man and woman to the sun and the earth, a comparison common to much mystical literature. This is an analogy also commonly found in early Hindu writings and in the Tantras.

ALEXANDER THE GREAT'S ENCOUNTER WITH A TANTRIC YOGI

Greek explorations of the nature of sexuality and the universe were influenced by interactions with Hindu Yoga philosophers, several of whom were known to have visited Athens. An early account of a Hindu Yogi, who apparently was a Tantric, comes from the time of Alexander the Great (356–323 B.C.E.), who encountered one in India. Yogis were known in Greek as *gymnosophistae*, or "naked philosophers."

A story is told how Alexander and his soldiers once came upon a group of Yogis engaged in philosophical debate. When his troops approached, the only reaction from the Yogis was the stamping of their feet. On Alexander's inquiry, he was told that this meant that "every man can possess only as much of the earth's surface as one can stand on, and after one's death, as much as it takes to be buried."

Alexander invited a particularly proficient Yogi, whose name may have been Kala Nath but was corrupted into Greek as Calanus, to live close by him while he keenly observed his activities. According to some accounts, Calanus was "a slave to fleshly lusts," which is a nasty way of saying that he was a Tantric.

Calanus became the teacher of Lysimachas, a Macedonian general, and a friend and confidant of Alexander. One day, Calanus asked for a funeral pyre to be prepared. He said farewell to the various generals with whom he was friendly, turned to Alexander, and said he would "see him again, in Babylon," so prophesying his death. The fire was lit and Calanus burned himself alive. Alexander left India and died in Babylon as prophesied.

Over subsequent centuries, this story of Alexander and the Yogi recurs throughout classical literature. What is not generally realized is how much influence both Hindu and Buddhist esoteric teachings had on Greek and subsequently Western philosophy and science. Greek medicine, for example, is largely based on Hindu medicine. The emerging Western science of sexology was thus inspired by Hindu, Buddhist, and Greek observations and speculations. From the time of Alexander the Great onward, Tantric ideas began to flood into the Western world.

THE MYSTERIES OF ELEUSIS AND LSD

The Greek mysteries of Eleusis were initiatory rites much sought after by the intelligentsia of ancient Europe. A sanctuary to the Great Goddess had been in existence in the town of Eleusis since the Bronze Age. Eleusis had a main temple of initiation with a "holy of holies" and tiers of seats that could accommodate up to three thousand initiates. From the sixth century B.C.E., Eleusis was dominated by the city-state of Athens, until it was finally destroyed by the king of the Visigoths around 395 C.E.

The mystery cult of the goddesses Demeter and Persephone was enacted at the sanctuary of Eleusis every fall. The Demeter and Persephone myths tell of a testing of marriage rites, journeys to the underworld, and the recovery of a mystic treasure. Since initiates were sworn to secrecy on pain of death and no literary accounts survive, the exact nature of the Eleusian mysteries is not clear. There is, however, strong evidence, published by R. Gordon Wasson, Carl

A. P. Ruck, and Albert Hofmann in their book *The Road to Eleusis: Unveiling the Secret of the Mysteries* (1978), that a natural form of LSD derived from ergot-infested wheat, barley, or the wild grass known as paspalum, was prepared as an intoxicating drink, stimulating intense mystic visions of the Great Goddess. This special drink was given after the required nine days of fasting. Interestingly, the Tantric Hindu *Nava Ratri* festival of the Great Goddess Durga, which, like the Eleusian mysteries also takes place every fall, involves participants in a nine-day fast followed by the partaking of *bhang*, a psychedelic drink made from specially prepared marijuana, spices, milk, and other ingredients.

At Eleusis, offering cakes took the form of the vulva or were bowl- or boat-shaped. The Eleusian mysteries were a spiritual experience with an erotic dimension. Fragmentary accounts tell of phalluses garlanded with flowers from the sanctuary of the Goddess, carried in processions to the shrine of Dionysius, the Greek version of Shiva.

The Eleusian mysteries are the early European equivalent to the fertility mysteries of early Sumerian and later Indian Tantric culture. All such mysteries celebrate the initiatory and visionary power of nature, in all of its "cascading of colors and ever-changing forms," as well as the vision of the seductive body of the Great Goddess and her intoxicating power. This vision, achieved through the ego-deflating and spiritualizing effect of a powerful psychedelic, strips the intellect of all reason, leaving only pure heart-consciousness and spiritual communion with the Great Goddess.

ZARATHUSHTRA, THE MAGI, AND THE CULT OF MITHRA

Zarathushtra (better known as Zoroaster) was a magi who lived sometime prior to the sixth century B.C.E. The magi were a tribe of priest–magicians who were active in ancient Iran. It was their job to lead all religious ceremonies and recite praise-hymns to the various gods and goddesses. The magi used sacred utterances, known as *mathra*, meaning "thought," as magical power phrases or spells, to which the Sanskrit word *mantra* meaning "protection of mind" is related.

Zarathushtra reformed and reorganized the ancient priestly

Stone sculpture depicting the naked torso of Mithra within a vagina and surrounded by zodiacal signs. Mithra has a phallus on his head and holds a knife and flaming torch. (From the Mithreum of Borcovicus [Housestead], in northern England)

rites and became the prophet of a new religion, Zoroastrianism. This religion promoted several cults, one of the most important being that of Mithra, the solar deity, whose name means both "covenant" and "friendship." Zoroastrianism had a very significant influence on Judaism, Christianity and Islam.

The cult of Mithra preceded—and might have been a precursor to—Christianity and was firmly established in Rome by at least 100 B.C.E. It was essentially solar oriented and iconographically phallic. Mithraic rites included baptism, resurrection, and a type of mass in which bread and wine were consumed as a sacrament. The chief Mithraic temple in the Western world was on the hill where the Vatican is now located. Another was established in London, England. December twenty-fifth, the winter solstice, was celebrated as the birthday of Mithra.

According to the eminent scholar Sir James Frazer, writing in his major work, *The Golden Bough: A Study in Magic and Religion* (1915):

> In respect both of doctrines and rites the cult of Mithra appears to have presented many points of resemblance not only to the religion of the Mother of the Gods but also to Christianity. The similarity struck the Christian doctors themselves and was explained as the work of the devil, who sought to seduce the souls of men from the true faith by a false and insidious imitation of it. . . . There can be no doubt that the Mithraic religion proved a formidable rival to Christianity, combining as it did a solemn ritual with aspirations after moral purity and a hope of immortality. Indeed, the issue of the conflict between the two faiths

appears for a time to have hung in the balance. An instructive relic of the long struggle is preserved in our festival of Christmas, which the church seems to have borrowed directly from its heathen rival.

Zoroastrian teachings declare that a cosmic dualism pervades everything. This dualism manifests as good and evil, expressed in everyday life as truth and lie, purity and pollution. Zoroaster ruled that a husband is obligated to have sex with his wife at least every nine days, that contact with a menstruating woman is polluting to man, and that semen is a spiritual sacrament.

Some Mithraic rites have parallels to those found in both Hindu and Buddhist Tantric tradition as well. Rites of the sacred fire, immersion in sacred waters, the receiving of initiatory names, the distribution of sacraments among worshippers, and empowerments by incantations and gestures are some examples of pagan spiritual rituals common to these ancient faiths.

ARYAN INTERACTION

Aryan tribes probably entered northern Pakistan and India en masse around 1700 B.C.E. These light-skinned horse-riding warriors were patriarchal cattle rearers whose origins, via Iran, were European. They raided the Indus Valley cities: evidence suggests they devastated them, scattering the darker-skinned Indians, whom later they termed *dasyus*, meaning "servants."

Most of what are generally viewed as the basic tenets of Hinduism, such as the caste system, holy cows, patriarchal priestly rites, fire sacrifices, and the self-immolation of widows, have their origin with the imported beliefs of the Aryans. There is no evidence that such tenets were held by India's indigenous people.

The priestly language of the Aryans was Sanskrit, the Vedas their sacred texts, and the thirty-three gods the focus of their worship, which was aniconic, meaning it was without images, taking the form of hymn singing. The Vedic gods addressed in these hymns included Indra, the heroic king of gods, the Sun, Moon, Wind, Water, Fire, the Dawn, and *soma*, an intoxicating drink made from a specific type of plant. The greatest Aryan spiritual rite was horse sacrifice, because of their nomadic culture's dependence upon the animal.

The Aryans interacted with the various Indian tribes they encountered, selectively absorbing much of their culture while settling on the best of their land. These invaders adopted the native Indian peoples' Yoga technology, their unique medical and scientific knowledge, their spiritual icons (*murthis*) in worship, their secret power phrases (mantras) and protective spells (*dharanis*), and many of their archaic methods of worship (*puja*). What they adopted eventually became transformed into their own, generally changed almost beyond recognition.

Pushed into remote and inhospitable areas, most of India's indigenous people were dispossessed, eventually becoming second-class citizens in their own land. This is the context in which, some three thousand or more years ago, the archaic secret Tantric teachings began to be redefined. They emerged about one thousand years later as "new" and radical spiritual teachings known as Tantras that had no place for elitism or sexism and embraced true democratic ideals. It took another three hundred years or so for the first Tantras to be written down.

Some Tantric teachings have been preserved only in mythology, in songs, dance, sculpture, painting, and in the arts of love. Traces of Tantric philosophy and ritual procedures are found in Hindu and Buddhist texts reaching back as far as the fifth century B.C.E. Early Indian medical and scientific writings, in particular, include data clearly based on Tantric beliefs. The first *written* Tantras probably date from between the second to fourth centuries C.E., but these exist only as fragments of far older secret teachings that have mostly been conveyed orally. Much of these teachings are concerned with the rites and practices of spiritual sex and how they can aid human evolution. In the following chapter, we will explore in detail these beliefs and writings from the period when Tantra blossomed forth as a religion, as cultural expression, and as a way of life.

3 THE NATURE OF TANTRA

Form is perceived by the eye; sound is heard by the ear; smell is experienced by the nose; taste is experienced by the tongue; objects are felt by the body and the mind experiences pleasure and so forth. These, which are worthy of adoration, should be served.

—*HEVAJRA TANTRA*

HUMANS ARE sensual beings. We crave sensual satisfaction from the first moment of our lives. A caress, the smell and sound of our mother, the taste of nourishment, the sight of a friendly face—all these delight the human spirit and allow it to evolve and express its unique potential. Unlike many spiritual paths that deny the senses, Tantras tell us that the senses are worthy of adoration and can be used as tools to help attain spiritual liberation. This radically different approach to spirituality is said to be the shortest, most difficult, and most dangerous path. It is also the most joyous and the most appropriate for the present time.

The sensual path to spiritual evolution is difficult because it requires self discipline, patience, and faith. It's not a solitary path, either, which means there's at least twice as great a chance of things going wrong. It's also difficult because there are not many familiar "signposts" on the way, and because it's new territory, with unexpected twists and turns as well as unusual features. And it's dangerous because it can give access to tremendous spiritual powers.

The sensual path is especially hazardous to persons who are spiritually lazy, who have little faith, who are doubters. This is a path which requires a heroic attitude for one to progress. This is a path that will continually test one's intelligence. The beauty is that we can all have access to unlimited intelligence and can easily experience unlimited faith once we adopt a positive spiritual attitude and recognize that we truly are immortal spiritual beings whose time for the completion of our evolution is *now*.

Humans naturally pursue pleasure and want to avoid suffering. We are hedonistic creatures, needing to learn how best to pursue pleasure intelligently and creatively. Tantra teaches how the pursuit of sensual pleasure can become an authentic spiritual activity. All it takes is a healthy body, an open mind, attentiveness to the teachings, a loving partner, and the earnest desire to attain spiritual liberation in this lifetime.

The Difference Between Hindu and Buddhist Tantras

Hindu and Buddhist Tantras generally teach different approaches to achieve the same goal. The emotional approach found in most Hindu Tantras requires participants to make drastic leaps of faith so as to connect as efficiently as possible with the divine power within, who is viewed as one's ultimate guide and initiator. Since this is perceived to be essentially female in nature, woman is the most obvious and accessible embodiment. She is therefore worshipped as a living goddess who has the power to endow spiritual illumination on her intimate devotee.

The intellectual approach outlined in most Buddhist Tantras demands tremendous mental self-discipline. No Great Goddess is recognized, just idealized spiritual qualities, known as "wisdom energies." It is the meditation techniques that, in most Buddhist Tantras, are viewed as the secrets. Chakras and mandalas are tools of Buddhist Tantra and are used primarily as vehicles of empowerment, as part of an intellectual process of initiation. However, as the higher levels of attainment are accessed, Buddhist Tantras commonly require the spiritual seeker to abandon intellect and embrace nonduality with passion.

Confrontation with superstitions and taboos, which are emotional issues, also plays a significant role in Buddhist Tantric practice. The *Hevajra Tantra*, for example, categorically views Wisdom as a female persona, a position far removed from mainstream Buddhism which generally considers woman as inferior. The *Hevajra Tantra* declares:

> Wisdom is called Mother, because she gives birth to the world,
> Likewise she is called washerwoman, daughter, or dancer.
> She is called washerwoman because she touches all things;
> Daughter because she yields fine qualities;
> Dancer because of her tremulous nature.

There are three different categories of Buddhist Tantra. These are referred to as father Tantra, mother Tantra, and nondual Tantra. These can be compared to Shaivite, Shakta, and Shiva-Shakti Hindu Tantras.

Both father and Shaivite Tantras take an absolutist, intellectual, and somewhat patriarchal stance to "the problem," which is how to obtain spiritual liberation as quickly and as efficiently as possible. Both mother and Shakta Tantras take an all-encompassing, devotional, and somewhat matriarchal stance to the same problem, which is mostly seen as the need to alleviate both worldly and spiritual suffering.

Both the nondual and Shiva-Shakti Tantras aim to eliminate any kind of emotional or intellectual obstacles. Their primary tasks are to stop all mental/intellectual chatter, eliminate all forms of discrimination (viewing even "clean" and "dirty" as the same), and manifest only spontaneously blissful behavior. This is similar to the behavior of innocently playful young children, a fashion in which the highest Siddha teachers of Tantra, both Hindu and Buddhist, commonly seek to behave.

Far too much has been made of the differences between Hindu and Buddhist spiritual teachings. To Hindus, Buddhism is a cult of Vishnu, for Buddha is viewed as one of Vishnu's incarnations. The Buddha was originally brought up as a worshipper of Shiva; in his own spiritual search, he associated primarily with Shaivites. His rejection of asceticism in favor of "the middle way," the avoiding of extremes, is a development or adaptation of orthodox Yogic teachings. At the highest level, Hindu and Buddhist Tantric teachings are virtually indistinguishable.

The Fivefold Structure of the Tantric Universe

According to Tantric tradition, we inhabit a multilayered universe that naturally has a fivefold structure. It is comprised of five elements: fire, air, earth, water, and space. On a simplistic physical level, the human body has five principal appendages: our four limbs plus our head. Each hand and each foot is also fivefold: four fingers and a thumb, four toes and a big toe. And we have five principle organs: brain, heart, lungs, kidney, and liver. Tantras teach that the fivefold divisions of both our body and the universe we inhabit have deep significance. The "branches" of our Tantric "tree of life" divide into five, again and again.

The five sense organs—the eyes, ears, nose, tongue, and skin—are the five principle tools of Tantra; seeing, hearing, smelling, tasting, and touching are their five principle functions, or *sensual raptures*. Loving intimacy and sexual intercourse invariably involves all five of these tools and functions in a delightful and joyous play. When it culminates in ecstatic sexual climax, it also has the potential to produce a physical body and incarnate a spiritual being—a magical and mystical activity indeed.

Our five sense organs are driven by five "subtle energies" referred to collectively as *pranas*, meaning "vitalities." These five principal *Pranas*, which are individually known as *Prana, Udana, Apana, Samana*, and *Vyana*, control inspiration, the ascending vitality, the descending vitality, the digestive vitality, and the entire metabolic process, respectively. They are visualized as being colored yellow, pale blue, orange, light green, and red, respectively. Tantra teaches how to use these vitalities so as to totally transform and illuminate one's whole being.

The consciousness principle or "knower" clothes itself in five "sheaths," known as *Koshas*. These are referred to as the physical sheath, the vital sheath, the sheath of ordinary human consciousness or mind, the sheath of the subconscious, and the blissful and ecstatic sheath of "love-consciousness." Access to the last sheath is what practitioners of Tantra seek.

According to Tantric tradition, the true spiritual seeker manifests five principal powers. These are faith, perseverance, recollection or mindfulness, contemplation, and discriminative awareness. And if we advance spiritually, we can achieve the five "supernormal cognitive powers," referred to as clairvoyance (the ability to see into the future), clairaudience (the ability to hear the future), telepathy (knowledge of the minds of others), miraculous abilities (inexplicable achievements), and knowledge of past lives.

The Five Primary Races

Tantric teachings tell of five primary races. Most specialists agree, recognizing five major and distinctive races from a common ancestor (presumably a couple or couples) who originally lived in Africa. The UNESCO (United Nations Educational, Scientific, and Cultural Organization) declaration on race states:

> All men living today belong to a single species, *Homo sapiens*, and we are derived from a common stock. There are differences of opinion regarding how and when different human groups diverged from this common stock.

All available evidence indicates a long period of separation of these five principle races from an ancient ancestral type of modern human. According to molecular biologists, the greater the number of genetic mutations found in a species, the more ancient it is.

The five major races or subspecies of modern *Homo sapiens* are, according to physical anthropologists:

> *Australoids:* dark-skinned aboriginal types, which include South Indians, native Australians, Melanesians, Papuans, and Negritos of South Asia and Oceania
> *Mongoloids:* yellow-skinned Oriental types, which include Chinese, Japanese, East Asiatics, Indonesians, Micronesians, Polynesians, Amerindians, Eskimos, and Finns
> *Congoids:* brown or black-skinned African types, which include most Negro and Pygmy people
> *Capoids:* very small-statured, distinctive, brown-skinned Africans, which include Bushmen and Hottentots
> *Caucasoids:* white or light-skinned European types, which include many Middle Eastern people

There are probably no ''pure'' races at present. American whites and blacks have about twenty-one percent of their genes in common. Cultural empowerment and renewal comes about especially when highly differentiated cultures mix. Cross-cultural and interracial alliances are welcomed, even sought after in the Tantric evolutionary world view, a scenario that will likely color the makeup of future generations in the twenty-first century.

Esoteric Tantric teachings also divide the people of the world into five distinctive types or ''families.'' These divisions are not based primarily on skin color but instead on types of spiritual personalities. However, when the different spiritual families are evoked or organized within the framework of a particular Tantric system, such as in a mandala, they are generally color-coded as yellow, blue, red, green, and white.

A color-coded Buddhist Mandala of typical fivefold structure. At the center is the mystic form of the deity, identified with the worshipper *(sadhaka).* Other manifestations are oriented to the four directions. Tibetan *thanka* painting on cloth, circa fifteenth century C.E.

Tantric teachings do not acknowledge the existence of any chosen people, sinners, or outcasts, and do not place any value on economic or social status. Tantras teach us to question everything, to break down limitations of caste, color, or convention and remind us of the need to awaken our spiritual conscience and act upon it.

Five Principal Chakras

The Sanskrit word *Chakra* means "wheel," "round," "circular," or "disk-shaped." In the Tantric tradition Chakras are subtle circular-shaped energy wheels or vortexes that play an important part in the mechanism of spiritual evolution. Their role is to refine and transform raw sexual energy into spiritual illumination.

Close scrutiny of the nature of reality reveals its circular nature. The earth spins on its own axis; all the heavenly bodies spin around in space; so do electrons and atoms. The seasons, days, and years progress in circular cycles. Consciousness moves from life to life, and even our thinking process has a circular nature.

There is no getting away from the reality of Chakras. We can't practice Tantra without knowing about them. When we refer to Chakras in the Tantric tradition, we invariably mean one of two things: energy vortexes in our subtle or psychic being, or circular gatherings of lovers performing mystical rites in-

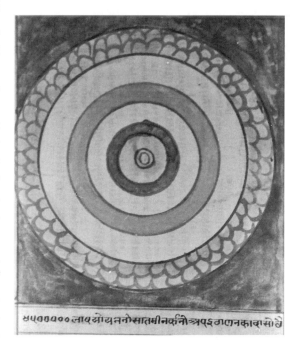

Tantric scientific diagram depicting the circular nature of reality. Manuscript painting on paper, central India, circa sixteenth century.

volving spiritual sex. Here we'll explore the meaning of Chakras as energy vortexes. Later we'll look into the meaning of Chakras as circular gatherings for sexual rites.

It's best to think of the Chakras of our being as plexuses, meaning junctions of life energy. Chakras are subtle, not physical, and cannot normally be seen. We should not expect to find them described in normal physical anatomy books. But we *can* sense them.

Just as in higher mathematics we work with imaginary numbers, which can be very effective in solving complex problems, in Tantra we work with Chakras, which cannot normally be seen or measured with instruments but have a subtle effect that produces results.

Chakras generate a field of force. Wherever consciousness is active in a process of transformation, a Chakra exists. This means there are many different Chakras, far more than the normal four, five, six, seven, nine, or twelve that we commonly find described by different Tantric Chakra systems.

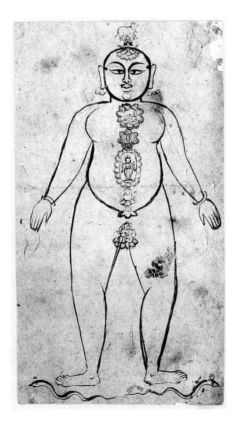

Tantric teachings view Chakras as crucial aspects of the evolutionary mechanism of spiritual liberation. They are hubs or whirlpools of subtle psycho-physical energy, located at different parts of our body. Some texts refer to them as lotuses with specific colors and numbers of petals. Such references are obviously allegorical.

Because of their complex nature, there has been a lot of confusion about Chakras. How many are there? Where are they? What are their colors? How many petals or divisions do they have? What are their names? And why do Tantric traditions of Chakras vary?

Tantric diagram depicting the Chakras as lotuses with a deity or spiritual power at their center. Drawing on paper, Rajasthan, India, circa eighteenth century.

It is important to remember that there are as many Chakras as human consciousness creates, which means Chakras can be infinite. They are part of the mystical reality and are always extremely personal.

Chakras are interfaces between earth and Heaven, between physical and spiritual realities. They are part of the microcosm–macrocosm relationship, and since they are driven by consciousness, their nature varies. Depending on the *focus* of consciousness, different Chakras are perceived.

Chakras reflect the diversity of human consciousness, so different Tantric teachers have developed different visions of Chakra systems. All evolve, however, from one simple fivefold view. Just as there are five principle *Pranas*, there are five principle Chakras of the human body. They commence in region of the sexual organ and terminate within the head.

The five principle Chakras described in Tantric texts are the sex Chakra, the assimilation Chakra, the navel Chakra, the heart Chakra, and the throat/head Chakra. As we shall see later, the head Chakra actually consists of three separate Chakras (at the throat, forehead, and crown of the head), but these are best considered, at least initially, as a single Chakra.

The sex, assimilation (also known as spleen), navel, heart, and throat/head Chak-

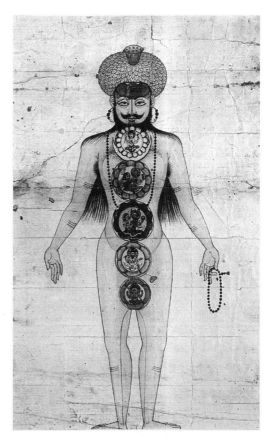

Tantric illustration of the principle Chakras, shown as lotuses of specific colors and numbers of petals, with spiritual powers at their centers. Painting on paper, from Nepal, circa eighteenth century.

ras are linked to the natural elements of earth, water, fire, air, and space, respectively, and are connected with the faculties of smell, taste, sight, touch, and hearing as well.

Tantras also link the Chakras to forms and colors: to the square, crescent, triangle, hexagon, and circle and to yellow, green, red, blue, and white, respectively. All these links are, in Tantric tradition, crucial to the process of consciously empowering one's spiritual evolution. They are used as tools to visualization, helping to direct the Kundalini upward, in an evolutionary direction.

If you sense carefully, you'll easily experience a plexus at the navel region. This is the solar plexus, correctly named since it is the center of one's subtle fire. If you fall hard on the solar plexus and the "fire" gets knocked out of you, panic sets in. It takes a while to recover. This fiery plexus is the source of transformatory energy, a minisun in your microcosm. This is the navel Chakra.

The head Chakra, another primary plexus, is the center or vortex of consciousness. It is vacuous like space and cool, mystical like an inner room. Tantras teach that the inner sun at the navel Chakra and the inner moon at the head Chakra interact with each other, rather like the actual sun and moon do. These inner heavenly bodies manifest solar and lunar characteristics, producing cycles of activity, tides and so forth, which have both physical and psychological influence.

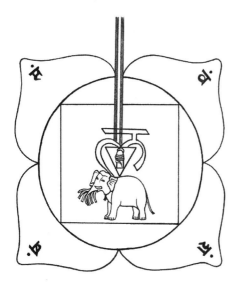

Traditional line drawing depicting the typical Hindu visualization of the sex Chakra. At the center, within a triangle, is a Shiva Lingam, encircled by a snake (the *Kundalini*). The seed-mantra *Lam* almost encircles the triangle and is contained within a square in which an elephant with seven trunks stands. Two subtle channels (*nadis*) rise upward. The four petals of the lotus Chakra have Sanskrit mantras on them.

Then there's the heart Chakra, emotional, mystical, unpredictable. Influenced by the organ we call the heart, which pumps the blood throughout our physical body, the heart chakra has both fluidic and airy properties.

Tantra teaches that our consciousness visits the heart Chakra from time to time. We become lighthearted or heavy-hearted according to what is on our mind; our heart Chakra becomes disturbed. Tantras advise us to cultivate dispassion, using breath control and sense withdrawal to help resolve conflicts between head and heart. Paradoxically, they also tell us to dive into this Chakra fearlessly, throwing caution aside but keeping spiritual faith in the certainty of gaining wisdom through loving experience.

We must not forget the sex Chakra, the secret place from where

Simplified Tantric representation of the Goddess as a female Yogi, with the spiritual powers or deities Brahma, Vishnu, and Shiva at the navel, heart, and head Chakras. Painting on paper, Rajasthan, India, nineteenth century.

the journey of Kundalini Shakti begins. This is the plexus of orgasm, an earthy basic center, untouched by reason, driven only by primordial need, by the instincts for reproduction, pleasure, and the fulfillment of sexual desire. This Chakra is likened to the fire in the bowels of the earth. Incredibly powerful, potentially world shattering, yet somehow maintaining balance. It is a Chakra driven largely by the powerful sense of smell.

Tantras teach that it is important to indulge the Goddess while consciousness is in this particular realm. It's important to please Her and channel Her tremendous creative powers to the purpose in mind; which is union with Shiva in the spiritual realm.

There is another Chakra between the sexual plexus and the solar plexus at the navel. It governs the assimilation of food and is driven by the sense of taste. Without proper assimilation of food, our body withers. This Chakra, then, can be thought of as our nourishing friend. It governs not only what is assimilated but also what is excreted. This is the assimilation or spleen Chakra.

Tantra is unique for its discovery of Chakras and their functions. Though other spiritual traditions preserve traces of Chakra knowledge, Tantra is the only way of life in which this knowledge is fully developed into a systematic aid to liberation. Together these five principle Chakras serve governing and evolutionary functions, helping to spiritually empower and refine raw psychophysical energies.

Tantra, Mantra, Yantra, and the Activation of the Chakras

In India today, mention of the word *Tantra* inevitably leads to the related Sanskrit words *mantra* and *yantra*. *Tantra-mantra*, *Tantra-yantra*, or *Tantra-mantra-yantra* are, in modern Indian culture, virtually synonymous. These three very similar, related words tell of the subtle and immensely potent interconnections between ourselves and the universe we inhabit. A person who perceives and can apply the interconnectivity of Tantra, mantra, and yantra has access to tremendous personal power and unlimited spiritual potential.

The sound of our breathing and our heartbeat are our most personal mantras, as is our most intimate name. Mantras are the keys to our identity; in Tantric tradition, they are used to unlock our personal power. They are power words or phrases, loaded with energy derived from spiritual realms. When they are repeated with willful spiritual intent, they focus, empower, and transform the psyche.

A mantra is by definition a protection of mind. It can be a personal prayer or chant, used in meditation, in ritual, and in all types of magical acts. All archaic spiritual traditions used them. In traditional Tantra, mantras are primordial vibrations, revealed originally as spiritual insights, then passed on from one initiate to another. By repeating such mantras, following initiation, minds are protected and connected, mental processes purified, and the spirit liberated.

The *Kularnava Tantra*, an important Hindu text, explains how a mantra gets its power:

> The perfection of a Mantra is caused by the power of transmission, by the teacher's grace, by the natural effect of the Mantra, and by the reciter's devotion.

Tantric diagram of a seed-mantra repeated, showing the emergence of organized forms as yantra. Manuscript painting on paper, Rajasthan, India, nineteenth century.

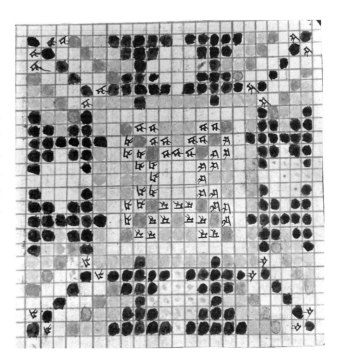

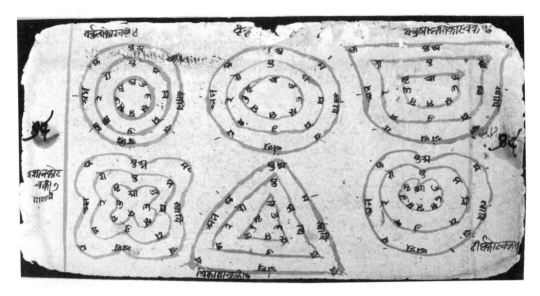

Tantric diagrams of seed-mantras creating organized forms or yantras by their focused repetition. Manuscript drawing on paper, Rajasthan, India, eighteenth century.

The first, simplest, and most potent Hindu mantra is *om*, which is comprised of three sounds—*ah*, *ou*, and *mm*, transcribed as *aum*. The threefold nature of *aum* or *om* reflects its triple interactions on every level, from the very subtle to the gross. From *om* follow all the other mantric seed-syllables, which, by their subtle and gross vibrations, manifest and define the invisible and visible universe.

The word *yantra* means "instrument." Our body is our sacred yantra, through which we communicate spiritually. In traditional Tantra, yantras are viewed as mystical diagrams, the tools of Tantra that define, contain, and channel what is normally considered undefinable and uncontainable.

In some traditions of Tantra, special postures, generally derived from Hatha Yoga, are used as yantras and are dedicated to specific tasks or functions. By a process of resonance with spiritual energies or divine powers, created through use of the human body as a yantra, the whole process of spiritual evolution can be sped up.

The use of mantras in conjunction with yantras enhances the whole process of spiritual evolution. This is a secret science and an occult art. It is an authentic ancient teaching derived from shaman-

Hindu Tantric representation of the Sri yantra, mystical symbol of the body with Goddess energies in place. Painting from Rajasthan, India, circa eighteenth century.

ism. For success in the use of mantra–yantra interactivity, initiation is key.

As can be seen here, oral evocations are inherently powerful and are used prolifically in Tantric practices. According to Tantric tradition, the five principle Chakras are activated by five seed-sounds (known as *bija mantras*). These are the sound *lam* in the sex center, *vam* in the assimilation center, *ram* in the navel center, *yam* in the heart center, and *ham* in the head center. In Tantric rites devised to awaken the Kundalini Shakti and guide the potent evolutionary energy through these five principal Chakras, these five seed-syllables are used. They are evoked at each of the centers.

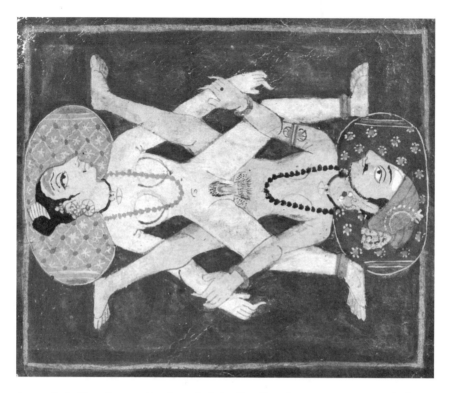

A couple in Tantric sexual union, their bodies forming a yantra or mystical diagram. Painting on paper, from Nepal, circa late seventeenth century.

The whole procedure of awakening and channeling the Kundalini energy is a mystical process, not a physiological one. Tantras teach different methods, some of which are closely guarded secrets. The identity, however, of the five primary Chakras—and the seed-sounds used to evoke and transform the Goddess energy at each of them—remains consistent. The overall picture of the relationships among the parts of the fivefold Chakra system looks like this:

Chakra	Element	Faculty	Seed-Sound
Head	Space	Hearing	*Ham*
Heart	Air	Touch	*Yam*
Navel	Fire	Sight	*Ram*
Assimilation	Water	Taste	*Vam*
Sex	Earth	Smell	*Lam*

A pentagram yantra with seed-syllable mantra of the Goddess at the center. Painting on paper, from Rajasthan, India, circa late seventeenth century.

A triangular yantra with central seed-syllable. Painting on paper, from Rajasthan, India, circa late seventeenth century.

The fivefold triangular yantra of the goddess Kali. Drawing from an Indian painting, circa eighteenth century.

These five principle Chakras and their "correspondences" are of prime importance to the Tantric practitioner and to anyone earnestly desirous of practicing spiritual sex. The elemental and sensual correspondences of these five Chakras are key to taming the "wild horses" of consciousness and empowering one's spiritual evolution. These are easily accessible truths that can be applied in a straightforward manner, with just enough mysticism to make spiritual sex interesting rather than mechanical.

The fivefold correspondences aid the process of self-realization, steering the raw sexual energy through the various stages of refinement down the Tantric path. These correspondences help focus the mind, help structure and organize the normally disorganized, and by the powers of resonance, speed up the evolutionary process.

The Five Conflicting Emotions, Faculties, and Sentiments

Buddhist Tantra texts list five conflicting emotions: desire, hatred, delusion, pride, and envy. These are sometimes referred to as the five poisons. We all know how desire drives us to all kinds of mischief, how hatred can be so destructive, how delusion can be so easy to see in others yet so difficult to see in oneself, how pride invariably leads to some kind of loss or fall, and how envy is such an unpleasant—even crazed—emotion. Tantra teaches us to transform these emotions or poisons into divine qualities or elixirs. This is done by applying the five faculties: faith, perseverance, recollection or mindfulness, contemplation, and discriminative awareness.

Five devotional sentiments are particularly important to the Tantric path of spiritual sex. These are peaceful devotion, service to the beloved, true friendship and loyalty, selflessness as when caring for a child, and erotic passion. By cultivating these five devotional sentiments as one approaches the practice of spiritual sex, success will be most easily achieved. There should be no secrets between lovers, no hidden agendas, no game-playing behavior. True intimacy can only occur when every consideration is given, when service and satisfaction is a pleasure and not a chore, when acts of love are uncomplicated, generous, and spontaneous.

Traditional Fivefold Tantra

Traditional Tantric practices, both Hindu and Buddhist, are most easily understood under the following five topics:

Asana: body posture; the use of Hatha Yoga techniques to relax and prepare the body for spiritual activity. Through correct use of *asana*, the body expresses itself as both yantra (through its posture) and mantra (through repetitious controlled breathing).

Pranayama: focused breathing practices that exerts control over the *Pranas*, which are the life-force.

Mantrayana: the repetition of mantras or "power words." These can be informal (such as the sound of breathing) or formal (esoteric power words received through initiation).

Yantrayana and Mandala construction: the use of mystical diagrams and mandala for focusing the mind, attracting spiritual powers, conveying initiation, and for occult purposes (such as charms or amulets).

Sadhana: spiritual practice; the blending of worldly and otherworldly intentions and energies, especially through controlled indulgence in the five senses.

In the Tantric lifestyle, the above five "limbs" comprise the complete, holistic spiritualized person.

The Five Families of Buddhas and Their Consorts

Stories of the life of Gautama, the historical Buddha who lived in the sixth century B.C.E., abound with accounts of his spiritual powers. Like Jesus, he used to perform miracles, such as walking on water, knowing the thoughts of others, making things or persons invisible, magically causing rain during drought, simultaneously appearing in several different places, in this way helping to convert unbelievers to his spiritual teachings.

Miraculous powers are Tantric attainments. The *Guhyasamaja Tantra,* which is an early Buddhist Tantric text, tells us that the Bud-

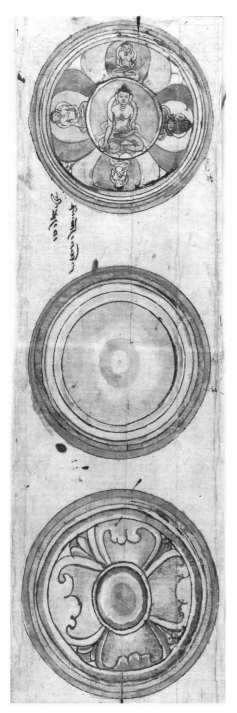

Left: Tibetan diagram showing five *dhyani* Buddhas, oriented to the directions, with encircling layers of spiritual radiance. From a painted manuscript, Tibet, eighteenth century.

Right: Tibetan diagram showing a central *dhyani* Buddha with consort and the emanation of Buddha families oriented to the directions. From a painted manuscript, Tibet, eighteenth century.

dha once sat in meditation and made five different hand gestures accompanied by specific mantras. By his spiritual power, he manifested himself in five different Buddha forms, colored yellow, red, green, blue, and white. Known as *dhyani* or "meditation" Buddhas, they each appeared seated on thrones, in intimate union with their consorts.

The five *dhyani* Buddhas and their consorts are the spiritual parents of the five families or lineages of Buddhas. The entire spectrum of Buddhist iconography—meaning all the spiritual powers, including past and future Buddhas, bodhisattvas, and divine beings—belong to one or other of these five *dhyani* Buddha families of Tantric tradition.

According to the *Sadhanamala*, an early Buddhist Tantric compendium of Tantric rites:

> The "Victorious Ones" or Dhyani Buddhas are called Vairocana, Ratnasambhava, Amitabha, Amoghasiddhi and Aksobhya. Their colors are white, yellow, red, green and blue, and they exhibit the "Wheel of Law" (*dharmachakra*), "Gift-bestowing" (*varada*), "Absorbed-in-Meditation" (*samadhi*), "Fear-not" (*abhaya*) and "Earth-witness" (*bhumisparsa*) mystic gestures.

Every spiritual system relies upon a philosophical system or "root view," which is the foundation of its esoteric practice. The Buddhist Tantric or *Vajrayana* systems all have as their root the doctrine of aggregates, the observed and experienced factors comprising the complex combinations of changing forces within a person. These are:

> *Matter:* the totality of all physical properties such as solidity, fluidity, heat, and motion.
>
> *Sensation:* the totality of all experienced feelings—painful, pleasant or neutral—that derive from the contact of our physical and mental organs with the outside world and give rise to sensations.
>
> *Perception:* the totality of all recognition, derived from the contact of the sense faculties with the external world.
>
> *Formation:* the totality of "compounded mentality," meaning karma-created mental formations and volitional activities. These bind us to a seemingly endless cycle of births and deaths.

This cycle is in need of spiritual purification so that we can be freed from it.

Consciousness: the product of a constantly changing flux of dominating properties such as eye-consciousness, mind-consciousness, matter-consciousness, and so forth, and is the totality of the four previously listed aggregates.

In Tantric Buddhist philosophy, each of the five *dhyani* Buddhas symbolizes one of these five aggregates. For visualization and ritual purposes, these five aggregates or *dhyani* Buddhas are assigned places at the four cardinal directions of a circle, with the Buddha Vairocana, symbolizing matter and the practitioner, at the central point. This structured circle of energies with assigned meanings is known as a mandala.

A mandala is a mystic protective circle and is encountered in Hindu and Buddhist Tantra, as well as in most other occult traditions, as a magical tool. Tantric initiations emphasize the importance of the mandala, which is an easy-to-comprehend, easy-to-visualize systematic representation of forces or ingredients being confronted or transformed.

In Tantric tradition, mandalas are generally intricate interrelated systematic structures that define relationships of forces, symbols, and all things. Orientation, element, color, form, sense, symbol, gesture, sentiment, mantra, and more are, in Tantric practice, laid out and approached through a fivefold mandala structure.

In Buddhist Tantra, the basic mandala of the five *dhyani* Buddhas, and of all the derived families of Buddha energies is laid out in the following way:

Orientation	Center	East	North	West	South
Buddha	Vairocana	Aksobhya	Amoghasiddhi	Amitabha	Ratnasambhava
Consort	Vajradhatvishvari	Locana	Tara	Pandaravasini	Mamaki
Color	White	Blue	Green	Red	Yellow
Element	Space	Water	Air	Fire	Earth
Symbol	Wheel	Scepter	Crossed scepter	Lotus	Jewel
Creature	Lion	Elephant	Garuda	Peacock	Horse
Mantra	*Om*	*Hum*	*Kham*	*Hrih*	*Tram*
Poison	Delusion	Enmity	Jealousy	Attachment	Egoism
Wisdom	Seed	Mirrorlike	Pervading	Discriminating	Equality
Yogini	Brahmani	Dombi	Rajaki	Narti	Candalini

Tibetan painting showing a central cosmic seated Buddha with consort, and a typical mandala structure, oriented to the directions. From a *thanka* painting on cloth, Tibet, seventeenth century.

For the sake of completeness, I have included esoteric Buddhist Tantric concepts as they relate to this basic *dhyani* Buddha mandala. The poison category relates to personality faults that can be corrected or purified by self-identification with the specific *dhyani* Buddha. The wisdom category lists types of wisdom attainable once the poison is purified. The Yogini category refers to the type of female

Yogi-consort who can help the purification process. For example, Dombi, which is the name for the washerwoman caste, means a Yogini who is direct, physical, and perhaps unsophisticated; Brahmani, who is from the high priestly caste, means the opposite; Candalini, also Kundalini, means a consort who is very passionate and has raw, untamed sexual powers; Narti is the dancer or artistic type, who is skilled in the subtle way she expresses herself; Rajaki, or Vajri, is the adamantine type, excellent in concentration, spontaneous in spiritual nature.

Intense or prolonged sexual intimacy generally produces an exaggeration of whatever lies beneath the surface of one's "normal" consciousness. Egoistic feelings or the opposite—a sense of emptiness—can be confusing, as can negative emotions such as jealousy, envy, or excessive attachment. Such things can totally destroy what may have otherwise been a progressive and liberating relationship.

If you have chosen to practice your spiritual sex in a Buddhist manner, you'll begin to identify with Buddhist spiritual powers. You'll discover them within your self. By identifying with a particular Buddha family, by using a specific gesture, mantra, or meditation approach, the protective power of the *dhyani* Buddhas will help your liberation. You'll be following a well-trodden path with plenty of signposts along the way.

The Five Faces of Shiva

Shiva is the "father" of Tantra Yoga, and Shakti is the "mother." In the previous chapter, we explored the archaeology and anthropology of both these archetypes over many thousands of years. Hunter-priest and mother-priestess, transcendental stud and materialistic holy whore, shaman and virgin—these are but some of the archetypal personalities that Shiva and Shakti have embodied over the millennia.

Shiva is the ruler of the universe, the Supreme Yogi. He has three eyes on each of his five faces, symbolizing the sun, moon, and spiritual fire—linked to solar, lunar, and occult forces and to the

Stone sculpture of a multiheaded Shiva with three eyes on each face, the third eye at the center of the forehead. Sandstone carving from Someshwar, Indian Himalayas, circa tenth century.

right, left, and central "psychic nerves channels" (*Ida*, *Sushumna*, and *Pingala*) of the subtle Tantric Yoga anatomy.

The three eyes also signify *om*, which is comprised of the three sounds *a*, *u*, and *m* and is the supreme seed-mantra that is a precursor of all spiritual activity that precedes every other mantra. The five faces are aspects of Shiva's popular five-syllabled mantra, which is *Na-mo-Shi-va-ya*. Shiva's five faces look toward the four cardinal directions, with the fifth face at the center, turned upward.

A supreme cardinally oriented phallic "transcendental Lord" similar to Shiva is found in other ancient cultures, such as

A cover for a Shiva Lingam, with five faces, the fifth face uppermost. Hammered copper, from Rajasthan, circa nineteenth century.

Five-faced Fang wooden carving
from Gabon, West Africa. Part of a
ritual drum used in prophecy.

Egypt and in West Africa. For example, among the Fang tribes of Gabon and the Dogon of Mali, directionally facing wooden sculptures of male rulers with transcendental attributes are known.

Gerald Massey (1828–1907), a brilliant self-educated writer, postulated an African origin to much of the common occult symbolism in classical cultures, outlining the evidence in his major works, *The Book of the Beginnings* (1881) and *The Natural Genesis* (1883). In his time, many of his conclusions, which were controversial and politically troubling, were ridiculed or ignored.

Kenneth Grant, the noted authority on Western magical tradition and especially that of Aleister Crowley, confirms Massey's insights. Writing in his fascinating book, *Cults of the Shadow* (1976), he connects the origins and practices of Tantra with some of the fetish cults of Western Africa, who have Shaivite-type festivals, phallic symbols and shrines, and magical liturgies and use mantras in their rites. He observes:

Traces of some of the most obscure magical languages are yet extant in some of the god names, place names, and ancient dialects of Africa. In the Western African "fetish" cults, for instance, are preserved some of the primal names of magical power that were carried over and integrated with Egyptian and Chaldaean traditions at a much later age.

Four-faced Fang reliquary guardian figure. Wooden carving from Gabon, West Africa, circa nineteenth century.

In Hindu tradition, Shiva's five faces symbolize the fivefold duties of spiritual entities. These are traditionally defined as creation, maintenance, annihilation, concealment, and blessing. According to Tantric lore, the first three—creation, maintenance, and annihilation or destruction—are the natural threefold process that all phenomena pass through. *Concealment* means the hidden spiritual potency that

remains and *blessing* means liberation from the cycle of birth and death.

Shiva's five faces also symbolize the mind, ego, intellect, material world, and soul. These five faces are linked to the five states in which the individual soul can be: waking, dream, deep sleep, cosmic delight, and spiritual ecstasy. *Waking* means the perception of the external world through the senses; *dream* means internal perception produced by the mind; *deep sleep* means the soul is in a state of nonapprehension; *cosmic delight* means when the soul experiences an ecstatic flash of spiritual essence; and *spiritual ecstasy* means the soul's perfection of ecstasy.

Shiva's five faces are also linked to the five primordial elements—earth, water, fire, air, and space—and to the five senses, five colors, five tastes, five sentiments, five shapes, and five *Pranas*. They have many other fivefold correspondences, such as the five original tribes of humanity, the five types of beings, and the five deities to be worshipped by Hindu Tantrics: the elephant-headed Ganesha, "remover of obstacles"; Brahma, the creator; Vishnu, the preserver or maintainer; Shiva, the transcendental Supreme Yogi, and Shakti, the Great Goddess.

Giant stone phallus at the Yoruba
holy shrine of Ife, Nigeria.

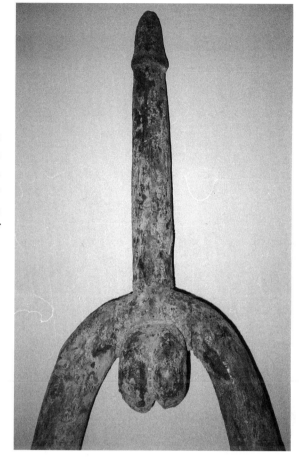

Wooden phallic effigy—a giant erect penis with two testicles below—carried on the shoulders during fertility festivals. From the Grasslands culture of Cameroon, West Africa.

Writing in his important book, *Shiva Mahadeva: The Great God* (1966), Vasudeva Agrawala, the eminent Indian scholar, emphasizes the significance of the Shiva correspondences:

> The five faces of the god Shiva point to a basic concept in which the whole cosmos is conceived to be rooted in a fivefold scheme at all levels of creation. . . . The three eyes of the god Mahadeva and his five faces are but significant symbols of the spiritual constitution of human personality: without them there can be no conception of any creative form of Pranic energy. One has, therefore, to understand the iconographic forms as the alphabet of a language that is universal and endless in time and space.

The Five Gods of Hindu Tantra

The elephant-headed Ganesha, "remover of obstacles." Stone sculpture from Khajuraho, central India, circa eleventh century.

Traditional three-headed image of Brahma the creator. Stone sculpture from central India, circa eighth century.

Traditional three-headed image of Shiva, the transcendental Supreme Yogi, with third eye clearly marked. Stone sculpture from Kashmir, India, circa nineteenth century.

Traditional image of Shakti, the Great Goddess. Wooden carving from South India, circa eighteenth century.

Painting of Vishnu, the
Preserver. From Nepal, circa
fifteenth century.

The fivefold correspondences—of color, direction, gesture, mantra, visualization and sequence—vary in different Yogic traditions.
Initiation into this mystery has traditionally been conveyed orally,
one-on-one. Those wishing to make rapid progress in their practice
of Tantra in the Hindu manner, with worship of the Great Goddess
and the transcendental Lord Shiva as the primary focus, should ideally connect with and take initiation from an established spiritual
lineage. Unlike Buddhist Tantra, which has a generally unified system of correspondences, Hindu Tantras tend to be more diverse in
their structure, offering both more variety and to the uninitiated,
the possibility of more confusion.

Traditional image of Shiva and Shakti, known as Uma-Maheshwara, depicting the Supreme Yogi and Cosmic Woman in playful intimacy. Above their heads are five Lingams. Stone sculpture from the Chandella culture, central India, circa eleventh century.

Shiva's mysteries can be accessed directly by self-observation, by perception, through Yoga, through meditation, and by participation in the rites of spiritual love. When we perform worship of self and others, using the five senses as our Tantric tools, we can experience the spiritual powers of Shiva directly.

Shiva: The Power of the Penis

Traditional representation of Shiva, the Supreme Yogi, phallus erect, a trident in his uppermost left hand. Stone sculpture from Nepal, circa sixteenth century.

According to Tantric lore, the immortal spiritual principle is known as Shiva, whose essence is transcendental. Shiva is idealized as the Supreme Yogi who can conquer death. Among Shiva's most important symbols are the upturned horns of a bull, the upturned crescent moon, and the trident. These three obviously related symbols are very archaic and, as we have seen, can be found in many different cultures. They mean "death transcended," the power over death through Yogic or shamanistic expertise—spiritual resurrection.

Another important symbol of Shiva is the erect male organ, the penis or phallus, known in India as the *Linga* or *Lingam*. This is an ancient symbol found in all pagan cultures. The icon of male sexual power, the Shiva Lingam symbolizes male sexuality exalted, controlled, and transformed into pure penetrating spiritual insight.

Lingam and Yoni: Shiva and Shakti

An ancient Hindu story tells how Shiva and his consort, Shakti, once had a dispute about which of the two sexes is superior. Each created a race of people. Shiva's creation devoted themselves exclusively to the worship of male energy. After a while their bodies became feeble, their limbs became distorted, their complexions took on mottled colors, and their intellects dulled. The people created by Shakti, the

Great Goddess, worshipped female energy. They were exceedingly handsome and after a while became powerful and wealthy.

This Tantric story reminds us that though Shiva-energy is powerful, it is unworldly. Shakti-energy is far more suited to mundane concerns. This story also brings to mind the Tantric saying that "Shiva without Shakti is a corpse," that the heavenly transcendental power has no potency unless it can interact with Goddess energy. Together, Shiva and Shakti are the perfect cosmic balance: Shakti expressing Herself through nature and with everything in this world, and Shiva dealing with everything in the next. In relationships between the sexes, it's wise to remember this original cosmic order. Woman is the natural ruler over worldly matters and earthly forces, whereas man predominates over transcendental or heavenly issues. And earth and Heaven are codependent, requiring a third entity, "space," to interact.

The Goddess Kali

Joseph Campbell (1904–1987), mythologist and scholar extraordinaire, brilliant author and television raconteur, has changed the way many now think of myths. He risked much when, in discussions with journalist Bill Moyers, he presented his essentially radical and heretical view of world mythology and spiritual philosophy in the important television series *The Power of Myth*, which was to become the highest rated public-television series in history. A student of the famous Indologist Heinrich Zimmer (1890–1943), who died suddenly at the peak of his career, Campbell took up some of his work and saw it through to publication.

Zimmer's *Myths and Symbols in Indian Art and Civilization* (1946), edited by Campbell, includes a vivid description and insight-filled interpretation of the Great Goddess manifestation known as Kali. Pointing to Kali's ambivalent Tantric character, he explained the unique iconography and potent magical symbolism:

> As the "Fairest of the Three Spheres of the Universe," the one and only "she," this majestic wonderful figure is the embodiment of man's desires and delights, the archetypal object of all longings

and all thought. In order that she may represent the *full* significance of Shakti-Maya, this alluring, ever-charming Eternal Female of our Soul has to be painted black, has to be clad with the symbols of destruction and death as well as the symbols of life.

Joseph Campbell traveled to Asia and met with Yogis and Tantrics. He became a devotee and enthusiastic promoter of the Great Goddess, somehow managing to maintain his traditional Christian beliefs while embracing paganism with passion.

The Dark Goddess and Tantric Magic

Joseph Campbell advised spiritual seekers to ''follow your bliss.'' To male Tantric initiates, bliss is generally identified with the Great Goddess in her mystical and magical aspect, more often than not idealized and embodied as woman. For female initiates, identification with the Great Goddess, in all her forms, is entirely natural.

''Shiva without Shakti is a corpse.'' Again, this well-known Tantric saying neatly expresses the truth of Goddess potency and the raison d'être of the Tantric lifestyle. Shakti is energy, power, and delight. Shakti *is* bliss. She is the dark and the light, every color and every female form.

Shakti, the Great Goddess, is Shiva's phenomenal power. Acts of magic require her assent and are driven by her power. According to Tantric lore, the goddess Kali is the highest expression of female spiritual power in this, the Kali Yuga, the dark age of egoism and materialism.

Kali reveals herself to devotees through the forms of nature and especially through women. She is the very essence of woman, sensual, pleasure-seeking, sometimes fickle, but always nurturing. Like nature, she can seem either cruel or benign. She is the Dark Secret of the Universe, an initiatory power, the Ultimate Shakti. Within the body, she is the Kundalini, the ''serpent power,'' the key to spiritual liberation. In the world, she is all women, all nature.

Kali's origins are in India's archaic matriarchal culture. Her radiant blackness protected the dark-skinned tribes who worshipped her and inspired fear and dread in their enemies. She was, originally,

Shakti in the form of a four-armed Kali, using Shiva to satisfy herself. From a traditional Tantric painting, Rajasthan, India, circa eighteenth century.

a warrior goddess, worshipped with blood sacrifice and offerings of flesh and liquor. She was always viewed as all-powerful, awesome, as mysterious as night, fierce, passionately sensual, demanding, and magically potent.

Variations on the name Kali for female divinity can be found in many ancient cultures outside India, which suggests that in the distant past, a common or related matriarchal religion pervaded much of the world. In prehistoric Ireland, people worshipped a powerful goddess known as Kele (her priestesses were known as Kelles); in ancient Finland, there was the all-powerful goddess Kalma; in the Sinai region of the Middle East, there was the goddess Kalu; and in ancient Greece, an aspect of the goddess was known as Kalli. These

Goddess Kali in the cosmic cremation ground of the phenomenal world, striding on the recumbent Shiva. Traditional Tantric painting, Company school, Bengal, circa nineteenth century. (In the Falk collection)

very similar names for the Great Goddess in different cultures were the result of the export of spiritual ideas and practices from India prior to the early invasions by light-skinned Aryans.

Some early Buddhists identified the Great Goddess with their Prajnaparamita, the "Perfection of Wisdom," conceived of as a multiarmed female "wisdom energy." Buddhist Tantrics viewed Prajnaparamita as the original Buddha-consort, and over time, developed this vision further. They viewed her as a saviouress, calling her "Tara, the Compassionate One, She who helps the devotee overcome suffering." As the dark four-armed Ugra Tara, with the dark blue *dhyani*-Buddha Aksobhya on her crown, she became the Wrathful Saviouress, externally fierce so as to ward off enemies and unbelievers, but internally compassionate, the embodiment of compassion and spiritual wisdom.

Indian Tantric Buddhists also knew the Dark Goddess as Shyam (the Dark One) and Kali. According to the noted Bengali authority on Indian Buddhist Tantra, Benoytosh Bhatta-charyya:

> Kali, according to Buddhist tradi-tion, is Kadi or Kakaradi, or, in other words, all the consonants of the alphabet. . . . All the consonants of the (Sanskrit) alphabet are deified in her.

The mystery of Kali's name, which begins with the first consonant of the Sanskrit alphabet, attached to the first vowel, is deep indeed. From Tantric tradition, we learn that the whole material universe is but an ex-pression of certain primordial sounds or vibrations. These are expressed by the consonants and vowels of the Sanskrit alphabet, combined together in different ways.

Sculpture of the Saviouress Tara, a Buddhist form of Kali. Pala stone carving from Bihar, Eastern India, circa tenth century.

Seed-syllables (*bija* mantras) and spells *(dharanis)* are the very fabric from which this universe is formed. From Tantric tradition, we learn that the garland of heads about Kali's neck symbolizes the letters or vibrations of the Sanskrit alphabet. From this, we can learn Kali's seed-syllables, names, and potent mantras, the tools by which we can transform ourselves and become one with Her.

Kali Ma, the compassionate Primordial Mother, can be timeless and formless, young and old, exquisitely beautiful and alluring as well as awesomely ugly and repugnant. She manifests as virgin and whore, young girl and sensual mature woman, a wrathful warrior queen and an old hag, nurturing mother and wicked witch. Kali is a paradox to those who do not know her well. She seems unpredict-able, yet to her devotees she is always reliable. For practices of Tantra magic, meaning Tantra-mantra, Kali is the ultimate ally. Her seed-mantras *kang* and *kling* are all-powerful and are used in many different Tantric rites.

Forms and Meanings of Kali

Over the centuries, many different iconographic forms and names for the Dark Goddess became known in India and surrounding countries. These icons were revealed in visions coming from spiritual practice, dreams, drugs, trances, or austerities, and all are variations of the one Great Dark Original Mother, Kali.

Kali is mentioned in the Hindu epic *Mahabharata*, described as "red-eyed, red-faced, garlanded with red, terrible to look at, and holding a noose." Here the color red indicates her sensual, sexual nature and her close connection with the life-force, blood—the sacrificial blood of offerings and the potency of menstrual blood—and Kali's transcendent power over death.

In the *Devi-Mahatmya* and several *Purana* texts of the medieval period, Kali is generally described as dark, witchlike, fanged, emaciated, and terrible to look at. A myth tells how the body of Devi or Parvati (daughter of the Himalayas and consort of Shiva the Supreme Yogi) was transformed and turned black, becoming known as Kali or Kalika. In this form, she terrorized the patriarchal demons who had begun to take over the universe. In her emaciated haglike form, she was the only divine power able to defeat two particularly egoistic demons named Chanda and Munda. After she defeated them, she made their spirits serve her and she became known as Chamunda.

Bhairavi is another well-known name for Kali. In the *Kalika Purana* text, the names Kali and Bhairavi interchange as if at a whim. Here Bhairavi is generally used when referring specifically to the Tantric consort of Bhairava (wrathful Shiva), especially when engaged in the "great rite" of sexual union. In north India, there is a tradition of calling twelve-year-old virgin girls Bhairavi when they are worshipped as the virgin Goddess in Tantric rites.

In north India, the Bhairavi form of the Great Goddess is most

Bronze casting of the multi-armed Hindu goddess Chamunda, the emaciated haglike form of Kali. From Nepal, circa sixteenth century.

commonly depicted as elderly, a *mata-ji*, emaciated, with eyes sunken, breasts shriveled or pendulous, hair upstanding and unkempt, but always ecstatic, "out of this world," and loaded with mystic initiatory power. The following is an iconographic description of the Bhairavi form of Kali:

> Disheveled hair, garland of human heads, face with long or projecting teeth, four arms, lower left holding a human head just severed, upper left holding a sword, lower right hand posed as if giving a boon, the upper right hand posed granting freedom from fear, deep dark complexion, naked, two corpses or arrows as ornaments in the two ears, girdle of the hands of corpses, three

eyes, radiant like the morning sun, standing on the chest of Mahadeva (Shiva) lying like a corpse, surrounded by jackals.

In Hindu Tantric tradition, followers of the Great Goddess are
told to view all girls and women, of whatever age, race, or color, as
the visible embodiments of her, at times worshipping with offerings
of worldly and sensual things in the hope of getting boons, mystic
powers *(siddhis)*, and spiritual liberation.

Bronze casting of the
virginal form of Bhairavi,
an aspect of Kali, from
South India, circa
seventeenth century. (In
the Spiesshofer collection)

Contemporary rendering of Yam Raj, the buffalo-horned Hindu ruler of death. His penis is erect. Woodblock print from Tibet.

Yam Raj, the buffalo-horned tribal and modern Hindu ruler of death, is said to live in the south *(daksin)*. Daksina Kali is the "remover of the fear of death" and remover of Yam Raj, and Mahadeva (the Great God Shiva, also known as Mahakala in his wrathful form) is her consort.

Daksina Kali sports on Shiva. She is his energy, his dark muse, his Shakti. Playfully and without any reserve, she takes her pleasure while he lies intoxicated beneath her. Sometimes she stands on him or dances around him, sometimes she squats on him, inserting his erect *Lingam* into her *Yoni* in wild sexual abandon.

She is the active power, time transcended. He is her support,

Large metal casting of Mahakala, a form of Shiva. Sino-Tibetan culture, circa seventeenth century. (Private collection)

depicted as white, pure consciousness, penetrating deep into the unknowable. The *Kamakalavilasa Tantra* sums up their relationship:

> Shakti performs all the physical needs of Shiva. Bodiless Shiva, being of the nature of pure consciousness, must have Shakti for his body.

Kali is the essence of bliss, the love-power. Shiva is delight incarnate, the root of all new creation. It is said that "the whole universe is created by the Shakti of Shiva." In the form of white Shiva and dark Shakti, Kali is to be viewed as *atma* (the self) and Shiva as *jiva* (the transcendental soul). Through spiritual practice and by identifying with this vision, self and soul become one.

Four-armed form of the goddess Kali squatting in sexual union upon the recumbent Shiva. Traditional Tantric painting from Nepal, circa nineteenth century.

Many different forms of Kali have been described, yet many more abound. As Maha Kali, the Great Goddess is most commonly visualized as ten-armed, ten-faced, with three eyes on each face, her complexion dark and shining. In this form, she destroys two particularly egoistic patriarchal demons, Madhu and Kaitabha.

As Kala Ratri, tawny-eyed, cruel, and fond of war, she wears tiger and elephant skins and holds an axe, a noose, other weapons, and a skull-bowl from which she drinks blood. Kali is the "night of destruction" at the termination of this world. She is the female spiritual power, always ready to defeat the last negative forces, so none can pollute the next world.

Forms of Bhadra Kali have sixteen arms, eighteen arms, or one hundred arms, all giving protection to her devotees. Bhadra Kali is always visualized as a giantess wearing a three-pointed crown ornamented with the crescent moon and a snake about her neck, her body draped in red and her mood jolly. She pierces the body of a buffalo with her lance, one of her many weapons. Hindu Tantrics believe that this is the form of Goddess that pervades the whole universe in the present dark age of materialism.

One of the most important places of Goddess pilgrimage and Kali worship is at Kalighat, in Calcutta. This is one of the "seats" of the Great Goddess. Here dark Kali is worshipped with sacrifices of specially selected goats and sheep and with liquor. After such rites, the offerings are viewed as special sacraments and are generally consumed by devotees.

The Kalighat Kali icon is most extraordinary. It mainly consists of her dark head, with three eyes exaggerated, her mouth wide and showing an array of teeth, her tongue extending downward and outward. In the 1960s, it inspired the lolling-tongue logo used by the Rolling Stones.

One cannot adequately describe the fervor of Kali's devotees at the Kalighat temple. The atmosphere there is always charged with mystery, magic, and occult energy.

Great Kali image, depicted squatting in sexual union on Shiva, within a cremation ground, yantras of the Mahavidya goddess powers all around. Metal casting from Nepal, circa seventeenth century.

Kali is considered to be the guru or teacher of the ten Mahavidya goddesses of Hindu Tantric tradition. Known as the ten fundamental cosmic powers, whose role is to create, maintain, and reabsorb the entire universe, these Mahavidya goddesses have, in Hindu Tantric tradition, specific names, mantras and yantras by which they are evoked through magical rites. They can best be understood as cosmic projections of female cosmic spiritual energy (Shakti).

The black goddess Matangi (one of the Mahavidyas) is another of the many potent forms of Kali. Matangi is dark black, her face fear-inspiring and angry, her three eyes reddened with intoxication, a crescent moon on her forehead. She can have from four to eighteen arms, holding various weapons as well as a trident and a pot filled with wine. She wears fine red silk clothes and is seated on a lion and/or a throne made of precious gems. Matangi is invoked by newlyweds, and Tantric Hindus believe that she bestows prosperity and happiness. It is believed that she originated from the dark fire of Kali's face.

Bhramari Devi is a dark goddess identified as another form of Kalika. Said to be "as brilliant as a million dark suns," she is surrounded by black bees that she holds in the first of her hands, others of which are in the "boon-granting" and "fear-allaying" gestures. She destroys egoistic demons while her bees make the seed-mantra *hring*.

Kali also became known and revered in Tibet. Known there as Lhamo ("God Mother"), several different forms of her are found in the Tibetan pantheon. One of her Tibetan names, Sri Devi, tells of her Hindu origin. She is the guardian goddess of Lhasa, the Tibetan capital, and is the chief protectress of the Gelugpa sect of Lamaism, of which the Dalai Lama is the supreme hierarch.

Kali is the wrathful protector of the Buddhist Dharma in Tibet, visualized at the base of the trunk of the "lineage tree" of several sects. She is the only feminine deity among the Buddhist Dharmapalas, the defenders of the law of Buddhism.

Krsnananda Agamavagisa, the Bengali mystic (born about 1500 C.E.), once had a powerful spiritual experience that caused him to popularize a new form of the Great Goddess Kali. Tradition has it that he went to bathe in a river near a cremation ground. He happened to disturb a dark-skinned tribal girl who, believing she was

Lhamo or Sri Devi, a Tibetan form of Kali, shown riding on a mule. *Thanka* painting on cloth, from Tibet, circa eighteenth century.

Black stone image of the four-armed youthful Kali, rendered much in the style of Krsnananda's vision. From Dinajpur (now called Bangladesh), circa sixteenth century. (In the Bumper collection, Calgary, Canada)

alone, had stripped nude and was washing herself. She was using a discarded skullcap from a nearby funeral pyre, had her long black hair untied, and was engrossed in her ablutions.

Embarrassed by Krsnananda's sudden presence, the girl stuck out her tongue in shyness (a reflex action still performed by village girls in India). Krsnananda, who had been trying to understand how best to comprehend the many varied forms of the dark Goddess, and how to get a direct vision of her, had a sudden spiritual insight. He viewed this tribal girl as a living Kali and took the vision of her naked dark body, long disheveled hair, extended tongue, and skull in hand as a new and especially potent icon of the Great Goddess. Using this insight as his meditation, he soon became perfected. He had images made of this new and potent form of Kali and worshipped them as his deeper self. He then spread word of this special form of Kali far and wide.

Around 1580, in his book known as *Tantrasara*, a "compendium of Tantras," he gave the following description of the Dark Goddess, which forms the basis of the typical East Indian Kali icon:

> Possessed of complexion like the color of sapphire, blue like the sky, extremely fierce, defeating gods and demons, three-eyed, crying very loudly, decked with all ornaments, holding a human skull and a small sword, standing on the moon and sun.

Christians who encountered statues of this Great Goddess in India viewed this particular goddess form as demonic. They did not understand the symbolism of Kali, who is portrayed as a very sexual young woman, her tongue out, protectively fierce but always compassionate. This iconographic form of the Great Goddess is an ideal of Tantric womanhood: sexually aggressive, playful, and magically potent.

To many Westerners unfamiliar with the inner meaning of wrathful metaphysical symbolism, Kali's many dark and fearsome forms can seem threatening. Tantra veils occult power to keep it accessible only to initiates. Just as knowledge of nuclear secrets needs to be kept away from those who might misuse it, Tantra conceals its potency behind scary symbols. To those for whom death and ghosts and witches hold no fear, Kali is always ready to share her special secrets.

Kundalini, the Goddess Power

Any close look into the Tantric tradition of spiritual sex leads to Kundalini, often referred to as the "serpent power." To many, *Kundalini* and *Tantra* are synonymous, Kundalini Yoga generally being viewed as an aspect of Tantra Yoga.

The Sanskrit root-word *kunda* means a "pool" or "bowl-shaped fire vessel." A *kundala* is a coiled earring and *kundalin* means "decorated with coils." The Kundalini is the inner and original source of evolutionary energy. Likened to a coiled snake, this potent energy is a raw sexual power that has a female character and is, in Tantric tradition, viewed as the Goddess power within the body.

The *Thirumandiram*, a Tamil South Indian work of Hindu Tantra, refers to Kundalini as an inner fire and the potent power of love:

> Light the fire of Kundalini;
> Melt your heart with divine love!

The Theosophical movement first manifested in the prudish Victorian era. Rather than explore or discuss India's secret teachings in context and without bias, Theosophist writers took a dualistic stance and separated Hindu practices into "pure" and "impure," along sex-

Traditional rendering of the coiled Kundalini, depicted as a snake with heads at each end. Painting on paper, from Rajasthan, India, circa eighteenth century. (In the Kieffer collection, Stamford, CT)

ual lines. They viewed celibacy and orthodox Hinduism as pure, and sexuality and the radical Tantric teachings as impure.

Theosophists were the first Westerners to write about Kundalini and popularize certain Tantric information. Unfortunately, they misstated the very simple Kundalini scenario as described in the Tantras, in which the Kundalini Shakti, viewed as a goddess power, rises up and seeks union with her lord, Shiva. They declared Kundalini dangerous, stressing the need for sexual continence by those who would or could awaken this inner psychic power. They desexualized and reinterpreted the Kundalini phenomena, both physicalizing and mystifying it.

Theosophy took the goddess out of Kundalini, leaving a pseudo-scientific, garbled version of the real teachings. Other Westerners copied them. To try to correct this confused situation, which nowadays generally includes complex correlations with glands, Yoga postures, deities, auras, and so forth, I'll share a brief look at the real meaning of the inner Goddess power and Her spiritual ascent—and I'll try to keep it simple.

The *Lakshmi Tantra* explains Kundalini in the following way:

> The Kundalini power (Shakti) contains the entire creation in a coiled and concentrated form. . . . She, Kundalini, the unfathomable, unfolds the worlds through the journey of creation and ultimately, as the Absolute Self, she finally comes to rest.

Kundalini is the creative power that resides normally in the sexual region. This is a female power, a goddess, unfathomable, creative, and inherently spiritual. In the Tantric view of reality, Kundalini, the raw, untamed sexual-energy goddess, seeks to be unified with the transcendental-consciousness god. Or to put it more simply, the inner Shakti, who normally rests in the sex region, seeks to unite with the inner Shiva, whose abode is the head. The goal is to unite Shakti with Shiva, so the two can interact together, completing each other as a ''cosmic couple'' or ''divine androgyn.''

Residing as she does in the ''base'' or sexual region, Kundalini has to rise up to reach her lord, whose place is the head, the seat of consciousness. When awakened, the inner Kundalini energy rises up and travels through a central, subtle nerve or channel, known as the *sushumna*, which connects the lower and upper regions of the human psycho-organism. At various points along her evolutionary journey upward, Kundalini encounters natural spiritual energy centers, the Chakras that were previously mentioned. This process is one of spiritual awakening and illumination. By it, the soul is switched on, illuminated, gaining full access to its spiritual potency, which can be either creative or destructive.

The Shiva text known as *Thirumandiram* explains Kundalini Yoga as a copulatory Yoga that, when correctly performed, leads to duration of sexual enjoyment as well as mastery of phenomenal reality.

Traditional Tantric rendering of the Kundalini as vital energy snakes, their bodies made of mantras. Diagram on paper, from Rajasthan, India, circa eighteenth century.

In the copulatory Yoga performed by the heroic couple, they drive the "coach of breath" upwards. It has "wheels," a left and right. By correct practice of this Kundalini Yoga, they collect the ambrosial heavenly waters. He, checking the urge to emit semen, they become all-powerful and never tire!

Most of the popular views on Kundalini have derived from the writings of Gopi Krishna. An Indian intellectual who had a "Kundalini experience" that lasted twelve years, Gopi Krishna (1903–1984) spent the remainder of his life writing about it. According to him, all great men became so because their Kundalini awakened and was directed creatively. This is another way of saying "behind or within every great man is a powerful woman."

For man, the easiest and most reliable way to advance spiritually is by devotion and service to woman. Because of the principle known as resonance, which is recognition that "like influences like," service to woman is in Hindu Tantric tradition also taken to be service to Kundalini. Delighted by the attention, the Great Goddess power is pleased; She grants both worldly and spiritual favors to her devotees.

No matter how beautiful or ugly a woman may be, the original archaic Tantras teach that man should always think of woman as a living goddess. Spiritual sex is one of the best ways of awakening and pleasing the living goddess. Spiritual passion is the driving force.

Kundalini is known to Buddhist Tantra, but is not seen in the same perspective as in Hindu tradition. This is because Buddhism, which evolved as a reformed cult of Hinduism, tends to be more intellectual than emotional.

In Buddhist Tantric tradition, Kundalini is generally referred to as Candali or Candalini. *Candali* means "a fiercely passionate woman," one who takes a dominant role and can initiate men into the sexual mysteries. Candalini is the name of a Yogini (female Yogi) who has the ability to transform egoistic sexual lust into the "wisdom of equality" by perfecting an inner Yogic process. Linked to the earth element and the color yellow, Candalini represents the refined intellect's ascendancy over the "animal passions."

Graveyard Goddesses and the Dakini Tradition

Traditional Indian image of a Dakini, depicted as a sensuous woman, dancing and drinking. Stone sculpture from Eastern India, circa eleventh century.

Female graveyard spirits or goddesses, popularly viewed as witches, figure prominently in both Hindu and Buddhist Tantras. Often animal or bird-headed, these beings, known as Dakini, are sky-fliers, credited with occult powers and the ability to move anywhere at will.

Dakinis are also initiatresses (female initiators) into the Tantric mysteries. Interestingly, Damkina, which sounds very similar to Dakini, is the name given to the "faithful wife and spiritual consort" of Ea, also known as Oannes, the Sumerian wisdom deity who "taught civilization to mankind."

A fascinating account of initiation conveyed by a Dakini is told in the life story of Padmasambhava, the Indian Tantric Yogi par excellence who brought Tantrism to Tibet. The story tells how, seeking initiation, Padmasambhava arrived at the sandalwood garden in the midst of a cemetery, where the Dakini resided in a "palace of skulls." When he arrived at the door, he found it closed.

A servant girl appeared, carrying water into the palace. Padmasambhava sat in meditation and halted the servant girl's water-carrying by his Yogic power:

Thereupon, producing a knife of crystal, the servant girl cut open her chest, and exhibited in the upper portion of it the forty-two Peaceful Deities and in the lower portion of it the fifty-eight Wrathful Deities. Addressing the Yogi, she said, "I see you are a fine Yogi, possessed of great power. But look at me; have you not

Traditional Tantric image of a Dakini, dancing ecstatically and holding a sword of wisdom, skull-bowl, and trident. Stone sculpture from Nepal, circa sixteenth century.

Traditional Tantric image of a Dakini, dancing ecstatically upon a recumbent figure as she holds a mystic chopping knife, skull-bowl, and trident staff. Behind her is a triangle, symbol of the sexual center. Wood sculpture from Tibet, circa sixteenth century.

Traditional image of Padmasambhava, holding a trident (symbol of Shiva) and scepter *(vajra)*, with his mantra *"Om ah hum: vajra guru padma siddhi hum"* written in Tibetan, repeated all around. Woodblock print from Tibet.

faith in me?'' Padmasambhava bowed before her, apologized and asked for the Tantric teachings. She told him, ''I am only a servant girl. Come inside!''

Entering the skull-palace, Padmasambhava saw the Dakini queen herself, sitting on a throne made of the sun and moon, holding a double-drum and a human skull-bowl in her hands, and surrounded by thirty-two Dakinis making offerings to her. Padmasambhava bowed to the enthroned Dakini, made offerings and begged her to initiate him. The one hundred Peaceful and Wrathful Deities then appeared overhead. ''Look,'' said the Dakini, ''these are the Deities. Now receive initiation!'' The Yogi replied, ''Inasmuch as all Buddhas have always had gurus, accept me as your disciple.''

The Dakini then absorbed all the Deities into her body. She transformed Padmasambhava into the mystic sound-syllable *Hum*. The *Hum* rested on her lips, then she conferred on it the blessing of the Buddha of Boundless Life. Then she swallowed the *Hum*; and inside her womb Padmasambhava received initiation of the secret Compassionate Savior. When the *Hum* reached the region of the Kundalini, the inner "serpent" fire, she conferred on him initiation of body, speech, and mind. She also granted him the special initiation which gives power to dominate all negative spiritual beings.

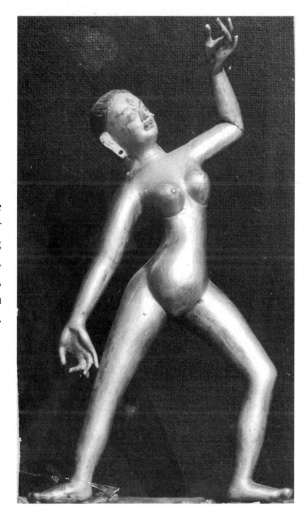

Traditional Tibetan image of an initiatory Dakini or Tantric consort, standing naked in dance posture. Hammered metal sculpture, gilded, from Tibet, circa seventeenth century.

Tibetan image of the Sarvabuddha Dakini ("the consort of all the Buddhas"), holding chopping knife, and skull-bowl. Metal casting from Tibet, circa fifteenth century.

Tibetan image of Vajravarahi Dakini ("the sow-headed initiatress"), holding knife, skull-bowl, and trident as she dances ecstatically. Metal casting from Ladakh, Western Tibet, circa sixteenth century.

This scenario, in which the Yogi Padmasambhava prostrates before the initiatress who then transforms and absorbs him into herself, is clearly sexual. It tells of the initiatory power of feminine divinity, here expressed as Padmasambhava's spiritual rebirth and his attainment of spiritual powers. In Tantric rites of sacred sex, the well-prepared spiritual consort can act as an initiatress into the mysteries of the unconscious and confer magical powers on her lover.

Trinities of Gods and Goddesses

Mesopotamian deities were generally organized into trinities, such as the sun deity (Shamash), the moon deity (Sin), and Venus (the goddess Innana). A similar custom of grouping pagan powers into trinities was followed in ancient Egypt, India, and Africa.

Such trinities could be viewed in different ways: as tridents (three deities standing side by side, together), as upward-pointing triangles (a base of two deities and a third deity at the apex), or as downward-pointing triangles (a single deity at the base, derived from a cosmic couple above). This system of visualizing cosmic powers as trinities, tridents, and triangles is deeply a part of Tantric tradition. It suggests that there is an alternate reality to the dualism or binary system that has been predominant in the Western world since early Christian times.

Though Christianity recognizes the potency of the trinity, it is kept in an esoteric context and has virtually no practical application. In Tantra, the Sacred Law of Three is recognized in every micro-cosmic–macrocosmic situation and is used constantly in everyday life and in spiritual work.

The Tantric Yoga teachings also recognize a triune or trinity of forces pervading the human psycho-organism. These have creative (referred to as *sattva*), maintaining *(rajas)*, and destructive *(tamas)* characteristics. In our body, the three expressions of the same forces produce "airy," "fiery," and "watery" temperaments (known as *vayu*, *pitta*, and *kapha*). In our breathing process, the three forces are mirrored as inhalation, retention, and exhalation. And in the subtle or psychic body, they manifest as the right subtle channel (known as *pingala*), the central channel *(sushumna)*, and the channel on the left *(ida)*.

In the iconography of divine powers, the three forces are the Hindu deities Brahma, Shiva, and Vishnu, whose consorts are the goddesses Saraswati, Kali, and Lakshmi. Together, these three divine powers control the five senses plus the mind:

Brahma: sight	Saraswati: sound
Shiva: mind	Kali: smell
Vishnu: taste	Lakshmi: touch

In traditional Tantra, spiritual powers are internalized. They are awoken from within, exalted and worshipped within the body, in the understanding that whatever is anywhere outside can also be found inside. The Tantric saying "What is here is elsewhere; what is not here is nowhere" expresses this truth exquisitely. In all basic Tantric rituals, after exalting the teacher or lineage of teachings, the first offerings are to the self and to the powers and deities within. Incense is lit and both body and spirit are worshipped—first the self, then any spirit or heavenly deity. Tantra has no concept of any external god or goddess. At best, only the human couple, at its most intimate moment, can be viewed as god and goddess. Here the sacredness of sex is self-evident.

4 TANTRA AND JUDEO-CHRISTIAN TRADITION

I looked back and behold there was a fair and glorious lady whose garments were all skye-color, and curiously (like Heaven) bespangled with golden stars. In her right hand she bare a trumpet of beaten gold, whereon a Name was ingraven which I could well read in but am as yet forbidden to reveal it. In her left hand she had a great bundle of letters of all languages, which she (as I afterwards understood) was to carry into all countries. She also had large and beautiful wings, full of eyes throughout, wherewith she could mount aloft and flye swifter than any eagle.

—CHRISTIAN ROSENKREUTZ, *The Chymical Wedding*

Tantra: The Interface Between Sexuality and Spirituality

The connection between sexuality and spirituality is compelling. Yet in the West it is too often overlooked. For most of the last two thousand years, Western culture has been molded by orthodox Judeo-Christian spiritual influences and values. These have been largely patriarchal and materialistic. Christians pray to God, "Our Heavenly Father" to "give us our daily bread," invariably forgetting to invoke the "Mother Goddess" whose domain is the earthly reality, in whose soil our cereal grains flourish and through whose flesh we are born.

The spiritual powers that brought each of us into worldly existence are not the exclusive property of any single culture or religion. They have been accessed by followers of all religions throughout his-

135

tory. The roots of Western spiritual life were once nourished by Celtic, Phoenician, Roman, Greek, Egyptian, Mesopotamian, and other pre-Christian "pagan" civilizations, all of which had connections with the rich ancient cultures of India and Africa. We need to reconnect with those roots and explore their relevance to today's reality. Tantra shows the way.

Belief in the immortality of the soul, in reincarnation, in the cosmic law of cause and effect (karma), and in spiritual powers or divine beings, idealized as gods and goddesses, are the cornerstones of Tantra. Such beliefs were once common in the West. However, orthodox Christianity has, over the centuries, attempted to eradicate them, instead promoting the idea that we live only a single life, followed by reward or punishment, Heaven or Hell.

According to orthodox Christian dogma, salvation supposedly comes only at the end of the world, on Judgment Day. This pessimistic, narrow-minded view of reality has for many generations held back spiritual evolution in the West and has been the cause of much suffering.

More and more people have abandoned orthodox Christian beliefs. Some seek solace in unorthodox or "heretical" Christian cults centered around charismatic church leaders. In many of these Christian cults, the hidden agenda has included the requirement that female followers have sex with the male charismatic leader. Jim Jones (involved in the mass suicide in Jonestown, Guyana, in 1978) and David Koresh (involved in the 1993 standoff in Waco, Texas, that ended with the deaths of 87 cult members) are examples of patriarchal Christian cult leaders who promoted such practices.

Many Westerners have become atheists or materialists. Others have explored different spiritual beliefs and systems, embracing astrology, reincarnation, karma, and modern paganism, as well as Yoga, meditation, and Tantra. Many have found that it *is* possible to keep one's Christian or Jewish faith and still explore spirituality in an eastern, New Age, or Tantric way. Though Tantra evolved in ancient India as part of the spiritual systems of Hinduism and Buddhism, Tantric teachings can also be found in Taoism and are present in both early Christian and medieval Jewish spiritual traditions.

Women's Rights and Tantra

One of the benefits of living in a democratic, open society is that we are free to make changes to situations that are unfair, that cause unnecessary suffering, or impede progress. Modern democracy enables us to break down barriers. As we approach the end of the twentieth century, sexual and socioeconomic barriers are still among the most crucial, urgently needing to be properly addressed.

It has taken a long time for Western women to acquire proper civil rights. Orthodox Judeo-Christian culture has for centuries viewed women primarily as property. Initially, women were considered to be the property of their fathers, and after marriage, the property of their husbands, whom the older marriage vow states women must "honor and obey."

In most Christian cultures, women were relegated to a secondary role. About two thousand years ago, St. Paul instructed Christian women to adopt a subordinate role to man. In Corinthians, he justified this teaching with the following argument:

> Man was not made from woman, but woman from man. Man was not created for woman, but woman for man.

A similar view is promoted in both Jewish and Islamic culture. Ibn Arabi, a twelfth-century Sufi mystic, stated:

> Woman occupies an inferior degree to that of man, confirming the Koranic Word that "As for men they precede women by one degree." There is a ternary of God, man and woman; man reaches out toward his Lord, which is his origin, as woman reaches out toward man.

As we approach the twenty-first century, such views are clearly no longer relevant or tenable. In all Tantric traditions, it is mandatory that women are to be honored. The *Lakshmi Tantra*, an important Hindu work, categorically states:

> A Tantric Yogi should never abuse a woman, either in deed, thought or speech.

The *Hevajra Tantra*, an early Buddhist work, echoes the same sentiment:

> He who is well versed in this Yoga always honors the mother, sister and all women. He must always remember that it is woman who gives birth, woman who nourishes, woman who is auspicious, woman whose grace bestows occult powers.

In most of Judeo-Christian Europe and America, women could not legally own property themselves until the late nineteenth century. Only among the Cathar communities of medieval Europe could women own property. In twelfth-century Cathar society, they could even function as priestesses of the heretical church. In Tantric tradition, women have *always* been viewed as initiatresses, as priestesses, and as living goddesses.

In most of the Western world, woman's emancipation took a long time. English women gained the right to vote only in 1918, and American women, only in 1920. By 1923, women obtained the right to divorce their husbands, but only on grounds of adultery. Since then, Western women have seen a steady increase in their rights, though crucial issues such as birth control and abortion are treated differently in different areas, with rulings dependent largely on political agendas. By contrast, in the Tantric tradition, woman has always been fully emancipated.

Tantra initially evolved in matriarchal societies, with woman controlling the economy, the family, and her own body. In these Tantric societies, woman was generally the instigator of sexual interaction and initiatress into the sexual mysteries. In Tantric sexual rites, woman has the "first right" of sexual satisfaction. The *Guptasadhana Tantra*, a Hindu work declares:

> Woman should always be worshipped. Firstly by washing her feet, massaging and caressing her. Then by worshipping her mouth, breasts, navel and her Yoni. She is always to be viewed as the goddess Shakti, while her devotee imagines himself to be Shiva. He should always ask her permission before having intercourse with her. He should treat her with consideration and see to her satisfaction. And when he offers his semen as an oblation, as a sacrifice, it is offered to the Great Goddess in the form of

woman. This behavior leads to the acquisition of all desired objects, freedom from disease, the love of women and the eight great occult powers.

Sex and the Church

Many of the obstacles to sexual spirituality have been built by churches. Birth control is a controversial subject for most Christians and is still totally unacceptable to the Catholic church. Women's right to abortion is a topic at the forefront of modern American politics. When Margaret Sanger (1879–1966) started the first birth-control clinic in Brooklyn, New York, in 1916, she was arrested. She was persecuted for many years under the Comstock bill. Introduced by Anthony Comstock (1844–1915) and his followers from the YMCA this bill made it a federal offense to use the U.S. mail to transmit any "obscene, lewd, lascivious, or filthy book, pamphlet, picture, paper, letter, writing, print, or other publication of an indecent character." The New York Society for the Suppression of Vice, also founded by Comstock, was endowed with police powers and became a formidable opponent of marriage manuals (the precursors of sexual how-tos), birth control, abortions, and any kind of even slightly erotic literature. Using entrapment and infiltration methods, Comstock's society arrested many and lobbied to send pharmacists to prison for selling condoms and other birth-control devices.

Almost without exception, Western leaders have chosen not to deal with sex frankly and openly. They have chosen not to explore, update, or redefine sexual knowledge in a modern spiritual context. For Western politicians, sex is a minefield best avoided—the less said, the better. As I write, there is much debate about how the sexual content of the Internet can be controlled and regulated, with politicians using this topic as a potential vote-getter. Moral issues, "family values," and the call to "just say no" to sex and eroticism are topics almost certain to attract votes in the current resurgence of puritanical fundamentalist Christian standards.

The right to complete freedom of sexual expression is still not in place. According to orthodox Judeo-Christian belief, the sole purpose of sexual intercourse is reproduction, which is legitimized only through legal marriage. Though such beliefs are changing, they are still the views of the majority of Westerners.

The Christian church had, in the Middle Ages, viewed it as a mortal sin to "embrace one's spouse solely for pleasure." The church taught that sexual intercourse should only take place in the "missionary" position, with woman on her back and man on top. All other sexual positions were considered unnatural and it was said that because in the ancient past women took an active role in lovemaking and "went mad and abused their husbands by riding upon them," God sent the great flood to destroy humankind. This type of sex-negative superstition-driven church propaganda has no relevance in today's world.

All nonprocreative sexual acts, such as masturbation, oral sex, sodomy, and homosexual lovemaking, were viewed by the church as unnatural and illegal. Thus, in America, as in much of Europe, "crimes against nature" such as oral sex, even when practiced in private by married couples, were until recently punishable by long terms of imprisonment. In some places, this law is still in force.

Dr. Bidder, a professor of biology at Cambridge University, argues that "the advocacy of a celibate life for spiritual people means that for two thousand years we have systematically bred out of our race people with spiritual potential." An interesting thought, one with which the orthodox Christian church has yet to come to terms.

For more than fifteen hundred years, the orthodox Christian church has stubbornly continued to view sexual intercourse as sinful, a lustful act with woman cast in the role of temptress. For those who embrace such values, the promotion of spiritual sex is likely to be viewed as threatening, "the Devil's work," and most definitely un-Christian. However, as we shall see, such views are very far from the truth. Christianity in its original form was a love cult in which sex was a spiritual sacrament.

Both Christianity and Judaism are Oriental religions with roots reaching back to Asia and ancient branches that embrace pagan and Gnostic systems of belief. In the rest of this chapter, we'll examine Gnosticism and its connections with early Christianity. We'll explore the mysteries of sacred sex in Christian and Jewish tradition. And we'll take a brief look at sacred sex and erotic symbolism in European alchemy and science.

Gnosticism, "Free Love," and the Bridal Chamber Mystery

The Greek word *gnosis* means "divinely inspired knowledge." Gnosticism developed its identity in Alexandria just before and during the early centuries of the Christian or "current" era, through a merging of spiritual currents and ideas. There were numerous Gnostic sects, both pagan and Christian. Egyptian and Sumerian mythology; Jewish mysticism; Mithraic, Manichaean, and Hellenistic mystery cults; and Hinduism all contributed to the emergence of Gnosticism as a radical and mystical form of religious expression.

Elaine Pagels, author of *The Gnostic Gospels* (1979), a fascinating account of the contents of some "lost books" of early Christianity that were excluded from the New Testament but were discovered in Egypt in 1945, writes:

> Gnostic Christians undoubtedly expressed ideas that the orthodox abhorred. For example, some of these Gnostic texts question whether all suffering, labor, and death derive from human sin, which in the orthodox version marred an originally perfect creation. Others speak of the feminine element in the divine, celebrating God as Father and Mother. Still others suggest that Christ's resurrection is to be understood symbolically, not literally.

She points out that Gnostic teachings, which are concerned with the nature of illusion, the search for enlightenment and the knowledge of divinity within, "sound more Eastern than Western" and suggests that the roots of Gnosticism may go back to Indian sources.

Followers of some Gnostic sects believed that Jesus had an erotic relationship with Mary Magdalene, to whom he gave secret teachings.

It's very likely that Jesus and Mary Magdalene were married. Nowhere in the Bible does it say that Jesus was not married, or that he was celibate. As a Jew and a Rabbi, for Jesus to be recognized as a spiritual teacher, he *had* to be married. An account in the New Testament of the Bible, in John 2:9–10, tells how, when Jesus and his mother were present at a wedding, he turned water into wine.

According to Jewish tradition, replenishing the wine is an obligation of the wedding's host and hostess. In the text, Jesus is referred to as the bridegroom by the master of ceremonies.

Mary Magdalene is the best candidate for Jesus' bride. During the early phase of his ministry she accompanied him everywhere, which would have been viewed as a disgrace if she was not married to him. It was to Mary Magdalene that Jesus first appeared after his resurrection.

The Gnostic Gospel of Philip states that Jesus "used to kiss Mary often on the mouth." The Gospel of Mary, another "lost text," rediscovered in 1896, suggests that Mary Magdalene, a former prostitute, was a visionary and spiritual teacher whose insights surpassed those of the apostles. Other Gnostic texts suggest that Mary Magdalene was the leader of a group of twelve female apostles and that she had extraordinary occult powers.

Apparently, many early Christian Gnostics promoted "free love." Irenaeus (circa 130–200 C.E.), an orthodox Christian bishop, wrote that some Gnostic Christian women "engaged in promiscuous sexual activities" as part of their religious practice. He also noted that Christian women "were especially attracted to heretical groups" and tells of a Gnostic churchman called Marcus who seduced women from his congregation by praying to "female divinity," following which he "initiated them" and told them to prophesy. According to Bishop Irenaeus, Marcus told them:

> Adorn thyself as a bride who is expecting her bridegroom, that thou mayest be what I am and I what you are . . .

Marcus himself tells how, in a vision, "the female divinity" descended upon him in the form of a woman, who explained the origin of all things, saying:

> I wish to show you Truth Herself; for I have brought Her down from above, so you may see Her without a veil and understand Her beauty.

All this suggests that such early Christians were following an ancient Eastern spiritual tradition in which suitable women were initiated as priestesses, were revered as prophetesses, and functioned as sexual initiatresses into a spiritual mystery cult of the Great Goddess.

Valentinus (who died in 161 C.E.) was another prominent Gnostic teacher and a poet. He claimed that Jesus shared certain mysteries only with his closest disciples and that these mysteries could only be taught to spiritually mature persons through a process of initiation. According to him, "matter is not separated irretrievably from the spiritual."

The chief sacrament of the Valentinians, the followers of Valentinus, was the "mystery of the bridal chamber," where the pious could witness the spiritual marriage rites between Sophia (the Gnostic wisdom goddess and "cosmic mother") and the Redeemer. It was believed that on such occasions, the faithful experienced mystical union with their personal angel. The Gnostic Gospel of Philip gives the following tantalizing account of the rites of the bridal chamber:

> Woman is united to her husband in the bridal chamber. Indeed, those who have united in the bridal chamber will never be separated. Eve separated from Adam because she was never united with him in the bridal chamber.

Gnosticism has since influenced many radical European and American spiritual seekers, as well as medieval alchemists, Rosicrucian initiates, and members of magical fraternities and secret occult organizations.

Simon Magus and Helena the Prostitute

Bishop Irenaeus wrote about an early Gnostic Christian known as Simon Magus, who "redeemed from prostitution a certain woman named Helena and elevated her to high esteem," adding that "the mystic priests belonging to his sect lead profligate lives and practice magical arts, employing exorcism, incantations, love potions, and charms."

Justin Martyr, a contemporary of Irenaeus, wrote:

> Simon was considered a God. Almost all the Samaritans and even a few of other nations worship him, and acknowledge him as the

First God; and a woman, Helena, who went about with him at that time, and had formerly been a prostitute, they say she is the "first idea" generated by him.

Simon Magus taught that God "emanated" a divine female or Goddess, the embodiment of the generative principle. According to him, it was she who gave birth to the angels, who then created the visible material world. Some Gnostic teachings suggest that the angels became jealous of their Divine Mother and "attracted her down to the earthly realm" where, throughout history, she was reincarnated as a series of women, one of whom was Helena, Simon Magus's wife.

Such early Christian accounts of Gnostic activities confirm that some Christians had been exposed to the most esoteric teachings concerning spiritual sex, reincarnation, and cosmology. Apparently, at one time there were many Gnostic Christians openly practicing spiritual sex.

The "Daughters of Satan" and "Original Sin"

Origen (circa 185–253 c.e.), who represented the Alexandrine school of church philosophers, was one of the main definers of early Christian theology. He argued that as spiritual beings left the proximity of God, the world manifested, and as they moved further away, human physical existence took form. He saw human evolution as "movement away from God." Origen believed that God sent Christ to lead the fallen back to him by denying and mortifying the flesh.

According to Origen, all women are the daughters of Satan, loaded with hereditary sin. He taught that the pious should abstain from all sexual intercourse. The following quotation from his writings explains his philosophy very clearly:

We think it both reasonable in itself and well pleasing to God to suffer pain for the sake of virtue, to undergo torture for the sake of piety, and even to suffer death for the sake of holiness . . . and we maintain that to overcome the love of life is to enjoy a great good.

Origen castrated himself "for the Kingdom of Heaven." Valerius, one of his foremost disciples, founded the first Christian sect of castrates in 250 C.E. This later became the inspiration for several Christian cults such as the Skopts, a medieval Russian sect whose members castrated and mutilated themselves. According to Skopt theology, original sin consisted of Adam and Eve's sexual union. In their extremist heretical view, Christ had already returned (as Origen?) and castrated himself, teaching that humanity could only be redeemed from original sin by following his example.

St. Augustine (354–439 C.E.) theorized on the relationship between sex and sin, writing that if it hadn't been for the temptation and original sin, sex in the Garden of Eden would have been without eroticism, lust, desire, or ecstasy. It would have been merely a bland mechanical process of procreation as the fulfillment of God's command to multiply. According to him, after humankind's fall from grace, sex was driven by lustful concupiscence and became a willful and sinful genital activity, without any spiritual worth other than for the production of Christian children.

The early church's fathers viewed all women as temptresses from whom all sinful thoughts originated and who blindly followed the example of their original ancestor, Eve. They denied or were ignorant of the story of Lilith, Eve's elder sister. This is not surprising because at the time, Jews were viewed by the church fathers as responsible for the crucifixion of Jesus and the Hebrew scriptures and ancient Semitic mythology were largely ignored.

Lilith, Adam, and Eve

Hebrew myth tells us that God made Lilith, the first woman, and Adam, the first man, simultaneously. He made them from the same piece of clay, breathing life into it. He then instructed them to "be fruitful and multiply."

The story goes that Lilith got on top of Adam and began to have sex with him. However, Adam reacted negatively, demanding that Lilith must lie beneath him, in the subservient position. Lilith refused to do so, arguing that because she was created from the same substance as Adam and at the same time, she was his equal. She refused to be subservient to Adam.

The myth goes on to tell how, sexually frustrated and dissatisfied with Adam, Lilith flies up in the air (she has magical powers) and makes her way to a cave in the desert. There she has sex with nonhuman spiritual beings, according to her desires, giving birth to many noncorporeal spirit offspring.

Adam is upset and complains to God that Lilith has deserted him. God then takes one of Adam's ribs and uses it to make Eve, a replacement wife. Eve is naturally subservient because, unlike Lilith, she is made from a part of Adam and after him.

Lilith learns about her replacement. One of her powers is that she can transform into any creature. She takes on the form of a ser-

European woodcut depicting Lilith as the serpent tempting Eve. From Cologne, Germany, late fifteenth century.

pent and tempts her sister Eve, who "eats of the fruit of the tree of knowledge of good and evil" (forbidden knowledge) and "sins."

The exact nature of this original sin is unclear. Since God had already commanded the first humans to be fruitful and multiply, having sex should not have been regarded as sinful. They were, after all, only obeying God's command.

Early images of the temptation of Eve show the serpent with the face and breasts of a woman, who is a magically transformed version of her sister Lilith. The serpent promises Eve that once she has eaten the forbidden fruit, she will "be like God." This suggests that Eve was promised the magical power to create anything at will. According to most early Christian dogma, Eve's original sin was her participation in the spiritual or sacramental power of sex.

Adam and Eve were expelled from the Garden of Eden, the earthly paradise, and the concept of original sin and sexual guilt was firmly established. It has confused and plagued many, instilling an association between sin and sex in untold numbers of Christians over the centuries.

Bishop Methodius and Spiritual Marriage

Bishop Methodius of Olympus was a contemporary of Origen. He declared sex to be unseemly but conceded that "if husband and wife rationed their embraces," marriage "need not necessarily be damning." According to him, sex for procreative purposes is acceptable only as the means to continue the human species, whereas sex for pleasure is a sin. This view was very popular among churchmen in Victorian times and, amazingly enough, is still common among many orthodox Christians today.

Bishop Methodius viewed spiritual union with Christ as a spiritual marriage. To a very large extent, this view drove the idea that, in the church, celibacy was holy. Though both Methodius's and Origen's teachings that Christians should deny the flesh and seek mystical marriage with Christ became the standard dogma of orthodox Christianity, many early Christians took an entirely different and much more radical view, somewhat similar to those held by followers of the Hindu Tantric tradition. Though normally celibate, on

specially selected occasions, they engaged in "love feasts" or sacramental sex, as a way to achieve spiritual union with God.

Carpocrates, Epiphanes, and the Sacrament of Lust

Carpocrates was a Gnostic Christian and a follower of Plato's philosophy, who lived in Alexandria, Egypt. Together with his son Epi-
phanes, he taught that one could achieve true spirituality only by
experiencing every pleasure life has to offer. He took the view that
the human spirit continues to reincarnate until it has exhausted its
desires. The followers of Carpocrates claimed to have been initiated
into secret teachings from a lineage of female adepts who included
Mary Magdalene and Salome, she of the dance of the seven veils.

Like Tantrics, the Carpocratians taught that everyone is inherently equal and has equal rights. They also taught that lust could
best be combated by allowing it to manifest and run its natural
course. "Lust is combated by the enjoyment of lust" was the essence
of Carpocratian esoteric teaching. This sounds very much like the
Tantric tenet that "one can rise by that which can cause one to fall,"
a saying at times used to justify hedonism.

Carpocratian Christians shared their property and even their
wives with each other. They held love feasts at which men and
women mingled together, eating, drinking, and making love. Partners were exchanged in the belief that possessiveness is sinful. This
was the original Christian free-love cult.

Clement of Alexandria gave the following account of a Carpocratian love feast:

> They gather together for feasts, men and women together. After
> they have sated their appetites, then they overturn their lamps
> and so extinguish the light that the shame of their adulterous
> "righteousness" is hidden, and they have intercourse where they
> will and with whom they will. After they have practiced commu-
> nity of use in their love-feast, they demand by daylight of what-
> ever women they wish that they will be obedient to the law of
> Carpocrates.

Carpocratians did not take part in love feasts with the aim of creating children. On the contrary, they viewed such lovemaking as sinful. They promoted various forms of continence, emphasizing the desirability of man's refraining from emission. If emission of semen could not be controlled, Carpocratian men were taught to withdraw, expel semen into their hands, and offer it up as a sacrament.

Manichaeism, the New Religion

Toward the end of the third century c.e., followers of Gnosticism became much more secretive. For a while Manichaeism emerged as the "new religion." Manichaeism tried to reconcile the teachings of Zoroaster (a magi or priest-magician who lived in Iran in the sixth century b.c.e.) with those of Christ and emphasized the irreconcilability of good and evil. If we can believe St. Augustine, who viewed the act of sex as disgusting and was among those who promoted the doctrine of original sin, Manichaeans engaged in a form of sacramental sex. Regarding them, he wrote:

> The Manichaeans partake of a Eucharist which has been strewn with human semen, in order that from it as from the other food they eat, the divine substance may be purged. It accordingly follows that whatever food they take, Eucharist or other, is to be purged in the act by human or other semen.

Nicolaitians and Phibionites

The Nicolaitians, an early Christian sect founded by Nicolaus of Antioch, promoted libertinism and sexual excess. The Nicolaitians were the inspiration for the Phibionites, another Gnostic Christian sect who flourished in the fourth century c.e. They produced many books and were active in trying to attract people to join their cause. Bishop Epiphanius (315–403 c.e.) described how some Gnostic Christian women who wished to convert him to their beliefs had tried to seduce him. He wrote the following fascinating account of a Phibionite communion service:

First, they have their women in common. And if a stranger appears who is of the same persuasion, they have a sign, men for women and women for men. When they extend the hand for greeting, at the bottom of the palm they make a tickling touch and from this they ascertain whether the person who appeared is of their faith.

After they have recognized each other, they go over at once to eating. They serve rich food, meat, and wine even if they are poor. When they thus ate together and so to speak filled up their veins to an excess, they turn to passion.

The man leaving his wife says to her: "Stand up and make love with the brother." Then the unfortunates unite with each other, and as I am truly ashamed to say the shameful things that are being done by them, because according to the holy apostle the things that are happening by them are shameful even to mention. . . .

After they have had intercourse, in the passion of fornication they raise their own blasphemy toward heaven. The woman and the man take the fluid of the emission of the man into their hands, they stand, turn toward heaven, their hands besmeared with the uncleanness, and pray as people called "Stratiotikoi" and "Gnostikoi," bringing to the father who is the nature of all that which they have on their hands, and they say: "We offer to thee this gift, the body of Christ." And then they eat it, their own ugliness, and say: "This is the body of Christ and this is the Passover for the sake of which our bodies suffer and are forced to confess the suffering of Christ."

Epiphanius's account goes on to explain that Phibionites offer up the menstrual blood of their women in the same way, calling it "the blood of Christ" and consuming it as a sacrament. Apparently, Phibionite lovemaking was dedicated to the pursuit of pleasure and mystical communion with the divine, rather than for the begetting of children. This account ends with the following assurance:

They take care of their bodies day and night, women and men, with creams, washings, and foods, and devote themselves to the bed and to wine. They curse the man who fasts because they say that one should not fast, for fasting is the work of the Archangel who made this Aeon. Rather they believe one should nourish himself in order that the bodies may be strong, so that they may give the fruit in its time.

The main tenet of Phibionite belief was that, because sexual intercourse is a unifying experience, it is blessed. They taught that sexual secretions are holy, provided they are collected and not wasted. They claimed that Jesus himself revealed these spiritual sexual secrets to his intimate disciples. Such Phibionite beliefs are essentially identical with the core philosophy of traditional Tantra.

A Phibionite tradition tells of how, accompanied by Mary Magdalene, Jesus once went to pray near the top of a mountain, and "took from his side a woman and began to have sexual intercourse with her." The story recounts that Mary is shocked and falls to the ground and is picked up by Jesus, who questions her faith. According to Phibionite tradition, Jesus then takes his ejected semen and offers it up to God as the ultimate sacrifice.

There were many other early heretical Christian sects with beliefs and lifestyles that seem related to traditional Tantra. The Adamites, Paulicians, Bogomiles, and the Khylisti are some of them. Unfortunately, most of what we know about these sects has come down to us through the filter of orthodox Christian legislators or commentators whose views were biased against them.

The Adamites: Tantric Nudists?

The Adamites, a heretical Christian sect that existed between the second and sixth century c.e., claimed to have regained the "original human condition of innocence," before Adam and Eve were expelled from Paradise. In their view, their society no longer was "tainted by original sin." Adamites worshipped in the nude, performing their services in secret churches, which they referred to as Paradise. Nudism, total freedom of sexual expression, and "common marriage," in which wives were shared, were the principal tenets of Adamite belief.

Adamite sects were suppressed for many centuries but reap-

peared in early fourteenth-century Bohemia as a Christian sect referred to as the Brothers and Sisters of the Free Spirit, also known as
Picards. The fifteenth-century Dutch master painter Hieronymous
Bosch was supposedly a member of this sect. Picards lived in a state
of total nudity and practiced a form of group marriage. They were
persecuted by the church and eventually disbanded or were completely destroyed.

The Paulicians and Bogomiles

The Paulicians were another early heretic Christian sect whose sexual practices reveal Tantric leanings. Centered mainly on the writings and alleged sayings of St. Paul the apostle, Paulicians blended
his teachings with a Gnostic and dualistic view of reality. St. Paul
taught that in Christianity, celibacy is superior to marriage, but also
advised that "it is better to marry than to burn with desire." He also
recommended that a husband should "give to his wife her conjugal
rights, and likewise the wife to her husband." St. Paul taught that
the human body is a part or "member" of Christ, and that by having
sex, "two become one flesh" in a spiritual bond.

Paulicians were dualists, believing in the twin forces of good
and evil. One of the main tenets of this sect was the belief that the
world was created by the Devil or an archdemon, whereas Heaven
was created by God. They also believed in the transmigration of
souls, commonly known as reincarnation.

Around the sixth century C.E., the Paulicians were expelled from
Armenia, where they had originally settled, and forcibly removed to
parts of Macedonia and Bulgaria. They were the precursors of the
Bogomiles, Christian heretic monks who by the ninth century were
being expelled from orthodox monasteries in Bulgaria and the surrounding region.

The Bogomiles were radically opposed to the orthodox church
and adhered to the principles of dualism. They promoted nudity and
the right to freedom of sexual expression. Their opponents accused
them of being sodomites or "buggers," though there is no evidence
that they promoted such practices.

The Bogomiles gained a large following in Bosnia, Herzegovina,

Dalmatia, and the Balkans until the thirteenth or fourteenth centuries. Apparently, they developed sexual disciplines and practices aimed at spiritualizing themselves and gained personal power that caused them to be viewed as a threat to Christian orthodoxy. After the Turkish conquest, many Bogomiles converted to Islam because they found it more tolerant than Catholicism.

Brethren of the Free Spirit, Khylisti, and the "Mad Monk"

The Khylisti were a Russian Christian sect who were outwardly orthodox but secretly heretical. They supposedly derived from an earlier orgiastic Christian sect known as the Brethren of the Free Spirit, which taught that "no action of the body parts below the girdle is sinful" and that when Christ arose from the dead he had sexual intercourse with Mary Magdalene. The following account tells of the activities of this heretical Christian cult:

> When they go to confession and come together, their priest preaches to them. He takes the most beautiful among them and does to her whatever he wills. The light is extinguished and the followers fall upon each other, as it comes about.

The Khylisti taught that man can actually become God by taking on the nature of Christ and woman by taking on the nature of the Virgin, through a mystical process of transfiguration. The main Khylisti transfiguration took place at a secret rite, held at midnight. For this occasion, men and women would gather together, naked except for a single white garment. A young woman, who was worshipped both as the Holy Virgin and the Earth Mother, was placed in the central position of a circle of Khylisti worshippers. "Naked as the day she was born," she would distribute a sacrament of dried grapes to all who participated.

The Khylisti danced in circles, all the men moving together in one direction in the middle, all the women moving in the opposite direction in an outer ring. The participants gradually worked themselves into a frenzy, sometimes aided by men and women whipping each other. At the peak of their excitement, everyone stripped and made love. Other than this rite, sex supposedly was taboo to members of the Khylisti sect and marriage was also forbidden.

Rasputin (circa 1868–1916), confidant of the Russian tsarina, spiritual healer and hypnotist, was a member of the Khylisti sect. Known as the "mad monk," his amorous and prophetic exploits are legendary. It is recorded that on his last day (in 1916), he had a wild party with gypsy musicians and spent the night with two women.

Spiritual Love, Dianism, and Tantra

The ancient Greeks knew of two kinds of love: *eros* (carnal love) and *agape* (spiritual love). The early orthodox Christians rejected the former and embraced the latter. Worried as they were about original sin and carnal urgings, many early Christians viewed continent marriage (marriage without physical sex) as the highest form of union between man and woman.

Dianism, inspired by Diana, the Roman goddess of chastity, had a following since the early days of Christianity. Unmarried virgins, known as *agapetae*, would become "spiritual wives" to members of the clergy, living intimately with them without any sexual connection. It was believed that this helped spiritualize monks. Between the second and sixth century, many Christians lived with *agapetae*, in the belief that this was an acceptable spiritual form of marriage, unsullied by carnal sin. Scuthin, an Irish holy man of the sixth century C.E., always slept with two virgins in his bed. St. Brendan also did so, but he soon abandoned the practice, as he found he could not sleep. Those who lived with *agapetae* were eventually viewed as heretics by the orthodox Christian church.

In this century, Mahatma Gandhi (1869–1948) commonly kept one or two virgin girls in his bed and slept with them without intimacy, believing that it helped to strengthen him and empowered his vow of celibacy. Omraam Mikhael Aivanhov (1900–1986), a Bulgarian mystic of the White Brotherhood lineage, explained this type of Tantric Dianism in the following way:

A Yogi starts out by studying the subject of love for years, meditating, fasting, doing breathing exercises. When he is ready, a young girl will be chosen for him, also well prepared, and he will live in the same room with her for four months. He puts himself entirely in her service, he thinks of her as divine, as a manifestation of the Divine Mother, and he doesn't touch her. Later, he sleeps on the same bed, still without touching her, for four months on the right side and for four months on the left. Finally, when they have acquired complete control, they begin to embrace and even to merge with each other, but with such great purity they can be together for hours with no emission.

Apparently, knowledge of this type of spiritual sex had made its way to parts of Europe by medieval times. Cathars and Troubadours are among those European mystical movements who may have been influenced by Tantric Dianism. There is more to this than the man's control of carnal urgings or sublimation of his sexual energy. Woman has the key role in this type of spiritual interaction. Tantra teaches that certain women, known as Yoginis, can, by intimate association, convey spiritual sustenance on a man. An eleventh-century Tibetan commentary on the *Chakrasamvara Tantra* puts it like this:

Recognizing a Yogini who both delights him and has the ability to convey spiritual power to him, the Yogi should be passionately attracted to her. He must worship and serve this Yogini, so she blesses him: otherwise spiritual attainments will not arise in him.

Sacred Sex in European Secret Societies

Secret societies devoted to the study and practice of occultism manifested throughout Europe during the Middle Ages, linking Egyptian mysteries, Druidism, Jewish and Christian mysticism, and Eastern philosophy to paganism, nature-worship and Oriental religions. The Cathars, Knights Templars, Troubadours, European Gnostics, Alchemical Fraternities, Rosicrucians, and Freemasons were among the many Eruopean groups apparently influenced by Tantric teachings. Several of them may have been influenced through interaction with

Romany people, the so-called gypsies who fled parts of western India following the brutality of the Moslem invasions and made their way into Europe. Others were perhaps influenced by European crusaders and merchants who were initiated into these teachings in the Middle and Far East and introduced them to intimates on their return.

Traces of Tantra in Medieval Jewish Mysticism

Traces of Tantra philosophy can also be found in medieval Jewish mystical teachings known as Cabbalism. Among the texts that have come down to us are Cabbalistic marriage manuals such as *The Letter of Holiness* and a text known as *The Book of Splendor*. Both of these fascinating medieval Jewish documents show a remarkably liberated and mystical view of sex, quite different from that found in orthodox Christianity during the same period. Some of the topics raised in these texts echo themes found in traditional Tantra. Even Hasidism, which is a radical Jewish spiritual movement that emerged in the Ukraine during the mid-eighteenth century, teaches that the pleasures of the senses are not sinful.

The *Letter of Holiness:* A Jewish *Kama Sutra*

Medieval Jewish mysticism was known as Cabbalism. Early in the thirteenth century, an anonymous Spanish Cabbalist wrote the *Iggaret ha-Kodesh*, a marriage manual known as the *Letter of Holiness*. In this, the author states:

> We who have the Torah believe that God created all in His wisdom and do not believe that He created anything ugly or unseemly. If we say that sexual intercourse is repulsive, then we blaspheme God, who made the genital organs.

The focus of the *Letter of Holiness* is "to teach sexual techniques helpful for producing learned sons." Reasoning that good sons are produced by good and harmonized seed, this text emphasizes that lovers should behave wisely and strive for pleasure when having sex. The text points to the importance of foreplay and recommends that a man ensures that his wife achieves orgasm first, as in Tantric tradition.

The *Letter of Holiness* refers to the existence of male and female spiritual powers, known as *sefirot*, who "come together in holy intercourse," brought about when married men and women make love. Cabbalist teachings explain how "both men and women emit when in a state of orgasm" at the peak of harmonious sex. These teachings state that sexual emissions are very much influenced by thoughts when a couple has sex; the *sefirot* are empowered by spiritual thoughts at this time. "Loss of seed" by lustful or material thoughts during sex is believed to be very inauspicious and potentially damaging to the spiritual powers.

The *Book of Splendor* and Sex on the Sabbath

The *Zohar* or *Book of Splendor* is a mythological Cabbalist text written by Moses de Leon toward the end of the thirteenth century. Like the *Letter of Holiness*, it teaches that well-performed acts of sex between Jewish mystics and their wives produces harmonious lovemaking between the spiritual beings known as *sefirot*, who bless them. However, the teachings state that clumsy or lustful sex causes disharmony between the *sefirot*, who then are disruptive and generally unhelpful.

Cabbalism tells how even the Creator has a spiritual consort, known as the Shekhinah, who has a twofold nature as Great Nurturing Mother and All-Powerful Destructive Goddess. Jewish mystics strive for mystical union with the Shekhinah, the evening of the Sabbath being viewed as the only appropriate time for this activity. Clearly, the Shekhinah of the Jewish Cabbalist and the Shakti (the divine female energy/goddess) of Hindu Tantric tradition are related.

The Hasidic View of Sex

Baal Shem-Tov (1700–1760), who lived in the Ukraine, was the founder of Hasidism, a Jewish movement that evolved among the poor, who resented domination by the educated wealthy elite. As with the Tantrics of India, this radical spiritual movement sought to break down economic and social barriers.

Shem-Tov taught through parables and emphasized the importance of spiritual enthusiasm and devotion. He taught that the pleasures of the senses are not sinful, because "man must serve God with his body as well as his soul." In this respect, his teachings echo a basic tenet of Tantra, which is the need for wholehearted and passionate devotion to spiritual pursuits, applying one's body as much as one's intellect.

European Alchemy and Tantra

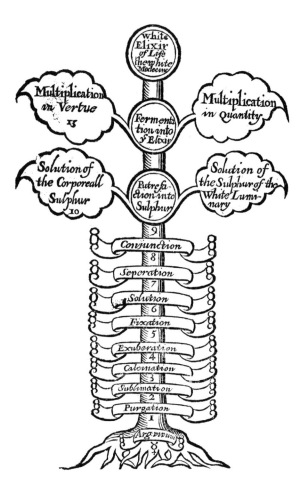

The link between Western alchemy and Tantra is apparent. Closer inspection of alchemical treatises and writings of those who immersed themselves in the mysteries of this almost supernatural discipline reveals the obvious connections. A book published in 1664 in England, with the title *Elhavareuna or the Rosie Crucian Medicines of Mettals*, written by John Heydon, sums up the stance of European alchemists in the middle of the seventeenth century. The author invokes the "High Priest of the Rosie Cross" along with "Hiarthas King of the Chaldeans, Jes-

Illustration from John Heydon's book *Elhavareuna or the Rosie Crucian Medicines of Mettals*, depicting an alchemical reversed Tree of Life with the "White Elixir" at the top.

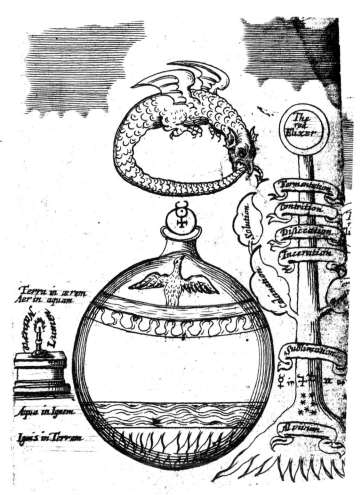

Illustration from John Heydon's book *Elhavareuna or the Rosie Crucian Medicines of Mettals*, depicting an alchemical Tree of Life with the "Red Elixir" at the top; this is an alchemical retort containing fire, water, and a bird (symbol of the soul) with a dragon above, eating its own tail (symbol of eternity, or "time transcended").

pion Prince of the Brackmans, Phroates the Indian Prince, Astaphon Duke of the Gimnosophists, Budda King of Babilon, Numa Pompillius King of the Romans, Zamolxides Emperor of Thrace, Abbaris Priest of the Hiperborean Jewes, Hermes Trismegist a King and Lawgiver of Egypt, Zoroaster the son of Oromasus King of Persia," stating "all these and many more were Lovers of these Rosie Crucians."

This list is quite revealing, since it touches on the Oriental and Indian connections with Rosicrucianism. The author then goes on to tell how while he was in a "sweet sleep," a vision appeared to him of a "lovely lady, but fifteen years old," who proceeded to transport him to a far-off island where she initiated him into the mysteries of

Illustration from John
Heydon's book
*Elhavareuna or the Rosie
Crucian Medicines of
Mettals*, depicting a
celestial goddess above an
alchemical retort with
dragon eating its tail, a
Tree of Life to the side.

alchemy. She showed him the "tree of the Sun and the other of the
Moon" and introduced him to the "Water of Life," which is "to the
fruit (of the Tree of Life) as if it were a woman." The author then
goes on to explain the Rosicrucian mysteries of quicksilver (mercury) and sulfur, with tables and charts showing alchemical transformations of base materials into gold.

Sexual imagery runs all through Heydon's book. *Mercury* and
sulfur, codes for semen and menstrual blood in Tantric texts, are
terms used almost casually. His book is clearly written for adepts,
for those who knew about the keys to Tantric symbolism.

In structure, Heydon's book resembles a Tantra. Covering a
wide range of topics, loaded with hidden sexual symbolism and sub-

tle meanings, it includes dialogue between celestial beings, visions, visualizations, detailed geomancy, and discussions on such arcane topics as supernatural effects, good and evil spirits, the charming of serpents, exorcism, the transformation of a human body into another shape, and so forth.

During the Inquisition, it was extremely dangerous to show any interest in occult or sexual matters. One could be tortured, burned as a witch, or have all one's property confiscated, so people formed secret societies and occult orders that enabled them to pursue their interests, sexual, occult, or otherwise, in a relatively safe context. There can be little doubt that Tantric knowledge continued to develop in Europe between the thirteenth and eighteenth century, mostly under the guise of alchemy, Rosicrucianism, and other hermetic traditions.

Sir Isaac Newton: Scientist and Mystic in the Tantric Tradition

Sir Isaac Newton (1642–1727) is generally viewed as one of the greatest of all scientists. What is not generally recognized is that he was also an alchemist obsessed by the occult. He was a Freemason and may have also been a Rosicrucian. Apparently, he was deeply interested in the early Gnostic "heresies."

Newton made his scientific discoveries following prolonged periods of meditation and spiritual introspection. He promoted the concept of ether, a hypothetical "subtle substance that permeates the entire universe," believing it to be a living spirit or spiritual substance. Some of Newton's writings, which show a subtle blend of science and mysticism, are reminiscent of ancient Tantras.

Alchemical treatises of Sir Isaac Newton's time are loaded with androgynous sexual symbolism and reveal strong Oriental influences from India and China. Interestingly, Sir Isaac burned a chest of his papers shortly before his death, most likely because it contained material that would have been misunderstood by his peers and might have cast the dubious light of sexual occultism on his purely scientific works.

Had Sir Isaac Newton been alive today, this brilliant man, who was a unique combination of scientist and mystic, could perhaps have enlightened us to the true goings-on among alchemical fraternities during those dark ages. From my perusal of the alchemical literature of his era, I am certain that what was being practiced by Newton and his associates was a type of spiritual sex derived from Indian Tantric teachings.

Sir Isaac Newton was the first to translate the seminal alchemical riddle known as the emerald tablet *(tabula smaragdina)*, as follows:

That which is below is like that which is above,
And that which is above is like that which is below,
To do the miracles of the one only thing.

This simple statement sums up the essence of Pythagoras's teachings and is very similar to statements found in a number of Tantric works. It can clearly be interpreted in many different ways, philosophically, alchemically, and sexually. It supposedly refers to the inherent bisexuality or androgyny of both man and woman, the understanding of which is at the foundation of Tantra philosophy.

It also refers to an ideal combination of sulfur and mercury, which in alchemical parlance can mean menstrual blood and semen, ovum and sperm. And it can mean both magical sex and alchemical apparatus used for distilling the ingredients of the "philosopher's stone." Interestingly, medical and alchemical Tantras, most of which originate in south Indian Siddha culture, commonly deal with the purification and combination of mercury and

Drawing of an Indian stone sculpture from Bengal, circa twelfth century, depicting the androgynous form of Shiva as Ardhanarishwara, the left side female, the right side male.

sulfur, and use apparatus and terminology similar to those used by Newton and other European alchemists.

Alchemy and Bisexuality

Herbert Guenther, an eminent professor of Oriental philosophy who has spent much of his career studying Buddhist Tantra texts, makes the following observation concerning the widespread acceptance of human bisexuality in his important book *Yuganaddha: The Tantric View of Life* (1972):

> The idea of bisexuality is met with all over the world, among the most primitive tribes as well as among the most cultured society.

Griaule, a prominent French anthropologist who studied the archaic Dogon culture of Mali, in western Africa said:

> According to the Dogon, from the outset, each human being is given two souls of different sex, or rather two principles corresponding to two distinct persons inside everyone. For the man, the female soul is lodged in the foreskin. For the woman, the male soul is housed in the clitoris.

It is because of this scenario that many African cultures have advocated both male and female circumcision, in the belief that by removing the other sex, the person can become more fully male or female. Though male and female circumcision are practices found in

Indian bronze casting of the androgynous form of Shiva, from south India, circa tenth century.

many ancient cultures, they are the result of the patriarchy taking over and using them for social control. In the true Tantric tradition, one embraces rather than negates the natural androgynous human condition, using it as a potent tool for spiritual liberation.

In his *Treatise on Passion*, the Tibetan former monk and hedonist Gedün Chöpel observes:

> Half of the body of a husband is his wife and half the body of a wife is her husband.

Carl Jung, the brilliant psychologist, made a similar observation in his *Psychology and Religion:*

> From time immemorial, man in his myths has expressed the idea of a male and female coexisting in the same body.

Jung even evokes Christian and Tantric parallels, using the term *anima* to mean "a psychic representation of the minority of female genes in a man's body," and quoting from the biblical book of Jeremiah:

> The image of God enveloped by the anima is the same as Gregory the Great's allegory of Christ and the church: "A woman shall compass a man" (Jeremiah 31:22). This is an exact parallel to the Tantric conception of Shiva in the embrace of his Shakti.

Large wood carving of an hermaphroditic figure seated on a throne. This "original ancestor" has prominent breasts and beard. From the Dogon tribe of Mali, west Africa, circa seventeenth century.

June Singer, a prominent Jungian psychoanalyst, used the natural androgyny of humans to advance a "new theory of sexuality." In her book *Androgyny: Toward a New Theory of Sexuality* (1976), she explored both alchemical and Tantric views of androgyny. Her account of spiritual sex à la Tantra is remarkably insight-filled. Regarding her "new theory," she wrote:

> Any new sexual theory developed for the years ahead must place sexuality in a far wider context than it has been seen in the Western world in modern times. The new era we are entering will require a shift from the exclusively personal viewpoint to one that includes the transpersonal, a shift from an egocentric position toward a universal orientation. . . .
>
> The new model of sexual consciousness will need to be inward-turning for, paradoxical as it may seem, in order to be aware of oneself as a cosmic being, one needs to discover the nature of his own essence. In the view of individual as microcosm within the macrocosm, the idea loses its strangeness. . . .

After some discussion of the Jungian psychological approach, she adds:

> The androgyn is a symbol of the Self par excellence. But more than that the androgyn is a representative in human form of the principle of wholeness. Each person, as an androgyn, has his or her unique combination of qualities. . . .
>
> Androgyny is the outcome of a dynamism based on the application of energy in an organic system that is open-ended and that interfaces with an open-ended universe.

The ideas of bisexuality expressed by Singer are inherently Tantric: a universe expressed by opposite yet perfectly balanced forces, both male and female, the spiritual and the sensual, heavenly bliss and earthly ecstasy, as one. In this way, the principles of alchemy, which sought to distill separate elements into one harmonious, concrete whole, were very much aligned with the ideals of Tantra.

The View of Sacred Sex in the West

In the West, sex has been viewed as spiritual, as a sacrament, only by unorthodox "heretics" and radicals. Over the centuries, many men and women who celebrated sex as a spiritual sacrament have been hounded, unfairly accused of crimes, physically transported to faraway places, tortured, jailed, and killed.

Sex is unquestionably a sacrament of love, a celebration of the natural urge for pleasure and for reproduction. It is amazing that Christianity, a religion supposedly founded on the simple view that God is love, could and did provoke such intolerance, such violence toward those who joyously chose to worship with sex as the ultimate sacrament.

Sex is a fact of life and should not be seen as sinful. The early Christians who offered up the "fruit" of their sex to God and the Goddess as sacraments were responding authentically to spiritual urgings. They were not perverts or heretics but rather were true believers who chose to worship in an unorthodox way. Many radical Gnostic Christians and Cabbalists boldly chose to worship "in the original pagan manner," offering up their pleasure and their most valuable resource to the spiritual powers. As we shall see in a subsequent chapter, many Tantrics practice sacramental sex in a manner very similar to the early Christians.

5 TANTRA IN THE WEST

Every man is the builder of a temple, called his body, to the God he worships,
after a style purely his own, nor can he get off by hammering marble instead.
We are all sculptors and painters, and our material is our own flesh and blood
and bones.

—HENRY DAVID THOREAU

Tantric Communities

THE TRANSCENDENTALISTS AND OTHER SPIRITUAL RADICALS

More than a hundred years ago, a radical spiritual movement known as the transcendentalist movement took hold among a small group of American intellectuals. Its followers questioned established Western views of religion, philosophy, and literature. Two of the movement's founders, poet Ralph Waldo Emerson (1803–1882) and writer George Ripley (1802–1880), had been ministers of the Unitarian church. Margaret Fuller (1810–1850), one of America's first female journalists and feminists, and writer-naturalist Henry David Thoreau (1817–1862) were other notable transcendentalists.

Followers of transcendentalism believed in the divinity of both humans and nature, in sexual and social freedom, educational innovation and the value of communal living; Thoreau developed a doctrine of passive resistance, advocating civil disobedience as a form of political protest; Ripley established an experimental cooperative community; Margaret Fuller showed that women can excel in intellectual pursuits. Dissatisfied with conservative orthodox Christian teachings, transcendentalists were radical spiritual optimists and mystics who recognized the interconnectedness of all life, taking it upon themselves to bring about positive change by the example of their own lifestyle.

The seeds of the American transcendentalist movement came from Europe, notably through Emerson's contact with the English romantic poet William Wordsworth (1770–1850) and the Scottish writer Thomas Carlyle (1795–1881). Another influence was the writings of Emanuel Swedenborg (1688–1772), the Swedish scientist and mystic who proposed that spiritual reality can best be approached through direct communion with the mystic manifestations of nature. A pioneer in human psychology and physiology, Swedenborg claimed to have experienced direct visions of spiritual realms.

A golden thread of radical spirituality runs through the works of Immanuel Kant (1724–1804), Swedenborg, Samuel Taylor Coleridge (1772–1834), Wordsworth, and Carlyle. This spirituality found in nature was the Holy Grail of Emerson, Thoreau, and the other American transcendentalists. Emerson, for example, viewed nature as "a visible manifestation of invisible spiritual truths."

The American transcendentalists translated and published key Hindu and Buddhist sacred scriptures, including the *Bhagavad Gita*, the *Upanishads*, and the *Lotus Sutra*. Their translations gave the emerging "new American paganism" an Eastern spiritual context. By so doing, the transcendentalists unknowingly prepared the ground for Tantra to become part of American culture in the century ahead.

Author Marilyn Ferguson accurately sums up the contribution, roots, and result of the American Transcendental Movement in her important book *The Aquarian Conspiracy* (1980). In it, she wrote:

> The Transcendentalists supposedly threatened the older order with their "new ideas"; but the ideas were not new, only the prospect of applying them in a society. The eclectic Transcendentalists had drawn not only from Quaker and Puritan traditions but also from German and Greek philosophers and Eastern religions. Although they were charged with having contempt for history, they replied that humankind could be liberated from history.
>
> They challenged the assumptions of the day in every realm: religion, philosophy, science, economy, the arts, education, and politics. They anticipated many of the movements of the twenti-

eth century. Like the human-potential movement of the 1960s, the Transcendentalists maintained that most people had not begun to tap their own inherent powers, had not discovered their uniqueness or their mother lode of creativity.

Before the Civil War intervened, Transcendentalism had almost reached the proportions of a national grass-roots movement. Apparently many Americans of the day were attracted to a philosophy that stressed an inner search for meaning. Although the Transcendental movement was overwhelmed by the materialism of the late nineteenth century, in various guises it entered the mainstream of world philosophy, to inspire giants like Whitman and Melville and to invigorate generations of social reformers.

Walt Whitman (1819–1892), probably the greatest of the nineteenth-century American poets, created poetry that embraced sexuality, racial diversity, democracy, and the spirituality inherent in all life. When his masterpiece, *Leaves of Grass* (first published in 1855) first came out, it was labeled an indecent book and caused his dismissal from a government position in the U.S. Department of the Interior. Times have changed.

Before we can truly be liberated from our history, we need to understand and learn from it. Nineteenth-century Quakers, ancient Greek philosophers, and Eastern religions may seem irrelevant to today's spiritual reality, yet many of the themes with which they dealt are pertinent to how Tantra evolved in the West. At this point, we'll pass over the intricacies of Greek philosophy and Eastern religion and instead focus on Christian cults such as Quakerism, Shakerism, Mormonism, and other radical spiritual movements that manifested in America during the last century. Our understanding of the roots of Tantra in the Western world, and in America in particular, must take into account the activities of these influential Christian cults.

RADICAL CHRISTIANS AND THEIR SEARCH FOR GUIDANCE

The transcendentalists and other American advocates of social and sexual change were actually radical Christians. Many were former church ministers who first turned to the Bible for spiritual inspiration and explored the writings of classical philosophers and historians for guidance. Knowledge about the spiritual function of sex was a prime concern of such radical seekers, but discussion of it in Western literature was hard to find prior to the twentieth century.

Many Christian cults, most notably the American Perfectionists, were inspired by the Cathars, a heretic Christian sect that appeared in parts of Europe at the beginning of the twelfth century. Perfectionists adopted many Cathar beliefs, one being that women naturally have a high spiritual status and can rightfully function as priestesses within the Christian church. In the twelfth century, Cathar women in France could also legally own property, a right that orthodox mainstream Christian women did not gain until the nineteenth century.

THE CATHARS AND SPIRITUAL SEX

Cathar priests and priestesses were both called *parfaits*, meaning "perfects," rising to their office through good works, austerities, spiritual initiations, and the practice of meditation. They believed in reincarnation, the immortality of the soul, asceticism, and nonviolence. Like Jesus, they practiced the healing arts in rites known as "the laying on of hands." They rejected the notion of the Eucharist and were opposed to the normal institution of marriage.

Cathars, American Perfectionists, and transcendentalists shared many common beliefs. Most were dualists, believing that the forces of good and evil have existed since the beginning of the universe and will continue to exist until the end. They did not follow the orthodox Christian view that evil was created by original sin, which supposedly entered the soul of humankind following Adam and Eve's expulsion from the Garden of Eden. Because Christian dualists did not subscribe to the doctrine of original sin, they viewed sex as a spiritual act.

Cathars practiced spiritual sex in the esoteric early Christian and Tantric tradition, using breath control, visualization, and other Yogic techniques. They practiced a form of *coitus reservus*, sometimes referred to as *karezza* ("little caress"), concerning which more detail shall follow shortly.

Cathars became rich and powerful, building their own churches and castles. They were eventually perceived as a threat to the orthodox Catholic church. The Pope ordered all Christian heretics "cleansed" and, beginning in 1209, organized massacres of Cathars followed, together with the confiscation of their property. By the fourteenth century, Catharism had been virtually exterminated. However, esoteric Cathar spiritual sex teachings survived among the Knights Templars, the Troubadours, and in the teachings of some secret societies and occult organizations that emerged in Europe between the late thirteenth and mid-seventeenth centuries.

QUAKERS, SHAKERS, MORMONS, AND CHARISMATIC PREACHERS

The roots of the nineteenth-century American transcendental movement are varied but undoubtedly reach back into both Quakerism and Shakerism. The Quakers, a seventeenth-century English Christian sect founded by George Fox, taught that because "God exists in every person," formal church structures and ministers are unnecessary. Persecuted in England, many Quakers came to America, where they were a potent political force until the American Revolution. Known as the Society of Friends, Quakers were committed to advancing pacifism and women's rights and denouncing slavery. Their goal of "inward experience of God" was closer to the Hindu spiritual approach than to orthodox Christianity.

Charismatic leadership has always been the cornerstone of new faiths and political movements. Early in the eighteenth century, a group of religious "visionaries" known as the French Prophets had created quite a stir in England. Their unique form of worship involved "divine possession," commonly of charismatic women who served as mediums or prophetesses who manifested ecstatic behavior such as uncontrolled shaking and dancing, and a form of sacred theater. These performances attracted large crowds and quite a number of converts. The sight of spiritually inspired women shaking and prophesying was certainly threatening to many orthodox churchmen, who labeled them promiscuous and saw their spirit possessions as "the Devil's work."

The Shakers, also known as the United Society of Believers in

Christ's Second Appearing, emerged out of the spiritual climate evoked by the French Prophets. They first manifested in England in 1747 within the Quaker faith and were called Shakers because of the uncontrollable trembling and shaking of church members while in spiritual ecstasy. When Ann Lee, an early Shaker who was referred to as Mother Ann, declared she had "received the feminine principle of God," she was imprisoned. Following a vision, she led a small group of her followers to America in 1774.

In post-Revolution America, Shakerism emerged as a radical spiritist Christian cult focused around the alleged divinity of Ann Lee, called "the Mother, Queen of Heaven, Elect Lady, and Bride of Christ." Shakers identified her with "the woman spoken of in the XIIth chapter of the Revelations of John, who was clothed with the sun, having the moon under her feet, and on her head a crown of twelve stars." She was viewed as the "Second Appearance of Christ" in the form of the "Spiritual Mother of all the children of the resurrection." To the opponents of Shakerism, Ann Lee was a witch, "in league with the Devil." On repeated occasions following Ann Lee's death, the "spirit of Ann Lee as Holy Mother Wisdom" possessed various Shaker women and gave spiritual messages and visions. Following Ann Lee's death, Lucy Wright gained the Order of Spiritual Mother in 1796 and helped reorganize Shakerism into a successful spiritual community.

During the course of their worship, Shakers evoked charismatic powers and "spiritual dispensations," which often included uncontrolled shaking, hopping, spinning, running, laughing, howling, and groaning, as well as speaking and singing "in tongues," excessive smoking, drinking, and nudity.

Like Tantrics, Shakers believed in the dual nature of God, the "Heavenly Father" and the "Eternal Mother." They promoted pacifism, the equality of the sexes, communal sharing of property, the value of "consecrated" work, and the confession of sins. They advocated total celibacy, and were against marriage. Their way of worship was a form of ecstatic shamanism leading to spirit possession and visionary experiences, common enough in "pagan" cultures such as India and Africa but definitely very threatening to puritanical America at the end of the eighteenth century.

Mormonism is another radical Christian cult that was established in the revivalist atmosphere of nineteenth-century America. Those were wild and strange times, when people explored spirituality as spontaneously as they explored the new territories of America. Mormonism was really an entirely new form of Christianity. Around 1824, when several of the local churches were experiencing revivalist activities, Joseph Smith Jr. (1805–1844), the founder of Mormonism, experienced his first vision. For a while, he made his living as a "money digger," meaning he used his alleged occult or visionary powers to lead landowners to buried treasure or valuable minerals. At times, Smith spoke to others of a spirit who could lead him to "plates of gold," a "Golden Bible" that would make him and his family rich and famous. Early in 1827, he married Emma in Harmony, Pennsylvania, where the Lutheran minister George Rapp had established a communal farm following a vision. Later that year Joseph Smith claimed to have recovered the Golden Bible after receiving a visitation from an angel called Moroni. The *Mormon Bible* purported to tell the history of lost tribes of Israel who reached America in pre-Columbian times.

Joseph Smith Jr. dictated his translation of the Golden Bible, initially to his wife and then to Martin Harris, an associate of his. No one ever got to see the original inscribed "plates of Nephi." The resultant *Book of Mormon*, which was first published in late March 1830, was unquestionably inspired by *View of the Hebrews; or the Tribes of Israel in America* (1825) by Ethan Smith, a pastor of the Poultney Congregational Church.

Joseph Smith's *Book of Mormon* soon became accepted as a divine revelation by many of his immediate family circle and associates. He started to organize his church soon after publishing his book and within a month had some thirty converts. As prophet of his Mormon church, Smith organized missionary activity, which quickly established a "new Zion" in Missouri, set up as a religious commune. Among the notable original Mormon doctrines is baptism of the dead, celestial marriage, and polygamy, the practice of a man having more than one wife at a time.

As with so many radical cults, the Mormons were persecuted, initially because of their strange beliefs, especially their advocating of polygamy, then because of their prosperity and political influence. Joseph Smith was jailed for an old offense related to his days as a money digger and shortly afterward, in 1844, assassinated. Brigham Young was then installed as leader, taking twenty-seven of his female churchgoers as wives. He moved the Mormon church headquarters to Utah, where it remains today. Because polygamy was acknowledged as a tenet of Mormon belief, Mormons were persecuted by the authorities, resulting in the passing of antibigamy laws by Congress in 1862 and 1882.

In 1879, the U.S. Supreme Court ruled against the Mormons, declaring that "religious freedom cannot be claimed as grounds for the practice of polygamy." In 1890, the Mormon church of Utah officially denied its members' rights to polygamy. At present, the Mormon Church, also known as the Church of Jesus Christ of Latter-Day Saints, has about eight million members worldwide.

Quakers, Shakers, and Mormons had different spiritual messages and different forms of religious expression, but they all valued spiritual experience over empty philosophical theorizing. They all wanted to experience ecstasy, to "feel the spirit move within" and sought visions and "spiritual dispensations." The spiritual and visionary aspects of these new Christian religions, which were initially focused around charismatic leaders, have much in common with modern religious cults.

REVIVALISTS, PERFECTIONISTS, UTOPIANS, AND FREE LOVERS

In the early nineteenth century, some revivalist church ministers in New England began to challenge conventional Christian doctrines of sin and human unworthiness, suggesting instead that people had the potential to achieve perfection on earth. This perfectionist view was radically different. It allowed for spiritual exploration, visionary experiences, "biblical communism," and bold sexual and social experimentation. The resultant American utopian free-love movement promoted equality of the sexes, embraced individualism, and sought to elevate sexual union to a spiritual art. This was the beginning of American Tantra.

Revivalists, perfectionists, and utopians started to set up idealistic communities, often inspired by spiritual visions. Following a vision of the angel Gabriel, George Rapp, a Lutheran minister, founded

Harmony, a communal farm in Pennsylvania. He attracted more than seven hundred followers, all of whom made vows of celibacy. Celibacy was but one pole of the new communal religious spirit that emerged during this period. Other perfectionists and utopians believed that freedom of sexual expression or free love was essential before the human spirit could evolve properly.

Robert Dale Owen, an advocate of the new spiritual socialism of the early nineteenth century, established the New Harmony utopian community, which was visited by Frances Wright, a Scottish immigrant free-thinker who was opposed to slavery, organized religion, and conventional marriage. Independently wealthy, she founded a large communal farm in 1862 near Memphis, Tennessee. Known as Nashoba and located on about two thousand fertile acres, this community brought both black and white Americans together, to work and to make love.

Frances Wright's opposition to slavery, organized religion, and marriage was, in its time, extremely controversial. Even more controversial was her belief that blacks and whites should be encouraged to cohabit and make love together. In *Intimate Matters: A History of Sexuality in America* (1988), a fascinating book, authors John D'Emilio and Estelle Freedman explain the situation in the Nashoba community:

> An interracial abolitionist community would itself have offended the majority of Americans, northern or southern, but Wright had even more radical intentions. She had come to the conclusion that only the amalgamation of the races would resolve the conflicts inherent in a biracial society. . . .
>
> Wright formulated one of the earliest defenses of free love to appear in America. She based her theory on the belief that individuals who mutually desired sexual union should be constrained neither by marital status nor by race. In her vision, sex could be a key to human happiness, but society kept it from becoming so. Writing in 1827, when the middle class had begun to embrace female purity, Wright affirmed sexual passion as "the best source of human happiness" and criticized public opinion and social institutions for warping this naturally "noble" instinct. In reaction to the growing public reticence about sexual-

ity, Wright initiated a century-long free-love attack on sexual silences. ''Ignorant laws, ignorant prejudices, ignorant codes of morals,'' she wrote, condemned ''one portion of the female sex to vicious excess, another to as viscious restraint and generally the whole of the male sex to debasing licentiousness, if not to loathsome brutality.'' Only the free expression of sexual passion would undermine those powerful constraints that subverted its positive force.

The Nashoba community closed in 1830 because of economic and social pressure. Frances Wright was years ahead of her time. Angry mobs continued to threaten meetings she held; she was labeled ''Priestess of Beelzebub'' and to many became a despised figure. She died in 1852, without proper recognition for her bold visionary activities. Amazingly, African-Americans had to wait until Congress passed the Civil Rights Act in 1964 before gaining basic liberties such as the right to vote.

In the early and mid-nineteenth century, other free-love communes existed for brief periods in America. In the 1850s, the Grand Order of Recreation, a free-love organization that met in a Broadway salon in New York City, was raided and its members arrested. The Modern Times free-love commune, run by Mary and Thomas Nichols on Long Island, was closed down following some negative press reports. Other free-love groups were set up in upstate New York; New England; Brimfield, Massachusetts; Berlin Heights, near Cleveland, Ohio; Texas; and elsewhere, created by enthusiastic sexual radicals, anarchists, and social reformers. Some were inspired by Christian revivalists, Perfectionists, and biblical communists. Others were influenced by the teachings of Charles Fourier, a French aristocrat and author of the book *The Social Destiny of Man*, which, in its time, had a wide impact among American intellectuals.

The American Fourierists founded capitalistic settlements. Their members worked in light industry, crafts, agriculture, and so forth. In these utopian settlements, industriousness was encouraged as the key to upward mobility. The quality of the living quarters and facilities made available to members was determined by their ability to produce for the community. In these Fourier communities, monogamy was discouraged. Sexual needs were apparently served by persons known as erotic saints, who were supposedly individuals free of possessiveness.

Brook Farm, situated in West Roxbury on the outskirts of Boston, was a Fourier-inspired community founded by transcendentalists in 1841. Referred to as the Brook Farm Institute of Agriculture and Education, it attracted many poets and writers within the transcendentalist movement, such as Ralph Waldo Emerson, Henry David Thoreau, George Ripley, Henry James, Margaret Fuller, and Nathaniel Hawthorne. People could earn their room and board by working on the farm, communing with nature while exploring their sexuality in a spiritual context. Eventually, in 1847, this experimental free-love community closed down.

THE SOCIETY OF PERFECTIONISTS: THE ONEIDA COMMUNITY

Soon after the American transcendentalists became established, John Humphrey Noyes (1811–1886), a young law student and son of a wealthy congressman, attended a revivalist rally and decided to devote his life "to the service and ministry of God." In 1834, he became convinced of his own spiritual perfection.

Following his visits to several free-love communes, in 1846 Noyes founded the Society of Perfectionists, whose members practiced Biblical communism and advocated free love. Noyes had noted that ecstatic Christian revivalist gatherings often led people to express what he termed "amative tendencies," meaning the desire for sexual intimacy. He saw a natural connection between ecstatic spirituality and the desire for sexual expression. He recognized the potential for spiritual sex, and what is most interesting, he saw it in a Christian context.

All members of the Society of Perfectionists, the spiritual community established by Noyes in Putney, Vermont, practiced what came to be termed "complex marriage" or "group marriage," in which both men and women married into the group as a whole. According to Noyes, by subscribing to group marriage, "each man is both the husband and brother of all the women, just as each woman is the wife and sister of all the men." Driven out of Putney by public opinion and charges of adultery, Noyes and his followers founded the Oneida Community in 1848 on 160 acres of good land on the Oneida Creek in Madison County, in upstate New York.

Noyes's community promoted equality of the sexes, freedom for slaves, and the humane treatment of laborers. Noyes taught a sexual technique that he termed "male continence," which members of the Oneida Community practiced as a religious rite. Many years later, he explained his thesis as follows:

> I conceived the idea that the sexual organs have a social function which is distinct from the propagative function, and that these functions may be separated practically. I experimented on this idea, and found that the self-control which it requires is not difficult; also that my enjoyment was increased; also that my wife's experience was very satisfactory, as it had never been before.
>
> The discharge of the semen, instead of being the main act of sexual intercourse, properly so called, is really the sequel and termination of it.

Noyes promoted his view that sexual intercourse without male orgasm is a spiritual activity, whereas when culminating in ejaculation, it is sensual. Whether or not Noyes knew it, he had discovered the ancient Tantric technique that was practiced centuries beforehand.

In the Oneida Community, children were conceived following "eugenic selection," the promotion of improved human breeding by selecting from healthy stock. Permission to have children was granted by applying to the Stirpicultural Committee and showing oneself to be mentally and physically healthy.

More than a hundred years later, John G. Bennett, the noted mathematician and student of the Russian mystic George Gurdjieff, commented on the value of eugenics, writing in a small volume entitled *Sex* (1975):

> It is a strange thing, which many people have noted, that we modern people breed almost indiscriminately, without reference to genetic considerations. For a hundred years now, we have been in possession of a great deal of knowledge about genetics and the rules for successful breeding which we apply with increasing success to almost every species of plant and animal life with

which we have concern, except our own. So we are able to produce greatly improved grains, fruits, flowers and animals of almost any kind that we require; and yet with the human race, on
the whole we do the opposite and with the indiscriminate mating
of men and women which is customary we encourage the proliferation of the less stable genetic patterns and breed out the ones
with higher qualities.

In the Oneida Community, children created by eugenic selection
were raised with the entire community as their parents and at adolescence were sexually initiated by an adult carefully chosen for the
purpose. Sexual propositions were always delivered through third
parties. The Oneida Community was not a sexually promiscuous society. There were no wild orgies. According to the laws of the Oneida
Community, every person had the right to refuse the caresses of a
person they disliked.

Noyes's book *Male Continence* was published in 1872. He wrote:

> As propagation will become a science, so amative intercourse will
> have place among the "fine arts." Indeed, it will take rank above
> music, painting, sculpture, etc.; for it combines the charms and
> benefits of them all. There is as much room for cultivation of
> taste and skill in this department as any.

More than a hundred years after Noyes's prediction of "amative
intercourse having its place among the fine arts," we are still far
away from realizing this vision. Only the Hindus of the era of the
sage Vatsyayana, author of the *Kama Sutra*—more than fifteen hundred years ago—could boast that their achievements in erotic arts
rank above or alongside the arts of music, painting, or sculpture.
Perhaps in the twenty-first century, a new sexual paradigm will
eventually allow for this vision to be fulfilled.

The Oneida Community existed for more than twenty-five
years and was industrious, prosperous, and socially successful. But
Noyes's theories always remained controversial. In 1875, he created
tension in his community by insisting that one of his sons should
eventually become his successor. Pressure on the community was
already mounting from Protestant clergymen and from Anthony
Comstock, creator of the Comstock antiobscenity bill of 1873. Com-

stock pointed out that much Oneida Community literature, which in his view was immoral, was being sent through the U.S. Postal Service and could therefore be cause for arrest. There was also a suggestion that Noyes could be prosecuted and imprisoned for having sex with underage girls.

By 1879, under extreme pressure from critics, the Oneida Community officially gave up practicing complex marriage and the following year discontinued communal ownership of property. Noyes eventually decided that, in the best interests of the community, he should retire to Canada. Before he left his free-love community, he wrote of it:

> We made a raid into an unknown country, charted it, and returned without the loss of a man, woman, or child.

Noyes died in Canada at the age of seventy-four and his body was returned to Oneida for burial.

The transcendentalists, the Oneida Community, and other Bible communist and free-love groups were radical pioneers who attempted to discover and define a new spiritual order in which sexuality and human rights could have free and creative expression. Unfortunately, the "new religion" of science and materialism took over at the end of the nineteenth century, before the bold experiments of America's radical mystics, who were ahead of their time, could be completed. They were would-be Tantrics, attempting to discover and define a new spirituality, a new spiritual paradigm for the century ahead.

Tantric Pioneers

The rise of sexual communities throughout the world could not have been achieved without the help of specific individuals who paved the way for the introduction and eventual acceptance of Tantric philosophy and practice in the Western world. What follows is an account of the most prominent of these people who, though from different times, brought Tantra from the little-known interior of Asia to every corner of the globe.

MARCO POLO'S ACCOUNT OF INDIAN YOGIS
AND TANTRICS

The Venetian traveler Marco Polo was probably the first European to write about Indian mysticism in his *Description of the World* (better known as *The Travels of Marco Polo*). Published in the late thirteenth century, it tells of "Brahmans and a certain men living under a rule who are called Yogis. They live longer than the others, as much as 150 or 200 years."

Marco Polo refers to Indian Yogis who used mercury products for longevity. He also wrote about the people of Kashmir and their attainments in the "magical arts," obviously impressed by personal experience:

> Their knowledge of devilish enchantments is something marvelous. They make their idols speak. They change the weather by enchantment and bring on thick darkness. They accomplish such marvels by magic and craft that no one who has not seen them could believe them. I may say that they are the past masters of idolatry and it is from them that idols are derived.

This European account tells of Indian occult powers (known in Sanskrit as *siddhi*) of a type generally associated with Tantra. Marco Polo locates this event in Kashmir, home of Kashmiri Shaivism, an evolved school of Hindu Tantra.

Marco Polo's writings also include a description of a Hindu ceremony in which temple women are used to "test the resolve of certain Yogi-probationers." His account describes an esoteric Tantric initiation rite:

> The maidens who are offered to the gods are brought in and made to touch the probationers. They touch them on various parts of the body and embrace and fondle them and instill into them the most earthly bliss. If the man thus caressed lies completely motionless without any reaction to the maiden's touch, he passes muster and is admitted to their Order. If on the other hand his member reacts to the touch, they will not keep him, but expel him forthwith.

Marco Polo's book had everything it needed—adventure, sex, and mysticism—to make it a best-seller. It is still in print today. His stories of long-living Yogis, idolatry, magic, and sacred temple maidens involved in strange sexual rites set the standard by which Indian mysticism in general and Tantra in particular would be described in the centuries ahead.

AN EIGHTEENTH-CENTURY SEXUAL "HOW-TO"

During the eighteenth and nineteenth centuries, one had to be either a churchman, a medical doctor, or an anthropologist to publish reference works that were sexually explicit. Descriptions of sexual acts generally had to be written in Latin to be acceptable and the sale of such publications were restricted to "members of the medical and other recognized professions."

In *The Mysteries of Conjugal Love Reveal'd*, originally published in Paris in 1712 and one of the earliest Western sexual how-tos, author Nicholas de Venette used an oblique but effective strategy to justify his work, writing the following in his preface:

> Had not the Books of the Ancients that treated of Love been unfortunately lost, either thro' the malice of Men, or injury of the Times, we might doubtless have increased our Observations about the Generations of Human Kind. . . .

"Observations about the Generations of Human Kind?" What the author is referring to is sex, plain and simple, but in the early eighteenth century, any direct mention of the word was considered taboo. The "Books of the Ancients that treated of Love" were not all lost, but most were unknown or untranslated and were not considered relevant to Judeo-Christian culture.

de Venette was bold enough to make the great (and at that time, potentially dangerous) leap forward and incorporate his own and others' experiences into his treatise, but this early eighteenth-century sexologist was careful to maintain some connection with classical Greek and Roman historical sources. He explained:

> Methinks our own Experience, in Conjunction with that of our Friends, may furnish us with a sufficient share of Knowledge, to

make a large Volume about the Orders Nature has prescrib'd for the production of Men, without having recourse to the Thoughts of the Ancients.

de Venette was remarkably direct and advanced for his time; his book includes detailed information on the clitoris and its role in lovemaking and a compelling argument that women can ejaculate during orgasm. Also, in his chapter entitled "After what Manner married People ought to caress," he poetically reveals the mystical extent of his observations concerning sex and woman, writing:

> Women are better versed in the Pliantness of Love than we, being they give themselves more up to Sensualities. Indeed their Passion is more violent, and their Pleasure of a longer Continuance, as Fire kept in green Wood.

One might wonder where this author got such opinions, which seem inspired by classic Hindu erotic lore. What is certain is that he was one of the first Westerners to attempt to write a truly direct and spiritual book about sex. His view of women being "better versed in the Pliantness of Love" was radical indeed.

SIR RICHARD FRANCIS BURTON AND THE *KAMA SUTRA*

Sir Richard Francis Burton (1821–1890), the famous Victorian Orientalist and traveler, contributed greatly to putting sexual practices into the proper context. He was particularly interested in both Oriental and African attitudes toward sex and was always inquisitive. While in India, he kept an Indian woman as his mistress. Burton returned to England and in 1873, where he and several friends founded the London Anthropological Society, which issued the periodical *Anthropologia*. Concerning this, he wrote:

> My motive was to supply travelers with an organ that would rescue their observations from the outer darkness of manuscript and print their curious information on social and sexual matters.

This periodical was instrumental in educating many Victorian persons of influence about the diversity of human sexual behavior.

Burton also cofounded the Kama Shastra Society, a small and

highly secretive organization that privately published the *Kama Sutra* (in 1883) and the *Ananga Ranga* (in 1885), the first ancient Hindu treatises on the arts of love to be translated into the English language. Amazingly, they could not be "officially" published in English until the mid 1960s, following a landmark court case. Sexual barriers like these continued to exist in the West until the "psychedelic" era. Then they came down with a crash, as we shall soon see.

THE OLIPHANTS, "SEXUAL MISSIONARIES"

Laurance Oliphant (1821–1888), was an English statesman and journalist who in 1865 became a disciple of Thomas Lake Harris (1823–1906), the American mystic. Oliphant and his wife traveled to India, where they learned Yogic breathing and other esoteric spiritual techniques. Upon their return to England, their *Sympneumata* was published (in 1885). In this book, some Tantric breathing secrets were revealed in English for the first time.

Eventually, the Oliphants moved to Palestine, where they taught esoteric sexual practices obviously inspired by Tantra and Yoga teachings. They liked to think of themselves as "sexual missionaries." In today's world, they would be termed neo-Tantric sex therapists. Some of the Oliphants' spiritual sex teachings survive in the kibbutzim of Israel.

PASCHAL BEVERLY RANDOLPH AND THE "WOMANHOOD OF GOD"

Paschal Beverly Randolph (1825–1875) was another individual who helped introduce Tantra to the West. An American writer and occultist who picked up some knowledge of sexual magic during his travels to Europe and the Middle East, he joined the Hermetic Brotherhood of Luxor. This esoteric organization based in Boston was a direct antecedent of the Ordo Templis Orientis, commonly referred to as the O.T.O., a European occult fraternity. In 1870, Randolph set up his own fraternity, which he called the Eulis Brotherhood.

Randolph's book *Magia Sexualis* was compiled by his followers from his notebooks and published after his death. The central thesis of this work is that all force and powers arise from the "womanhood of God." He also emphasized the magical power of sex.

Randolph seems to have been influenced by a combination of European alchemical thought, Cabbalism, Arabian erotica, and Hindu Tantra. He introduced many new or little-known words to try to redefine esoteric concepts. *Volancie* (exercise of the will), *decretism* (a dictatorial quality), *posism* (bodily attitudes or postures that are signs of particular thoughts), and *tiroclerism* (the power to evoke clear images with the inner sight) are some such terms.

Randolph was a Tantric initiate of sorts. His main focus was the use of sex to empower magical acts. He subscribed to the male continence and sexual magnetism theories in vogue with American free-love groups of his time, but also believed that a woman's orgasm should coincide with the man's emission, declaring that "only in this way will the magic be fulfilled."

Randolph prescribed long periods of preparation for some of his recommended sexomagical rites. But he seemed to have had a rather chauvinistic view of women, using them in his practice of sexual magic. He listed the following five separate aims that members of the Eulis Brotherhood could pursue during their sexomagical procedures:

1. Realization of a project, desire, or precise order
2. Provocation of supersensual visions
3. Regeneration of vital energy and strengthening of "magnetic power"
4. Production of an influence to subject a woman to a man or a man to a woman
5. Liberation of "charges" of psychic and fluidic force to saturate certain objects

These aims are rather similar to those found in traditional Indian Tantric teachings.

During the late nineteenth century, Randolph was influential among such emerging American occult organizations as Theosophy, which incorporated a wide range of mystical beliefs and hidden teachings passed on from ancient times. Theosophists were among the first Westerners to publish Indian Tantric material and bring concepts such as reincarnation, karma, and *mahatmas* to the wider American public.

THE THEOSOPHICAL SOCIETY AND A TANTRIC PUBLICATION

The Theosophical Society must take credit for introducing many Westerners to oriental spiritual teachings. Founded in New York in November 1875 by Helena P. Blavatsky (1831–1891), this organization's published aim was "to promote universal brotherhood, study all the great religions, philosophies, and sciences, and to investigate unexplained laws of Nature and the psychic powers of human beings." This was virtually a mandate to explore Tantra.

Madame Blavatsky, who was known as H. P. B. to her intimates, was a colorful and enigmatic character. Her father was German and she married a Russian. In 1851, she was supposedly initiated by a certain Master Morya in London. She traveled to India and Tibet (1867–70) before settling in London, where she wrote *Isis Unveiled* (in 1877) and *The Secret Doctrine* (in 1886–87), two occult works based on Hindu teachings but interpreted in her own rather peculiar spiritualist manner.

The Theosophical Society became a major movement, almost a new religion or cult, with centers in many of the world's largest cities. The society published a translation of Patanjali's *Yoga Sutras*, the classic Hindu Yogic text, and one of its earliest productions was *Nature's Finer Forces*, Swami Rama Prasad's translation of a Bengali (East Indian) Hindu Tantric treatise.

The Theosophical Society can hardly be viewed as a Tantric organization, but it did disseminate information of relevance to seekers after Tantric truths. Many Westerners who became involved with the Tantrik Order in America, founded in 1906, were introduced to Indian mysticism through the activities and publications of the Theosophical Society.

THE GOLDEN DAWN AND *NATURE'S FINER FORCES*

The story of how Tantra became part of Western occult tradition is inexorably linked to an occult organization known as the Golden Dawn. Originally the German occult order Die Goldene Dammerung, the Golden Dawn was, in 1887, established in England by William Westcott, a Freemason and Rosicrucian. He received permission to do this from Anna Sprengel of Nuremberg, who was the last adept of the German organization.

In 1891, MacGregor Mathers took control of the Golden Dawn. Working in conjunction with the poet W. B. Yeats, Mathers refined and reorganized the order's rituals. Swami Rama Prasad's Tantric treatise *Nature's Finer Forces*, published by the Theosophical Society, became required reading for Golden Dawn initiates.

The Golden Dawn was an important focal point for many would-be occultists and neo-Tantrics, such as Aleister Crowley, who eventually succeeded Mathers as the order's chief adept.

Because of *Nature's Finer Forces*, the Golden Dawn began to take on a distinctly Tantric flavor. Rituals that had originally been adapted from those of Freemason and Rosicrucian type took on a more magical and sexual character. Crowley, concerning whom more detail follows in a subsequent section, was largely responsible for adapting the rites of the Golden Dawn along neo-Tantric lines. Later, Crowley formed his own cult, becoming infamous as "the wickedest man alive."

SUPERSTAR SWAMI VIVEKANANDA

Any exploration of Tantra in the West inevitably leads to Swami Vivekananda (1862–1902), the first "superstar Swami" to visit America. Born in Bengal but educated abroad, this fascinating man was a renunciate monk and the main disciple of Sri Ramakrishna. A great scholar and student of both arts and sciences, Vivekananda was also a practicing Tantric, yet he kept this aspect of his spiritual life very private. Tantra was the source of Vivekananda's charisma and power; it was the secret spiritual system that enabled him to achieve so much in such a short time.

In May 1893, Vivekananda traveled from Bombay to Vancouver, Canada, en route to Chicago, to represent Hinduism at the Parliament of Religions. This event was to be part of the World's Colombian Exposition, commemorating the four hundredth anniversary of Columbus's landing in the Americas. The Parliament of Religions opened in Chicago on September 11, 1893. Swami Vivekananda's address to the "sisters and brothers of America" brought cheers from the audience.

Vivekananda was well educated, eloquent, handsome, charming, and tremendously charismatic. Most important, for the time, he presented his arguments in a scientific way. For the first time, Hinduism had a credible face to the American public.

Swami Vivekananda became the honored guest of many wealthy and influential Westerners, impressing them with his compelling personality and his learned and accessible presentation of Hindu spirituality. He spent two years explaining Hinduism to Americans, touching on deeper subjects such as Yoga and Tantra. He taught principally in Chicago, Detroit, Boston, and New York. In 1896, he returned to India via England, where he also attracted followers. His book *Raja Yoga* was published in 1897, helping to introduce concepts of Yoga philosophy to a wider audience.

In 1899, Vivekananda made his second and last visit to the West, spending most of his time in the United States. It was during this trip that he was able to connect with several Americans on a more esoteric level. Among those was an American going by the Hindu name Shastri, soon to become better known as Pierre Arnold Bernard, Dr. Bernard, P. A., or "Oom the Omnipotent," the founder of the Tantrik Order in America.

Swami Vivekananda, whose picture is prominently featured in the *International Journal: Tantrik Order*, wrote of Bernard:

> There is no greater whirlpool than the mind of man, and he is indeed an artist who can hold in hands its twists, its turns, its gambols. Such a one (Shastri) Bernard has proven himself to be.

Swami Vivekananda returned to India in 1900 and died on July 4, 1902. Of his Tantric initiations and practices, very little is known. For example, it is not known whether Vivekananda ever practiced advanced Tantric rites with a consort. In his time, when India and much of the world was under the sway of puritanical Victorian values, it would have been extremely difficult to admit to involvement in activities such as spiritual sex. Nevertheless, his endorsement of Pierre Bernard and the Tantrik Order of America, which was unquestionably a venue where spiritual sex was practiced, suggests that he may have personally participated.

Picture of Swami Vivekananda, as reproduced full page in the "International Journal: Tantrik Order," 1906.

THE TANTRIK ORDER IN AMERICA

Sometime prior to July 1906, several prominent Americans, well informed about Yoga, got together and formed the Tantrik Order in America. This event most likely was inspired by the arrival in California of Swami Ram (Swami Ram Tirath), a young and highly qualified Tantric Yogi and Sanskrit specialist, from India a couple of years earlier. Another influence had undoubtedly been Swami Vivekananda's visits to America and his interactions on an esoteric

Swami Ram Tirath, one of the main persons responsible for bringing Tantra to America.

level with several Americans who had already acquired some knowledge about the Indian mystic arts and sciences.

The Tantrik Order in America was founded by Pierre Arnold Bernard, together with several other people. Pascal Warren Tormes was named secretary and Robert Emile Young, director; Young made the official registration in Washington, D.C. and in Canada. The date of registration was given as July 1906 and their first production was the *International Journal: Tantrik Order*, published from St. Louis, dated October 16, 1906.

Published by the Tantrik Press, New York, the *International Journal: Tantrik Order* is a comprehensive compendium of information pertaining to Tantra. It is truly remarkable how much data was brought together and published at a time when very little information on the Tantric tradition was available in the West and when prudishness prevailed.

Pierre Arnold Bernard is listed as the "first American Primate" of the Tantrik Order of America. The organization was firmly established in New York City and eventually made its base in Nyack, New York, when Bernard acquired large estates there. Many prominent Americans and Europeans became associated with Bernard and his Tantrik Order.

DR. BERNARD, THE FATHER OF TANTRA IN AMERICA

Dr. Bernard, the "father" of Tantra in America, was born into a middle-class American family with roots in California, in 1875. Very little information has survived about his family or his childhood, but apparently his father divorced and remarried more than once. He was brought up largely by relatives. Perhaps this is part of the reason why, when he came into his own, he chose to hide his real origins and created a fictitious identity and fanciful biography, which he nurtured throughout his life. For example, at some point he began to use the name Peter Coon, giving his birthplace as Leon, Iowa; newspaper reports commonly gave this as his true birth name and place, though no evidence has surfaced to support such claims. It seems likely that Peter was actually Bernard's given first name and that he chose to change it to Pierre to add a distinctive and European flavor to his persona.

While still in his teens, he worked his way to India, fascinated by "the ancient Sanskrit writings and the age-old Indian methods of curing disease of mind and body." He studied in Kashmir and Nadia, Bengal, and after some years was given the title Shastri, meaning a knower of the Hindu teachings (*shastras*). Such an achievement, even today, is hard to come by.

Returning from India, Bernard traveled widely throughout America and, by his own account, worked in various occupations, as a barber, an acrobat, a salmon packer, and a fruit picker. While in California, he studied medicine with help from a relative and became a keen student of hypnotism. He also evolved his own special technique of self-induced hypnosis.

It is not clear when or why Bernard started to call himself Dr. Pierre Arnold Bernard. Some reports suggest that he did this to add respectability and to associate himself with the illustrious French doctor, Claude Bernard (1813–1878), founder of both experimental physiology and pharmacology. As far as I am aware, there is no evidence of Bernard actually getting a formal medical degree, but it is a fact that he was extraordinarily knowledgeable about Western medicine and could hold his own among eminent doctors.

Pierre Arnold Bernard had several brothers and half brothers, many of whom survived him. Another well-known Bernard, Theos, who became a physician, scholar, and author on Yogic topics, was his nephew. In the 1930s Theos married Viola Wertheim, one of the daughters of Jacob Wertheim, the tobacco magnate.

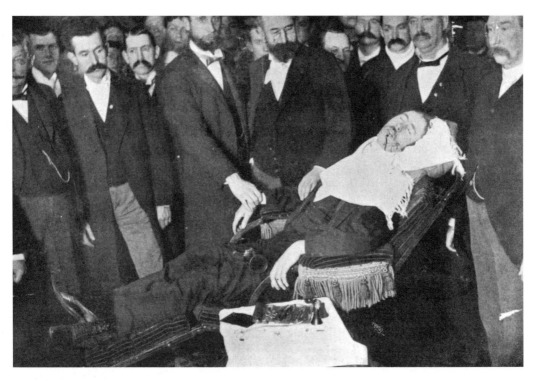

Dr. Pierre Bernard demonstrating the Kali Mudra (the counterfeiting of death) before an audience of physicians.

We know for sure that Theos Bernard spent considerable time in India. He was one of the first Americans to perfect all the Hatha Yoga postures and wrote an excellent book about his Yoga experiences. He visited Nepal and Tibet, and received formal training as a Lama while in Lhasa (1936–37). He collected many fine Tibetan paintings, Tantric sculptures and ritual items, and had the basic three hundred–volume Tibetan Buddhist reference library (known as the *Kangyur* and *Tengyur*) carried on muleback to India and shipped to America for use in a proposed meditation center near Santa Barbara, California. He was, in 1947, tragically murdered by bandits near the Spiti monastery, on the border of Tibet.

By the turn of the century, Dr. Pierre Arnold Bernard became famous for his demonstrations of self-hypnosis, Yogic trance, and immunity to pain. Of this, Dr. Daniel McMillan of the University of Michigan wrote:

> The self-induced state of hypnosis performed by Dr. P. A. Bernard is the best counterfeit of death I have ever witnessed in my thirty-eight years of experience in the active practice of medicine.

In November 1900, Pierre Bernard demonstrated *Kali Mudra*, in which "the entire organism is sunk into the deepest lethargy that actually precedes death" before forty physicians and surgeons. Apparently, he had done this on previous occasions, because the captions to the photographs of the event mention that this demonstration was "for the last time."

It has been claimed by the press that Bernard "picked up the rudiments of Yoga from Hindu students." It is certain that, while in California, he connected with Swami Ram Tirath, who had the esoteric knowledge he needed. Of Bernard, Swami Ram wrote:

> My friend Pierre Bernard (Shastri) . . . has attained the highest office of Vedic learning and is the recipient of the greatest honors a Sanskritist can achieve. He perfectly understands our doctrine both in principle and practice. . . .
>
> Dr. Pierre Bernard compares most admirably with the Brahmanical Tantrik High Priests of India; he is most earnest and sincere, is more energetic and has knowledge just as extensive. *In my opinion he is one of the most profoundly learned men on earth today* [italics added].

This is a strong endorsement, coming from a highly qualified Hindu Yogi mathematician. It suggests that rather than being a showman or charlatan, as was so often proposed by detractors, Bernard was the real thing, an American Tantric Yogi with both intellectual and spiritual powers.

One press account has Bernard saying that "his system, called Tantra, came from a Syrian named Hamati who had studied in India," adding that he "sat at the feet of Hamati for eleven years before branching out on his own." Salvais Hamati is listed as one of the founding officers of the Tantrik Order in America, so it may be that Bernard did acquire some esoteric knowledge from this man, but little is known about him.

Pen-and-ink sketch from a painting that portrays the ongoing work at the Tantrik Order in America. The name of Hamati appears around the seal, along with the names Bernard, Norton, DeLois, and Tuell, all of whom were founding members.

In 1904, Bernard ran a clinic in San Francisco. By 1905, some of his close associates were calling him "the loving teacher," "the Boss," "Doc," P.A., or Oom. He attracted his first students in Tacoma, Washington, and Portland, Oregon. He also taught in Seattle, where he initiated some into the Tantric tradition; it is possible that Bernard's Tantrik Order was first established there. Also in 1905, Bernard established the Bacchante Academy in San Francisco.

According to the press, which at that time was particularly biased against anything uncommon and Oriental, this academy "catered to young women interested in learning hypnotism and 'soul-charming' " (described as the "mysteries of the relations between the sexes"). There were hints of sexual scandal, soon followed by the San Francisco earthquake of April 18, 1906, which put the Bacchante Academy permanently out of business.

In 1909, Dr. Bernard moved to the East Coast and lectured at the Biophile Club, in New York City. Around this time, he became a Freemason and rose high in their ranks. In 1910, he opened his Oriental Sanctum on West 74th Street, New York. This was a twofold operation: downstairs, a form of Hatha Yoga was taught, while upstairs, there was an area where Tantric initiations took place. Once again, there was scandal, this time brought by two young girls, Zella Hopp and Gertrude Leo.

Charges of kidnapping were filed and Bernard was held in jail, in the New York "Tombs," for more than three months. The press had a field day, naming Bernard "Oom the Omnipotent." It seems he was a bit of a womanizer; according to one knowledgeable informant, "the younger they were, the better he liked them." Eventually, both women left New York State and the case was dropped through lack of evidence. Apparently, the charges had been motivated by jealousy on the part of other female admirers of the Tantric doctor.

Dr. Bernard overcame the scandal and went on to open the New York Sanskrit College at 2379 Broadway in New York City, advertising lessons in Yoga and in the Sanskrit language. Once again, there were rumors of strange goings-on. There were reports of "wild Oriental music" and "women's cries, but not those of distress." A newspaper report of the time recounts the result of a raid on Bernard's New York Sanskrit College:

Investigators found Dr. Bernard calmly smoking a cigar, wearing a worn black cutaway coat, gray striped trousers, a pale blue scarf, [and] turquoise cuff links and sporting a curled black mustache. Surrounding him were Hindu statues, delicate models of temples, photographs of Swamis, Eastern symbols and signs, some plaques of snakes swallowing their tails, and a marble bust of himself. He greeted his visitors cordially and introduced them to a dark-skinned good-looking young man with an English accent who was smoking a bulldog pipe and said he was Pandit Shastri. "I am conducting a perfectly respectable Sanskrit school," said Dr. Bernard.

Dr. Bernard opened another clinic at 62 West End Avenue, in the office of a former New York City health commissioner. At about this time, he met and married Blanche DeVries, an exotic dancer and Yoga student of Dr. P. C. Bannerji, noted Hindu and Western-trained physician. Together, Bernard and DeVries launched what the press described as "a highly successful health-system of Tantrism, embodying Hatha Yoga, dancing, and psychophysical education." Blanche DeVries (1891–1984) went on to become a prominent Yoga teacher, opening her Living Arts Center in New York City in 1945.

In 1918, Dr. Bernard took over the 72-acre Maxwell estate, a property in Upper Nyack that had been leased to the Riverhook

School, an academy for young ladies. He renamed it the Braeburn Country Club and established his utopian "Tantric community" there. The realtor with whom Bernard dealt, was, apparently, quite frightened by him; at the time Bernard was described as "heavily muscled, with a large head covered with close-cropped hair, and with grayish-green eyes that were so sharp they seemed to fix whatever fell within their point of focus, the way the pin of a collector fixes a butterfly."

The spectacular property which became known as the Braeburn Country Club fea-

Bust of Dr. Pierre Bernard, from his sanctuary.

tured a three-story brick Georgian mansion containing some thirty rooms. At its peak, it was described as "embracing pasture land and wooded mountain side, sweeping down from the brow of the Palisades to within five hundred feet of the river. Its residential park with wide lawns and private driveways encloses two large manor houses and three cottages. Here stands the picturesque old Brick Clubhouse, said to have been built by a French pirate in 1825 with bricks imported from France. The walls are three and a half feet thick and a smuggler's tunnel once led from the cellar out beneath the highroad to the water's edge."

Another of Bernard's major purchases in Nyack was a fabulous property known as The Moorings. It consisted of an English country house with half-timbered cottages at either side, sloping lawns right down to the banks of the Hudson river, and rare trees, exotic gardens, a swan pond, a beach and a marine landing.

In addition to his Nyack centers, Bernard also opened "Tantric clinics" in Cleveland, Philadelphia, and Chicago; an exclusive establishment for women only, at 16 East 53rd Street in New York City, and a "Tantric summer camp" for men only in Westhampton, on Long Island in New York State.

One of Bernard's principle teachings was what he called the Art of Reversion. "I'll teach you," he told his audience, "to reverse your circulation, not once but several times a day. Many ills afflicting the average human arise from our static habits of posture. We are the only animals who constantly go about head up and feet down, never altering the position of our internal organs or the stresses we place upon our muscles." Bernard was also an advocate of colonic cleansing, utilizing both Indian Ayurvedic and Western techniques for this purpose, and always keeping his own specially trained physician on hand to supervise the procedures. Bernard also taught *mulabandha*, the Yogic activity in which the anal sphincter is brought under the control of the will.

Apparently, Bernard also believed that sexually unresponsive or what he termed "desensitized" women could be helped by a form of partial circumcision in which the clitoral hood was surgically removed. Obviously a controversial procedure—believed by some to improve female sexual responsivity by exposing the clitoral glans to more direct stimulation—the rumors of these and other "sexoyogic" procedures and activities undoubtedly contributed to his no-torious reputation.

The police raided Bernard's clinic at 62 West End Avenue, fol-lowing complaints from neighbors, and, according to a *Town and Country* reporter, found "luxurious furnishings and the usual men and women gyrating on mats." Dr. Jenkins, Bernard's influential associate there, came to his defense and no charges were brought.

Now above reproach, Dr. Bernard's 53rd Street New York City Tantric clinic became a resounding success. According to *Town and Country* (April 1941 issue):

> Every hour of the day limousines and taxis drove up to the en-trances of the Doctor's New York clinics. In the marble foyer be-hind the wrought-iron portals of 16 East 53rd Street, a pretty secretary handled appointments. Properly recommended novi-tiates paid an advance fee and were given a physical examination by a house doctor. Then they were led to private rooms, handed Annette Kellermann bathing costumes, and told to disrobe.
>
> The rooms were decorated in different color schemes and bore on their walls such mottos as "Cleanliness is next to godli-ness" and "A clean colon ensures a clean mind." When the new patient was ready, a young woman instructress appeared in a gaudy robe covering a pair of silken tights the same color as the mat on the floor. Standing at rigid attention, heels together, she did a front somersault which wound up in a headstand, then doubled over backwards, and ended by sitting between her legs. Next she instructed the newcomer in the simple Yoga exercises of rolling the stomach and touching the toes. Finally she adminis-tered a high colonic irrigation.
>
> As students progressed they were taught breathing and bending exercises and, when possible, how to stand on their heads. Among the female teachers at this time were two of social prominence, Mrs. Loring Andrews and Mrs. Hannah Prince, daughter of the late Walter Scott Hobart, millionaire California sportsman, who were known solely by their lodge names of Miss Hawley and Miss Raleigh. Besides teaching, they performed me-nial tasks around the establishment.
>
> The men's lodge, run by a Mr. Corbin, who was said to have

been Mr. Everit Macy's chauffeur, was not so sumptuous as the women's, but was as completely equipped.

When a new student had completed several advanced courses, his teacher took him (or her) aside and explained that a body of serious-minded people were pursuing their studies in an incorporated country club at Upper Nyack. If he seemed interested, an interview was arranged with Dr. Bernard, and if a careful scrutiny showed the applicant's character and past to be satisfactory, he was allowed to pay an initiation fee, and join.

Apparently all who joined the Braeburn Country Club were given lodge names. There were more than one hundred members, including many society women and securities brokers.

On Saturday and Sunday nights, Dr. Bernard gave lectures, at times embellished with theatricals. The strange stories about Bernard in the New York press and the unusual goings-on at his Braeburn Country Club caused local Nyack residents to spy on his Tantric cult. They called the state police, who raided the premises. The raid, like the one before it in New York City, uncovered nothing more sensational than a class of men and women dressed in bloomers and sandals doing Yoga exercises on the lawn. Outraged, several

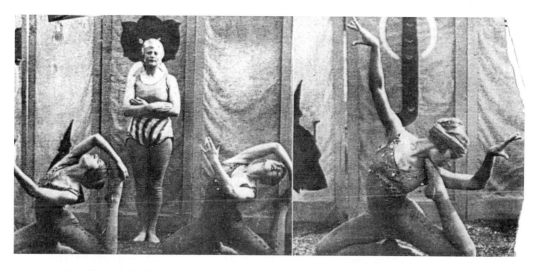

Mrs. Hannah Hobart Prince and Mrs. Loring Andrews doing Yoga exercises at the Nyack Tantra Center. (Photo by Charlotte Fairchild.)

prominent members came to the club's defense. Again, no charges were brought, and that was the last of the raids on Dr. Bernard.

In 1920, Dr. Bernard and his associates bought a 76-acre South Nyack estate at a cost of more than one hundred thousand dollars and incorporated it as the Clarkstown Country Club, with Sir Paul Dukes, the former English secret service agent, as its elected president. Some financial help for this purchase supposedly came from Mrs. William K. Vanderbilt, whose two daughters, Margaret and Barbara, were club members (Margaret married Dukes later that year, while Barbara married Bernard's longtime assistant). An indoor swimming pool was constructed and the stables and coach house were turned into a theater and meeting rooms.

This was some country club! The 1935 illustrated commemorative volume *Life: At the Clarkstown Country Club, Nyack, NY* gives the following overview of the Club's philosophy and activities more than fifteen years after it first opened:

> This is a place where an attempt is made to translate the business of living into an art. It provides every form of country life enjoyment, and at the same time offers facilities for the further development of the individual, a "new deal" in both mind and body. Here the ideal is expressed in terms of balanced living, in contrast to the "lopsided" development so current in these days. Through all the Club's varied activities (like beads strung on a thread), runs the central idea of a more intelligent and joyous way of life.
>
> There are six fine tennis courts, indoor and outdoor swimming pools, gardens of many kinds, a cabin cruiser for trips on the Hudson and a splendid sports stadium brilliantly lighted for night events. The Club has its own theater, its lecture hall—seat of the year-round Open Forum—and an extensive research library. For those interested in astronomy a powerful telescope has been mounted on the Club House roof; for the physical education department there are two gymnasiums; for indoor sports, billiard and card rooms; for artists, studios, and for children, a play-room.
>
> But this is less than half the story. The unique plan of study and self-development which the Club features is the other, the more important half.

This may best be called a type of adult education, though it differs markedly from all that generally goes by that name. To this end foreign and scientific movies and travel films are alternated with lectures, of which a hundred and fifty are delivered annually by leaders in varied fields of learning, the arts, philosophy and scientific endeavor. This department, known as the Open Forum, is managed by the Club's founder, an authority on Vedic literature and ancient Eastern systems of thought. The attitude of the group is a liberal one; the common purpose is the search for truth. All creeds mingle freely, without any sense of compulsion or prejudice.

"As much or as little as one desires" is the rule for all this. Some may seek here merely country air and a rest from business, others, a new point of view; one comes for lunch, another for a life-time.

The combination of so many factors essential to living, study, health and fun, all interwoven into a single fabric, saves many an hour and much expense. Formalities in dress and procedure are not stressed, and all members, from eighteen years to eighty, enjoy the friendliness and warmth of a congenial country home.

The Clarkstown Country Club had its own dairy and chicken farm, an orchard, kitchen gardens, wells, laundry, construction center, garage and service station. Various types of accommodation were available to Club visitors. There were sparse but inexpensive student dormitories as well as luxurious suites, done in English, French, Spanish or Italian modes—maid or nurse services were also available. Single rooms cost $2 a day and up; double rooms $4 a day and up. There were weekly, monthly or seasonal rates, "with special prices for week-ends and holidays." The minimum monthly rate was $100 for room and meals.

Gradually, Dr. Bernard ingratiated himself with the residents of Nyack. He joined the local volunteer fire department, and the chamber of commerce and patronized local merchants. Many more adjoining properties were added to the club and new buildings were constructed, some designed by Blanche DeVries. A steady stream of distinguished people came to visit, including such notables as Leopold Stokowski, Major Francis Yeats-Brown, Augustus Thomas the playwright, the Panama Canal engineer Henry Goldmark, Sir Hubert Wilkins, and Dr. Francis Potter. Many wealthy followers of the Tantric teacher bought costly homes nearby.

Over subsequent years, membership in the Nyack Tantric community grew to over four hundred. The library contained over seven thousand volumes, including "the finest collection of Sanskrit lore in the United States." Many of the premises were decorated with fine rugs, exotic furniture, and rare Asian works of art, including Buddhist and Hindu sculpture and paintings.

Dr. Bernard started a zoo on the club grounds, collecting various animals, including a llama, a chimpanzee, a lion, a white peacock, and seven elephants. He imported three of the elephants, named Buddha, Juno, and Babe, direct from India. He employed animal trainers to teach the elephants to "ride tricycles, play chimes, walk planks, and dance in a ballet." On occasions the elephants were rented or loaned to showmen, conventions, and individuals such as Frank E. Gannett, who used them in the publicity for his presidential campaign.

Dr. Bernard held an annual circus under a huge tent erected on the club grounds, with club members trained as acrobats. The 1929 circus included a "dance of death" by his wife, Blanche DeVries, who, according to a press account, was veiled and "rose up from a coffin and performed a belly dance." She was followed by Dr. Bernard himself, dancing with his "sacred baby elephant."

Hindu festivals were held periodically, the exotically costumed guests seated around low tables covered with gold cloths and loaded with fresh fruit. During Tantric ceremonies Dr. Bernard sat on a throne, wearing a turban, baggy pants, a silk robe, and flourishing a scepter. Some items on the showbill read thusly: Dance of the Five Senses, Africana, Budhamass Festival, Super Women and Supper Women, The Baseball Dance, Birthday of Krishna, Blue Lotus Ballet, Chinese Opera, Yoga Postures, or Dance of Maya-Yama (Illusion of Death).

Lavish weddings and anniversaries were celebrated in grand style at Dr. Bernard's Nyack Tantric club. In December 1925, a Pittsburgh society couple celebrated their tenth wedding anniversary at Dr. Bernard's Nyack center. According to published news reports:

Members wore dark hooded robes over fancy-dress costumes and marched in a solemn procession carrying lighted candles. Two crape-draped coffins were carried in behind the honored couple. After further somber ceremonies, the coffins were suddenly turned upside down to serve as buffet tables, all removed their outer robes, and a great celebration took place.

Apparently, Dr. Bernard also helped develop baseball from simple amateur club games into a professional business. He is credited with organizing some of the first games played under the artificial lighting of his Nyack stadium. He helped train professional boxers, teaching them Yoga breathing and concentration techniques. In 1939 heavyweight boxer Lou Nova joined Bernard's Tantra club and trained under him for his title fight against Max Baer. He established a dog-racing organization in Nyack, built and opened an airport in the area, and in 1931 became president of the State Bank of Pearl River. At his peak, his total net worth was estimated at twelve million dollars. Fine cars were among the things he liked to collect: he owned classics such as a Rolls-Royce, a Stutz, a Pierce-Arrow, a Minerva, a Packard, a Lincoln, and a Stanley Steamer.

Dr. Bernard loved to smoke expensive cigars and in later years dressed in tweeds. Over the entrance to his Nyack estate, which at one time totaled about 200 acres, was the following inscription cut in stone:

> Here the philosopher may dance,
> And the fool wear a thinking cap.

During World War II, Bernard closed his center at Nyack and turned the estate over to the Wertheim family, who used it to house refugees from Nazi Germany. Eventually, as the founding members became elderly, the club's organization fell apart.

To the end, Dr. Bernard was an excellent Yogi and the first Westerner to introduce Tantric teachings to a wide audience. He was said to be "the most amazing and vari-colored personality who could lecture on any religion with singular penetration and discernment, who knew the human body, anatomically and every other way to such an extent as to amaze veteran surgeons and physicians, and at the same time, knew the theory and practice of Yoga best of anyone

A painting from Dr. Pierre Bernard's Nyack center, showing "an American Tantrik in the practice of his Yoga." He is performing fire sacrifice *(havan)* by a stream.

in America." Of himself, he once said, "I'm a curious combination of the businessman and the religious scholar," adding, "I'm just a man of common sense, in love with beauty."

His legacy still remains to be properly accessed. He died in the French Hospital, New York City, on September 27, 1955, at the age of eighty. His obituary gave the cause of his death as "a weakening brought on by fatigue from a summer heat wave."

Following Dr. Bernard's death, the remaining Nyack estates were dispersed. In 1977, his widow sold the bulk of the library together with important artwork. In 1980, I helped a New York art dealer move some boxes from his gallery storage to the street, for disposal. One box broke open to reveal many copies of the difficult-

Logo of the Tantrik Order in America. It is made up of a winged globe within two interlaced triangles (symbolizing the union of male and female) encircled by a snake biting its own tail (alchemical symbol of rebirth in eternity).

to-find *International Journal: Tantrik Order.* Soon, books from the Nyack Tantric library also emerged. I followed the trail and located other books from the Nyack Tantric library, ritual items, and important Buddhist and Hindu sculptures and paintings. I have since redefined the formerly defunct Tantrik Order, reestablishing it on the TantraWorks Internet Web site.

The following quote from Dr. Bernard sums up his philosophy of life:

> Respect the conscience of others and never impose on them, even the truth. Break not forcibly the yoke of slaves who love their yoke. Be devoted always, never too zealous. If souls rejoice in their folly, it is cruel to deprive them of it without restoring their reason. . . . The light shines for all men coming into the world; but all have the right to open or shut their eyes as may please them.

Ceremonial goblet or chalice, used in Tantric high rites at the Nyack Tantra community.

ALEISTER CROWLEY, NEO-TANTRIC

Aleister Crowley (1875–1947) was brought up under the severe rules of the Plymouth Brethren, an extremist Christian sect. He had an unhappy childhood but was brilliant at his studies, well educated at Kings College, London, and Trinity College, Cambridge, where he became interested in poetry and pagan religion.

Crowley inherited money in his youth, which enabled him to be

Aleister Crowley as he appeared in the frontispiece to one of his self-published magical tomes, *The Equinox: The Official Organ of the A. A.*, volume I, no. III.

financially independent for many years. He rejected Christianity and advocated hedonism as a religious duty. He studied alchemy and medieval magic(k), especially Hebrew mysticism and the Cabbala.

Aleister Crowley was a fine poet and an accomplished mountaineer. Introduced by George Cecil Jones, a chemist and pharmacologist with interests in mind-altering substances, in November 1898 Crowley joined the Hermetic Order of the Golden Dawn, an occult organization whose chief adept was MacGregor Mathers.

In the spring of 1899, Aleister Crowley met Allan Bennett, a leading member of the Golden Dawn who had considerable influence on him, introducing him to Yoga. The same year, he bought Boleskine House in Scotland on a large estate. In 1900, he studied Hatha Yoga in Mexico, and in 1901, he traveled to San Francisco, Honolulu, Japan, China, and Ceylon. There he joined Allan Bennett, who was practicing Yoga with P. Ramanathan, the solicitor-general

of Ceylon, an advanced Shaivite Yogi known by some as Swami Par-
ananda.

After Ceylon, Crowley went to India, visiting Burma and climb-
ing in the Himalayas. Apparently, he might have met the Tantric
Yogi Swami Sabhapaty (who was born in 1840) during this 1902
visit to India and received initiation from him. Other Hindus who
are said to have initiated Crowley into Tantra are Brima Sen Pratap
and Sri Agamya Paramhamsa.

By late 1902, Aleister Crowley was in Paris and in 1903 he was
living in Scotland. He married Rose Kelly in August 1903 and shortly
thereafter traveled to Egypt. In Egypt, Rose ''became oracular'' and
was given special magical status as his ''scarlet woman,'' meaning
the sexual consort with whom he practiced his ''magick.'' Much of
Crowley's most important work was achieved at this time. His spe-
cialty was sexual magic; there can be little doubt that he derived
much of his inspiration from India's Tantric tradition.

During the winter of 1905–06, Aleister Crowley was again
traveling, this time across China. By 1910, he was divorced and had
become a member of the Ordo Templi Orientis (known as the O.T.O.)
founded at the turn of the century by the wealthy and well-traveled
Austrian Freemason Dr. Karl Kellner (1850–1905), another Tantric
initiate.

In 1912, Crowley became ''magically involved'' with Leila Waddell and very active in the O.T.O., which was an amalgam of Scottish
Masonry and an occult organization known as the Hermetic Brotherhood of Luxor. The same year he was appointed grand master of
the O.T.O. and made its ''special delegate to America.''

Between 1914 and 1918, Crowley lived in America and was
helped in his magical rites by a series of women. In 1918, he was
living in Greenwich Village, New York. During this and subsequent
periods he became notorious, with stories circulating about him as a
''sex, dope, and demonism guru.''

In 1920, he founded the Abbey of Thelema at Cefalu, in Sicily,
but this was closed down by the local authorities following publication of his *Diary of a Drug Fiend* in 1922. Sensational stories in the
English popular press characterized him as ''the wickedest man
alive'' and grossly exaggerated the goings-on in what was in essence
his own cult. Following the Cefalu fiasco, Crowley was viewed by

the public at large as a pariah. Publication of *The Confessions of Aleister Crowley*, in six volumes (from 1929 onward) did not help his image.

A maverick of the magical arts, Crowley experimented with just about everything, including a wide range of drugs, psychedelics, and experiencing every imaginable type of sexual scenario. He took enormous risks. A brilliant and fascinating man, he authored many books and treatises. His philosophy, put simply, was: "Do what thou wilt shall be the whole of the Law." It got him and many of his followers into trouble. Nevertheless, the Ordo Templis Orientis and the Crowley cult is still growing, with followers in many countries.

It has recently been suggested that the big secret of Crowley's O.T.O. was the consumption of the *Yoni Tattva* as the culmination of spiritual sex rites. The *Yoni Tattva*, or "vaginal essence," is in Tantra traditionally taken to be a mixture of female sex secretions, semen, menstrual blood, wood ash from a sacred fire, and clarified butter *(ghee)*. It was consumed ceremonially and in the O.T.O. was credited, as in the Tantric tradition, with imparting magical powers *(siddhi)*. Curiously, in all his writings, which covered a vast range of occult lore, Crowley never mentioned any of the Tantric publications from Sir John Woodroffe (also known as Arthur Avalon). This might have been because he did not wish to acknowledge his organization's indebtedness to the Tantric tradition.

A curious account of a European woman's experiences of Tantra in India was published in 1936, under the title *The Secrets of the Kaula Circle*. The author, Elizabeth Sharpe, who had lived in India for about twenty-five years, refers to a European who "called himself by a number" (later, she gives the number as 666), who apparently was involved in sexual rites in India "with the help of the Lamas." This can only be Aleister Crowley, also known as "The Beast 666," and seems to confirm that Crowley did indeed receive Tantric instruction in India.

In many ways, Aleister Crowley was way ahead of his time. He recognized the need for a "modern paganism" but saw himself as its primary prophet. His radical and paradoxical behavior and his outspoken no-holds-barred style contributed to the popular misconceptions about him, yet his widespread contribution to Tantra in the West was certainly influential.

GEORGE GURDJIEFF, ARCH-TANTRIC

George Ivanovitch Gurdjieff (1873–1949) was another individual who, in his own way, contributed to the coming of Tantra to the West. He was a mystic and sometime psychotherapist, part Russian and part Armenian, who traveled extensively through much of the Middle and Far East. This enigmatic character developed his own unique philosophical and spiritual teachings, some of which were obliquely based on Indian and Tibetan Tantra. In 1922, he established his Institute for the Harmonious Development of Man at Fontainebleau, France.

Gurdjieff's major published work, *All and Everything: Beelzebub's Tales to His Grandson*, loaded with allegory, includes fascinating esoteric data presented in his unique style. His explanations of a mysterious implanted organ, "Kundabuffer," is clearly an allegorical reference to Kundalini, the "serpent power" of Tantric tradition. And his "Sacred Law of Three" and his commentaries on the "Cosmic Octave" are precursors to truths found in Tantric texts.

Gurdjieff was a highly charismatic and brilliant man who attracted many interesting and influential students, John G. Bennett, architect Frank Lloyd Wright, artist Georgia O'Keeffe, writer Katherine Mansfield, and journalist and mathematician P. D. Ouspensky being among the better known. Though neither he nor his students formally acknowledged the Tantric content of his teachings, there can be little doubt that Gurdjieff re-

George Gurdjieff, at the Prieuré
near Fontainebleau, France.

ceived Tantric initiation. He is also known to have had a "disturbing sexual effect" on certain people and was sexually active with several of his female followers.

He incorporated Tantric-type breathing, complex ritualized body movements, visualizations, music, and other esoteric techniques in his work. Along with Pierre Bernard and Aleister Crowley, he helped introduce esoteric Tantric techniques to the West.

The Science of Sexology

In the West, the study of sexuality was greatly restricted by the teachings of the church. In the sixteenth century, Gabriel Fallopius described the Fallopian tubes and the clitoris. Until 1677, human semen was not closely examined and spermatozoa were only observed following the discovery of the properties of lenses and the invention of microscopes. The human egg was discovered only as recently as 1829. To most people in the medieval period and right up through the Victorian era, sex remained a mystery.

The science of sexology, which emerged in the West only in the twentieth century and is still being defined, focused almost exclusively on the physiology and psychology of sex. The spirituality or mysticisim of sex was virtually neglected.

In 1914, William Carpenter and others founded the British Society for the Study of Sex, later transformed into the British Sexological Society. The Institute of Sexual Science, founded in Berlin by Magnus Hirshfeld (1868–1935), opened its doors in 1919 but had a relatively short life. In America, the Institute for Sexual Research at the University of Indiana was established as late as 1947.

The two Kinsey reports, *Sexual Behavior in the Human Male* (1948) and *Sexual Behavior in the Human Female* (1953), with Alfred C. Kinsey (1894–1956), a professor of zoology, as the principal author, were the first large-scale empirical studies of sexual behavior. They helped define American sexual habits in the middle of the twentieth century and set the stage for the sexual revolution.

The Kinsey researchers were hounded by the police and attempts were made to prevent publication of their findings. Their studies detailed habits and frequencies of sexual behavior such as petting, masturbation, oral sex, intercourse, and orgasm. However, the Kinsey reports were based solely on analysis of the self-reported sex lives of 5,300 white American men and 5,490 white American women, hardly the comprehensive study of human sexual behavior suggested by the book titles.

In 1966 Drs. William Masters and Virginia Johnson published *Human Sexual Response*, their best-known work on human sexuality. Working in a clinical laboratory setting, they used polygraphlike instruments to record the sexual responses of about seven hundred different Americans through some ten thousand male and female orgasms. Their work was also biased, drawing only from a narrow demographic sample and focusing on only physiological observations.

PIONEERS IN THE PSYCHOLOGY OF SEX

The idea that sex can be a spiritually liberating activity has only recently been acceptable in mainstream Western thought. Sex has mostly been viewed as a problem to be researched, commented on, and treated only by qualified professionals, such as medical doctors, psychologists, or psychiatrists.

Havelock Ellis, Sigmund Freud, Wilhelm Reich, and Carl Jung were all brilliant and highly qualified professionals who contributed to the sexual revolution and, in their own way, helped the acceptance of Tantra in the West. Their various scientific studies on the psychology of sex helped demystify human sexual behavior and shaped the way we view sex today. Because of their vast influence on Western culture in the twentieth century, an understanding of their respective backgrounds, views, and contributions is helpful to comprehend the context in which to view spiritual sex at the present time.

HAVELOCK ELLIS'S VIEW OF THE SPIRITUAL FUNCTION OF SEX

Havelock Ellis (1859–1939), an Englishman, was the pioneer of modern sexual psychology. His *Studies in the Psychology of Sex* was published in seven volumes between 1897 and 1928 but was banned in England. In America, these books were available only to doctors, psychiatrists and other "professionals" until 1935. Working more as an anthropologist than a psychologist, Ellis documented the diversity of human sexuality. He was among the first Westerners to promote women's right to a fulfilled sex life.

Ellis was also the first Western sexologist *not* to view homosexuality (which he termed "sexual inversion") as unnatural. He took the primary physiological function of sex to be reproduction but also wrote of a secondary spiritual function that he believed "furthered the higher mental and emotional processes." It is this function that Tantric teachers developed and that practitioners of spiritual sex seek to activate.

Ellis was an enigmatic and highly strung man who suffered from premature ejaculation. According to his biographers, who relied on the evidence of his writings and those of his most intimate friends, he never experienced complete sexual intercourse. An advocate of "open" marriage, he married a lesbian and lived with her and another woman for a while, but was unable to overcome his feelings of jealousy.

Havelock Ellis cultivated numerous intimate friendships with women, many of whom adored him. According to him:

> The complete spiritual contact of two persons who love each other can only be attained through some act of rare intimacy. No act can be quite so intimate as the sexual embrace.

This observation puts Ellis in a league almost on his own. In his day, he was one of the very few professionals who saw a connection between sex and spirituality.

Ellis was perhaps the first European to experience psychedelics like mescal, introducing the drug to his circle of intimate friends. He loved to tell the story of his good friend John Barker Smith, who while on a mescal trip came face to face with God. Recognizing this was an opportunity not to be missed, he asked God to tell him the meaning of the universe. According to Smith, God gave the answer in a single word: "Reproduction." Tantra teaches that there is far more to the meaning of the universe than reproduction. Had John Smith come face to face with the Goddess instead of God, he would surely have been given a much more interesting answer: "Spiritual evolution!"

SIGMUND FREUD AND HIS RENEGADE DISCIPLES

No one in the twentieth century has had a greater influence on Western views on sex than Sigmund Freud. Freudian concepts influence much of the advertising that in turn influences many of our habits. We use terms such as *libido, complex, Freudian slip,* and *ego* quite casually, but we rarely stop to think what Freud's work was really about. A brief look at both his life and his theories is helpful to our understanding of what relevance, if any, his work may have to the subject of spiritual sex.

Sigmund Freud (1856–1939) was brought up in Austria and was a contemporary and, for a while, a rival of Havelock Ellis. One of his earliest publications was on the interpretations of dreams (in 1899), in which he developed a unique methodology that became formalized as psychoanalysis. Psychoanalysis is a method in which, using free association of thoughts, memories, and sexual ideas, a transference—a shift or release—of feelings could take place. Infantile sexuality was pivotal to Freud's theories, especially the connection between sexual and aggressive instincts, which he saw as the cause of psychological complexes. He studied neurology and the unconscious mind and was one of the first to explore the links between sexual repression and neurosis.

Freud recognized the compelling power of the sexual impulse. In everyday achievement and in the practice of spiritual sex, it is the sex impulse that drives us. His Oedipus and Electra complexes, built around the idea that a child desires exclusive attention or even a sexual connection with the parent of the opposite sex, and shows hostility and rivalry toward the parent of the same sex, is the foundation on which Freudian psychoanalysis rests.

Freud's own life was extremely complex; one could almost call it tortured. Born in a Jewish family, he suffered both anti-Semitic persecution and economic hardships. For many years, his ideas were treated with considerable hostility. He suffered from cancer of the jaw for nearly two decades, underwent numerous operations, and used cocaine as both a painkiller and a general panacea, believing wholeheartedly in its efficacy.

It cannot be denied that Freud's discoveries and theories have had a considerable influence. In the twentieth century, they have been key to the evolution of psychology as a science. For many people with complex neurotic problems, Freudian psychoanalysis has been helpful, even though tedious and costly. One might well wonder about the advisability of spending so much time and money on analyzing the past. Why couldn't positive results have been achieved by other means, more efficiently, and faster?

One of the main reasons may well be that, unlike Ellis or Jung, Freud never addressed the spiritual aspects of sex. He never explored the healing inherent in having a healthy and spiritualized sex life. To him personally, and in life in general, sex was always a problem. He tended to avoid dealing with either his own sexual complexes or his personal spiritual inadequacies. Had he been able to apply his brilliant mind to unraveling the connections between sexuality and spirituality, people in the Western world might by now have been in better mental health. They would have been able to benefit from spiritual as well as psychological insights.

It is rightfully said that the "measure of a teacher is to be found in his disciples." Sigmund Freud had many illustrious followers, including his own daughter Anna, who became a brilliant psychoanalyst specializing in the psychology of children.

Freud was an extremely difficult man. Both of his most intelligent disciples, Wilhelm Reich and Carl Jung, soon fell out with him, disputing aspects of his theories and establishing their own schools of psychology. Each of them, in their own way, set the stage for Tantra to become adopted by Western culture.

Both Reich and Jung were great explorers into Tantric truth. Wilhelm Reich's life work focused on the power and dynamics of the orgasm, the key topic of modern Tantra in the New Age. Carl Jung focused on the unconscious mind and its spiritual and mythic potential, aspects that are crucial to any practical involvement in Tantra as a lifestyle. A brief look at the lives of these two illustrious early followers of Freud indicates how Tantra can take on a different character according to focus.

THE CONTRIBUTIONS OF WILHELM REICH AND CARL JUNG

Wilhelm Reich (1897–1957) was born and brought up in Austria. While still in medical school, he met Sigmund Freud and became one of Freud's most brilliant assistants, working with him in the new science of psychoanalysis.

In the mid-1920s, Reich developed his theory of orgiastic potency, in which he advocated "full surrender to the sensations of pleasure during sexual embrace" in the belief that this resulted in mental health. He documented the existence of "character muscular armor" made up of defensive character traits that are accompanied by muscular spasms. He observed that full orgasmic relief broke down the muscular armor and restored mental health.

Reich opened sex clinics in Vienna and Berlin, offering sex education, therapy, and information on hygiene to large numbers of people. Later, he moved to Scandinavia but was eventually attacked by the press for his belief that repressive attitudes to sex are the cause of both mental and physical disease. Reich relocated to America, where his ideas had developed a following. In 1942, he published his major work, *The Discovery of the Orgone: The Function of the Orgasm.*

In America, Wilhelm Reich gradually became alienated from mainstream psychiatry. Rivals and law-enforcement officials suspected him of involvement in some type of "sex racket." After conflicts with the U.S. Food and Drug Administration (FDA) over products he was promoting that used "orgone energy," he was tried and convicted and his books and apparatus were destroyed by court order. He died in jail in 1957.

During the sexual revolution of the 1960s, Reich's ideas found wide acceptance. His concept of orgiastic potency and his use of it to heal mental and physical problems points to the spirituality inherent in sex. He demonstrated "sexual healing" to be a practical and liberating experience. Many of his discoveries have a relevance that can be truly appreciated only when viewed in a Tantric context.

Carl Jung (1875–1961) was born in Switzerland, where he completed medical training and practiced psychiatry. His own studies of word association led him to Sigmund Freud, who influenced him greatly. Jung had mystical inclinations, experiencing dreams and visions loaded with mythological and spiritual symbolism. After a falling-out with Freud over theoretical disputes about the significance of human sexuality, Jung developed his own psychological insights into a systematic science, which became known as Jungian psychology.

Believing that the Freudian view of the sexual impulse or libido was imbalanced, reductionistic, and limiting, Jung proposed that the libido could assume different forms and move in different directions. He suggested that the sexual impulse moved principally in either inward or outward directions, *inwardly* meaning "toward the unconscious," into the realm of images and ideas, and *outwardly* meaning "toward the world of people and things." This view led him to categorize people as introverts or extroverts.

In *Psychology and Religion*, a major work of his most pertinent to our understanding of the dynamics of spiritual sex, Jung wrote:

> The East bases itself upon psychic reality, that is, upon the psyche as the main and unique condition of existence. . . . It is a typical introverted point of view, contrasted with the equally extroverted point of view of the West. . . .
>
> Introversion is, if one may so express it, the "style" of the East, an habitual and collective attitude, just as extroversion is the "style" of the West. Introversion is felt here as something abnormal, morbid, or otherwise objectionable. Freud identifies it with an autoerotic, "narcissistic" attitude of mind. . . .
>
> In the East, however, our cherished extroversion is depreciated as "illusory desirousness" . . . culminating in the sum of the world's sufferings.

Jung proposed that the unconscious psyche consisted of two principle layers, which he termed the personal unconscious, comprised of repressed mental data accumulated throughout one's life, and the collective unconscious, made up of inherited universal symbols common to all humanity. He suggested that even deeper layers of the unconscious operate independent of time, space, and causality and are the repository of paranormal powers. Here, Jung was grasping at esoteric levels of truth and communication, attempting to apply psychological science to understand spiritual arts and mysticism. What he was referring to was the domain of Tantra.

Jung traveled to India and was deeply impressed by Indian spiritual teachings, writing:

The philosophy of the East, although so vastly different from ours, could be an inestimable treasure for us too; but, in order to possess it, we must first earn it.

Jung wrote detailed and informative commentaries to W. Y. Evans-Wentz's *The Tibetan Book of the Great Liberation* (in 1939) and *The Tibetan Book of the Dead* (in 1953 and 1957), as well as an essay on Yoga for a Sri Ramakrishna Centenary publication (in 1936) and a foreword to Dr. Suzuki's *An Introduction to Zen Buddhism* (in 1939). This was by no means the full extent of his contribution to the acceptance of oriental spiritual teachings in the West.

Jung's work in the understanding of dreams, symbols, and mythology also has great value. He was an extraordinarily brilliant and perceptive man, a pioneer in spiritual psychology. Concerning sexuality, he wrote:

> Our civilization enormously underestimates the importance of sexuality, but just because of the repressions imposed upon it, sexuality breaks through into every conceivable field where it does not belong, and uses such an indirect mode of expression that we may expect to meet it all of a sudden practically everywhere. Thus the very idea of an intimate understanding of the human psyche, which is actually a very pure and beautiful thing, becomes besmirched and perversely distorted by the intrusion of an indirect sexual meaning. A direct and spontaneous expression of sexuality is a natural occurrence and, as such, never ugly or repulsive. It is "moral" repression that makes sexuality on the one hand dirty and hypocritical, and on the other shameless and blatant.

It is unfortunate that Jung never personally pursued Tantric initiation and did not return to India after his first visit. He did, however, embrace Eastern mysticism and helped introduce the West to many of its symbols and concepts, such as the spiritually integrating power of mandalas, so important to Tantric thought and practice.

BRONISLAW MALINOWSKI, MARGARET MEAD, AND SEX IN TRIBAL CULTURES

Some anthropologists and psychologists working in Western cultures took the opportunity to test the various "new" theories of sexuality in different contexts. So-called primitive or tribal matriarchal societies offered the most challenging possibilities because they functioned so differently from Western patriarchal norms. The problem was that, in the twentieth century, not many of the few surviving matriarchal societies were free from significant Western influences. Christian missionary activity had reached almost everywhere and changed most tribal cultures.

Bronislaw Malinowski and Margaret Mead were the two principal anthropologists who, in the early part of this century, boldly chose to explore human sexuality in tribal societies, where matriarchies prevailed and much Freudian psychological theory was irrelevant. Such societies, freed from the influence of Christian guilt and inhibitions, revealed the underlying playful and spiritual nature of human sexuality.

The Polish scholar Malinowski (1884–1942) was one of the first and most thorough anthropologists to explore the meaning of human sexuality in matriarchal cultures. Malinowski made prolonged visits to the Trobriand Islands in the Pacific between 1915 and 1918, scientifically documenting sexual views and customs in a matriarchal society for the first time.

Like Margaret Mead, Malinowski sought to explore the anthropology of sex in matriarchies in the belief that in such a context Freud's sexual theories would not be applicable. In 1932, he published his book, *The Sexual Life of Savages: In North-Western Melanesia*, based on these studies. Havelock Ellis wrote the preface. In this important volume, Malinowski introduced Western scientists to a tribal culture in which sex was indeed relatively freed from complex Freudian neuroses and from inhibition. Interestingly, there were no sexual "abnormalities" in this culture.

Margaret Mead (1901–1978) did work similar to Malinowski's in many ways, continuing the exploration of the anthropology and psychology of sex in non-Western cultures. Her major books, *Coming of Age in Samoa* (1928), and *Sex and Temperament in Three Primi-*

tive Societies (1935), helped redefine "natural" human sexuality and place it in perspective.

In Tantric tradition, the oldest Tantras are termed mother Tantras, testament to their evolution in matriarchal tribal societies, the old or "original" way of evolving spiritually. At their foundation is the acceptance of the natural equality of the sexes and an understanding of the extraordinary differences between woman and man. When woman is free to be herself, as man has been over the past three thousand years or so, sex automatically takes on a more spiritual dimension.

The pioneering anthropological work of Malinowski, Mead, and others has been an inspiration. It has allowed consideration of an alternative to the guilt-ridden aggressive patriarchal cultures that have dominated for so long and have been the cause of so much neurosis and pain and suffering. If there is a lesson to be learned here, it is that the liberation of female power is crucial to the establishment of a new paradigm of human behavior for the twenty-first century. Only when woman is truly free can she realize her true potential as a spiritual and sexual being. Only then can she truly embody the Great Goddess.

Tantra in American Culture

TANTRA IN AMERICA IN THE LATE 1950s

The late 1950s spawned the American beatnik movement, led by poets and writers such as Jack Kerouac, Lawrence Ferlingetti, Gregory Corso, and Allen Ginsberg. During this period, social, sexual and spiritual conventions were broken down in the name of art and freedom. Writers and poets wrote more directly than ever before about subjects like homosexuality, drug experiences, hedonism, atheism, and anarchy. Some explored Oriental philosophy and religion, finding relevant answers to their radical leanings in Zen philosophy and in Tantric teachings.

Exponents of the new "beat" hedonism took Tantra as an example. Its unconventionality and its supposed sexual license seemed particularly attractive. Here at last was a well-established philosophy of life that seemed to embrace many of the ideals of the late 1950s and early 1960s. Tantra took on a new meaning.

DRUGS AND THE SEXUAL REVOLUTION

The fact that the sexual revolution was to some extent triggered by consciousness-transforming drugs cannot be denied. Many of its luminaries had experience with such drugs in their search for self-knowledge. Madame Blavatsky, founder of the Theosophical Society, commonly smoked hashish, as did Sri Ramakrishna. Sigmund Freud, who defined much of modern psychotherapy through his theories on sexuality, used cocaine regularly. Havelock Ellis, Freud's rival, is known to have used mescal, introducing the poet W. B. Yeats and others to it. Aldous Huxley used both mescaline and LSD. The infamous Aleister Crowley, whose "magickal" cult is increasingly popular and whose writings were a major influence in the sexual revolution, used many different drugs, including psychedelics.

Marijuana was a major influence on American music all through the birth of the blues, jazz, and rhythm and blues. Its consciousness-transforming and mind-expanding effect also helped break down inhibitions about sex.

In Hindu Tantric tradition, marijuana and its derivatives, *bhang* (an intoxicating drink made from marijuana, milk, and spices) and *charas* (a form of hashish) are common sacraments, their use associated with Shiva, the "Lord of Yoga." Deep rhythmic music is another ingredient of both Buddhist and Hindu Tantra, helping evoke an atmosphere for ecstasy.

By 1960, knowledge about psychedelics was being widely disseminated in America. Aldous Huxley was lecturing on psychedelic visionary experience, Zen promoter Alan Watts, beat poet Allen Ginsberg, and Harvard professors Timothy Leary, Ralph Metzner, and Richard Alpert were all sharing their views on how psychedelics could and would change the world. By 1962, LSD took over from psilocybin and mescaline, soon becoming the psychedelic drug of first choice.

LSD was so powerful, it broke down every barrier, shattering many an ego. Along with the advent of the birth-control pill, which was commercially available by 1961, it contributed much to the sexual and spiritual revolution of the sixties, helping blend sex and religion into a mystical experience. It opened the doors to a reassessment of the practical relationship of spirituality and sex.

Only since the onset of the sexual revolution has the view of sex as a natural, sin-free human activity become more acceptable. The advent of the birth-control pill separated sex from procreation and opened up new territories of sexual exploration. Many years ago, Marshall McLuhan made the following observation and prediction about the effect of the birth-control pill:

> The Pill makes woman a bomb. She creates a new kind of fragmentation, separating sexual intercourse from procreation. She also explodes old barriers between the sexes, bringing them closer together. Watch for traditions to change!

Many Christians still see sex as sinful, linking it to lust rather than viewing it as an act of higher love. Promote sex as an inherently spiritual activity and you'll still find that opinions are divided. Some people still feel uncomfortable associating sex with spirituality, some are intrigued and want to know more, and others accept the connection without question. This book is, obviously, primarily for those who accept the connection between sex and spirituality and want to explore it.

TANTRA IN THE PSYCHEDELIC SIXTIES: A YOGA OF SEX

The radical no-nonsense nature of Tantric teachings made them very attractive to the sixties generation. Psychedelic mind-expanding drugs, uninhibited sex, and the quest for spiritual experiences took on new meaning when viewed in the context of Tantra. Tantra helped legitimize the sixties experience, helped give it spiritual *and* political meaning. There was no turning back.

By the early 1960s, *Tantra: The Yoga of Sex* (1964), by Dr. Omar Garrison, was published. In this popular book, the author presented a greatly simplified overview of Tantra as a manual of sexual liberation, a secret doctrine, and Yoga of sex. His book was the first Western Tantric sex manual. In it, he promised:

> Through wholehearted study and application of the sexual prin-
> ciples of Tantra Yoga, man can achieve the sexual potency which
> enables him to extend the ecstasy crowning sexual union for an
> hour or more, rather than for the brief seconds he now knows.

All this was rather sexist—the offer of enhanced sexual potency
for men, of hour-long orgasms or ecstasies for *him*. What about
women? What could the "Yoga of sex" offer them? It was not until
the 1980s, when the New Age movement was fully manifesting,
that women started to take up the challenge that Tantra teachings
so radically promoted: the role of woman as the embodiment of the
Great Goddess, sexually liberated and multiorgasmic.

TANTRA AS A SPIRITUAL ART FORM AND SCIENTIFIC METHOD

In the late sixties, Tantra was redefined yet again and was promoted
as a particular art form known as "Tantra art." The person largely
responsible for this was Ajit Mookerjee.

Ajit Mookerjee (1915–1990) was a Bengali whose enthusiasm
for Tantra was unbounded. For many years, he was the director and
curator of the Crafts Museum in New Delhi, India. Collecting, re-
searching, conserving, and exhibiting Indian art and craft was his
passion. For over two decades, he assembled diverse and fascinating
objects and began to separate out and put together items he viewed
as Tantric. These became the basis for the Ajit Mookerjee Collection
of Tantric Art.

In 1966, Mookerjee's exquisite volume *Tantra Art: Its Philosophy
and Physics* was published. The book was a resounding success and
opened the eyes of many of the sixties generation and others to a
whole new way of looking at Indian art. Because the art published
in Ajit's book was abstract as well as figurative and erotic, many
modern artists, their dealers, and their collectors were attracted to
it. Ajit's Tantric art seemed to give meaning and direction to certain
types of contemporary art.

In 1971, Mookerjee published his follow-up book, *Tantra
Asana: A Way to Self-Realization*, dedicated "To Me and Thee." This
book was as equally fascinating and well produced as his previous
book; his view of Tantra had expanded. In this second book, he fo-

cused on Tantra *asana*, ''the (Tantric) science of psycho-Yogic poses, based on the conception of the universe and of man's role in it.''

In this second volume, Mookerjee added to his previous definition of Tantra, redefining his position to explain the subject of his latest volume:

> Tantra itself is unique for being a synthesis of *bhoga* and Yoga, enjoyment and liberation. There is no place for renunciation or denial in Tantra. Instead, we must involve ourselves in all the life processes which surround us. The spiritual is not something that descends from above, rather it is an illumination that is to be discovered within.

I knew Mookerjee well and worked with him on a number of projects. He was infectiously enthusiastic about things and people that took his fancy. His collection, with which I became very familiar, consisted of sculpture, paintings, and ritual objects.

Ajit Mookerjee was a great believer in ''art as *sadhana*,'' meaning ''art as spiritual practice.'' He loved to associate with traditional Tantrics; because he was a Brahmin, this meant he had to risk being labeled a radical by his peers. He was an ardent believer in the Great Goddess and dedicated his works to Her. On one occasion when I was visiting his house, a *sadhu* (renunciate) woman dressed in red arrived and settled herself in the corner of his yard.

Ajit prostrated himself before the woman, garlanded her with flowers, and ordered sweets and drinks for her. She started to verbally abuse him, yet he took it all with a smiling face. Later, he told me she was a Tantric practitioner, that she had once been his wife but had left him to pursue her spiritual liberation. He told me that he knew she was really a living goddess and that quite often what she said came true. He added that though she sometimes spoke to him harshly, he felt honored that she remembered him and visited his house. He said that undoutedly she was helping him, that her anger was a blessing in disguise.

To Ajit Mookerjee must go most of the credit for focusing Western minds on the visionary aspects of Tantra and for promoting it as a valid art form. His view of Tantric art was not so much centered on its eroticism but rather on its power. He continually pointed to the awesome potential inherent in true spiritual art, defining this as art created through spiritual discovery. He believed such art to be "loaded with the Power of the Goddess" and told me that in his considered opinion, such art actually *is* part of the body of the Great Goddess.

Ajit Mookerjee's amazing art collection was widely exhibited in Europe, and much of his Tantra art became known in international circles. His definition of Tantra, explained in *Tantra Art: Its Philosophy and Physics*, was really straightforward, emphasizing its experiential and scientific aspects, together with its linkage to the acquisition of spiritual power:

> Tantra is both an experience of life and a scientific method by which man can bring out his inherent spiritual power.

Albert Einstein (1879–1955), the physicist, Nobel prizewinner, and discoverer of the theory of relativity, once declared the Hindu icon of the dancing Shiva to be the "best metaphor for the workings of the universe." He was referring to the hieroglyphic and transcendental nature of this particular icon, which expresses a number of cosmic truths on different levels simultaneously. Such is the nature of Tantric art.

TANTRA: THE PHILOSOPHY OF SEX AND CULT OF ECSTASY

The sixties view of Tantra as the Yoga of sex was augmented by the publications of Philip Rawson, a curator at the Gulbenkian Museum of Oriental Art at the University of Durham, England. He promoted Tantra both as a philosophy of sex and as an art form.

In 1968, Rawson's book *Erotic Art of the East: The Sexual Theme in Oriental Painting and Sculpture* was published. Interestingly, the general editor was Dr. Alex Comfort, who also wrote the introduction. Four years later, he would finally get his *Joy of Sex: A Gourmet Guide to Lovemaking* published, a book which went on to become a worldwide best-seller.

Philip Rawson has a "Tantrism" chapter in the India section of his book. In it, he writes:

There is an important strand of thought running through Indian religion which has attracted the fascinated attention of many modern Western and Indian students. This can broadly be defined as Tantrik, and involves religious rituals in which sex plays the fundamental part. Tantrism is sex as philosophy, philosophy as sex.

In 1972, *Tantra*, a major exhibition of Tantric art, opened at London's Hayward Gallery. Sponsored by the Arts Council of Great Britain, it primarily featured objects from the Ajit Mookerjee collection, with other items loaned from museums, dealers, and Tantric art collectors. The catalog was organized by Philip Rawson and carried his introduction and other explanatory text. In it, Rawson states:

> Tantra is a special manifestation of Indian feeling, art, and religion. It may really be understood, in the last resort, by people who are prepared to undertake inner meditative action. There can be no quick and easy definitions. . . . There are so many variations of practice and belief. However, there is one thread which can guide us through the labyrinth: all the different manifestations of Tantra can be strung on it. This thread is the idea that Tantra is a cult of ecstasy, focused on a vision of cosmic sexuality. Life-styles, ritual, magic, myth, philosophy, and a complex of signs and emotive symbols converge upon that vision. The basic texts in which these are conveyed are also called Tantras.

The sexual revolution, psychedelics, and the search for new meanings to life's mysteries all contributed to the interest in Tantric art in the sixties. Tantric symbols appeared everywhere, on T-shirts, buttons, posters, and on record albums. Mandalas appeared on pop concert posters. Tantric art designs were painted on several of the Beatles' cars. Jimi Hendrix had Tantric Yantra diagrams painted on his guitar and on his cheeks. And several important modern painters, such as Matta, Appel, Paul Jenkins, Francisco Clemente, and others took up Tantric themes in their work. From the sixties onward, many Westerners began collecting original Indian and Tibetan Tantric art with a passion.

ALEX COMFORT AND *THE JOY OF SEX*

One of the ways that sexual barriers have been broken down in the West has been through the publication of sexual how-to books. Undoubtedly the most successful of all has been *The Joy of Sex: A Gourmet Guide to Lovemaking* by Dr. Alex Comfort, first published in 1972, now with more than eight million copies in print.

Joy of Sex was not Comfort's first erotic work. In 1961, his *Darwin and the Naked Lady* was published and drew attention to the value of Indian erotology. And in 1964, following in the footsteps of Sir Richard Francis Burton's translation of the *Kama Sutra*, Comfort's *The Koka Shastra and Other Medieval Indian Writings on Love*, another Hindu erotic classic, was published.

In the introduction to his English version of the *Koka Shastra*, Comfort points out that India and most other cultures have a rich and refined body of erotic literature, whereas Judeo-Christian culture does not. He wrote:

> The Sanskrit textbooks on the art of love form a continuous sequence from remote antiquity to the sixteenth century A.D. or later, and on to the present time in vernacular versions and inspirations. Most great cultures, as well as many tribal societies, have had a literature of this kind—our own Judeo-Christian tradition is almost unique in lacking one.

Comfort then explains how, because of our culture's fear and rejection of sexuality, people interested in sexual topics had to turn either to the classics of antiquity or to certain ecclesiastical or medical writings.

Comfort's *Joy of Sex* and its sequel, *More Joy of Sex: A Lovemaking Companion to the Joy of Sex*, gave many people permission to explore their sexuality, and to have sexual adventures without feeling guilty. The tremendous success of his books indicates the great need for sexual liberation that many people seek.

TIBETAN TANTRIC TEACHERS IN THE WEST

There are now many Tibetan Lamas and monks living permanently in the West. They all teach Tantric forms of Buddhism, with emphasis on peaceful and wrathful forms of meditation. Along with Buddhist teachings has come Tibetan language and liturgical instruction. Temples, monasteries, and meditation centers have been built across America. Tibetan Tantrics have introduced the peaceful and wrathful deities to the Western world and promoted their rites. As with all popular religions, the Tibetan form of popular Buddhism rests largely on faith. Linguistic skills are also necessary if one truly wishes to penetrate into the deeper level of meaning of traditional Tibetan Tantric rites and ceremonies.

In Tibetan monasteries and meditation centers in the West, Tantric Buddhism is gradually being redefined. Many Westerners are interested in learning about spiritual sex practices in the Tibetan Tantric tradition, but very few Tibetan Lamas are sexually experienced. Those in the *Gelugpa* ("yellow hat") sect, of which the Dalai Lama is the supreme hierarch, take vows of celibacy. Others, such as those of the *Nyingmapa* and *Sakyapa* sects, can have wives, and there is a *Kargyudpa* tradition of Yogis having sexual consorts. But in general, Tibetan Lamas treat sex either as solely a means for maintaining family lineages or as an energy requiring sublimation through Yogic disciplines.

In Tibetan Tantra traditions, spiritual sex practices are generally kept secret. They do exist, but most Tibetan Lamas have chosen to avoid discussing or practicing them with their Western followers. One of the rare exceptions was the late Chögyam Trungpa, who was among the very first Lamas to establish Tibetan Buddhism in the West and who himself broke tradition, had affairs, married, and produced children. A high Lama of the *Kargyudpa* lineage, he lived his life as a Tantric *siddha* master, flouting convention and courting controversy. Yet his spiritual teachings maintained their integrity and his initiations had lasting power.

As Tibetan teachers become more familiar with Western culture, it is hoped that some will find ways to openly address the increasing interest in spiritual sex. Westerners who follow a Tantric path are not generally interested in learning how to sublimate or transform their sexual longings; they'd prefer to find out how to have a better and more spiritual sex life. They want to be taught how to use sex for achieving both sensual and spiritual gratification. They want to empower their spirituality with earthly Goddess energy. Or they are looking for unconventional yet meaningful forms of sexual expression.

Some are seeking spiritual sex union with Dakini or Dacca "mystical consorts," looking for initiation through sex. Others want to experience greatly prolonged—"oceanic" or "total body" orgasm. And there are those who have had and want to repeat "out of body" sex, or sex as a high form of spiritual sacrament. These are earnest spiritual seekers with "sex-positive" attitudes, who have totally outgrown conventional Western norms.

It is my expectation that Tibetan Tantric teachers will eventually deal with the Western obsession with sex, directly. I hope they will share some of the deeper sexual secrets of Tantric Buddhism. Original explicit Buddhist texts on Tantric sexual rites and procedures are available and have been translated into English, but much remains obscure. What is needed is explanation and practical guidance.

AN OVERVIEW OF THE NEO-TANTRIC PHENOMENON IN THE WEST

The American transcendentalists boldly embraced a broad humanistic and spiritual view of reality that broke down barriers and opened up unlimited creative possibilities. Quakers, Shakers, Mormons, Revivalists, and Perfectionists opened Christian communities to new spiritist visionary ecstatic experiences. Frances Wright's radical initiative in founding the Nashoba interracial free-love community early in nineteenth-century America was exceedingly bold and, with racial tension on the increase, her theories may be of value today. Fourierists and other utopian "free-lovers" introduced different ways of handling social, economic, and sexual needs, as did John Humphrey Noyes and his Society of Perfectionists.

The American Perfectionists were would-be Western Tantrics whose main goal was the attainment of spirituality, harmony between the sexes, and good works. No matter how much doubt, rumor, and innuendo has been brought to bear on these little-known Christian sects, their achievements live on. All helped prepare the ground for Tantra to become part of Western culture.

The Oliphants, "sexual missionaries" at the end of the nineteenth century, contributed to the relaxed sexual atmosphere found in many of Israel's kibbutz communities today. Paschal Randolph's Eulis Brotherhood, which emphasized the magical power of sex, was a synthesis of many converging traditions, had a significant influence on American Rosicrucian beliefs, and helped establish Tantra in America. The American spiritualists also helped in this respect, opening up people to the reality of certain psychic phenomena, attributes of the human psyche long familiar to Tantric tradition. Theosophists, although largely unknowingly, also contributed.

The journey of Tantra and neo-Tantra to the West was also aided by the Hindu Swamis Vivekananda and Ram Tirath, without whose contributions many of us would still be in the dark. And we must not forget Dr. Pierre Bernard, the father of Tantra in America, the principal founder of the Tantrik Order. A man until now largely forgotten, this brilliant and colorful character had an extraordinary life that would no doubt make a fine movie. Hounded by the press, persecuted, loved, and hated, he was let alone only after amassing great wealth and influence. He surely exemplifies the Tantric teachings.

Then there was the enormous contribution made by such occult organizations as the Golden Dawn and the OTO.

Aleister Crowley, George Gurdjieff, and the American beatnik movement—neo-Tantric, arch-Tantric, and Tantric "tricksters," respectively—all share a common ground with Tantra. Tantra in the West would not be what it is today without their contribution. Add to this mix consciousness-transforming drugs such as marijuana, mescaline, and LSD, plus the influence of jazz and rhythm and blues, and we reach the new dimension that Tantra took on in the psychedelic sixties.

On its journey to the West, Tantra was touched by many different influences: brilliant intellectuals, artists, musicians, and radical thinkers.

There are presently many teachers of Tantra in the West. Universities offer degree courses in philosophy or Indology, with Tantric topics as the main attraction. Harvard University puts out the *International Journal of Tantric Studies*, with its own Web site on the Internet. *Tantra: The Magazine*, the New Age leader of the Tantric media phenomena, touches more and more people with each issue.

There are now many Tantra home pages on the Internet, with Tantra hot links, Tantra talk venues. And there is plenty of sex on the Internet, most of low order, but some striving for the spiritual heights.

The Tantric lifestyle and spiritual sex is here to stay. Tantra is needed to help harmonize relationships between the sexes and between races; to complete the liberation of women; to enhance communication, interaction, and mutual respect; to heal the wounds or disappointments of the past; and to define the new spiritual paradigm for the future. By viewing sex as a sacrament and learning how to use the powerful Tantric "spiritual software" of our senses and soul, people of every color and culture can expect a future filled with meaning and joy.

6 TECHNIQUES FOR MASTERING TANTRIC SEX

Sexuality is not mere instinctuality; it is an indisputably creative power that is not only the basic cause of our individual lives, but a very serious factor in our psychic life as well.

—CARL JUNG

ACCORDING TO Tantric tradition, sex goes beyond reproduction, having the power to convey feelings of pleasure and loss, the ability to advance one's spiritual evolution, and the potential function of initiating magical or occult spiritual powers.

Spiritual teachers have traditionally viewed the pursuit of physical pleasure as potentially dangerous. One can get so attached to pleasurable feelings that one becomes addicted to them, and feelings of attachment inevitably lead to fears of loss. Almost every spiritual path, then, emphasizes the desirability of sexual continence—almost every spiritual path, that is, except Tantra.

Tantras teach that we can rise by those same activities that commonly make us fall. The *Hevajra Tantra* categorically states:

> That by which the world is bound, by that same its bonds are released, but people are deluded and know not this truth. A person deprived of truth will never get perfected.

In Tantra, we traverse the dangerous yet short path to spiritual evolution. We pursue physical pleasure without succumbing to hedonism. The difference is very subtle, yet crucial. When pursued without attachment, without clinging, without "expectations," the physical pleasures can be liberating. Tantra shows the way.

The earnest desire for spiritual liberation drives all true Tantric activities. It is the psychic fuel, the positive power, energizing and illuminating. The liberating power of sexual interactions pursued without attachment is the antidote to worldliness, lethargy, and, ultimately, the dread of death.

Tantras require practitioners of spiritual sex to cultivate heroic and optimistic mental attitudes. And there's the application of physical techniques whereby the normal involuntary process of sexual orgasm can become controlled while remaining joyously spontaneous. This is a science and art unique to Tantra.

Sexual Potency

Men reach their peak of sexual potency at about age eighteen; women reach their peak at about age twenty-eight. This fact contributes to the difference between male and female sexual behavior. Young men tend to seek sex earlier than women their own age. Of course, as novices, they tend to be clumsy and overeager to prove their manhood. Adolescent male sexual behavior tends to be aggressive and insensitive, and women, especially young women, generally don't appreciate it. This is why, in matriarchal tribal cultures, young men are commonly sexually initiated by older women. Once they learn the laws and procedures of sex, they can take a partner of their own age or younger.

Women commonly don't experience full sexual satisfaction until they are fully mature, which generally is not until their late twenties. A young woman who engages in sex with a young man is easily sexually disappointed and spiritually hurt by the "wham, bam" attitude to sex the prevails among inexperienced male adolescents, which is partly why, in most tribal societies, young women are sexually initiated by older men who are sexually experienced, emotionally mature, and spiritually aware. Traditional Tantra uses such scenarios creatively, setting up sexual rites and initiations in such a way that these natural differences between man and woman are adjusted for and balanced.

Tantra teaches—and physiological studies confirm—that man's orgasmic ability is very limited, whereas woman's is considerable. Generally, in a healthy person, it takes between five and thirty muscular contractions for orgasm to be reached. Man invariably reaches orgasm faster and has fewer contractions than woman. Spiritual sex techniques are designed to address and balance this scenario also. Choice of sexual posture, with woman in the dominant role, allows man to switch from physical to spiritual focus, prolonging his staying power. Use of Yoga locks (*bandhas*), breathing techniques, pressure points, mantra repetition, and visualizations help aid a man's retention of semen. For these techniques to work properly, it is important for the woman to understand them and aid in their application.

In Tantric sex, foreplay and afterplay, using body, speech, and mind, is tremendously important. Spoken compliments, commands, and noises of love, part of carefully orchestrated sexual scenarios requiring both mental and physical attention, together enhance and potentiate the sexual act. Tantric spiritual sex techniques include methods for man to suppress the urge to reach orgasm until woman is fully turned on and opens up to her awesome potential as initiatress into the sexual mysteries.

Here again, the considerable differences of physiology between women and men is apparent. Women need to learn to come easier and more frequently. They can best do so by being truly free to explore their natural and awesome sexual power. Sensual exploration, self-pleasuring (masturbation), being empowered to take their pleasure without feeling guilty, and being treated as a goddess and worshipped by their partner are some of the best ways for women to experience spiritual or oceanic orgasms.

It can also be very helpful if, before having sex, a couple discusses their respective expectations. They should try to agree on "the menu" and should also agree on signs or words that inform the other to either slow down or speed up. Ideally practiced, spiritual sex should take time. Only then can a couple truly reap the benefits!

Marriages and Sexual Contracts

Spiritual sex is a deep commitment. In Tantric tradition, this is generally formalized through either marriages or sexual contracts. In orthodox Vedic-style Hinduism, eight different forms of marriage are recognized, including such categories as "marriage by abduction" and "marriage by purchase."

In the Tantric tradition, only *two* forms of marriage are recognized. Both can either be just for a limited duration—for a specified period of time, such as a day and night, a week, a month, a year, or several years—or forever, meaning for life, beyond even death. These are referred to as Brahma marriage and Shiva marriages, respectively.

Brahma marriage is essentially patriarchal. Its focus is procreation and ultimately in the distribution of property by descent to offspring. Its main feature is that the wife is always chosen by the man and must come only from a family of equal status. Polygamy, though uncommon now in India, is acceptable in Brahma marriage. Followers of Brahma marriage commonly perform Tantric rites solely in a symbolic way, without physical participation in the sacraments of sex.

Shiva marriage is of a much more matriarchal style. Social status is ignored when choosing a partner according to Shiva's tradition. In this type of marriage, woman can be the instigator of the marriage rite. Color and caste barriers have no relevance to Shiva marriage. Polygamy is acceptable, provided the primary wife is in agreement, in which instance she is considered both husband and sister to other wives.

Followers of Shiva marriage indulge in sex and share sacraments as a Tantric high rite. Tantric Yoga techniques are practiced to avoid premature or excessive loss of semen. Though welcomed, offspring are not considered crucial. In the Shiva form of marriage, unconventional lifestyles predominate.

Contrary to much that has been erroneously written about Tantra, casual sex is not part of the Tantric lifestyle. In the Tantric tradition, *every* action, and especially sexual acts, have consequences. Tantra teaches that even mere thoughts can create consequences.

Those of us following the Tantric tradition employ mantras, which purify our thoughts as well as our bodies. Mantras are viewed as protectors of the mind and liberators of the spirit from bondage. The *Kularnava Tantra* states this position very clearly:

> In the world there is no other sacrifice superior to the sacrifice known as *Japa*, which is the repetition of Mantras. By so doing, one can attain the four goals of human existence; these being spiritual merit, worldly prosperity, sensual pleasure, and liberation.

Tantric sexual contracts are agreements that should be based on an exchange of dialogue that communciates what each expects of the other both sexually and materially. Ideally, these sexual contracts should be declared in front of a sacred fire, burning candle, or lamp, which is considered to be a witness.

The proposed duration, conditions, or promises of this Tantric contract should be expressed aloud. At this time, favorite food and drink should be shared and a positive, playful, sex-positive attitude cultivated. This is no dreaded "until death do us part" Judeo-Christian marriage contract, nor is it supposed to be a prenuptial agreement in any materialistic sense.

Following Tantric sexual contracts, neither person owns the other, yet each must perform service for the other, according to the terms of the agreement. Specific roles, such as initiator, initiatress, teacher, student, mistress, master, and so forth, as desired, should be defined and agreed to. New names can also be taken, just for the duration of the contract. This type of sacred-sex scenario can be a moving and delightful experience, embuing everything that is done subsequently (whether sexual or otherwise) with lasting meaning.

Such Tantric contracts allow participants to shed habitual or negative personality traits and take up new and more spiritual ones. They help expand the limits of what is or is not possible, empowering the relationship, even if it be for only a short duration. When the agreed term is completed, both participants can either revert to their previous condition or move into new ones.

Self-Liberation and the Yoga of Sex

Carl Jung once explained how Eastern spiritual teachings differ substantially from Western ones:

> The Christian West considers man to be wholly dependent upon the grace of God, or at least upon the church as the exclusive and divinely sanctioned earthly instrument of man's redemption. The East, however, insists that man is the sole cause of his higher development, for it believes in self-liberation.

A similar and expanded view of the differences between Western and Eastern religions was put forward by the eminent writer Amaury de Riencourt. In his book *Sex and Power in History* (1974), he explains the dilemma faced by followers of Western masculine-oriented religions:

> The unquestionably masculine character of Western religions in contrast with those of the East springs basically from the full acceptance in the West of an objective reality that, in the East, is viewed fundamentally as an illusion: the absolute dissociation of all human beings from the higher divinity. There was in the West (until the advent of psychoanalysis) no conscious problem of identification, of rediscovering one's deeper, divine self; the Western problem was how to *relate* to divine powers *outside* oneself, and how to develop one's ego in the process. In the East the problem was how to extinguish the ego, an essential step on the way to the discovery of one's fundamental identity with the unindividualized divinity within the self. This has striking consequences in terms of the relations between masculine and feminine principles.

This explains, in a nutshell, why in Eastern religions relationships between men and women are more balanced, based ultimately as they are on the unindividualized divinity within.

Yoga is a spiritual discipline that has self-liberation as its goal. Meaning "to join the mundane with the spiritual," Yoga uses many different techniques to achieve this same end. Most of these techniques are practiced alone, in total isolation from worldliness. They require a lot of discipline and are impractical for most people at the present time.

In the so-called decadent era in which humanity now finds itself, sex can be an extremely potent and effective form of Yoga. Referred to as Tantra Yoga or spiritual sex, this is a joint venture between man and woman. It is also an adventure, requiring a certain amount of courage, a lot of sensitivity, and the willingness to explore territories previously unknown.

The *Kama Sutra* and Tantra

The *Kama Sutra* is the earliest surviving example of a written Hindu love manual. It was compiled by the sage Vatsyayana sometime between the second and fourth centuries C.E. His work was based on earlier *kama shastras* or "rules of love" going back to at least the seventh century B.C.E. and is a compendium of social norms and love customs of patriarchal northern India.

Vatsyayana's *Kama Sutra* is valuable today for his psychological insights into the interactions of love and his structured approach to the many diverse situations he describes. He defines different types of men and women, describing what he terms "equal" unions, and gives detailed descriptions of many love postures.

The *Kama Sutra* was written for the wealthy male city dweller. It is not—and was never intended to be—a lover's guide for the masses, nor is it a "Tantric love manual." About three hundred years after the *Kama Sutra* became popular, some of the lovemaking positions described in it were reinterpreted in a Tantric way. Because Tantra is an all-encompassing sensual science, lovemaking positions can be considered relevant to spiritual practice.

Generally, Tantras recommend the use of only a few different love postures during spiritual sex. Five principle positions, all of which are found in the *Kama Sutra* and have many variations, cover what is normally recommended:

Man on his back, woman on top
Woman on her back, man on top
Woman and man on their sides, facing each other

Woman with her back to the man
Seated positions, normally face-to-face

Vatsyayana's *Kama Sutra* is divided into seven parts: general remarks, amorous advances, acquiring a wife, duties and privileges of a wife, relations with other men's wives, courtesans and occult means, and an appendix. The appendix includes detailed formulations of substances familiar to Ayurvedic (Indian indigenous medicine), with the emphasis on virilifics and aphrodisiacs. Some magical procedures of a type that in later times would be described as Tantric are also found in the last chapter of Vatsyayana's work.

The terminology used by Vatsyayana is context-specific. For example, when he uses the word *Yoga*, he is referring to sexual intercourse; the word *Tantra* means to him "method," "technique," or "mechanics"; and the word *yantra* means the sexual organ "utilized as an instrument," or a dildo or "artificial love device." *Lingam* specifically refers to the male sex organ, while *Yoni* refers to the female.

It is unfortunate that the *Kama Sutra* has generally been viewed in the West as a book of Hindu love postures, or as *the* Tantric sex manual, which it is not. Nevertheless, the *Kama Sutra* is continually popular. A recent survey of the twenty-five most popular search topics on the Internet found that more than half were *Kama Sutra* entries pertaining to sexual positions or practices such as oral sex, described in detail by Vatsyayana. Internet queries under the headings *Tantra* and *sacred sex* are also remarkably commonplace.

The popular Western perception of the *Kama Sutra* as a Tantric sex manual has been the cause of so much misunderstanding about Tantra. In fact, this important work on Hindu eroticism has hardly any resemblance to any known Tantra, nor do Tantras resemble it. Nevertheless, it is the earliest surviving sexual how-to and set the stage for many others, including those in which sexual techniques, postures, potions, charms, and superstitions were promoted over the centuries.

Five Principal and Five Evolved Sexual Positions

As previously mentioned, despite the popular view that the *Kama Sutra* is a book of Tantric sexual positions, the truth is that neither Hindu nor Buddhist Tantras *emphasize* sexual positions. Positions are described in Tantric texts, but the emphasis is generally on other things that aid spiritual success, such as mental attitude, breathing techniques, mantras, ritual gestures, ritual ingredients and procedures, timing of rites, visualizations, and so forth.

Obviously, there are many possible variations of the five spiritual sex positions (woman on top, man on top, side postures, seated postures, and postures in which the woman has her back to the man). There are also exotic or adventurous sexual activities involving standing, kneeling, being on all fours, group sex, partners of the same sex, and so forth.

Mutual oral-genital sex, with man on top—one of the "evolved" positions. Ivory carving from Eastern India, circa sixteenth century.

Five "evolved" sexual positions are common in rites of Tantric sex. These are oral-genital positions:

The woman stands, squats, or is seated over the man, facing him, her Yoni at his mouth.

The man stands, squats, or is seated, as the woman, kneeling or seated, faces him and pleasures his Lingam with her mouth.

Man and woman lie together in "69" position, in mutual oral-genital contact, the woman on top.

Man and woman lie together in "69" position, in mutual oral-genital contact, the man on top.

The man lies or sits, with the woman standing, sitting, or squatting above him, her back turned to him as she faces his feet.

There are some natural sequences of spiritual sex positions. Because it generally takes more time for a woman to become sexually turned on than a man, Tantra teaches that the first sex positions to be selected should be those that give woman maximum stimulation. This varies from person to person, so a certain amount of experimentation may be necessary before the most stimulating positions are found.

Man generally becomes sexually excited very quickly and often comes too fast. For him, positions that create *minimum* physical stimulation should be chosen first.

Most Western men seem to feel they have to prove their manhood by being vigorous lovers. They commonly take on a dominant role and try to please their partner with vigorous thrusts. This commonly results in their coming before their partner is truly satisfied.

From a classical Greek sculpture: woman on top of man, her back turned to him— one of the "evolved positions."

Classical Indian sculpture depicting a man orally pleasing a woman. Stone carving from Orissa, eastern India, circa thirteenth century.

Service to woman is the cornerstone of Tantra. Many Tantras suggest that spiritual-sex sessions should commence with the man orally servicing woman. One of the several different positions already described should be chosen. He should lovingly kiss and lick his partner's Yoni and she should tell him what she likes, guiding him so that he can give her the most pleasure. She should guide his rhythm and should be sure to look directly at him from time to time.

Then she should sit or squat on him, riding his erect Lingam, pleasuring herself with it. During this phase, the man should concentrate on retention. He should not thrust up toward his partner but instead lie recumbent, doing *mulabandha*, which is anal constriction. This has the effect of helping avoid premature ejaculation, concerning which more will be discussed later.

Tantras emphasize that woman must be free to take her pleasure and should initially take an active role in rites of spiritual sex. Once she has come for the first time, positions may be switched, but when switching positions, it is important to avoid interruption of intimacy.

After woman has "ridden" her man, if he sits up, they will easily be able to move into the Tantric sitting position, facing each other, looking into each other's eyes, without withdrawing.

Seated positions do not allow for much movement. She sits on his Lingam, legs around his back, her breasts and mouth easily ac-

Woman on top. Terracotta from the Gupta dynasty, central India, circa fifth century.

cessible to his mouth, her back and buttocks easily reached by his hands. In seated sex positions, intimacy is enhanced.

In the Tantric seated sex position, with woman seated on the lap of the man and facing him, she is still in control. She should use the *mulabandha* Yoga technique to rhythmically grip his Lingam with her Yoni. In this position, the Kundalini can awaken most easily and be directed upward. The sensation is indescribable.

From the seated position, it's very simple for woman to lie back and ask her partner to make love to her with him on top. This is a position in which the man can take a more dominant role. Moving her legs wide open or back over her head, he can penetrate very deeply and pleasure her inner recesses.

When tired, the couple can easily roll into a side-by-side position. Still face-to-face, side positions easily allow total relaxation and intimate "blending" into each other. Focus should be on the breath, each breathing and "absorbing" the other.

Without withdrawing, the man should turn his partner so her back faces him. This allows parts of the Yoni to be reached by the Lingam that may not have been accessible by other positions. Once this position has been fully explored, they can very easily move into the "69" mutual oral reverse position, so they can feast on the sacraments of sex.

In *The Poets of the Powers* (1973), an important book on the South Indian Siddha traditions of Tantra, Kamil Zvelebil, an eminent European Indologist, summarizes hints given him by one of his Yogi informants. After outlining details of recommended holistic health

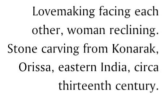

Lovemaking facing each other, woman reclining. Stone carving from Konarak, Orissa, eastern India, circa thirteenth century.

habits, such as eating only fresh foods and chewing well, taking sun-baths, breathing deeply and rhythmically, getting eight hours of naked sleep with the head to the north, taking walks regularly, and cultivating a positive mental attitude, his informant refers to sex. These are his recommendations:

> Regular and frequent sexual intercourse is beneficial. However, be master, not slave in your sex life. Oral-genital sex is not harmful; on the contrary, it is often desirable. Visualize yourself as the creative Shiva, and your partner as your (i.e., Shiva's) Shakti, energy. Let her lie on you, and drink your sperm; let you suck her discharge of pleasure *(curatanir)*.

Choice of sex positions should ideally be predetermined, or at least there should be some mutual understanding about preferences. Ideally, the woman's partner should bring her to a series of orgasms, which will become more and more liberating as she becomes familiar with the mystical oceanic experience of spiritual sex.

Partially seated lovemaking, the woman reclining and supported by cushions. Indian miniature painting, circa nineteenth century.

Seated sacred sex position. Here the couple embodies the celestial Buddha Vajrasattva and his consort Vajradhatvishvari. They are in the classic *Yab-Yum* ("father–mother") position of Tibetan Tantric tradition. Silk appliqué hand-embroidered hanging from Tibet, circa early nineteenth century. (Private collection)

Playful seated sacred-sex position. Here the couple embodies Radha and Krishna, the divine couple of Hindu "Vaishnav" Tantra tradition. Ivory from Bengal, circa eighteenth century.

The five principal sexual positions and the five evolved ones should be experimented with so that clumsiness ceases to be part of position-changing. These principal positions are natural expressions of the fivefold Tantric truth. They are the "five limbs" of spiritual sex, the steps in the dance of sensual ecstasy and spiritual liberation. To some, the dance is instinctual. For others, a little choreography and a certain amount of playful practice can work wonders.

Alice Bunker Stockham and the *Karezza* Technique

Alice Bunker Stockham (1833–1912) came from an American Quaker family. Brought up in Michigan, she studied medicine and was among the first women in America to become a doctor. She was a pioneer in obstetrics and a staunch advocate of women's rights.

Dr. Stockham drew much of her inspiration from John Humphrey Noyes and his Oneida Community. She tried to adapt some of his teachings for ordinary society. Unlike Noyes, she did not advocate orgasm for women. She emphasized "soul communion" and taught that in men, sexual energy should be "trained into channels of usefulness and power." She learned about free female sexuality from her studies of the Nayars, a Dravidian East Indian matriarchal tribe that practiced polyandry, meaning multiple husbands for each woman.

In 1883, Dr. Stockham self-published her book *Tokology* in which she promoted "natural childbirth" and a sexual "continence" method she called *karezza* (Italian for "little caress"), which was undoubtedly inspired by Oriental lovemaking techniques described in both Islamic and Tantric esoteric literature. Arabs called this technique *imsak*. It was one of the main sexual secrets of the Cathars, Knights Templars, the Troubadours, hermetic secret societies, and European occult organizations during the Middle Ages.

Karezza was explained by Dr. Stockham as "sexual intercourse between a male and female in which no coital movements are used, taking an hour or more to perform." For success, it required "an act of will on the part of both the male and the female." She wrote:

> *Karezza* consummates marriage in such a manner that through the power of will, and loving thoughts, the final crisis is not reached, but a complete control by both husband and wife is maintained throughout the entire relation. . . .
>
> During a lengthy period of perfect control, the whole being of each is submerged in the other, and an exquisite exaltation experienced. This may be followed by a quiet motion, entirely under full subordination of the will, so that at no time the thrill of passion for either party will go beyond a pleasurable exchange. Unless procreation is desired, the final propagative orgasm is entirely avoided.

Various versions of *karezza* were promoted. Among them was Zugassent's discovery, popularized by author George N. Miller in his novel *The Strike of a Sex and Zugassent's Discovery*, which was published by Dr. Stockham in 1890. Other forms of sexual continence disciplines, such as alphism, dianism, and "sexual communion," were experimented with by associates and followers of Dr. Stockham. Many of these disciplines and sexual techniques have, in the New Age era, been promoted as the teachings of Tantra.

In 1896, Dr. Stockham's major book, *Karezza: Ethics of Marriage*, was published. Concerning *karezza*, she wrote:

> Men who are borne down with sorrow because their wives are nervous, feeble, and irritable have it in their power, through *karezza*, to restore the radiant hue of health to the faces of their loved ones, strength and elasticity to their steps, and harmonious action to every part of their bodies.

Alice Stockham was a remarkable American woman who was years ahead of her time. Her pioneering work in human sexuality is little known today, despite the fact that in her time her books created widespread excitement and were translated into Russian, German, and Swedish. In the face of AIDS today, when monogamy is advised, and with interest in Tantra on the rise, her very straightforward and practical teachings have much to offer those wishing to spiritualize their love life.

Sacraments and *Siddhis*

According to Tantric tradition, spiritual sex and the products or sacraments of sex so produced can lead to occult powers. Occult powers are not the goal of Tantric practice, yet they very often herald spiritual success. Occult powers can corrupt and distract one from the higher spiritual goal, yet they are nature's gifts, to be neither denied nor exploited. By occult powers I mean inexplicable phenomena, such as telepathy, the power to make something come about by one's wishes, visions of the past or future, and all types of superhuman feats. Ideally, one should neither feel attached to such phenomena nor allow the ego to be boosted by them but instead cultivate an expectant but disinterested attitude. Such powers are traditionally referred to as *siddhi*, which is also the name of a Hindu goddess.

Orthodox Hindu Yoga philosophy teaches that there are five circumstances conducive to the attainment of *siddhi*. These are:

> Gifts from birth, coming from spiritual activities in a previous life or lives
>
> Austerities, which burn up obstructing karma and free the latent divine powers within
>
> Mantras, which purify the psyche and attract spiritual powers
>
> Certain "magical" substances (*ausadhi*), such as rare plant and mineral drugs (some of which are of an alchemical nature), which have empowering properties
>
> Prolonged periods spent in *samadhi*, meaning in deep spiritual meditative union with the divine

Tantrics add to these five the power of woman as Goddess incarnate. According to several Tantras, when a woman is worshipped as goddess and is pleased by the devotee, she can convey occult powers or *Siddhis* spontaneously, as a form of blessing or spiritual empowerment. This is another powerful Tantric secret.

The power of Tantra to bestow magical and supernatural gifts on those who practice it will be explored further in the next chapter.

The Worship of Woman

Men are the "products" of women because every man (and woman) was born through the body of woman. According to Tantric teachings, the worship of woman is the recognition of her true spiritual and creative power.

Tantras teach that woman must always be honored. Ideally, she should be viewed as a living goddess. In the *Lakshmi Tantra*, the Great Goddess herself declares:

> If a Yogi meets a beautiful and shapely woman, he should visualize me, Lakshmi, in her.
>
> He should envisage her vital air (*prana*) as the sun, and her soul as the Higher Self.

He should envision her beauty and charm as celestial fire.
He should always visualize the gifted woman as identical with
   me, the Great Goddess!

This type of visualization is extremely simple and creates a conducive and naturally spiritual atmosphere.

A Tantric text tells the story of the immortal Hindu sage Vasistha, who once paid a visit to northeastern India, on the borders of China. He was astounded to find the Buddha there, eating, drinking, and in erotic dalliance with a number of exquisite-looking ladies.

As Vasistha was wondering how such behavior could possibly be appropriate in someone as enlightened as the Buddha, he heard a celestial voice. The voice said, "Such is a form of worship which is suitable for persons who exalt the Great Goddess. This type of Tantric worship requires participants to vow never to blame or beat women. This type of worship should be performed only while in a naked condition and should be accompanied by the best of food, drink, and other sensual offerings." The Buddha himself then called to Vasistha and told him, "Woman should be worshipped because all the gods and goddesses reside in her body!"

A commentary on the *Chakrasamvara Tantra*, an important early Buddhist Tantra, clearly explains how worship of the female partner should proceed:

The skillful spiritual seeker, who is heroic and pure,
Should worship the Yogini's perfect lotus vagina.
He should worship it with mind well focused on it,
Lovingly attending to her every need.
Then he should unite his sexual organ with hers,
Pressing into her passionately,
So as to join their spiritual essences.
Then he should pleasure her luscious lotus flower, knowingly.
Uniting the two most secret subtle veins,
Deep within their beings,
Yogi and Yogini should exert themselves in the arts of love.
Wisely choosing the five principle positions,
They should enjoy their erotic pleasure like king and queen.
Joining their juices in the reverse union,
They will conquer the worlds and achieve all spiritual wishes!

Authentic Tantra is a spiritual cult in which the exaltation of woman is paramount. By this approach, woman is empowered to indeed be a living goddess whose every expression has a creative, auspicious potential. A look, a smile, a gesture, acceptance, playfulness, satisfaction—these are just some of the techniques the awakened divine spirit in woman can use to spiritually initiate her lover. When the goddess in woman becomes one with her god, everything is possible.

Spiritual Sex in the Moon-Elixir Tantra

The *Chandamaharosana Tantra*, known as the "Moon Elixir," is an important and relatively early Buddhist work. Its teachings were followed by several Chinese emperors. The following explicit account of the secret sexual practices of this particular Tantric tradition includes fascinating details of erotic trade and high theater:

> He should bring the woman into his presence and seat her before him. Each should gaze steadily at the other, evoking their mutual desire for sex. Concentrating on that delightful and enjoyable view, each should keep their minds focused. Then the woman, the Goddess incarnate, should utter the following words, which will awaken pleasure in the man:
>
>> You are my son and my husband, my brother and my father. I am your mother and wife, your sister and your niece. For seven lifetimes, you have been my slave, my lowly servant. I purchased you with cowry shells. I am your mistress.
>
> He should fall at her feet ardently, press his palms together, and make obeisance to her.
> Then she, in his embrace, should kiss him again and again. She should then give him a light blow to his head, playfully. And she should offer him the sweet saliva of her mouth. She should command him to suck her Lotus, and when he does so, she should roll her eyes and moan. Placing her cherry-red lips on his mouth, she should press his heart region with her sandalwood-scented breasts.

Looking at him directly, she should playfully pinch his chest and command:

Lick my secret sexual flower. Taste my urine! O Son, be a slave as well as a father! For I am your official wife, as well as your royal mother!

After commanding him to take refuge at her feet, she asks for the pleasure of his Vajra penis. Showing him every detail of her precious Lotus vagina, she tells him:

Come onto my sensual reclining form! I am filled with desire; put my feet on your shoulders. Look at my luscious body! Make your throbbing diamond-hard Vajra weapon of love enter into the heart of my silky soft Lotus! Give thousands of loving strokes to my fleshy three-petaled Lotus love-flower. Insert your precious Vajra and sacrifice your mind with pleasure!

Listening to her description of the pleasure he gives, he should become motionless, meditating on this pleasure.

After going through the five main sexual postures, he should kiss her forehead, eyes, neck, ears, armpits, hands, and breasts. He should rub and suck her nipples. Having her lie on her back, he should kiss her stomach, saying:

This is where I once used to live.

He should caress and titillate her lovely Lotus with his hand, admire it, kiss and slavishly lick it; savoring the exquisite odor, he should lick her Lotus clean. Then he should say:

Just as I recently entered through this sacred door, so too have I emerged in numerous past lifetimes.

He should then eat the white and the red of her Lotus flower and kiss and lick her feet, as if he were her slave. It is optional whether he should emit semen or not, but whatever he does, he must keep his mind wholly focused on pleasure. If he does secrete, afterwards he should kneel before her and lovingly lick her Lotus. Then he should politely ask the Wisdom Woman to stand up and he should flatter and kiss her. After lovingly hugging her, they should both feast on fish and meat, he being sure to first offer the food to her. They should drink some fortified wine or some milk, to aid in the increase of desire. Then the divine couple, the living god and goddess, should begin their lovemaking again. By this repeated procedure, Great Pleasure, spiritual liberation and occult powers are obtained!

This type of Tantric erotic theater has many different variations. A couple should agree beforehand what is or is not "on the menu." If there truly is an atmosphere of total trust, the expectations for the encounter can be left open. If woman is put in charge and there is an understanding that she will endeavor to open herself up to her natural, intuitive, and goddesslike nature, Tantric sacred-sex encounters need only a minimum amount of scripting.

To Come or Not to Come: The Supreme Sacrifice

The key topic for a man who engages in spiritual sex à la Tantra ultimately will always be "to come or not to come." This is a mystical rather than empirical choice; for many practitioners, it is a continuing source of confusion.

One must view traditional Tantra, whether Hindu or Buddhist, first of all in its original cultural setting. Celibacy was always a prerequisite for persons involved in regular Hindu Hatha Yoga practice and was also mandatory for Buddhist monks. So Tantric sex teachings were often taken to be allegorical, referring to symbolic inner unions rather than to actual physical male–female interactions.

Such an approach largely defeats the whole purpose of Tantra, which always was the radical shortcut to spiritual illumination, rather than the safe but long route requiring lifetimes to complete. Because sex is the cause of human existence and the driving force of human achievement, the authentic archaic Tantric view is that one must confront and gain mastery over this primordial power and apply it creatively. Tantra teaches that the urge for sex should not be denied or sublimated but should instead be used to obtain spiritual blessings.

In both Hindu and Buddhist cultures, there have always been those who view the descriptions of Tantric sex as purely allegorical, reflections of inner Yogic processes, unions without any physical intimacy. There are those who view Tantra as the spiritual path of sexual intimacy but teach that man should strive never to come. Finally, there are those whom the goal of Tantra is for a man to come as many times as possible.

The first scenario is for people of little spiritual faith who really have a problem seeing sex as a spiritual activity. Before they can effectively practice spiritual sex, they need to raise sex to a spiritual dimension. They need to purify their minds and their bodies; they need to qualify or spiritualize their lifestyle. This is best done by making drastic changes in lifestyle: by associating with spiritually minded persons; by following a vegetarian diet; by reading about spiritual subjects, by taking up physical Yoga, Yoga breathing, and meditation; and by cultivating a new sex-positive and spiritual-positive attitude. During this phase, it is best to avoid sexual activity. In going through this phase, it is best to view Tantric teachings as allegorical. Much spiritual benefit can then be achieved.

The second scenario of striving never to come is extreme and counterproductive. This is different from semen conservation, which is an important requirement before true Tantric rites can be effective. But this doesn't mean a man should *never* come. Many Tantras recommend that man should conserve his semen, in the belief that this strengthens and spiritualizes him. In the sexual technology of true Tantric Yoga, men learn to consciously withhold, to circulate the sex energy within, and to sexually satisfy their partner. Only then should they decide whether to come. For a man, coming or not coming can be crucial. Generally, once a man has come, it's all over for a while. Most men can, at best, come only a few times without feeling drained, exhausted, and "out of it." Women, however, are naturally multiorgasmic. Tantra teaches that a woman's orgasm is infinite, like the ocean. This doesn't literally mean that a woman can keep on coming forever; even oceans have a limit. In contrast to man, woman is naturally multiorgasmic and can come much more frequently, so for a woman to be truly satisfied, for her to truly bestow blessings on her partner, the man ideally needs to withhold.

The third scenario, in which a man endeavors to come as much as possible, is extreme and will ultimately be debilitating. Semen is a finite and precious substance. It is the essence of life, a man's most intimate and ultimate resource. Both Buddhist and Hindu Tantras teach that a man should not spend his semen carelessly. It is the highest sacramental substance, as will soon be seen.

The main goal of Tantric sex is to advance one's spiritual evolution. Physical pleasure is not the primary goal. Spiritual evolution should ideally be a pleasurable activity, but it is important not to get distracted by it. Tantric teachings therefore advise ''earnest spiritual desire'' over the desire for pleasure alone.

Tantric sex proceeds from one of two basic stances. The first advocates withholding the release of sex cells, namely the sperm and the female sexual discharge, with the aim of building up sexual power within the body. Followers of this approach use various mental and physical techniques to avoid orgasm and seek to circulate the resultant waves of sexual energy and hold the sexual secretions within the body. These include letting the woman take the active role, holding the breath as one approaches the urge to ejaculate, pressing the area between the scrotum and anus, gripping the teeth and swallowing saliva, distracting oneself from the rising pleasure sensations by using visualization, and consciously ''reversing'' the outward-moving tendency of the semen by use of Yoga.

The radical Tibetan monk Gedün Chöpel gives the following very concise description of the Tantric retention technique:

> When the fluid arrives at the root of the male sex, the lower parts become heavy and numb; at that time, imagine the expanse of the sky and pull inward strongly, whereby its reversal will be certain. Close the lower gate (the anus), and turn the tongue and eyes upwards. Contract the joints of the feet and hands, and tighten the fingers strongly. Pull in the stomach to the backbone. These are physical techniques that should be done.

In his book, Kamil Zvelebil's Yogi informants gave the following instruction on how man should control the urge to ejaculate:

> When the sperm is about to flow, one should seize the penis with the middle fingers of the left hand at its root in front of the anus and, pressing hard, expel slowly his breath through the nose, at

the same time performing contractions of the anal muscles in the *asvinimudra* or *mulabandha* (Yogic names for this technique), drawing them inward and upward.

This south Indian Tantric technique is easily learned and is most effective.

The alternate view is to allow the natural "wisdom" of the body to fulfill its own karma, not suppressing the natural urge to come when ready but instead doing so with a mixture of focused intent and spontaneous joy. Those who pursue this type of Tantric sex experience the mixing and exchange of sexual energies and secretions. They can become complete, feeling physically nurtured, emotionally fulfilled, and spiritually evolved by exchanging or trading sexual secretions or sacraments with each other.

Oral Pleasure: A Path to Enlightenment

In normal male–female sexual intercourse, the male essence is "extracted and absorbed" by the female; the vagina "consumes" the penis's emitted semen. In fellatio, which is oral stimulation of the penis and the most common form of oral sex practiced, the mouth is the consumer. In either case, though man may think he is "having" a woman, in truth, it is she who is having him. To put things very simply, merely from the perspective of sexual interaction, Tantric sex is the reverse of the normal scenario. How? In Tantric sex, the man refrains from coming for as long as possible. His aim is to help his consort come very profusely. Oral–vaginal intercourse (cunnilingus) precedes and commonly follows genital intercourse. The emphasis is initially on the male absorbing as much as possible of his partner's sexual fluids.

Exchange of sexual discharge also takes place in Tantra, by using such Yogic techniques as *vajroli mudra*, in which fluid is absorbed or "sucked" back into the genitals, and by prolonging contact so absorption can take place directly through the skin surface.

Mutual oral sex, using the *soixante-neuf* ("69") position, referred to in Indian Tantric texts as *kakila*, "the crow" or "throat jewel" position, is another Tantric sacramental rite that is focused on absorption of sexual fluids.

Gedün Chöpel, whose *Treatise on Passion* has recently been translated into English by Jeffrey Hopkins and published as *Tibetan Arts of Love* (1992), describes this posture:

> With pillows for his rear and his head, the man lies down from the end of a bed. The woman mounts him according to the opposite method (with the head toward the feet). With thighs and cheeks touching, they join in that position. Through sucking and moving their tongues, strong bliss burns simultaneously in both for a long time. In whisper, this is called *mukhamaithuna* (oral union). By another name, it is the wheel of whirling pleasure. . . .
>
> These deeds (of oral sex) are described in the treatises of Female Sky Travelers for the sake of satisfying extremely passionate men and women who can hold the constitutional essences in their bodies without emission:
>
> > When the self-arisen blood (the female essence) goes inside
> >   the man
> > And when the essence of the moon (the male essence) dissolves inside a woman,
> > Superior power and bliss are definitely achieved.
> > They become like Shankara (Shiva) and Uma (Shakti).

Exploring the subject of cunnilingus in traditional Tantra, Miranda Shaw, Tantric scholar and author of the important book *Passionate Enlightenment: Women in Tantric Buddhism* (1994), explains the scenario:

> Although the man and woman both perform (the) Yogic process (seen in Hindu Tantra and Yoga as well), "mixing their essences," the Tantras (both Hindu and Buddhist) place somewhat more emphasis upon the man's absorption of female fluids. The *Hevajra Tantra* says that "spiritual women, or women belonging to the five Buddha families, are bestowers of *siddhi*, and their sexual fluid is adamantine, so worshipping them, a Yogin drinks it." The same text instructs the man to take a vow to continue to absorb the female essences in all future lives, until enlightenment is reached.

Sexual secretions are, in both Hindu and Buddhist Tantric rites, treated as spiritual sacraments. They are the treasured product of the night's bliss, not waste to be washed away without so much as a spiritual thought.

The Five Tantric Nectars: The Sacraments of Sex

Tantra also teaches that our body produces five types of special secretions, referred to in secret texts as "nectars." These are different from the five nectars of *orthodox* Hinduism, which are sugar, honey, milk, clarified butter *(ghee)* and curd, normally mixed together in equal qualities and sipped on sacred occasions.

Tantra views the human body as both special and sacred. It is special because birth as a human is the culmination of a sequence of births and is the "highest physical form," said to be difficult to achieve. The human body is sacred because it contains divinity and all the divine forces within it. The temple of the body is a traditional Tantric concept.

Everything that comes from a temple is taken to be sacred, provided the temple is treated as such, with a spiritually focused consciousness inhabiting it—and provided its owner takes good physical care of it, following proper rules of health and hygiene.

Tantras offer radical and unorthodox solutions to life's situations. They teach how to confront duality head-on. Clean and dirty, good and bad, acceptable and unacceptable—these are relative, judgmental, and culturally driven concepts that can impede the rapid spiritual advancement that Tantrics seek.

Unlike orthodox Hinduism, which is obsessed by what is "pure" and what is not, there is no such concept in authentic Tantra traditions. The *Chandamaharosana Tantra* expresses the position clearly:

> Never should the practitioner think in terms of "pure" or "impure";
> Never should he think in terms of "edible" or "inedible";
> "To be done" or "not to be done"; in terms of "suitable for lovemaking" or "unsuitable for lovemaking";

By so doing, the Yogi is cursed and all *siddhis* (powers) will leave
   him!

Most Western cultures usually teach that sweat, saliva, urine,
sexual secretions, menstrual blood, and excreta are unclean; yet
Tantric teachings tell us that, provided our body is well nourished,
healthy, and clean, all its products are sacred and have special uses.

Nature has a use for everything. Leaves fall from trees, rot, and
become compost, which, like manure, works wonders on our crops.
The Tantric Yogis of the past looked to nature for inspiration and for
answers to life's mysteries. Like most young children, who in their
innocence have a fearless and experimental attitude to just about
anything, Yogic scientists were fascinated by the products of the
body. They asked themselves: "Could they have a special use?"

Tantrics sought out the special properties of all our bodily products. They inquired into the properties of sweat and tears; nail clippings and ear wax; the different kinds of hair, from head, beard,
eyebrows, eyelashes, nose, armpit, pubic area, and so on. They explored every facet of the body and its products and they formulated
magical uses for everything.

They zeroed in on five particular products of the body, referred
to in both Hindu and Buddhist Tantric texts as the "five nectars":
saliva, urine, sexual secretions (semen and vaginal emissions), menstrual blood, and excrement. These five are, in the highest Tantric
teachings, viewed as spiritual sacraments and used in mystical rites
as aids to spiritual liberation.

These five nectars are consistently referred to in both Hindu and
Buddhist occult tradition and are the deep secret of many Tantras.
Their use as spiritual sacraments goes against the grain of orthodox
Hinduism and Buddhism. Tantras, however, argue that if our body
is truly our temple and is properly tended and nourished, then all
our bodily products must be sacred substances endowed with divine
properties. Hold off judgment for a while as we examine the scientific facts about what these five nectars actually consist of and what
their known properties are.

The properties of saliva change frequently during the course of
a day and night. Saliva contains valuable trace elements and many
different enzymes, which are secreted food specifically, meaning according to the foods we eat. Saliva enhances taste and breaks down

food and its enzymes aid digestion. Saliva also has healing properties, which is why animals lick their wounds.

It's not tremendously strange to associate saliva with pleasure. Thoughts or even mention of our favorite food commonly makes us salivate. So does both sex and certain Yoga practices, such as the Yoga headstand.

When we soul-kiss, or French-kiss, we exchange saliva and enjoy it. When we practice particular Hatha Yoga or meditation techniques, we discover that we produce special salivas, which we are taught to swallow, thinking of them as a blessing, a special elixir.

Hindu medical texts refer to the healthful and spiritual power-enhancing properties of fresh human urine. Urine is also a bodily product, but it's rare to find people who treat it as a sacrament. Yet Uropathy, or urine therapy, which is the drinking of urine for health reasons, though alien to most Westerners, has an illustrious record, especially in Asia. It is gradually becoming accepted by some people in the West, notably because of its proven antibody activity.

Human urine has consistently been shown effective against various microorganisms, bacteria, and viruses. Before the advent of modern medicines, urine was commonly used to counteract infections and to alleviate or cure a wide range of medical problems. For example, a small amount of a baby's own urine was commonly used to cure mouth infections such as thrush.

Fresh urine is naturally antiseptic and has some uniquely positive qualities. It normally contains water (ninety-five percent), urea, uric acid, creatinine, ammonia, sodium and potassium chloride, magnesium, and phosphorus, as well as carbohydrates, amino acids, vitamins, minerals, hormones, antibodies, antigens, and sexual pheromones (which cause sexual attraction). One of the present uses of human urine is as an additive in the manufacture of certain expensive perfumes.

According to a recent scientific study, melatonin, which is a sleep hormone secreted by the pineal gland, is secreted into the urine at night. This substance has the reputed special property of slowing down the aging process. According to studies, it also lowers the risk of cancer and heart disease and alters the pattern of brain waves in a way that enhances meditative practice. This explains the logic of Yogi's practicing uropathy.

Uropathy has proven very successful in treating a wide range of health problems, including obesity; allergies; heart disease; arthritis; eczema; amebic dysentery; tooth and eye problems; spastic muscle problems; fungal, viral, and bacterial infections; *Salmonella* infections; tetanus; diphtheria; cholera; malaria; and cancer. It has also been helpful in relieving painful AIDS symptoms.

The U.S. military recommends the drinking of one's urine as a survival procedure. Apparently, human urine has no known toxic or poisonous effects. It has been said that urine is an exact hologram of a healthy or diseased body and contains the exact combination of substances the body needs at any particular time. Tantra teaches that the urine of a healthy person contains substances that contribute to the maintenance of health. Conversely, a sick person's urine contains secretions that can help cure his or her particular health problem.

Advocates of uropathy recommend that a small quantity (no more than a glass) of urine be drunk as a medicinal potion in the morning, following a night's sleep. Urine should be drunk fresh, not boiled.

For many years, Mahatma Gandhi drank some of his own urine, believing in its special health-giving properties. And Morarji Ranchhodji Desai (1896–1995), the Indian prime minister who died at the age of ninety-nine, credited his good health and longevity to his habit of drinking a glass of his own urine every day.

Tantras also refer to a more intimate form of urine drinking. This takes place during rites of spiritual sex, when urine is loaded with hormones, in which context it is valued for both its sacramental and medicinal benefits.

When most women come "properly," they emit or "ejaculate." It is only recently that this fact has become accepted in Western culture; in the East, however, most of the ancient teachings on sexuality refer to "female emission."

Female emission is obviously different from male ejaculate. It can be far more profuse. Recent studies have shown that female orgasmic "ejaculate" is a combination of juices secreted from Skene's glands within the vagina, together with bursts of urine. Laced with hormones, vitamins, minerals, and lubricants, the slightly acidic vaginal juices, combined with all the products found in urine, make up the normal female emission.

Multiple orgasms, which are much sought after in most rites of Tantric sex, especially from prolonged oral stimulation of the clitoris and the inner "secret spot" (the G or Grafenberg spot, on the front wall of the vagina, about one third of the way up), commonly results in a sudden release of urine, which Tantric texts emphasize *should be drunk*. This practice is known as *amaroli*.

Many Tantras recommend *amaroli* as a high sacrament, stating that the urine be drunk directly "from the lips of the Yoni" as the culmination of intimacy. The "lotus nectar" of the precious consort, released by her as an embodiment of the Great Goddess during a high rite of Tantric sex, can have a wide variety of flavors, each credited with specific transcendental and magical properties.

In the secret Siddha Yoga teachings concerning Tantric sex, three distinct types of vaginal emission are recognized, referred to as *suratham* ("winelike juice"), *sronitham* ("blood-tinged"), and *suklam* ("ejaculate"). As a woman is sexually satisfied, these three distinct fluids are secreted, in sequence.

The *Hevajra Tantra* advises a Yogi to distinguish a suitable consort by noting

Squatting woman emitting urine.
Wood carving from eastern India,
circa eighteenth century.

her different aromas, especially that of her vagina. Describing a good female candidate for rites of spiritual sex, the text states:

> Her breath smells sweet, and her perspiration smells pleasant like musk. Her lotuslike vagina has the subtle fragrance of the blue lotus but can instantly change to that of a pink lotus. The scent of her sexual discharge is exceedingly fragrant and delightfully varied.

Medical science only recently discovered that, like animals, humans have a tiny area within the nose that reads and reacts to the body's sexual scents or pheromones. This highly sensitive organ, within the tip of the nose and quite separate from our normal olfactory sense, is both species- and gender-specific, meaning it picks up only human pheromones of the opposite sex. What we experience as sexual attraction is largely driven by our receptivity to certain pheromones or sexual scents. In most people, it is an entirely unconscious phenomena.

More often than not, modern women seek to mask their natural scent with deodorants, or perfumes, the ingredients of which are nowadays invariably synthetic. If a woman is healthy, her own natural sexual scents should be a turn-on for her partner. They are an important part of her sacramental and magical power. Tantra teaches that such assets should be used, not masked.

In the Tantric view, both female and male sexual scents are keys that unlock the doors to erotic passion and empower fulfilling and lasting spiritual sex experiences. Some Tantric texts recommend the use of specific natural oils and fragrances to augment rather than mask sexual scents: for women, musk, patchouli, and jasmine are particularly recommended, and for man, camphor, sandalwood, and ambergris.

It is the view of mainstream science that sex cells are generated specifically for the purpose of reproduction. Sex cells are either small and very competitive mobile units that become sperm or large immobile ones that become eggs. Sperm and egg contain tremendous latent potential and when they connect together, physical transformations take place and spiritual forces are awakened. Tantra recognizes the potent creative power of sperm and egg, in all their different manifestations. They are referred to as "the powers of the white and the red."

The male ejaculate with live sperms is alkaline. Sperm goes through many different stages in its creation. Every part of a man's body contributes to its production: the food he digests, the air he breathes, genetic data, his thoughts and his natural spirituality—all are integral.

Sperm is produced mostly by the seminal vesicles, the prostate, and Cowper's gland. Calcium, iron, phosphorus, magnesium, sodium, potassium, chloride, ammonia, ascorbic acid, citric acid, lactic acid, phosphatase, fructose, cholesterol, urea, proteins, amino acids, multivitamins, hormones, pheromones, and a myriad of micronutrients are found in healthy semen, which Tantra views as a man's most precious possession.

Many men waste their sperm through casual sex, expelling it carelessly, thoughtlessly. We tend to view ejaculate as "yucky," as something to be washed off after sex. Ejected semen is commonly flushed down the toilet or thrown in the trash in condoms without so much as a thought. It is treated as a waste product; yet it is a scientific fact that sperms are living organisms that continue to survive for many, many hours after ejaculation. They commonly live for forty-eight hours in the moist, warm body of a woman, but they have been known to stay alive for as long as eight days.

Scientific tests done by Cleve Backster (one of the main developers of the polygraph lie-detector test) have shown that, until it finally dies, ejaculated sperm maintains a subtle psychophysical connection with its "owner," rather like a child with its mother. If, for example, a sperm is burned with acid, other ejected sperms from the same man will show a reaction, even though kept far removed. Interestingly, sperms also "fight" if brought into contact with sperms from another man. These fascinating facts, recently demonstrated by modern science and in a BBC TV series on reproduction, drive the logic of certain rites of Tantric magic that use semen.

In Tantric tradition, sperm is sacred, a sacrament. Semen is highly nourishing and has potent antibiotic and vitalizing properties. Many different tribal people view it as a sacred substance, rubbing it on the body in initiation rituals or for psychic protection, eating it as a sacrament, and so forth.

Sperm is a relatively easily renewable resource, whereas the female egg is not. A normal man's ejaculate contains around five hundred million sperm but a woman's body readies a single egg each month. Her monthly menstruation is part of the process of egg "renewal." In Tantra, as with the Gnostic Christians, menstrual blood is, like sperm, viewed as a sacrament.

There is an almost universal taboo about menstrual blood in patriarchal cultures. Menstrual blood is commonly viewed as polluting, yet it consists of the disintegrated ovum, the lining of the uterus, vaginal cells, valuable nourishing products, lecithin, and prostaglandins, as well as potent antitoxins and rejuvenating substances such as refined and potentized iron and arsenic.

Human excretus is, according to Tantric teachings, likened to the ashes of a sacred fire. If we digest our food properly, the excretus will be very minimal. The excretus of a healthy person who is careful with diet should smell good. It's because we generally combine foods with more consideration for taste than for digestion that in modern times excretus is commonly so unpleasant. Other reasons are overeating, excessive stress or eating at inappropriate times.

For those truly living the Tantric lifestyle, their excreta should be minimal and smell fragrant. We are what we eat, or, to be more precise, we are what we digest. Wise use of resins, fruit, herbs, and select spices totally eradicates the potential for viral contamination in human excretus.

Sacred pills given out by high Tibetan Lamas during special rites of initiation are known as "nectar pills." Texts state these should be made from special herbs and minerals (usually myrobalan and purified mercury and sulfur—cinnabar), together with the five nectars—saliva, urine, sexual discharge, menstrual blood, and excreta.

At its best, small doses of human excretus can have some valuable qualities, notably immune-strengthening ones, which is why it is included as one of the five Tantric nectars. In the West, patented and proven pharmaceutical products, such as the Swedish-made Ventrux-Acido are beneficial because of the intestinal bioculture *(Streptococcus faecium)* they contain.

The Baul Rites and Sex at Menstruation

Rabindranath Tagore (1861–1941), the Indian poet and author from Bengal, wrote on Hindu philosophical themes. His Nobel prize for literature, awarded in 1913, helped Hindu culture become better known in the West.

Tagore loved to associate with the Bauls, who are radical minstrels from Bengal whose enigmatic songs deal with Tantra, sexuality, life, and the pursuit of spiritual liberation. In the 1960s, American beat poet Allen Ginsberg and folk and pop singer Bob Dylan both had friendships with Bauls, bringing some of them to America.

The Bauls of Bengal have what is known as the three-day rite, which takes place at the onset of a woman's menstrual period. Meticulous cleanliness is kept, and diet is checked, with heavy proteins such as meat, fish and lentils, as well as garlic, onions, and strong spices being avoided. Lamps are lit together with incense, flowers are offered, and a Tantric type of lovemaking takes place over a period of three days.

Parts of the body are anointed with minute amounts of feces, sometimes mixed with some yellow turmeric paste, as a symbolic gesture of overcoming outward aversions and of inward dualities. There is also the belief that this helps the body, strengthening immunity. Small amounts of urine, menstrual fluid, semen, and female sexual secretions are mixed together with ashes from the sacred fire, milk, camphor and yogurt, or wine, and drunk as a sacrament. A Baul ecstatic song declares:

> By practicing these rites,
> All suffering will be overcome!

It is a fact that most female mammals have sex only when they are in heat, close to the time of menstruation. In most cultures, a menstruating woman is considered unclean. Tantrics seek to remove this superstition, which has been used for so long and in so many patriarchal cultures to manipulate and control women at the time when they are most potent sexually.

Some Tantras recommend sexual interactions at the time of a woman's menstruation, with partners being fortified by intoxicants such as red wine to break down inhibitions and taking part in mutual oral-genital acts, including prolonged licking of the consort's clitoris, sucking the vaginal lips, "drinking her secretions" together with urine sipping, and a general atmosphere of childlike, playful daring.

Obviously, in today's reality of AIDS and sexually transmitted diseases, such a scenario can be considered only if partners are absolutely sure about each other's sexual history and lifestyles and with a lot of emphasis on hygiene. Because so many Tantras, both Hindu and Buddhist, tell or hint at the great significance and value of partaking of the five nectars or sacraments of sex, one must accept them to be a genuine secret.

The *Yoni Tantra* is very explicit about the value of intercourse at the time of woman's menstruation and of the partaking of the special sacraments. The following quotation is very clear, without the normal obscuration found in many other works:

> Having seen the Yoni full of menses, after bathing and reciting one's Mantra 108 times, a man can become Shiva on earth. Reciting the Mantra, he should offer semen and the flowers of the Yoni (the menstrual blood). Naked and offering meat and wine, he should have intercourse with that Yoni. The Yoni water is of three types, which should be mixed with wine and offered. Mixing the secretions of Yoni and Lingam with this special water and with wine, this elixir should be sipped. Nourishing himself with it, he should caress and pleasure the Precious Lady. Pleased, by this and by the offering of clothes, perfumes, and jewels, the miraculous Great Goddess will surely bestow every power!

The Meaning of Sacrifice in Tantric Tradition

We have already understood that Hindu Tantras view repetition of mantras as a form of sacrifice. So if mantras are repeated during the sexual act and at the time of orgasm, this is an additionally potent form of sacrifice. This is another Tantric secret, a way of accessing power most efficiently.

Sacrifice is a concept familiar to all ancient spiritual systems. Whether in present-day Africa, the culture of the Old Testament, in Druidism, in ancient Greece and Rome, in Babylon, predynastic China, Sumeria, Haiti, or Brazil, sacrifice is at the core of all religious rites. Hindu Tantra views man's emission of semen at the culmination of the sexual rite as the most precious form of sacrifice. So do the Yorubas of Nigeria, as well as people from other west African tribes and others from different ancient high cultures.

In all pagan cultures, animals were sacrificed to the gods, goddesses, spirits, and ancestors. In this context, the "higher animals"—bulls, lions, elephants—were viewed as particularly fine sacrifices. The highest sacrifice of all was believed to be humans. In the Old Testament of the Judeo-Christian Bible, we read of many sacrifices, including Abraham's willingness to sacrifice his own son to the Hebrew god Jehovah.

Throughout much of the surviving tribal world—in Africa, India, and South America especially—blood sacrifice is routine. Some Tantric practitioners still offer blood sacrifices on occasions, such as during the *Nava Ratri* festival at the autumnal equinox, when various creatures (especially buffaloes and goats) are beheaded in the name of the Great Goddess Durga/Kali. But blood sacrifice is not a very common practice among evolved Tantrics, who offer fruit, vegetables, and other types of nature's precious products to the Great Goddess instead. Then there are those who offer a more mystic, more personal sacrifice—the sacrifice of living semen.

The sacrifice of living semen is one of *millions* of potential human beings. This is not to be taken lightly, for the conscious sacrifice of semen to fully satisfy the desires of the Great Goddess is the highest rite of Tantra.

Tantras teach that before such sacrifice, the semen should be potentiated by periods of conservation and must be healthy, from following correct diet and lifestyle. This higher sacrifice should occur only when the consort, who is viewed as a goddess incarnate, is herself sexually ready. Ideally, it is she who takes what she needs, when the time is ripe. The question of whether to come or not to come, then, needs no answer.

In this chapter, we have covered a lot of territory. Some of the concepts, especially the requirement that man put service of his partner first, may seem strange in this culture. But remember, for several thousand years, woman has been serving man: serving him his food and his sex, serving as the mother of "his" family. For most of this time, until very, very recently, she's had no rights, being treated as the property of her father, brother, or husband. This patriarchal attitude has caused a deep emotional and spiritual hurt that needs to be addressed.

Omraam Mikhael Aivanhov, the Bulgarian-born mystic, made the following prediction:

> Woman will transform the world. That it hasn't happened yet is because she is unaware of her mission.

Women all over the world have been claiming their rights in the last few decades. They are becoming more influential, more powerful. They are becoming economically and politically liberated. One hopes that with the aid of the new Tantric paradigm, they will be spiritually liberated as well. Only then can we expect to see Aivanhov's prediction that woman will transform the world fulfilled.

Nature is both a transforming and balancing power. After every storm, there is calm; after the hurricane or the floods, there is new

An intimate couple. Their bodies are intertwined as one. Wood carving from west Africa.

growth. Tantra, which is nature's secret science, is based on the balancing of opposites. Male and female energies and attributes, heat and cold, expansion and contraction, and a myriad of other opposites need to be well balanced for our spiritual evolution to proceed properly.

Male–female interactions also need to be balanced, not one-sided. Tantra teaches that just as the vulva is to be worshipped, so is the penis. If woman is to be treated as goddess incarnate, man must act and be treated as a living god. Only then can the right atmosphere be created for spiritual sex to bear its fruits.

Sacrifice is part of the balancing process. We serve one another, and by so doing, we sacrifice in many different ways. We sacrifice our selfishness and are left with selflessness, a higher spiritual quality. In the Tantric tradition, we sacrifice the fruit of our sex, when it is ripe, and we gain both worldly and spiritual powers.

7 THE MAGIC OF SPIRITUAL SEX

The significant act was of sexual union, understood as a rite in sympathetic mystical accord with the continuing creative act, now and forever in process, of the world becoming.

—JOSEPH CAMPBELL, *Mythologies of the Great Hunt*

SEX CAN be a magical and mystical experience. Since the beginning of spiritual awareness, mortal humans have sought to become one with the divine, to become all-knowing, spiritually powerful, perfect. Tantra teaches that divinity is found within. We don't need to search outside; divinity is at the core of our being, a spiritual light that manifests as a mystical and magical divine fire.

Tantra teaches that the body is a sacred shrine to the divine, a microcosm, or complete miniuniverse that is the reflex or mirror of the macrocosm, the universe at large. One of the first steps on the path of Tantra is "worship in the temple of the body," which is worship of the divinity within. This chapter relates some different forms of Tantric worship that can often result in the awakening of powerful magical powers.

The Magical Myriam Cult and Its Tantric Secret

Within both man and woman is an erotic power or fire that can be evoked. Tantra teaches how, through breathing and meditation practices, this spiritual fire can be induced to blaze up in a controlled and contained way and can be used creatively to empower one's spiritual evolution and refine consciousness.

The inner erotic spiritual fire of Tantric tradition has tremendous magical potential, meaning it has unlimited and inexplicable power. It is the power of the Great Goddess, and a hot or sexually ripe woman is its physical embodiment.

Giuliano Kremmerz is the pseudonym of Ciro Formisano, an Italian nineteenth-century occultist who promoted the cult of the Myriam, which he defined as the mystical "holy wisdom fire" embodied in woman.

According to Kremmerz, every man has his own special woman or Myriam, a kind of magical initiatory muse who can help bring about his spiritual integration. He also spoke of the magic fire of sensual ecstasy, called by him *pyr*, which can be ignited between man and woman and can awaken the highest spiritual powers from deep within.

The Myriam rites practiced within the Kremmerz cult incorporated Dianism, in which erotic charge was built up and sublimated. The techniques that Kremmerz taught "to keep the holy fire burning strongly and to fuel it" were surely taken from both Cathar and Tantric traditions.

Initiates of the Kremmerz cult slept with their special woman, treating her as a divinity, serving her and doing everything possible to please her. Erotic gazes, caresses, kisses, "breath-drinking," and intimate embraces were part of the highly stimulating repertoire of techniques of sexual dalliance used by members of the Myriam cult.

Adepts were taught to inhale a woman's breath in specific ways, accompanied by contemplation of its special scent and mystic qualities. This is reminiscent of techniques outlined in such Tantric texts as the *Swara Tantra*, which states:

> While embracing the lady, inhale by the right nostril the air coming from her left nostril. He should savor the sweet scent of her exhaled air, contemplating it to be endowed with initiatory qualities. He should practice this secret rite between the hours of midnight and three A.M., to get the most benefit. This will cause her to bestow magical powers on him. And if he has her inhale with

her left nostril the air from his right nostril, she will become in-
fatuated with him.

Followers of the Kremmerz cult sought to awaken and be magically empowered by the erotic charge created by such sexual practices. Not much is known about the culmination or results of the
cult's practices, except that "alchemical transformations" and the
"mysteries of mercury and sulfur" were their focus.

Now in alchemical parlance, *mercury* means "refined semen"
and *sulfur* is both menstrual blood and female sexual discharge, referred to in some Indian Tantric texts as *rajas*. Tantra teaches that
sulfur and mercury—female and male sexual discharge—when carefully refined and combined knowledgeably, produce magical substances that can convey mystical powers.

Tirumular, a Siddha Yogi and alchemist who lived in south India
some time in the seventh century C.E., wrote a book of Tantric secrets
called *Tirumantiram*. In the section on "inner alchemy," he declares
male semen (*velli* in the Tamil language) to be the "essence of the
moon" and the "inner silver." He says that female discharge (*pon*) is
the "essence of the sun" and the "inner gold." In this text, Tirumular explains that spiritual sex is the blending of lunar and solar substances within the "alchemical vessel," which is the human body.
Magical powers and self-realization are the result.

The magic of spiritual sex is the most difficult aspect to write
about. Why? Because it is so easily misunderstood. Over the course
of history, there have been so many sensationalized accounts of sexual magic, so many half-truths and distortions and claims, so much
mystification.

Alchemical and medical Tantric texts tell us that the correct
combination of purified sulfur and mercury produces *siddha makradwaj*. Made from "sublimate" of mercury and sulfur combined
with other ingredients, this is a potent immune-system strength-
ener, a vitalizing tonic, aphrodisiac, and rejuvenating medicine. It is
also credited with aiding longevity and is one of the most guarded
secrets of Siddha Yogis and Yoginis.

Supernatural Acts and Magical Powers

Tantras commonly list six supernatural acts (sat karma) attained by proficiency in secret rites. These are:

> Propitiation of bad karma—from previous births or negative celestial influence—including all acts of healing (shanti).
>
> The power to stop the action of any person through his or her body or mind (stambhana).
>
> The power to make any person subservient and bring him or her under control (vashikarana).
>
> The ability to magically cause separation by creating ill feeling (vidvesana).
>
> The ability to torment, through the creation of pain, shame, or discomfort (uccatana).
>
> The power to kill an enemy by magical means (marana).

Mantras, yantras, mystic gestures, breath control, and visualization are used to acquire the ability to perform these supernatural acts.

A common component of many Tantras are vashikarana formulas that are credited with the power to magically control, fascinate, or bewitch someone of the opposite sex. There are literally thousands of such formulas in Tantric texts. Use of semen or menstrual blood, nail clippings or pubic hair, cremation dust, and so on, empowered by recitation of specific mantras for a specific number of times, is common. The empowered article, mixed in food or drink, is secretly given to the person whom one wants to affect.

Texts and traditions declare that Tantrics can acquire various magical powers (siddhis). These are normally obtained by developing metaphysical concentration (dharana), practicing meditation (dhyana), and perfecting equanimity (samadhi).

Irresistible will, dominion over the elements, reducing or increasing one's size, invisibility, longevity, lightness and levitation, and fulfilment of any desire are some of the siddhis obtainable through proficiency in Tantra. No wonder Tantrics have been feared.

Tantric Sex Rites in the Emperor's Palace

During the early period of Mongol rule in China in the late thirteenth century, Kublai Khan established his capital in Peking and had foreign advisors, one of whom was Marco Polo. This was when the Tantric cult of sexual energy was introduced into Kublai's court. The following is a contemporaneous account of the sexual rites performed in the emperor's palace:

> The Emperor practiced the secret method known as "Discipline in Pairs," which are arts of the bedchamber. He summoned Indian Tantrics to direct the ceremonies. They all took several girls of good families for the practice of these disciplines, which they called "sacrifice." The Emperor daily followed these practices, with numerous women and girls, and found his joy this way. He selected some from among his concubines and had them perform the Dance of the Sixteen Dakini and Consorts. The sixteen girls who participated in this sacred dance wore ivory crowns, long red and gold tasseled robes, had their hair braided in very many long tresses, and held skull-bowls in their hands. The Emperor's brothers and his close companions all took part in these rites, naked and in intimate embraces, performed in front of the Supreme Ruler.

This colorful account, written by one of the Emperor's favorites, suggests that the magical rites of sacred sex had been introduced to China directly from India.

An Early European Account of Tantric Sexual Rites

In 1807, Abbé Dubois, a French missionary and traveler throughout India, finished his manuscript *Hindu Manners, Customs and Ceremonies*, which though filled with inaccuracies, contained some valuable material. His publication was probably the first account written in a European language of the Hindu Tantric sexual rite known as *Shakti puja* (the worship of Shakti, the female power). Abbé Dubois gave his version of the sacred Hindu ceremony, but could not resist judging it an orgy:

The ceremony takes place at night with more or less secrecy. The least disgusting of these orgies are those where they confine themselves to eating and drinking everything that the custom of the country forbids, and where men and women, huddled together in indiscriminate confusion, openly and shamelessly violate the commonest laws of decency and modesty. . . . Under certain circumstances, the principal objects which form the sacrifice to Shakti are a large vessel full of native rum and a full-grown girl. The latter, stark naked, remains standing in a most indecent attitude. The goddess Shakti is evoked, and is supposed to respond to the invitation to come and take up her abode in the vessel full of rum and also in the girl's body. A sacrifice of flowers, incense, sandalwood, colored rice, and a lighted lamp is then offered to these two objects. . . . As usual the meeting winds up with the most revolting orgy.

Dubois's account correctly outlines the basic scenario of Goddess worship in the Hindu Tantric tradition; however, he chose to take a sex-negative view of what is clearly a celebratory sexomagical scenario similar to those performed by the early "heretical" Christian sects. After accurately describing the magical Tantric ritual known as *Shakti puja*, he makes the mistake of characterizing it as a "revolting orgy."

There are two basic varieties of Hindu Tantric Goddess worship, referred to as *kumari puja* and *Shakti puja*. Both are rather similar in structure; however, the first type does *not* involve any sexual contact, whereas the second may. Both of these important rites have tremendous magical implications that should not be overlooked when embarking on the path of Tantra.

We'll take a look at both types of Tantric Goddess worship because versions of these rites could so easily be incorporated into the modern lifestyle. Why not exalt and "worship" woman openly, as part of spiritual culture? Why not recognize the goddess living within every woman? For far too long, worship in the West has been exclusively male-oriented, directed to the "Heavenly Father" without regard for the female divine powers. The time has come for this situation to be corrected.

Virgin Worship and Goddess Worship

The Sanskrit word *kumari* means "virgin girl." In India, as in other "pagan" cultures, sex is exalted and honored in all aspects. Tradition has it that *all* deities and spiritual powers are pleased with *kumari puja*. Because they are pleased, they grant favors, prayers, boons, and powers.

Puja translates as "worship." Yet *puja* actually means the ancient matriarchal tribal style of spiritual rite, involving offerings of sensual and worldly things. *Puja* is the Tantric way of pleasing divine powers. In the Tantric tradition, the effectiveness of *all* other

A *kumari* or sacred virgin, dressed up and wearing elaborate Tantric makeup. Contemporary event in Kathmandu, Nepal.

spiritual procedures, such as repetition of mantras and sacrifices, and all magical rites, are enhanced by performing *kumari puja*. Contrary to so many biased Western accounts, *kumari puja* does not involve any sexual activity.

In this rite, a maiden or virgin girl is honored and entertained. A *virgin* is meant to be a young woman who has had no sexual interaction with man. A *kumari* is defined as a pure girl between five and twelve years of age who has yet to have her first menstrual period. A girl ideally aged seven, eight, or nine is selected and treated like a princess. She is placed on a high chair or podium and sensual things—flowers, incense, perfume, makeup, sweets, a silk scarf or dress, a mirror, jewelry, and so on—are offered her. She is fêted. Music is played, as *puja* is performed in her honor as the young virginal embodiment of the Great Goddess.

She might sing or dance or laugh or cry. Whatever she does is seen as a blessing, as the playful yet empowering activity of a young goddess. Anything she touches and returns to the worshippers is considered to be empowered. Some Tantric texts advise giving her thread to spin or cloth to weave. The thread will be used to string beads for mantra recitation or for tying protective amulets. Anything woven or prepared by a *kumari* will be treated as sacred, used to contain ritual items, or employed in sacred rites.

Kumari puja is followed by a feast for the Great Goddess, which culminates in the presentation of a fee to the girl, traditionally in gold, silver, or pearls. The greatest benefit of *kumari puja* is thus believed to come about if the girl is subsequently sponsored to aid her future, such as for her ongoing education or marriage.

Shakti puja is another form of Great Goddess worship. There are numerous varieties, but in every one of them, a sexually mature woman is the object of veneration. The texts state that ideally a woman should be chosen for this rite who is "endowed with special qualities." She is highly honored, "worshipped" with the five sensual types of offerings—things related to the enjoyment of the five senses—and feasted with her choice of food, drink, and whatever else she desires.

The Shakti or "living goddess" can be young, single, married, with or without children. In each instance, she represents the Great Goddess and is honored as such. As far as is possible, her wishes are followed. When she is pleased by the offerings made to her and responsive to the "worship," she is asked for boons, which commonly manifest in the form of spontaneous magical acts. These can take different forms but commonly are specific gestures, looks, even verbalizations. *Shakti puja* may or may not culminate in sex. This depends entirely on the "living goddess" herself, who will let it be known what her wishes are.

Shakti puja has been badly misinterpreted by Western writers. This beautiful spiritual rite has been treated as a decadent excuse for a feast, for an orgy. More often that not, *Shakti puja* takes place one-on-one or among a very limited number of intimate devotees. On special occasions, however, such as particular phases of the moon or at the autumn or spring equinoxes, this Tantric rite may involve a larger number of participants, where the assembly of the sacred Chakra take part in the sacraments of sex communally.

An English Churchman's Account of Tantric Sex

Following Dubois, the Reverend William Ward described various aspects of Hindu Tantra. He referred to Tantras as texts and even mentioned the sacred Chakra circle of initiates. He pointed to the differences between "right-handed" and "left-handed" sexual rites in Tantric tradition, but considered them both shocking. Though he was judgmental in his bias and his use of Sanskrit terminology was inaccurate, Ward did describe rarely seen Hindu Tantric rites:

> Many of the Tuntrus [Tantras] contain directions respecting a most extraordinary and shocking mode of worship, which is understood in a concealed manner among the Hindus by the name of Chukra [Chakra]. These Shastrus [*shastras*] direct that the person who wishes to perform this ceremony must first, in the night, choose a woman as the object of worship. If the person be a *dukshinacharee*, he must take his own wife; and if a *vamacharee*, the daughter of a dancer, a *kupalee*, a washerwoman, a barber, a *chandalu*, or of a prostitute; and place her on a seat or mat; and then bring broiled fish, flesh, fried peas, rice, spirituous liquors, sweetmeats, flowers, and other offerings, which as well as the female must be purified by the repeating of incantations. To this

succeeds the worship of the guardian deity; and after this, that
of the female, who sits naked. . . . She [the woman] partakes of
the offerings, even of the spirituous liquors; and of the flesh. . . .
The priest then—in the presence of all—behaves towards this female in a manner which decency forbids to be mentioned; after
which the persons present repeat many times the name of god,
performing actions unutterably abominable and here, this most
diabolical business closes.

Ward's account was the start of puritanical reportage about
Tantric sex in the English language. As a direct result of such ac-
counts, Tantra came to be viewed as decadent and demonic by most
Victorian Britishers and by many Western-educated Indians.

Fivefold Sexual Rites

Hindu Tantra has a "high rite," referred to as the rite of the five
essentials or the *pancha makara*. We'll look at the details of this important rite shortly. However, before we do, it will be valuable and
relevant to become familiar with other sexual rites and how they
were first recounted by Westerners.

In the 1830s, a young English army officer by the name of Edward Sellon (1818—1866) wrote about Tantric sexual rites in India,
describing them as shocking. This was the same author who wrote
several crude pornographic novels, publishing them without
apology.

Sellon spent ten years in India. His "serious" work, *Annotations
Upon the Sacred Writings of the Hindus*, was published in 1865. His
interpretation of Indian Tantricism was crude and his Sanskrit corrupt, but he did accurately recount some of the basic tenets and
practices of sexual Tantra. He wrote:

All the principal ceremonies comprehend the worship of Sacti, or
POWER, and require, for that purpose, the presence of a young
and beautiful girl, as the living representative of the goddess. This
worship is mostly celebrated in a mixed society; the men of
which represent Bhairavas, or Viras, and the women, Bhairavis
and Nayikas. The Sacti is personified by a naked girl, to whom

meat and wine are offered, and then distributed among the assistants. Here follows the chanting of the Muntrus and sacred texts, and the performance of the Mudra, or gesticulations with the fingers. The whole terminates with orgies amongst the votaries of a very licentious description. This ceremony is entitled SHRI CHAKRA, or PURNABISHEKA, THE RING or full initiation.

The Kauchiluas are another branch of the Sactas sect; their worship much resembles that of the Caulas. They are, however, distinguished by one particular rite not practiced by the others, and throw into confusion all the ties of female relationship; natural restraints are wholly disregarded, and a community of women among the votaries inculcated.

On the occasions of the performance of divine worship, the women and girls deposit their julies, or bodices, in a box in charge of the Guru, or priest. At the close of the rites, the male worshippers take each a julie from the box, and the female to whom it belongs, even were she his sister, becomes his partner for the evening in these lascivious orgies.

Later, he refers to worship of the female and male sex organs, the Yoni and the Lingam:

The worship of Sacti (as already observed) is the adoration of POWER, which the Hindus typify by the Yoni, or womb, the Argha or Vulva, and by the leaves and flowers of certain plants thought to resemble it. Thus in the Ananda Tantram, c.vi., verse 13, we find an allusion to the Aswattha, or sacred fig-tree (the leaf of which is in the shape of a heart, and much resembles the conventional form of the Yoni, to which it is compared). . . .

In the mental adoration of Sacti a diagram is framed, and the figure imagined to be seen inside the Vulva. This is the Adhamukham, or lower face, i.e., the Yoni, wherein the worshipper is to imagine (mantapan) a chapel to be erected.

All forms of Sacti Puja require the use of some or all of the five Makaras: Mansa, Matsya, Madya, Maithuna, and Mudra, that is flesh, fish, wine, women, and certain mystical twistings or gesticulations with the fingers.

Such are some of the peculiar features of the worship of POWER (or Gnosticism) and which, combined with the Linga

Puja (or adoration of the Phallus), constitutes at the present day
one of the most popular dogmas of the Hindus.

Following this colorful description, Edward Sellon comments
that ''Sacteya ideas have found their way into the monasteries and
convents of Italy!''

Sellon's 1865 description of these Tantric sexual rites are remarkably similar to accounts of European ''witches' Sabbaths''
practiced by followers of Wicca or paganism. The common ingredients are worship of a naked woman and/or her vagina as the embodiment of the Great Goddess, adoration of the penis, feasting with
meat and wine, gesticulations, repetition of magical power phrases,

A high priestess of Hindu Tantric
tradition, depicted with three
heads, wrathful yet erotic, and
holding a human skull-bowl. She
is seated upon a crawling naked
man, identified as a high-caste
Brahmin by his hair tuft.
Miniature painting from
Rajasthan, India, circa
eighteenth century.

general lascivious behavior or sexual abandon, promiscuousness, and the attainment of supernatural powers. Add to this the common theme of meetings held at midnight or later, circular gatherings around a central high priestess or guru figure (who might well wear a horned headdress), and a high altar with sacrifices. Such scenarios have generally been defined as ungodly orgies with no redeeming features. No wonder Tantra has acquired a bad name.

The Cult of the Sexual Circle

In her 1936 book *The Secrets of the Kaula Circle*, Elizabeth Sharpe categorically states that "the cult of the circle is already in vogue in Europe, in secret places" and details the extraordinary story of Mary de la Mont (a pseudonym), who married an Indian Tantric Yogi-Lama at the age of 26 and lived in India for many years, leaving a diary and other writings at her death.

Sharpe described the magical rites of the Tantra circle as follows:

> The "Kaula" circle is the circle of the worshippers of the left-hand path, whose secret none but they of this circle have known till now. In this circle, the woman is the "mother"—but all her desires are fulfilled: that is the vow.
>
> Few women come through the ordeal pure, unstained: for it is believed that the husband is born of the mother, and the mother and the wife are interchangeable terms in the circle.
>
> The outer court of the temple of the goddess was heaped with raw flesh, fish, and these, with wine, were given to those of the outer circle.
>
> Man after man, woman after woman passed by me, singing, reeling and dead drunk. . . .
>
> I, still, remember that inner courtyard: stark naked men and women, who, from time to time, with excruciating yells, leapt to their feet, shaking their heads backwards and forwards, the women with loosened locks falling in black disorder about their heaving, shaking breasts.
>
> A voice would then cry out in deepest scorn the sonorous

Sanskrit Tantrik verse: "Let their desires be satisfied." And there would be a perfect orgy of bestiality.

This account closely follows the style of earlier descriptions of this sacred rite by Abbé Dubois, the Reverend William Ward, Edward Sellon, and others. Like their accounts, the scenario described by Elizabeth Sharpe is highly dramatized, using loaded language (*raw flesh*, *dead drunk*, *stark naked*, *orgy of bestiality*) to create a negative bias.

It is unfortunate and unfair that virtually all Western writers' accounts of Tantric-type sexual rites have been described in similarly negative ways. The news media is another culprit, generally covering "pagan" or spiritual-sex stories with negative headlines loaded with innuendo. SEX CULT, WITCHES' COVEN UNCOVERED, NAKED ORGIES, DEVIL WORSHIPPERS, and variations of these headlines occur quite frequently. They help sell newspapers and are effective in fanning the flames of patriarchal paranoia.

Such headlines and their accompanying luridly told stories both create and maintain a hysterical atmosphere about rites of sacred sex, making mainstream acceptance of pagan practices exceedingly difficult.

With the advent of neo-Tantra as the pop religion of the twenty-first century, we can expect to see CULT OF THE SEXUAL CIRCLE newspaper headlines. It's inevitable that there will be incidents generating press coverage.

Freedom of religious expression is our inalienable right. When groups of Goddess devotees gather for sexual celebrations, they are following time-tested spiritual traditions that once existed in most cultures. Just as political emancipation and women's rights have finally become accepted, so, eventually, must spiritual-sex rites.

"Right-" and "Left-handed" Tantric Rites

In traditional Hindu Tantra, what is commonly referred to as "right-handed" (*daksina*) rites do not generally result in actual sex. These are symbolic rites of sacrifice, usually performed only by a couple married under the Brahma type of ceremony, the woman sitting to the right of the man. The goal is an inner union, the awakening of the Kundalini Shakti, directing the energy upward through successive Chakras to union with the Shiva consciousness. This internal Yoga or union ideally results in an "inner" coming that produces what Tantra refers to as nectars.

The nectars are subtle secretions within the glandular system, triggering a series of metabolic processes that affect the midbrain. Adrenochrome, serotonin, endorphins, and a substance similar to LSD are some of the complex products naturally produced within the body by this type of Kundalini Yoga.

What are referred to as "left-handed" (*vama*) Tantric rites generally culminate in sacred sex. In these rites, the woman sits to the left of the man and participates in a series of ritual acts involving purification; offerings of sensual things, such as incense, flowers, flames of a lit lamp, and music; food, such as grains, fruit, fish, and meat; wine, liquor, and perhaps marihuana products. In such rites, the man and woman do not necessarily have to be life partners. They may only be "married" or have an agreement for the duration of the rite. They embody Shiva and Shakti, Great God and Great Goddess, and the culmination of the rite is spiritual sex.

Some Tantras emphasize that for "left-handed" rites, there should be an unconventional choice of consort. Traditional Hindu society has for long been hierarchical, with the focus on caste; Brahmins mix only with Brahmins, workers (*sudras*) with workers, and so forth. Because true Tantric teachings are radical in approach, such caste barriers must come down and taboos must be confronted and overcome.

In *vama* or "left-handed" Tantric rites, it is recommended that unfamiliar or unconventional couples pair off: Brahmins with sweepers or washerwomen and so-called untouchables, household servants with the high-class mistress of the house, politicians with prostitutes, light-skinned with dark-skinned, and so forth. This crossing of social barriers, leveling the field of play by intermixing caste, color, and roles, has the effect of democratizing and potentiating the whole experience of spiritual sex, giving it validity and power, deeply touching all participants.

The Witches' Sabbath, Dakinis, and Sky-Flyers

The Reverend William Ward's early nineteenth-century English-language account of the Tantric worship of female Shakti power is reminiscent of European stories of the witches' Sabbath. These stories tell of secret nocturnal gatherings or witches' covens of men and women who could "fly through the air" and who performed magical sexual rites. Common themes are of a leader wearing animal horns, altars with sacrificial offerings, groups of thirteen men and women in a circle, inverted crosses, strange drugs and potions, chanting, and dancing, all culminating in wild orgies.

The Catholic church originally denied reports that witches could fly. In 1000 C.E., an official proclamation declared the flight of witches to be "an illusion produced by the devil." From the early thirteenth century onward, following the persecution of Cathars by order of the Pope, heretics were fair game. By the mid-fourteenth century, witch trials were taking place in much of Europe. After

Ritual intercourse among plants. This ancient painting on a vase from Cyprus, circa 600 B.C.E., depicts the celebratory and magical traditions of sacred sex in the culture of the Mediterranean. (In the collection of the British Museum, London, England)

1480, the Catholic church forbade anyone to doubt the truth of witches' magical flight; the church kept changing its position to suit its changing agenda.

It has been estimated that between 150,000 and 500,000 people, the majority of whom were women, were convicted of witchcraft and burned to death between the late fourteenth and seventeenth centuries. Most were tortured and "confessions" were obtained; following the burnings, all their property was confiscated by the church.

Witches' Sabbaths were supposedly held weekly, at the time of the full moon, and at the solstices and equinoxes. Evidence from folklore suggests that the witch cults of Europe were not part of a heretical or organized anti-Christian movement but were vestiges of pre-Christian pagan beliefs involving a horned god, goddesses, and sex as a sacrament, combined with Tantric magical practices introduced from the East.

It has been suggested that medieval accounts of witches flying on broomsticks come from associations with the pagan rites of the Greek lunar goddess Hecate, whose priestesses were midwives who carried brooms. Some authors suggest that witches used broomsticks as dildos in magical rites and anointed them with "witches' ointments" composed of plant drugs such as belladonna, stramo-

Sex as a sacrament: a sacred "orgy" scene from the European pre-Christian era. Drawing from a stone carving, on an Etruscan ash urn from Chiusi, Italy. (In the Louvre, Paris, France)

nium, and aconite, which, when in contact with skin, can produce sensations of flying.

Tantric beliefs, sexual practices, and magical rites were also introduced to Europe by the Romany people. These people, later known as gypsies, were Hindu Tantrics who fled Rajasthan and surrounding regions of India in the eleventh century, following repeated Moslem invasions. They settled into parts of present-day Europe, especially in Romania, Transylvania, Bulgaria, and the Balkans. Some of them became known for their skill in such occult arts as clairvoyance, fortune-telling, and "wishing."

Rajasthan was the home of several Tantric cults, notably the cult of the Dakinis, female sky-fliers or witches. The earliest Indian textual mention of the name *Tantra*, which dates from 423 c.e., is also associated with the word *Dakini*. However, just as Tantra has a far more ancient but secret history, so have Dakinis.

As previously mentioned, Damkina is the name of the "faithful wife and spiritual consort" of the Sumerian secret wisdom-deity Ea. Also known as Oannes, Ea was half man and half fish, rather like a particular incarnation of Vishnu, the Hindu god of preservation. This Sumerian concept is more than forty-five hundred years old.

The similarity of the names Dakini and Damkina, together their both being associated with wisdom powers, strongly suggests that they are versions of the same spiritual entity.

As seen in Chapter 3, in Indian Tantra, a Dakini is a special kind of magical attendant or associate of the dark goddess Kali. Like Kali, Dakinis have a twofold nature: they are exceedingly erotic and attractive, but they can also appear furious and ugly. They are the guardians and initiatresses into the occult mysteries. They can be embodied in woman or they can be a female spirit who appears in dreams or visions.

Rakini, Lakini, Kakini, Shakini and Hakini are, in Indian Tantric tradition, the specific names of Dakinis who rule over the Chakras of the subtle Yoga body. They each have three eyes and several arms (denoting their different attributes) and are color coded. As the Kundalini awakens and rises up the central "channel" of the subtle body, she transforms into each of these Dakinis, in sequence.

Indian Tantric texts tell of five aspects of Shiva the transcendental Yogi, uniting with the five Dakinis: Hari with Rakini, Rudra with

Depiction of a Bhairava or male Tantric adept as an embodiment of the wrathful Shiva, three-headed and multiarmed, seated in Yoga posture. Stone sculpture from Nepal, circa fifteenth century.

Lakini, Isha with Kakini, Sadashiva with Shakini, Shiva with Hakini. This is reminiscent of the Buddhist Tantric tradition in which persons from the "five families" unite with five different-colored Yoginis. At a certain point in the evolution of Tantra, the names Yogini and Dakini became synonymous.

The male equivalent of Dakini is Daka, who is described as a wrathful form of Shiva, also known as Ghosha or Bhairava. In Tibetan Tantric tradition, Dakas are Siddhas, meaning adepts, who are both wrathful and wise. If a Dakini is a witch, then a Daka is a male witch or wizard.

Dakas and Dakinis, Shivas and Shaktis, Bhairavas and Bhaira-vis—these are all idealized Tantric men and women who practice spiritual sex as the ultimate act of liberation and self-realization. They gathered in circles for their magical rites, and superstition has it that they could fly in the sky.

Dakinis, Shakinis, Bhairavas, and Bhairavis evoke feelings of both awe and terror among orthodox Buddhists and Hindus. Mere mention of their names creates a reaction of awe because of the spiritual achievement and supernatural magical powers connected with them, of terror because of the frightening symbols associated with them—bones, cemetery dust, human skull-bowls, and so on—and also because of their association with spirits of the dead, occultism, and witchcraft.

Tantric initiates of the Dakini cult met in circular gatherings in secluded places at specific times each month. These rites were commonly led by naked priestesses, who personified the Great Goddess and were worshipped while at the center of a circle of male and female celebrants who feasted and made love. The purpose of such rites was the pleasuring of the Great Goddess and the attainment of magical powers such as clairvoyance, clairaudience, invisibility, "flying," and longevity.

Psychedelic drugs such as datura (jimsonweed) and *charas* (a potent form of hashish), as well as wines specially fortified with herbs and resins, helped remove inhibitions and break down social barriers. They must have aided in the establishment of an intimate and magical atmosphere.

Alchemical preparations and aphrodisiacs, such as specially purified and prepared cinnabar *(siddha makradwaj)* were used, together with musk and amber, which were mixed with the sexual sacraments and consumed in the name of the transcendental Shiva and the Shakti goddess.

Gatherings of Dakinis and Dakas, Bhairavis and Bhairavas, and Yoginis and Yogis took place mostly in out-of-the way locales. Cremation grounds, forest clearings, and hilltops were especially favored. Circular stone enclosures open to the sky were built at various places in India. Known as "sixty-four-Yogini temples," they commonly have sixty or sixty-four carved-stone images of Yogini/Dakini goddesses, set into niches around a central Shiva icon. These

The Ranipur Jharial Tantric temple. This circular sacred enclosure, open to the sky, has a central image of a dancing Shiva/Bhairava surrounded by sixty-four images of Yoginis/Dakinis. Central Orissa, eastern India, circa tenth century.

temples were used as places of Tantric initiation and were used for high rites of spiritual sex.

During the many years I spent in India, I was able to visit most of the known Yogini temples. They vary in size and type of location. Hirapur, the smallest, is not far from the coast of Orissa, in eastern India. It contains exquisite carvings of Yoginis dating from the time of many important Siddhas, in the Pala dynasty (circa tenth century). The main female image is called Mahamaya, a wrathful dark-colored goddess who is normally kept covered by a veil. Ranipur Jharial, another much larger circular sixty-four-Yogini temple, is in a desertlike area of central Orissa, built atop a huge black rock. Villagers living nearby assured me that on certain nights, witchlike Dakinis could be seen flying through the air.

In her important new book, *Passionate Enlightenment: Women in Tantric Buddhism*, Miranda Shaw gives a concise overview of Tantric communal assemblies. She writes:

Tantric feasts, or communal assemblies *(ganachakra;* Tib. *tshogs kyi 'khor-lo)* are one of the paradigmatic Tantric practices. The feast is an elaborate esoteric ritual that unfolds in many stages. . . .

The participants don special insignia, like bone ornaments and crowns, and use musical instruments of archaic design— such as skull drums, thighbone trumpets, and conch horns—for inducing trance states. Practitioners sit in a circle and partake of sacramental meat and wine served in skull cups. The feasts also provide an occasion for the exchange of ritual lore, the ritual worship of women *(stripuja),* and the performances of sexual yogas. The feast culminates in the performance of Tantric dances and music that must never be disclosed to outsiders. The revelers may also improvise "songs of realization" *(caryagiti)* to express their heightened awareness and blissful raptures in spontaneous verse.

She points out that women "commonly presided over Tantric feasts and staged them alongside men," giving several historical examples.

The Hindu version of a related circle rite is known as Bhairavi Chakra. A part description is given in the *Mahanirvana Tantra,* translated and published by Arthur Avalon (Sir John Woodroffe) in his book *The Great Liberation* (1913). Excluding the lists of requirements, rituals, mantras and visualizations, the following abbreviated excerpts are particularly pertinent. Like many Tantras, it takes the form of dialogue:

Sir Devi (the Great Goddess) said:

> What is the Bhairavi Chakra, and what is the Tattva Chakra? . . .

Sri Sada Shiva (the Supreme Yogi) said:

> O Devi! In the ordinances relating to Kula worship I have spoken of the formation of Circles. That should be done by the excellent worshippers at times of special worship.

Traditional Hindu representation of a Bhairavi or Tantric witch, naked, with long hair, fangs, and a third eye. She holds a skull-bowl and is accompanied by dogs or jackals. Miniature painting from Rajasthan, India, circa eighteenth century.

O Dear One! There is no strict rule relating to the Bhairavi Chakra. This auspicious Circle may at any convenient time be formed. I will now speak of the rites relating to this Circle, which benefits the worshippers, and in which, if the Devi be worshipped, She speedily grants the prayers of Her votaries. . . .

The text describes preparation of the place and a jar, which should be worshipped as if the deity is in it. Then Ananda Bhairavi and Ananda Bhairava, youthful Yogic forms of the Great Goddess and Great God who are identified with the human couple performing the rite, are evoked and worshipped. Wine is sanctified with mantra, followed by other ritualistic ingredients, also sanctified. Shiva then says:

> In this Circle there is no distinction of caste nor impurity of food. The Vira (heroic) worshippers in the circle are My image; there is no doubt of that. In the formation of this Circle there is no rule as to time or place or question as to fitness. The necessary articles may be used by whomsoever they may have been brought. Every kind of food becomes pure immediately when it is brought within the Chakra. . . .

After declaring that in this Circle "each should follow his own calling" and giving assurance that by one year's practice of this rite "one will conquer death," Shiva goes on to describe the *Tattva Chakra:*

> It is called the Divine Circle. . . . A devout believer in Brahman should be Lord of the Circle. . . . O Great Queen! There is no rule of caste in the Brahma Circle, nor rule as to place or time or worthiness. . . . Therefore should those excellent worshippers perform the rites of the Tattva Circle with every care for the attainment of spiritual merit, fulfillment of desire, wealth, and Liberation!

In 1921, Margaret Murray, an Egyptologist, published her book, *The Witch Cult in Western Europe.* She argued that European witchcraft was an organized cult with origins in ancient times. Her follow-up book, *The God of the Witches* (1931), further developed her ideas, which rapidly gained a following. In 1949, Gerald Gardner, a self-proclaimed British witch, published *High Magic's Aid,* which gave details of witchcraft rites and practices. He followed with *Witchcraft Today* (1954) and *The Meaning of Witchcraft* (1959), in which he introduced the concept of Wicca, the neo-pagan religion of modern witchcraft.

Writing in *The Woman's Encyclopedia of Myths and Secrets* (1983) and referring to writings of Naomi Goldenberg, Barbara Walker gives the following very concise overview of how Western witchcraft or Wicca theology differs from Christianity:

1. The female principle is deified, equal to, or greater than the male.
2. Body and soul are seen as one and the same; one cannot exist without the other.
3. Nature is sacred, not to be abused or "conquered."
4. The individual will has intrinsic value and is not to be subordinated to the "revealed" will of a deity.
5. Time is circular and repetitive; existence is cyclical; the figures of the Triple Goddess symbolize constant repetitions of growth and decay.
6. There is no original sin, and no hard-and-fast separation of "good" and "evil."
7. Sexuality, spontaneity, humor, and play activities may be incorporated into ritual, where the experience of pleasure is regarded as a positive force in life, rather than a temptation or a sin.

With a few additions, such as recognition of the immortality of the soul, the laws of karma, the efficacy of mantras, and body worship *(kaya sadhana)*, these seven beliefs are those of the Tantric tradition.

Today, most neo-pagans follow variations of Wicca teachings. Wicca is a booming cult with many similarities to neo-Tantra. Surveys done in the 1940s produced the amazing estimate that "half the literate white population in the world today believe in witchcraft," and a 1978 Gallup poll estimated that ten percent of Americans believe in witches. If a poll were done today, the figure would most likely be higher, depending on how one defines *witchcraft* and *witches.*

There are literally hundreds of pagan, neo-pagan, and Wicca Web sites on the Internet. See the last chapter, "Tantra Database," to explore this fascinating phenomenon.

Magical Methods in the Tantric Tradition

Tantras teach that supernatural influences may be controlled or transformed by means of worship *(puja)*. In most instances, it is a matter of recognizing the influence, knowing its name and the secret mantras for propitiating it, and knowing what it likes.

Tantra teaches that until we wake up and take charge of our own destiny, we are influenced by the cosmos. Constellations and planets are believed to have influence on karmic situations, meaning the situation in which one finds oneself as a result of some past action; therefore, constellations and planets are propitiated.

The "nine planets" of Indian and Tantric tradition (Hindu and Buddhist) are not precisely the same heavenly bodies we refer to as planets in Western cultures. Special emphasis is on the sun and moon, which are first and second among the nine. Mars, Mercury, Jupiter, Venus, and Saturn are five more planets. Then there is the "dragon's head" (known as Rahu, which is the "ascending node") and the "dragon's tail" (known as Ketu, the "descending node"). Tantra teaches that all these nine important planetary influences, which are thought of as personalities, are linked to and can be propitiated by wearing specific gemstones.

Among the various gemstones linked to the nine planets are rubies (the sun), pearls (the moon), coral (Mars), emeralds (Mercury), yellow sapphires (Jupiter), diamonds (Venus), blue sapphires (Saturn), hessonite (Rahu), and cat's-eye (Ketu). Constellational astrology, in which a person's entire horoscope is consulted, is used by Tantrics to broaden the effectiveness of gem magic. Once the right combination of fine-quality gemstones is chosen, a special piece of jewelry or amulet can be made, empowered, and worn.

Propitiation of planetary influences is

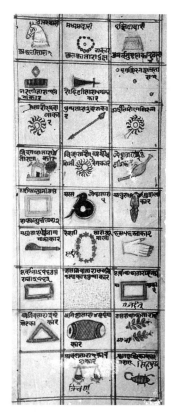

Hindu chart depicting constellations believed to govern individual destiny; 27 constellations are considered especially significant. Manuscript from central India, circa seventeenth century.

best effected by empowering the gemstones with instance-specific mantras, meaning mantras selected to achieve specific ends. In the case of planetary propitiation, the required number of repetitions (*japa*) of the mantra for it to be effective is one thousand times the period of a particular planet. For example, the secret books declare that the sun has a period of six years, so six thousand repetitions of the selected mantra should be recited.

The same tradition has it that negative planetary influences can be propitiated by fire sacrifice of specific ingredients. These are things that the planet "likes" or "eats," such as certain grains, oils, fruits, fragrant incense, and so forth. The number of times that articles should be offered into the fire should be one tenth the number of repetitions specific to each planet. For example, in the case of the sun, which requires six thousand repetitions of its mantra, there should be six hundred oblations into the fire.

This type of planetary and constellational gem therapy is an exact Tantric science. It is alive and well even today. In Asia, it is considered routine to consult a specialist in planetary gemology if one wishes to positively influence one's destiny. Seven- or nine-jewel talismans, referred to as *kavacas* (meaning "armor"), are considered to be highly effective in Tantric tradition.

Magical rites of propitiation can employ written mantras. They are written with specific types of ink (saffron, milk, soot, blood of different kinds, and so on), on specific types of material (birch bark, paper of certain kinds, cloth, skins), with particular types of pens (feather, bone of different kinds, metals), and can be worn or written on the body, eaten, placed at strategic locations, and so on. There is no end to the varieties of procedures and materials employed in Tantric magic.

Correspondences are considered to exist between the body and the outer world. The nine planets are, in some Tantric traditions, linked to the nine orifices of the body, to nine sentiments, and to nine metals. Certain types

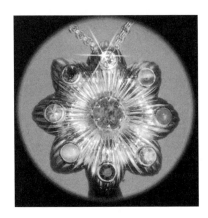

Contemporary nine-gem Tantric talisman.

Tantric magical love charm with male and female figures linked by a common scepter *(vajra)* and the seed mantra *hum*. From a Tibetan Woodblock print.

of breaths, gazes, gestures, meditations, and mantras may be used to reinforce or empower the effect.

Mantra and yantra are key to the propitiation or transformation of negative influences. In Tantric tradition, there is a complex lore of correspondences used to bring about resonance so the desired effect can be rapidly achieved.

This is not the place to get into great detail about the multitude of substances used in Tantric rites or their myriad applications. But dipping into a rather typical Tantric text, we would find mention of semen, menstrual blood, nail clippings, nose dirt, earwax, mother's milk, camphor, excretus, cemetery dust, urine, teeth of certain kinds, bones, shells, hair of innumerable types (person, cat, dog, camel, elephant, to name but a few), burned clothing, oils of every type, lamp soot, herbs, leaves, threads of every color, powder of burned ants, bees, parts of crows, metals of every kind, fruits, flowers—the list could go on forever. All such substances are, in Tantric tradition, used with magical intent, empowered with mantras to bring about precise effects. This is sorcery at its most thorough.

Tradition has it that magical charms, if well chosen, work because of natural correspondences—the "doctrine of signatures," a type of radionics—and because of their natural cosmic resonance. Their success also surely depends largely on the spiritual attainments and powers of the Tantric charm preparer.

Tantric magic has been known to work wonders. It can also be like fool's gold, illusory, good for nothing but fuel for superstition.

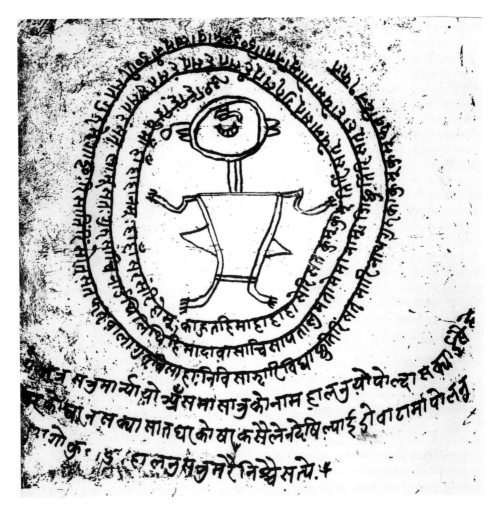

Magical charm composed of a central figure encircled by mantras and invocations. From Nepal, ink on paper, circa nineteenth century.

Obviously, great discrimination needs to be brought to all scenarios where Tantra magic is in play. In my time, I've seen enough to say that Tantra magic works wonders, provided one is aware that nothing's for nothing. If one selflessly puts in the necessary *intent* along with effort, there is virtually no limit to the reach or possibilities of Tantric magic.

The Tantric Great Rite of the Five Essentials

The Hindu Tantric Great Rite of the Five Essentials is a beautiful and moving experience. It is a particularly potent kind of spiritual-sex feast, a celebration, when divine powers are invoked. Contrary to normal Western descriptions of it as a sexual free-for-all or orgy, this sacred *maithuna* rite normally is a well-organized, focused celebration of both sensual and spiritual love.

Like most marriages, this high rite normally involves a man and a woman. It takes place in a carefully chosen place, in front of a sacred fire, which can mean anything from a simple burning flame or small brazier of wood chips and charcoal to an open bonfire, Yogi's *dhuni* fire pit, or formal fire altar. This fire should be located so that participants in the rite can, when required, circle it.

Only carefully chosen clean ingredients should be used for a sacred fire. No garbage or foul-smelling ingredients, such as kerosene or diesel oil, should be included. Ideally, there should be only natural and pure ingredients, including some fragrant woods such as cedar or camphor, tree resins, or beeswax. The lighting should be done with the mind spiritually focused, preferably accompanied by a mantra or prayer. Once lit, the fire should be lovingly tended.

The basic principle of the Great Rite is a ritualized blending of inner and outer fivefold Tantric correspondences, culminating in a high act of spiritual sex. This is no casual spiritual-sex party. First, there should be discussion, to determine the right selection of ingredients and choice of setting, time, and participants. Most important of all, a clearly defined program should be agreed to and the proposed sexual menu discussed.

The Tantric Great Rite of the Five Essentials is also known as the *pancha makara*, the "five M's," or the Tantric Eucharist. Why? *Pancha* means "five" and *makara* is the name of a mythical beast, a combination of various creatures. This rite truly is a combination of creatures and things of different realms.

The five M's are traditionally cereal grains (known as *mudra*), fish (*matsya*), liquor (*madya*), meat (*mamsa*), and sexual union (*maithuna*). These are all Sanskrit words, their interpretation rather generalized. Each category can be further broken down into five different things: five types of grain, five types of fish, five types of meat, five different sexual positions, even five types of men or women. There can also be five types of incense, perfume, sweets, aphrodisiacs, music, fruit, jewelry, silks of five colors, and so on. The variations are endless, as with any very special feast.

Everything to be included in this fivefold rite has to be carefully selected for quality, meticulously cleaned, and artfully laid out. Participants should prepare themselves by both physical and mental cleansing, the first by thorough bathing, the second by meditation. Subtle use of natural fragrances, especially sandalwood, musk, jasmine, patchouli, or amber oils, is recommended. They help to create an exotic and spiritually receptive atmosphere.

The rite of the five essentials is sometimes referred to as the Tantric Eucharist because everything is consecrated somewhat in the manner of Christ's Last Supper. During the Catholic reenactment of this event, sacraments are venerated, much as they are in the Tantric rite of the five essentials.

Everything consumed during this high magical rite is viewed as a substance endowed with spiritual power. This rite is not a feast in the normal sense of the word, because no large quantities of food or drink are consumed. The emphasis is on small but specially prepared tidbits of cooked grains, fish, and meat and well-chosen, high-quality liquor, such as fine wine or cognac. The emphasis is on quality—ideally, *spiritual* quality—rather than quantity.

The primary purpose of the rite is to awaken the normally dormant spiritual powers and satisfy them. These inner deities or spiritual powers are like honored guests invited to a great celebration. They are Shiva and Shakti, Mahadeva and Mahadevi, Great God and Great Goddess, Buddha and the wisdom-energy, Bhairava and Bhairavi.

These are the cosmic couple, honored guests at the Tantric feast. They are attracted by the spiritual atmosphere, the sacred fire, the incense and perfume and flowers, and by all the fine and colorful things. They are also attracted by the music, the self-confidence of the participants, the ritualistic atmosphere, and by the sacraments that are mentally offered to them before being consumed—and they are attracted by spiritual sex.

The couple sits in front of the fire, the woman to the man's left.

The sacred fire, being tended to by a Yogi, contemporary India.

This mirrors the natural layout of male–female forces in the human body: the left side female, the right side male.

The ingredients for the feast and laid out, using small containers to hold them. Both man and woman should honor each other and the fire by bringing the hands together in the traditional Hindu *namaste*, bowing or touching each other's feet. The sacred fire should also be bowed to, acknowledging it as a spiritual presence, ideal, or guru.

One by one, the feast ingredients are brought to the fire and a small portion thrown in. The rest is shared, man feeding woman, woman feeding man. When doing this, it is important to think that it is actually the Great God and Great Goddess who are being fed. The grains, fish, and meat, which have all been prepared beforehand in the way agreed, are all consumed while cultivating a joyful yet spiritually serious atmosphere. The chosen music helps to create intimacy and the liquor or other intoxicants (depending what has been selected) break down barriers. Soon, the spiritual feast is in full swing.

Following consumption of the sacramental food and drink, the couple encircles the sacred fire three and a half times. Whoever is most senior in years leads the way. The three and a half circles around the fire remind the couple of the three and a half coils of the Kundalini in Her dormant state, before awakened.

Tantric teachings emphasize the value of spontaneity over rigid dogma. The fivefold high rite should not become labored by overemphasis on ritual. Good communication, both before and during

An erotic scene depicting spontaneous sacred sex. Carved stone freize from Khajuraho, India, circa eleventh century.

the rite, is essential, especially as participants move to the culmination, which is the sexual interaction. However, some people thrive on ritual, and the gradual buildup of organized and precise procedures generally creates an enhanced atmosphere of expectancy that can in itself be erotically stimulating.

Participants in the high rites of spiritual sex will do well to remember the physiological differences between the sexes. Sexual arousal is generally much slower in woman than in man but lasts much longer. Woman's capacity for orgasm is much greater than man's, which is why, for him, Tantric teachings emphasize techniques for retention. Tantra compares the Yoni of woman to a sacred fire that takes a while to get going, flames up when fed, consumes all that is offered into it, and cools down very slowly.

The high rite of spiritual sex takes place on three levels simultaneously. There is the inner or subtle level, which is the awakening of the goddess and god energies within; the Kundalini Shakti or sexual power rises up, and passes through and illuminates the five Chakras

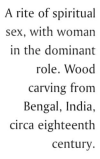

A rite of spiritual sex, with woman in the dominant role. Wood carving from Bengal, India, circa eighteenth century.

one by one, culminating in union with the awakened Shiva or transcendental consciousness principle. During this process, it is helpful to visualize the sequence of elements—from earth at the sex center, to space at the crown—accompanied by their colors, forms, and seed-mantras, as defined previously.

Then there is the outer or physical level: sexual intimacy between woman and man, with woman as the sex initiatress and man as the student. During this phase, the woman is in control and should feel free to "use" the man for her pleasure. He must treat her as the Great Goddess incarnate, doing whatever she asks. Only when he has fully pleased and satisfied her should she present him with his reward, which is whatever has been agreed upon beforehand, or what happens spontaneously.

Finally, there's the outer but subtle level, with both woman and man sexually fulfilled and still in playful intimacy, communicating as Shakti and Shiva, largely nonverbally. This is when the transcendental qualities of Shiva consciousness manifest, when anything is possible and when Shakti honors her Lord. This is the most potent time of all, when the five nectars, the secret sacraments of sex, are used. This is when Tantric magic happens, when wishes are fulfilled and spiritual powers are obtained.

Tribal Gatherings and the Magical Atmosphere

Since the sixties, many pop concerts have taken on the characteristics of pagan festivals. They have become tribal gatherings, with the performing artists as the priests and priestesses. I'm sure I couldn't give better examples than the original Woodstock festival or Grateful Dead concerts.

The charged, erotic atmosphere, heightened perhaps by drugs but certainly by rhythm and shared beliefs, is compelling. People forget themselves and become part of the group phenomena. The experience can be unforgettable, a type of initiation, a timeless and magical experience.

In the future, Tantra may make deep inroads into mainstream pop culture. Why? Because people strive for participation in magic. They long to be part of a transcendental group experience. Witness

the "acid house" and ecstasy parties that have been such phenomena. Witness revivalist church meetings, the power of gospel events,
the Catholic High Mass (all the better if it's in Latin). Witness how
opera and Shakespeare and pop music spectaculars, complete with
laser light shows, have taken on almost magical and mystical dimensions as we approach the end of the twentieth century.

Right now, many people's magical focus is on winning the lot-
tery using lucky numbers, birthdates of friends or children, and
every possible variety of superstitious practices. The majority of
people believe in magic, in the influence of the stars, in good and bad
luck.

Fortune-tellers, card readers, crystal gazers, astrologers; Hindu,
African, and Haitian seers; phone and television occult consultants;
spirit channelers, dowsers, and pendulum readers are all doing
rather well from the present trend for occult guidance.

Tantra is a sensually satisfying and exotic way of life. Magic is
very much part of the Tantric reality. According to Tantric teachings, every day and night is filled with magical possibilities, unseen
forces, known and unknown powers. Every moment, every breath
is a unique opportunity.

The magical atmosphere of the Tantric lifestyle has a lot of implications. How can we learn to use it to fulfill our dreams? How can
we use it to empower our spiritual growth? The next chapter will
explore exactly how Tantra can and will affect lives in the next century and beyond.

8 TANTRA IN THE TWENTY-FIRST CENTURY

That unity of culture and nature, work and love, morality and sexuality for which mankind if forever longing, this unity will remain a dream as long as man does not permit the satisfaction of the biological demands of natural (orgiastic) sexual gratification.

—WILHELM REICH

CONSIDER, FOR a moment, how much the world has changed over the past one hundred and fifty years or so. Hygiene was poor; health and education services were abysmal. People moved about in horse-drawn carriages at best. Communication over distance took forever.

There was no electricity, no phone service, no cars or planes, no recorded music, no radio or television, no MTV or CNN or Internet. Poverty and malnutrition were rampant. Child labor was common. Life expectancy was low. Most marriages were arranged. For the majority, human rights were virtually nonexistent. Patriarchal attitudes ruled. There was a predominantly uptight and prudish attitude about sex.

Then, in 1876, Alexander Bell invented the telephone. In 1879, Thomas Edison produced the first commercial lightbulb and electricity was introduced to our homes. Karl Benz's invention of the automobile came in 1886, and within a relatively short period of time, planes were flying and innumerable other marvels of the late twentieth century were being tested.

The first use of radio was in the early 1920s. Television was commercialized as recently as 1939, and the nuclear bomb was dropped on Hiroshima in 1945. These and a myriad of other inventions have totally changed the world and the way we live.

The human egg was first recognized by Western science in 1829. Gregor Mendel, an Austrian monk, discovered the basic laws of genetics in 1865. American women gained the right to vote in 1920, birth-control pills were commercially introduced in 1960–61, and the Civil Rights Act prohibiting racial discrimination came into being as recently as 1964. All these and other momentous discoveries and events have totally changed the lives of so many of us this century.

The twentieth-century revolution in science and industry gave us sewing machines and cameras, record players, records and transistors, refridgerators, microwave ovens, tape recorders, washing machines and televisions, electronic calculators, cassette players with headphones, fax machines and CD players, followed by the new digital reality of computers, CD-ROMs, e-mail, the Internet, and virtual reality.

All this and more was invented by the incredible minds of brilliant individuals, created from the consciousness of innovative and inquiring people who pushed aside the boundaries limiting what "could" be done. These people had imagination and energy and wouldn't take no for an answer; their consciousness was both focused and expansive.

All of the imaginative creations of the late nineteenth and twentieth centuries have been inspired by inner truths and scientific principles perceived by the human mind, our own "biocomputer." *All* were generated from the genius of human consciousness—and that genius has hardly been developed yet.

In the twenty-first century, Tantra will "come out of the closet," taking its rightful place as the most relevant tool to aid spiritual evolution for both men and women. It will awaken and empower the latent genius within each of us. How? By helping us reprogram our biocomputer with the spiritual software that Tantra offers.

The Human Biocomputer and the Science of Tantra

In his groundbreaking book *The Human Biocomputer: Theory and Experiments* (1967) neuroscientist John Lilly wrote:

> All human beings, all persons who reach adulthood in the world today are programmed biocomputers. No one of us can escape our own nature as programmable entities. Literally, each of us may be our programs, nothing more, nothing less.

Pointing out that our central control system simultaneously processes hundreds of thousands of programs operating in parallel, Lilly suggests that "new areas of conscious awareness can be developed, beyond the current conscious comprehension of the self." He wrote:

> With courage, fortitude, and perseverance the previously experienced boundaries can be crossed into new territories of subjective awareness and experience. New knowledge, new problems, new puzzles are found in the innermost explorations. Some of these areas may seem to transcend the operations of the mind-brain-computer itself. . . . New knowledge often turns out to be merely *old and hidden* knowledge after mature contemplative analysis.

Tantra *is* old and hidden knowledge. It has been around for a long time, existing below the surface of our normal conscious mind, residing deep within our cells and permeating every part of our spiritual being. The "programming" with which most of us have been brought up, however, has repressed this knowledge, relegating it to the realms of the unconscious.

We can access Tantric knowledge by reprogramming and fine-tuning our biocomputer. By exploring our true spiritual potential as dynamic and creative sexual beings, we can rid ourselves of confining sex- or gender-negative conditioning. By using the tools and techniques of Tantra, we can eliminate entrenched role limitations and become truly spontaneous and transcendental. We can reverse the downward spiral of the loss of spiritual values and meaning in life that the twentieth century has wrought. When we do so, we will become brighter—more self-confident and "spiritually luminous." Our consciousness will become spiritually empowered by the Great Goddess, by the nurturing and all-knowing genius that exists deep within.

True Genius in the Tantric Tradition

True genius is the ability to perceive solutions to seemingly insurmountable problems. According to Gopi Krishna, author of *Kundalini: The Evolutionary Energy in Man* and many other books, genius has a biological basis, which is the "evolutionary energy" known as Kundalini. As we have seen, this "serpent power" of Tantra tradition is sexual in origin and is the most jealously guarded secret in history.

The power of genius is usually dormant and needs to be awakened before it can manifest. This secret and essential sexual power can be defined and channeled into all types of creative works. Tantra is the scientific and mystical "software" that allows us to do so, using our bodily "hardware" as the vehicle.

Herbert Guenther, author and eminent professor of philosophy, summed up the reality of Tantric understanding when he wrote:

> What the Tantras have to say must be lived in order to be understood. But to live and to understand needs courage and perseverance, like everything that is great.

In the twenty-first century, interest in Tantra and spiritual sex will increase exponentially. Why? Because Tantra is both scientific and artistic, intellectual and emotional, worldly and spiritual, empirical and mystical. Because Tantra is the tool of *true* genius, awakening our latent spiritual potential, integrating our head and our heart. Because spiritual sex, wisely practiced using the tools of Tantra, resolves our natural and sacred androgyny and imparts a joyous and creative way of life, free from guilt and inhibition. And because, as we approach the twenty-first century, the time for Tantra has truly arrived, as we become a single world culture in need of a new spiritual direction.

New Versions of Old Discoveries Will Shape Our Future

The living human brain is an awesome entity. It processes literally *millions* of computations at any instant. It has approximately two million visual inputs and one hundred thousand acoustic ones. It has been estimated to contain at least thirteen billion neurons. Despite all this, we normally use less than twenty percent of our brain. We are only just beginning to discover how it works, how we "compute," what kind of "software" runs *us*.

We're still a long way from building a truly intelligent computer that rivals the human brain. This is one of the big goals of computer science. The living brain and its thought processes have only recently been explored by modern science with any degree of efficiency.

New scanning technology now allows specialists to track emotions, thoughts, visualizations, and so on, viewing the results on a screen, yet for several thousands of years, Tantric adepts have been active in these areas, scanning their consciousness from within. These adepts have been discovering and evolving consciousness expansion and contraction techniques and testing visualization, self-hypnosis, and spiritual empowerment methods, from which modern Western science and culture can learn much.

Existing self-hypnosis, guided imaging, and remote viewing psychological techniques will, in the twenty-first century, undoubtedly be further developed. Sensory deprivation and enhancement environments, ultrasound, virtual reality, pulse and brain-wave entrainment technology, neural computer-chip implants, and a whole new range of consciousness-transformation devices will produce transcendental experiences entirely new to the Western world. Some of these experiences will be sexual.

Most, if not all, will likely be "new" versions of old but little-known discoveries—the discoveries of Tantra Yoga.

Fluctuating field electric pulse devices *already* exist that can produce feelings of sexual arousal or profound mystical experiences. Recently, Dr. Michael Persinger, a neuroscientist at the Laurentian

University in Ontario, discovered that if a solenoid pulse device was targeted to penetrate deep into the right hemisphere of the brain's temporal lobes, the recipient experienced the feeling that a "negative presence such as an alien or devil" exists in the left side of their body. Conversely, when targeted on the left hemisphere, "subjects sensed a benevolent force such as an angel or a god."

Obviously, such perceptions of spiritual entities are colored by religious and cultural superstitions. What is fascinating, however, is that these scientific experiments confirm what the secret Tantra Yoga technology has long taught: that spiritual forces exist *within* each of us, not somewhere outside ourselves. They also confirm that inner spiritual forces can be invoked by focused pulses (as with mantras) and originate within our subtle anatomy.

In the twenty-first century, synthetic orgasmic and ecstatic experiences will, with fluctuating-pulse and related technology, become easily accessible. Fluctuating-pulse gadgets will likely be built into helmets, pillows, chairs, the seats of cars, and so forth. As a result, for some, "good sex" may mean cerebral sensual experiences without genital arousal or physical orgasm. They'll just hook up and put on the gratification device, adjust the dials, and enjoy prolonged oceanic orgasms without any physical sexual interaction.

Because of the advent of such sexual-gratification devices, there'll likely be the option of sharing synthetic sex experiences with people of any gender or number, in shared virtual environments— even remotely, perhaps through devices attached to pagers or Internet terminals. The prospects are both intriguing (virtual orgies with no physical contact) and disturbing. Without a doubt, if it can be done, some people will do it.

Nevertheless, it is my belief that in the twenty-first century, even with the availability of these types of sexual gratification devices, simulated sex will not replace intimate human interaction. Why? Because there can never be a substitute for the high level of romantic love that Tantra offers. Because as evolving humans, we'll always crave more intimacy and better and more meaningful interpersonal communication. Because as we become more familiar and comfortable with our innate spiritual power, our senses will be finer tuned. And because our innermost divine essence (the god and goddess within) will demand higher and higher levels of sensual gratification. We'll seek out more refined, better, and higher loving, rather than a wider interactive sexual bandwidth.

Tantra as a Sensual and Spiritual "Software" System

The unraveling of the genetic code, biological and genetic engineering, and new discoveries in medicine, psychology, chemistry, physics, and mathematics will contribute to our physical and mental evolution in the twenty-first century.

There'll also be many new discoveries in the field of computers and computer technology. This is an aspect of human achievement for which the twenty-first century will be famous. Look back just a few years and review the incredible advances in computer hardware and software. These advances are increasing exponentially, and they will continue to do so.

Advances in computer technology tend to mirror human evolutionary advances. Many of these advances or sudden breakthroughs have been, at one point or other, triggered by consciousness-expanding drugs. Visit Silicon Valley and other areas where computer technology has blossomed; talk to developers of both hardware and software and you'll find, as I did, that consciousness-expanding drugs such as LSD have been key to the whole process. Not only that, if you explore deeper, you'll find that many of the prime innovative developers of both hardware and software have a knowledge of and interest in Tantra.

Why? Because LSD and other consciousness-expansion drugs are some of the tools of Tantra. Because these sacred substances help turn the mind inward, help in the discovery and exploration of the self. By doing so, they reveal the way our own supercomputer, the one we carry on our shoulders, works.

In a recent interview in *Tricycle: The Buddhist Review*, Terence McKenna, ethnobotanist, author, and student of psychedelic shamanism, states:

> Buddhism, ecological thinking, psychedelic thinking, and feminism are the four parts of a solution. These things are somewhat

fragmented from each other, but they are the obvious pieces of the puzzle. An honoring of the feminine, an honoring of the planet, a stress on dematerialism and compassion, and the tools to revivify and make coherent those three (the tools being psychedelic substances).

Yet again, it is new versions of old discoveries that show the way. Honoring of the feminine is an ancient tradition, as is honoring of the planet and emphasizing the spiritual over the materialistic. Psychedelic substances have been around for a very long time and in many different cultures. Much evidence suggests that in ancient times, they were the impetus for sudden bursts of spiritual insight, leading to cultural enrichment.

In the years ahead, there'll be a steady flow of faster and more intelligent computers, organic computer chips, fluid-state processing, more innovative operating systems, total-feedback interactive learning programs, better-designed computer interfaces, virtual reality applications, and so forth. If we truly get smart, we'll learn to make computers that mirror the way the best of us think. In this area also, Tantra has much to contribute. For Tantra has, over untold centuries, been following a direction wholly driven by the inner–outer interface.

This is encouraging and leads me to believe that, in the future, some important advances in computer technology will most likely be derived from taking a closer look at traditional Tantric data.

Try entering esoteric key words such as *Tantra, Shiva, Chakra, karma, Sumeria,* and so forth into the Internet address search engines and you'll be amazed how many companies and individuals in the computer business apparently feel connected to metaphysical concepts.

Tantra Will Help Human Rights Flourish

We live in a society still colored by racism and sexism. Slavery in America was done away with in 1863, yet economic slavery still prevails, especially among so-called minorities. The Universal Declaration of Human Rights was passed by all member states of the United Nations in 1948, but today, much of the "civilized" world is plagued by innumerable violations of these same principles.

The right to freedom of religious expression is an indelible part of the U.S. Constitution, yet many laws and rulings, such as the antibigamy acts of 1862 and 1882, the 1879 U.S. Supreme Court ruling that declared that religious freedom cannot be claimed as grounds for the practice of polygamy, and laws against oral sex, homosexual acts, and the private use of consciousness-expanding drugs, all of which restrict or penalize what is essentially intimate behavior between consenting adults, are still in place. Add to these the laws governing abortion; American women are still fighting for the right to do as they wish with their own bodies.

Most Western women still have a hard time getting their share of available resources and often have to endure disrespect, in the workplace and in their homes. One might ask what this has to do with Tantra in the twenty-first century. The truth is, it has everything to do with it.

Tantra is the only way of life that *begins* by breaking down barriers enslaving the oppressed and *requires* that woman not only be treated as equal to man but be exalted as well. By emancipating people from mental slavery and spiritually liberating women as well as men, authentic Tantric teachings offer a positive future for those who embrace them.

Elizabeth Stanton (1815–1902), Matilda Gage (1826–1898), and Susan B. Anthony (1820–1906), Margaret Sanger (1883–1996), Simone de Beauvoir (1908–1986), Kate Millett, and Germaine Greer are some of the Western women who, in the nineteenth and twentieth centuries, paved the way for women's rights to be recognized and adopted. If further progress in women's rights is to be made in the twenty-first century, there will be a need for inspired female leadership.

Much will depend on how quickly the inspired teachings of Tantric traditions enter the mainstream of political thinking and how these teachings are understood—which ultimately means how women and men will evolve in the way they interact in intimate situations.

Tantra teaches a no-nonsense approach to the problems we are facing. The Tantric way of solving problems rests in having an un-compromising and vital spiritual approach to life.

Tantra also teaches a no-nonsense approach to death. Tantrics are not intimidated by thoughts or superstitions or talk of death. We embrace and welcome death, and when the time comes, we are ready to embark on the immortal eternal journey, confident that our spiritual essence will live on. If we *truly believe* in the eternity of the human spirit, we will become better people—fearless and wiser.

By confronting the reality that Tantra teaches, by truly understanding (both intellectually and emotionally) that death is a doorway to an eternal spiritual realm of infinite possibilities, we'll grow up. We'll become kinder, more respectful, and considerate to the elderly, who are closest to the transcendental doorway of death. We'll evolve spiritually and become better able to communicate with our partners and loved ones in a truly spiritual and loving way.

As Tantrics, we also embrace and revere sex and can deal directly with this ever-so-sensitive topic, lovingly and without psychological complexes, fear of inadequacy, or superstitions. Sex and death are the two poles that define the limits of the Tantric domain. Between them lies every thing and every action in this world and the next.

If we claim our rights according to the teachings of Tantra, we'll understand and explore the full spectrum of life in all its natural diversity. We'll intuitively learn, with help from our loving and fearless superstition-free partners, how to care for our elders and how to teach our children. We'll also learn how to promote and conserve good health and prosperity, how to nurture the environment we live in, and how to bring about the meaningful and lasting changes that will usher in the Golden Age.

Tantra: The Engine of Political Change

Tantra is a potent force for change. It has had and will continue to have potent political consequences.

When Tantra first appeared in caste-ridden India about sixteen hundred years ago, it had a liberating effect. It offered a new spiritual democracy. Anyone, no matter what caste or skin color, was eligible to practice Tantra, provided they had earnest desire and could find a teacher.

Tantra became the driving force in India's golden age of culture from the fourth to eleventh centuries C.E. During this period, great centers of Tantric learning were built, with huge libraries and art galleries dedicated to the science and art of spiritual sex. Innumerable temples were erected, many of them covered with the most exquisite sensual sculptures. The form of woman as goddess was openly exalted. The temples, monasteries, and universities were bastions of high spiritual culture. But their wealth, sensuality, and exaltation of woman was a thorn in the side of the emerging patriarchal Muslim nations.

India was invaded. Monasteries and temples were ransacked, ruined, and burned. Millions were killed or enslaved. Sacred statues were beheaded. Goddess images were smashed and mutilated. Many of the Indian Tantrics who survived moved to neighboring countries such as Nepal and Tibet.

The Tibetans took to Tantra in a big way. Their long-existing animist and shamanist beliefs prepared them well. Tibetans became the Tantric gurus of Chinese emperors. The emperors funded the construction of new monasteries, temples and libraries, sponsored monks and nuns, and innumerable Tantric paintings, images, Tantras, mantras, and yantras were created. For about one thousand years, Tantra grew and grew in Tibet, but disaster struck again.

In the 1950s, China invaded and devastated Tibet. Driven by nonspiritual materialistic communist ideology, Chinese leaders took over. Millions of Tibetans were killed or uprooted. Numerous Tibetan women were sterilized or relocated and forced to marry Chinese men. Innumerable monasteries, books, paintings, and sacred statues were once again destroyed. The Dalai Lama and many other Tantric High Lamas fled to India and the West.

It's hard to predict how the Tibet–China political situation will be resolved in the near future. Much will depend on spiritual and political leaders. Currently, the Dalai Lama and the present Chinese administration seem to be at loggerheads. There are ongoing squabbles about the recognition of incarnate High Lamas. In Tibet, Tantra cannot be practiced openly.

The human-rights situation in Tibet today is abysmal, but

change is inevitable. It will be driven by Tibetan Tantric leaders, who will inspire a new spiritual democracy. My prediction is that in the twenty-first century, this will result in major breakthroughs in resolving the political and religious status of Tibet.

India is currently going through troubling political times; change is evident everywhere. Recently, for a brief while, India had a fundamentalist Hindu government. Hindu pride is a vibrant, growing movement.

The Indian people as a whole have had an exceedingly hard time for much of the last one thousand years. Invasions from Moslems, the British, and even the French and Portuguese, restrictive colonialism, aggressive Christian missionaries, forced conversions, and the recent influx of aggressive Western business interests have overshadowed the native culture.

Chronic overpopulation, poverty, loss of traditional values, advertising-driven materialism, and the adoption of Western ways have caused upheaval in India, especially over the past fifty years. Truly, it's time for a change in India. Can it be change à la Tantra?

In his important book *The Tantric Tradition* (1965), Agehananda Bharati, an Austrian Hindu monk turned American professor of cultural anthropology, accurately explains the place of Tantra in modern Indian society, pointing out:

> Indian authors who study Tantrism [Bharati names a few] do so with a persistent apologetic note which, to our feeling, jeopardizes the advancement of Tantric studies in the area most germane to them. I have yet to meet an Indian-born scholar who stands squarely by the Tantric tradition. They seem to feel that Tantrism may be studied and written about provided their own identification is Vedantic or otherwise orthodox, either in the classical or modern sense; in other words, if they conform to the official culture of India, which is decidedly non- and anti-Tantric.

The official culture of India about which Bharati writes is the reaction to years of colonial rule, which, for its leaders' own ends, shaped India into a single large nation administered in the British Westminster version of democracy.

Divide and conquer, unite and rule—this was the practice applied by the colonial power that proved deadly to true Hindu culture, which once celebrated sex and sensuality as the highest form of art.

India is the world's largest democracy, and Tantra is at the root of Indian culture. Perhaps in twenty-first-century India, Tantra will finally take on a new and changed relevance.

The change is inevitable. In India, the stage is set for some radical political and social changes. With Tantra in the wings, the play should be both interesting and filled with promise.

That Tantra is a potent force for political change is also evident from events in Romania in recent years. During the later part of the oppressive communist Ceauşescu regime in the 1980s, Yoga was viewed as a threat to the state and those who practiced it were persecuted. The result was an upsurge of interest, led largely by Gregorian Bivolaru, who introduced Tantric teachings in his Yoga school despite being arrested, tortured, and imprisoned. Copies of *Sexual Secrets* and other Yoga and Tantra publications available in the West were smuggled into the country, translated, photocopied, and distributed.

The student movement blossomed. The MISA Yoga organization founded by Bivolaru began to spread its spiritual, nonpolitical, nonsectarian message of Tantra. It became an underground movement with more than ten thousand members. In 1989, the dictators were removed and the government changed.

Today, the MISA Romanian school of Yoga and Tantra has become firmly established, with more than twenty-five thousand registered practitioners. This movement's aim is to use Tantric teachings to revive and restore Romania's spiritual and cultural heritage. Though still largely viewed as a threat by many of the ruling authorities, Tantra has earned a level of recognition and respect, in Romania, if only for its large numbers of proponents.

Similar stories but with different players are told of Tantra in the former USSR, Yugoslavia, Poland, Czechoslovakia, in South Africa, and in Japan. In the former USSR, Yoga, Tantra, and occult teachings have become very popular, filling the void left by years of nonspiritual communist ideology. In South Africa, the revived interest in native spiritual traditions, animism, shamanism, Yoga, meditation, and Tantra helped empower individuals to take political action leading to the removal of the apartheid system—quite an indication of how, with the right application, Tantra can be used to create positive transformation.

Traditional Tantra has been known in Japan for about one thousand years, having been introduced there through contact with China and India. Nowadays, many "new" and highly successful Japanese religions are actually Tantric cults, using its initiatory techniques and empowering mantras.

Tantric Health Care and Medicine

Americans spend almost $14 billion annually on alternative medicine, yet we are only just beginning to integrate time-tested natural-health systems such as Chinese herbal medicine, acupuncture, Ayurveda, massage therapy, and other "alternative" treatments into our lifestyle. As we do so, many new natural drugs and therapies are being discovered.

In the twenty-first century, a whole new range of "smart" drugs will become available. These will no doubt include mood transformers, antidepressants, and consciousness enhancers, as well as potent new superfoods and psychovitamins. We'll have a wide choice of antioxidants, free-radical scavengers, immune-system boosters, longevity elixirs, learning enhancers, aphrodisiacs, and sensory stimulators. These are just a few of the developments we can expect in the century ahead, and Tantra has much to contribute in all of these areas.

One of the phenomena of the twenty-first century will be increased life expectancy and better quality of life for the elderly. Advances in sex hormone–replacement therapy will help overcome menopause and impotency problems normally associated with aging, allowing the elderly to have more active sex lives and conferring other benefits. This is an area to which Tantra can also contribute, because the ancient, natural, sex-enhancing ingredients and formulas outlined in Tantric texts will generally prove to be preferable to synthetic man-made versions.

In the twenty-first century, many of the new discoveries in medicine will undoubtedly be rediscoveries or developments of old discoveries, from research into the texts and techniques of traditional Indian medicine and especially from Tantra. Detailed research into Ayurveda and Siddha medicine and into the alchemical and longevity Tantric sciences known as *Rasayana* and *kaya kalpa* will also yield phenomenal results. Some of this work has already been started, but much has yet to be achieved.

Rasayana, the "way or science of essence," is a Tantric branch of Indian Ayurvedic and Siddha medicine that has yet to be thoroughly explored in the West. An ancient and largely secret science discovered and promoted by Yogi doctors and alchemists, it has an illustrious history, supported by at least two thousand years of research.

Rasayana is a category of Yogic and Tantric medicine dealing specifically with problems and issues of immunity, sexuality, and longevity. Because these are topics of key interest now and will continue to be in the years ahead, Western scientists would be wise to take a good look at authentic *Rasayana* theory and practice.

Some work on *Rasayana* has progressed in India in recent years, with considerable success. Also, there are a few doctors using *Rasayana* drugs in the West. A recent example is a well-known Ayurvedic herb, fruit, and mineral mixture known as *Chyvanprash*, based on a formula reputedly created by Chyvan Rishi, a Yogi sage who, at an advanced age, married a young woman and needed to enhance his vitality so as to sexually satisfy her.

When tested by Western science, it was found that *Chyvanprash* has enormous concentrations of easily assimilated vitamins and minerals, together with antioxidants, free-radical scavengers, and a whole spectrum of other highly potent healing substances. Proven effective in the treatment of a wide range of diseases, from the common cold to impotency and chronic fatigue syndrome, it is now available in the West under a number of different brand names (such as Amrita Kailash). Some are fortified with *Rasayana* preparations that include specially treated pearls, gold, diamonds, and other precious minerals.

An ancient Ayurvedic formula for treating liver disorders, which was discovered by Tantric scientists, is now mass-marketed. Available under the trade name Liver-52, it has proven to be tremendously effective in treating drug abuse, alcoholism, and disorders of the liver such as hepatitis. Another Ayurvedic substance, known as *shilajeet* (a form of mineral pitch), has recently been proven effective treatment for a wide range of urinary and sexual dysfunctions.

The considerable popular success of Ayurvedic and other Indian holistic-health system promoters, such as Dr. Deepak Chopra, gives cause for hope that traditional *Rasayana* or an updated version of it will become widespread in the West in the not-too-distant future.

Kaya kalpa, meaning ''bodily immortality,'' is a Tantric branch of Indian Siddha medical knowledge less well known than *Rasayana*, either in India or the West. This is the secret Siddha Yogic technology of the body that can enhance longevity. Originally developed in the ancient past, practitioners of this advanced holistic health technology use a wide range of techniques and substances, based on principles of cellular purification and nourishment.

Growth and decay are natural processes that normally occur at their own pace. Cell life is naturally dynamic, interactive, and constantly changing. In living tissue, energy is normally polarized into anabolic and catabolic reactions. Anabolic cellular changes lead to growth and catabolic to decay. The Tantric techniques explored and perfected by the science of *kaya kalpa* are built around means that reverse and regulate these processes.

Thus far, there has been only limited attention given to this important branch of Siddha medicine in the West, but some very valuable work has been done and is ongoing. Dr. Raam Pandey, one of the foremost innovators of traditional *kaya kalpa* treatments, has had clinics in America for more than a decade that have produced significant results. I expect research into *kaya kalpa* to flourish in the years ahead as more and more people become aware of the unique opportunities these Tantric treatments offer.

Tantra, Sex, and the Information Superhighway

It's hard to believe what the information revolution has achieved in the past decade. The whole world has suddenly become interconnected. Every area of human interest, every subject, from the most mundane to the most esoteric, has become accessible to virtually anyone anywhere in the world—and this is still just the beginning.

People are reaching out and beginning to understand. Thanks

to the information superhighway, it has become possible to explore even formerly taboo subjects such as Tantra, paganism, and spiritual sex. We can now explore these subjects in cyberspace without having to show our face. In October 1996, entering of the word *Tantra* in a popular Internet search engine produced thousands of different documents. By the time this book is in the stores, there will no doubt be many more entries under this category.

We can now chat online with people we'll most likely never get to meet. We can do so without inhibitions, peer pressure, or cultural or social censorship. How-to sex books like *The Joy of Sex*, which was written by a person very familiar with Tantra, gave millions permission to explore and experiment with their sexual preferences. So did the advent of X-rated movies and videos, as well as personal ads and phone dating services, which list categories of choice, from "women seeking men," to "men seeking women," "gay," "multiples," "anything goes," "mistresses wanted," "oral," "bondage and domination," and other categories. Interestingly, there has been a considerable increase in recent years in ads from people looking for or offering services in the "fetish," "multiples," or "anything goes" categories. This suggests that sexual variety or diversity will be a key interest in the twenty-first century.

Sex toys and phone sex are both phenomena of the 1980s and early 1990s. Undoubtedly, there will be new, more advanced sex toys in the twenty-first century. Phone sex will also continue to develop, especially through the Internet, and will be developed alongside live on-screen video scenarios. The effect will be to expand the possibilities, add variety and, of course, increase revenue. A form of sacred prostitution or ritual sacred sex with skilled professionals—at a distance, over the Internet—might prove to be very popular.

Sex services are a huge part of the Internet reality. As with sex in person, diversity rules. Every possible variety of sexual activity is now discussed and made available on the Internet. For example, a single randomly accessed adult site gave two hundred fifty-two "naughty links" in categories ranging from nudism to fantasy, others including seduction, sex images, kinky, fetish, leather, rubber, sadomasochism, bondage, domination, feet, gay, lesbian, bisexual, transgender, piercing, cross-dressing, dildos, handcuffs, corsets, muscle worship, wrestling, hair, high heels, French maids, spanking, swingers, polyamory, body art, lace, silk, and golden showers, along with erotic art, fantasy fashion, goddess worship, and, of course, Tantra.

The enormous variety of sexual fantasy scenarios offered in the published media, over the phone, and on the Internet tells us that nowadays, in sexual scenarios between consenting adults, nothing is off limits. This concurs with the *Kama Sutra*, written almost two thousand years ago, which categorically states: ''Once the Wheel of Love has been set in motion, there is no absolute rule.''

Using the information superhighway, we can get on with finding out who we really are, what we believe and are truly interested in, what our sexual fantasies really are, and how we want to live them out. We can do this interactively and anonymously, irrespective of country borders, provided we don't allow the Internet to become regulated.

There are so many areas in which Tantra can contribute: to physical, mental, and spiritual health; to business, economics, and education; to the environment, human relations, and the care of the aged; and to sport, entertainment, and recreation, to mention but a few. Tantra is a creative science and a fine art. Like the universe, it has no limits. One hopes that in the years ahead, Tantra data on the information superhighway lead earnest spiritual travelers directly to their goal.

Sexual Psychology and Tantra

In the twenty-first century, sexual psychology will have to evolve so it can keep pace with a whole new range of sexual experiences. As spiritual sex inspired by Tantra tradition becomes more popular, a new spiritually oriented form of sexual psychology will emerge. It is already beginning to happen.

Sexual surrogates, meaning skilled and sensitive ''sexperts'' trained to use psychology in a sexual way—at times leading to intimate interactions—are proving effective in treating sexual dysfunctions such as premature ejaculation and frigidity.

In the 1990s, commercial sexual services such as phone sex,

dating listings, and sensual massage have taken on more spiritual dimensions. There has been an upsurge of services offering "sacred-sex chat rooms," "goddess worship," and "Tantric massage," as well as Tantra "encounters," seminars, and weekend couples retreats in exotic settings. This trend will obviously develop further in the twenty-first century.

Several movies and videos produced recently, such as *Sacred Sex, Tantra Love: Eastern Secrets of Intimacy and Ecstasy for Western Lovers* and *Tantra: The Art of Conscious Loving*, along with modern interpretations of classics, such as *Kama Sutra: The Art of Love*, and mainstream self-help sex guides, such as *Discovering Extraordinary Sex* and the *Better Sex* video series, have proved commercially successful. All this helps break down barriers and establish better dialogue and understanding between people.

Freudian and Jungian psychology have had tremendous influence on the twentieth century, especially on advertising, where sexual symbolism rules. This is because our mind, which is the most erotic of our senses, is insatiable and is so easily influenced. Consider, for a moment, the effect of advertising on consciousness in the twentieth century. Consider how sexual imagery is used in advertising and the effect of it on sexual psychology: Nowadays, image is everything. People are no longer satisfied with how they look or what they have. They want to have perfectly sculpted bodies, look like models, wear the latest fashions, and drive the most recent model cars. The majority of people are highly influenced by the icons that advertising offers.

Today, to most people, "goddesses" are sex symbols, sex goddesses, created largely from skillful publicity. They are movie, fashion, and music stars, living idols whose every move is followed by the media. But it is rare for such media goddesses to exemplify spiritual ideals.

Marilyn Monroe, Brigitte Bardot, Ursula Andress, Bo Derek, Diana Ross, Naomi Campbell, Cindy Crawford, Madonna, and many other movie, fashion, and music celebrities have, in their time, become known as sex goddesses. Why? Because sex sells, and because the predominant Judeo-Christian patriarchal media has developed a skewed perspective on what women's roles really should be: Career woman or housewife, promiscuous whore or virginal bride, caring mother or hot mistress? These are but some of the paradoxical roles into which the mass media has cast women.

As a result, most of our modern sex goddesses have become superficial media icons. Rather than focusing on their spiritual qualities, many of our most talented female stars are ultimately promoted as dumb blondes or bitch goddesses. Something strange is going on here.

One measure of the direction that our culture is leading us is the type of intimacy or sexual services that people are looking for and the differences between ads from women and men. The majority of personal ads from women emphasize they are looking for an idealized man, for the romance found in romantic novels, for an intimate, caring relationship leading to marriage. Personal ads from men are most commonly for good-looking, sensuous, or exotic women—model types or mistresses—rather than for marriage or a lasting relationship. And ads from both gay men and gay women have increased dramatically over the past decade.

Fetishism, sadomasochism, domination, bondage, spanking, golden showers, and a myriad of other sexual variations are very much a product of our Western Judeo-Christian culture. They indicate interest in sexual ritual, in the desire for working through obsessions and neuroses, and in the desire of some men to recognize woman as a living goddess, serving and pleasing their mistress.

A recent Web survey of what people mean by and expect from the phrase *modern goddess* revealed that respondents were mostly men (99%), 48% of whom were between 31 and 45 years old, 27% between 23 and 30, 13% between 18 and 22, and 12% 45 and over. Of these men, 40% were married, 30% single, and 10% divorced; 85% were heterosexual and 8% were bisexual or "bicurious." Most "want desperately to be of service to women," 42% like to be humiliated, and 40% "dream of golden showers."

Amazingly, 78% admitted they "find it frustrating trying to find a woman who will let herself be worshipped," 60% are "not embarrassed by [their] drives," 99% like themselves, and a *massive* 85% "fantasize about doing more experimental game-playing and genuine female worship."

Summing up, the compiler/author of this fascinating but anonymous Web survey (Modern Goddess Survey, which had more than ten thousand visitors in the few months its site was listed) wrote:

> The one thing that becomes clear after all this is that ours is a secret society, closely guarded and withdrawn. 73% do not tell friends about their interest in female worship nor [sic] of fetishism. . . . We still manage to objectify women through our photo worship and serve them only in brief spurts with our own agenda, our own palette of desires to stand in the way of their true empowerment. We need women to whom we can submit and do so with absolute abandon . . . to trust in their leadership and guidance more than our own.

Such scenarios also indicate that in the West, there is a drastic breakdown in communication between men and women with respect to sexual expectations. Because of Judeo-Christian patriarchal programming and ingrained superstitions, many women still don't feel comfortable mixing sex and spirituality. In the twenty-first century, as Tantra becomes better known, this situation will surely change.

Thanks to psychoanalytical advances and the advent of New Age consciousness, more Western women than ever before are becoming interested in being "goddesses." They are searching for ways to experience their spiritual potential and their inherent initiatory sexual power. This evolving interest also indicates the desire for sexual experimentation and playfulness, which, when embarked on as acts of enhanced intimacy and love, can be extremely liberating.

This is another area with which Tantra can help. In such dynamic interactive relationships between the sexes, proper communication is paramount. Attitude, sensitivity, and spiritual awareness are tools that allow spiritual role-playing to bear potent fruits.

Increased interest in Tantra can help redefine woman's role as living goddess. This should develop an entirely new perception of woman and an entirely fresh sexual psychology. In the new paradigm, the emphasis will be on intimacy and the spiritualizing of sexual relationships.

Temples of Tantra in the Twenty-First Century

Christianity has its churches and cathedrals, Judaism, its synagogues, and Islam, its mosques. Tantra has always had its temples, secret altars, and special holy days.

As Tantra becomes better known in the West, it's likely that we will start to see Tantric temples. Already there are several rather private ones, as well as virtual ones on the Internet. See the next chapter, ''Tantra Database,'' for several links to these virtual Tantra temples.

It will be interesting to see what the Western public's reaction to temples of Tantra will be and how these temples turn out. We have an inalienable right to freedom of religious expression, so why shouldn't Tantrics worship openly, just like followers of other faiths?

About one thousand years ago, during the Chandella dynasty in central India, fabulous Tantric temple complexes were built at

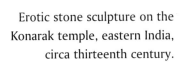
Erotic stone sculpture on the Konarak temple, eastern India, circa thirteenth century.

Couple standing in intimate embrace, the man supporting his consort with his hands beneath her feet. Stone sculpture on the Konarak temple, eastern India, circa thirteenth-century.

Erotic stone sculpture on a Khajuraho temple, central India, circa eleventh century.

A couple in intimate spiritual sex embrace, with a second woman to one side pleasuring herself. Sandstone sculpture on a Khajuraho temple, central India, circa eleventh century.

Khajuraho. Other impressive complexes were built at Konarak, on the eastern coast. These architectural masterpieces were covered with sculptures depicting myths, gods, goddesses, and scenes of everyday life, together with the most exquisite and imaginative erotic sculpture.

In his book *Erotic Spirituality: The Vision of Konarak*, featuring photographs by Eliot Elisofon of the Konarak and Khajuraho Tantric temples and erotic sculptures, writer Alan Watts reminds us that ancient Indian ideals of sexual love differ considerably from ours. Explaining that in the *Kama Sutra*, intercourse is a complex and elegant ritual, an act of mutual worship between god and goddess, he points out that most of the erotic sculptures on India's Tantric temples are *standing:*

> One of the most striking features of the Konarak (and Khajuraho) images is that these couples are not "going to bed" or "sleeping" with each other. They are standing or sitting—unless we are to imagine the temple walls as floors. Furthermore, they are not completely naked, but ornamented with crowns, necklaces, bracelets, and bangles, and, in many scenes, they are not alone. This suggests that what they are doing is not perceived as lewd or dirty, or something that should be done in private. Their lovemaking is more a sort of ritual dance.

An intricate group sex scenario, the woman on her head, the man supported by two other women. Stone sculpture on a Khajuraho temple, central India, circa eleventh century.

Another intricate group sex scenario, the man on his head, the woman supported by two other women. This type of erotic scene is interpreted by Tantrics as indicating Yogic control over the life-force and the reversal of the normal outward dispersal of sexual energy. Stone sculpture on a Khajuraho temple, central India, circa eleventh century.

A couple standing in an intimate "dance" of spiritual sex. Stone sculpture on a Khajuraho temple, central India, circa eleventh century.

Gilded metal casting of a Tantric *yidam*, or initiatory couple, symbolic of the union of wisdom (the woman) and means (the man), from Tibet, circa seventeenth century.

Gilded metal casting of the Tantric initiatory sacred-sex couple of Tibetan tradition known as the *yidam* Chakrasamvara (also the name of a Tantra). The man stands and is multiarmed. From Tibet, circa sixteenth century.

Gilded metal casting of the Tantric initiatory sacred-sex couple of Tibetan tradition known as the *yidam* Hevajra (also the name of a Tantra). The man stands and has sixteen arms, symbolic of the vowels or primordial sounds. From Nepal, circa sixteenth-century.

Similar depictions exist in most Tantric and Tibetan art. Couples in intimate embrace invariably wear elaborate crowns and ornaments and are either seated or, more commonly, standing. This indicates mastery of the erotic arts: lovemaking without much physical movement, and retention and concentration of vital energy, rather than mindless dispersion.

Many of India's Tantric temples were destroyed or badly damaged by Moslem invaders. The British viewed the surviving erotic sculptures as pornography, and until very recently (until the temples became tourist destinations), most Indians were embarrassed by them. Even Mahatma Gandhi tried to have the Khajuraho Tantric temples closed down.

Painting on cloth depicting the Tantric initiatory sacred-sex couple known as Kalachakra (also the name of a Tantra). Both stand and are multiarmed. *Thanka* from Tibet, circa sixteenth century.

Metal casting of the Tantric initiatory "cosmic couple" known as Guhyasamaja (also the name of a Tantra). The man is seated, with his consort in intimate embrace on his lap. From southern Tibet, circa twelfth century.

America now has quite a number of Hindu temples, but as far as I am aware, none of them are decorated with erotic sculpture. Even America's museums tend to shy away from displaying sexually explicit sculpture; very few sculptures of Lingams and Yonis are publicly exhibited.

As the interest in Tantra increases, Tantric temples will undoubtedly be established in the West. Will they be adorned with explicit erotic sculptures? Will they be staffed by priestesses and sacred prostitutes? Will the sexual sacraments of Tantra tradition be celebrated within their walls? Maybe.

In the twenty-first century, some Tantric temples might have birthing rooms supervised by matriarchal midwives and Tantric doctors. Perhaps there'll be Tantric schools, with curriculums specializing in Yoga, health, Tantric art, science, music, and the erotic disciplines. There could be special Tantric ashrams, where elderly people can go to prepare for death, and Tantric cremation grounds, so we no longer need to use valuable land for burials. Only time will tell.

Most Christians celebrate one day a week, generally Sunday, as a holy day. This is, really, the celebration of the life-giving sun—sun-

Painting on board, used to top a ceremonial offering, depicting the original "Father–Mother" (Tib: *Kuntu Zangpo–Kuntu Zangmo*) seated in sexual union. From Tibet, circa eighteenth century.

An orgy of erotic activity portrayed on a Tantric temple in Nepal. It symbolizes the unbridled "union of the six senses" (the five senses plus the mind). Wood sculpture from the Kathmandu Valley, Nepal, circa eighteenth century.

day—traditionally viewed as the day celebrating the "Heavenly Father." In Christian tradition, there is no time set aside for the Great Mother. This is a situation that needs to be corrected.

Tantrics traditionally view two days a week as sacred. These are Saturdays, dedicated to Shiva, and Tuesdays, dedicated to Shakti and all forms of the Great Goddess. Tantrics also celebrate the solstices and the equinoxes: spring and autumn for Shakti and winter and summer for Shiva. This is a tradition that, as the working week shortens in the twenty-first century, could easily become part of Western culture.

Tantric Initiation in Cyberspace

As twenty-first-century technology and traditional Tantra influence each other, a whole new range of technospiritual activities will likely emerge. For instance, it is likely there will be less desire or need for one-on-one Tantric initiations.

Modern people are already very wary of the traditional guru–disciple setup that Tantric teachings have for thousands of years required. Our culture has not adequately prepared us for it. Also, it seems that in the West, there has been quite a bit of abuse of the traditional Tantric initiatory scenario, by both gurus and by their followers.

In the first few years following publication of *Sexual Secrets*, I received numerous letters from earnest spiritual seekers. Most wanted to know how or where to obtain Tantric initiation. This phenomenon has continued.

I did not have the time to reply to all the letters I received over the years, and it was extremely difficult for me to give much guidance to those who persisted with their requests. Other than pointing them to books, basic Yoga techniques, and places of Tantra pilgrimage in India and Tibet or suggesting they try to meet certain people (whom I was reluctant to have bothered by people I did not know), there was very little I could do to help.

Times have changed.

Mantras of initiation and the accompanying visualizations are already available on Tantra Web sites, put together by people well versed into Tantric lore and connected to time-tested spiritual lineages. It will only be a small step for customized mantra audio clips to become available for downloading over the Internet.

In traditional Tantra, context-specific mantras are selected by the teacher and imparted to the student, generally as part of a spiritual bonding rite. Once heard, the mantras are repeated in a rhythmic way, with focused intent. Correctly applied, they produce a type of fluctuating inner pulse or field, resonating as primordial vibrations that evoke and channel latent spiritual powers within. Both peaceful and wrathful, passive and aggressive, mantras take on "personalities" which drive our innermost longings and transform our fears.

Cassette tape audio and video recordings have, in the latter part of the twentieth century, proven to be very effective aids for teaching languages, for training salespeople and personnel, enhancing self-esteem, and reprogramming of a wide range of personal attitudes. The fascinating power of sound and the potency of the focused word or power phrase has, in the twenty-first century, become popular everywhere—in advertising, in sales, in politics, and in the entertainment industry. That such techniques can be highly effective for psychological reinforcement or spiritual evolution cannot be doubted. Even the power of prayer has been scientifically shown to bring about positive results in healing and character reinforcement.

In the twenty-first century, digital technology, computers, miniaturized addressable satellite terminals, and the Internet will be applied to all these areas.

Virtual Tantra initiations, perhaps with mantras fed directly into the brain through entrainment devices, are already totally feasible. From the technical standpoint, there are no major obstacles. The potential for various types of online Tantra initiations is obvious, but it will take a combination of imagination, cooperation, technical know-how, and Tantric knowledge to make it happen. Much will depend on feedback, true seekers, and people like you and your willingness to open up, know yourself, and to ask yourself those most intimate and at times difficult questions and share honestly.

For a Tantric teacher to effectively convey initiation, he or she must know the candidate very well. Initiation is interactive. For "remote" initiations to work, there should first be a process of getting to know the candidate. In the twenty-first century, we can expect that candidates for Tantric initiations over the Internet will be required to participate interactively in cyberspace before being granted access to download customized initiation packets of data.

The New Tantric Sexual Paradigm

What will be the new sexual paradigm in the century ahead? To understand the problem, we should first take a brief look at the roots of traditional Western culture.

Ancient Greek culture, on which Western culture is largely based, was strongly masculine. In general, Greek men had a contemptuous view of women. The *hetairai*, who were generally well-educated courtesan love priestesses and followers of the goddess Aphrodite, were virtually the only respected women in this culture. The Greek version of democracy, which is so often held as an ideal in the West, was never truly democratic.

The data of modern embryology reveals that in humans, femaleness is in fact the original fundamental life-form. *The male evolves out of the female.* Contrary to the teachings of the book of Genesis in the Bible, all creation was, originally, female.

In relation to size and body weight, women's brains are larger than men's. Women are generally far healthier than men and are quicker to recover from physical illness. They are also better at recovering from psychological or emotional stress. At the present time, in all countries of the world, life expectancy for women is greater than for men. What is this situation telling us?

It is telling us that, far from being the weaker sex, woman is in fact stronger than man. Woman just needs to recognize this and exert her strength in a spiritual way.

All the evidence suggests that in ancient times, men stood in awe of women. The mysteries of childbirth and nurturing were compelling. The cosmic connections between woman and nature were intuited. The power of woman was perceived to be closely interconnected with magical control over nature. In this context, woman had the dominant role in spiritual evolution.

Stereotyped gender roles have indeed changed. More women than ever before are working. Many are taking on jobs previously held only by men. Women are rapidly gaining both economic and political influence. They are also becoming more conscious of their innate sexual and spiritual power.

As women gain more and more economic, political, and spiritual influence, does this suggest that women will take over from men as the dominant force of twenty-first-century society? Perhaps.

In the West, much will depend on the Christian church and on whether church leaders are able to embrace the new sexually expressive spiritual feminism that Tantra advocates. Much will also depend on how Westernized Tantra develops in the years ahead.

Attitudes toward, feelings about, and uses of sex have already changed drastically. Culturally driven sexual superstitions and patriarchal manipulation of gender roles are rapidly being abandoned. Our sexual paradigms have altered. With the advent of birth control, sex ceased to be primarily linked to procreation. It is now okay to have sex purely for pleasure, and more and more people feel comfortable viewing sex as a spiritual activity.

Women have more access to men than they once did. Sex roles are changing. Interestingly, recent statistics show that though men still have more extramarital affairs than women, some major changes are taking place. One study in 1996 reported that young wives are apparently now more unfaithful than young husbands.

The pituitary gland, situated in the head, is key to the manufacture and release of sex hormones in the body. Our bodies are veritable chemical factories. We produce a wide variety of substances (including some powerful drugs) that govern our functions, moods, and sexual interactions. Tantric Yoga and meditation techniques enable conscious control of the pituitary and other glandular secretions. Sex function is linked to overall health. There can be little doubt that, in the twenty-first century, sex hormones and prosexual drugs (substances that improve sexual interactions) will become even more important.

As conventional standards of sexual behaviour change, the unconventional will become conventional. Sexually aggressive men and women will redefine gender roles in the twenty-first century. Both men and women will have more freedom of choice about whether to be aggressive or passive in their intimate relationships. As Western culture adapts to these role changes, it will become spiritually enriched.

The Future of Sex, Love, and Marriage

In the twenty-first century, what will be the future of sex, love, and marriage? Will marriage disappear entirely or will entirely different forms of marriage become the norm? We can be sure that marriage as we have known it will change.

In both primitive and sophisticated societies, marriage has invariably been an economic alliance rather than an erotic one. It has generally been based on family alliances, social necessity, and the desire to legitimize offspring.

The *Laws of Manu*, a Hindu work of encylopedic scope compiled about two thousand years ago, has a lot of data on marriage. Of course, Manu's laws relate to a time in the distant past, when patriarchy and the caste system prevailed. Nevertheless, it is a wisely written book based around spiritual values; as such, it has some relevance today.

Manu lists eight different ways of marrying women. The first six are said by him to be right for a priest, the last four for a ruler and for a commoner or a servant:

> When a man adorns his daughter and gives her as a gift to a learned man of good character whom he has summoned
>
> When a man, while in the course of a sacrifice, adorns his daughter and gives her as a gift to the officiating priest who is properly performing his duties
>
> When a man gives away his daughter after receiving from the bridegroom a cow and a bull, or two cows and bulls, in accordance with the law
>
> When a man gives away his daughter after adorning her and saying, "May the two of you together fulfill your duties"
>
> When a man takes a girl, after giving as much wealth as he is able to her relatives and to the girl, because he wants her himself
>
> When a girl and her lover join with one another because they want to, out of desire

When a man forcibly carries off a girl

When a man secretly has sex with a girl while she is asleep,
    drunk, or out of her mind

All of the types of marriage recognized by Manu are the result
of decisions made by man. Only the sixth category, "when a girl and
her lover join with one another because they want to, out of desire,"
directly involves woman in the choice. In orthodox Hindu tradition,
as in Judeo-Christian teachings, woman is viewed as the property of
her father. This is a scenario that is now drastically different.

Marriage vows have been redefined, and they will no doubt be
redefined further as both women and men become more liberated.
The usual marriage vows of Christian origin to "love, honor, and
obey" now commonly omit *obey*. All kinds of new vows are being
developed, reflecting new perspectives on what is or is not expected
of a marriage. In the twenty-first century, we'll need to be very clear
about what we expect of each other in a relationship. For those who
choose marriage, whatever vows are proposed should ideally be discussed and fine-tuned so as to avoid disappointment.

Monogamy, polygamy (people of either sex having more than
one spouse), polygyny (a man having more than one wife), polyandry (a woman having more than one husband), group marriage, polyfidelity, polyamory, serial monogamy, closed relationships, and
open relationships are just some of the ways that men and women
have lived together.

In 1904, French scholar and novelist Remy de Gourmont, writing in *The Natural History of Love*, observed: "In most human races
there is a radical polygamy, disseminated under a show-front of monogamy."

In the West, the Christian church has largely been responsible
for virtually eradicating formal polygamy, which in Western culture
is illegal. What has taken its place is serial monogamy: People have
monogamous relationships, break up or divorce, and begin another
relationship.

Tantra teaches that love comes in one of two basic forms: conventional and unconventional. In the normal Western lifestyle, *conventional* means within the traditional marriage of a single man and
woman, and *unconventional* means a couple living together without

marrying, the relationships of a married man with his mistress or a married woman with her paramour, homosexual or lesbian couples, and group relationships such as two or more women living with a single man or vice versa.

Conventional love very often eventually becomes restrictive or limiting. It can become routine or boring. What was once a passionate and highly sexual relationship becomes virtually nonexistent. This commonly leads to separation, divorce, or infidelity. Unconventional love very often can be empowering. It can be stimulating and exciting.

As we approach the end of the twentieth century, for many people, unconventional love is already taking the place of conventional love. More and more couples are living together without marrying. Same-sex relationships are on the increase. "Family values" are changing. What is this situation telling us?

It is telling us that if we truly wish to sustain an intimate relationship, we need to add some unconventionality to our lifestyle. This doesn't mean that when we're in a relationship, we need to look for sex "on the side." Neither does it mean we should become sexually promiscuous.

Most people can benefit from adding some variety to their sexual activities. Most can benefit by a bit of sexual experimentation. Here, too, Tantra has much to contribute.

In the sixties, we saw a lot of sexual experimentation, including open marriages, in which couples agreed to allow each other outside relationships, and group marriages. This and other variations of polyamory or polyfidelity are still being experimented with and might eventually become formalized in Western society within a legal and socially acceptable framework. Same-sex marriages is another hot topic currently under debate.

Women are rapidly gaining political and economic liberation. The traditional housewife is becoming more rare. As women take on most of the roles and responsibilities that were once exclusive to men, will women take on "wives" to run their homes? What will be the meaning of *family values* in the twenty-first century? Will the majority of children be brought up by surrogate mothers? Will communal family care become part of Western culture?

In the kibbutz system in Irsael, all children in a community are

separated at an early age from their families and brought up together, with parents rotating as their "minders" and teachers. The
children live in fully integrated children's houses. Sexes are not seg-
regated; young men and women commonly share the same dormi-
tory. Sex is openly discussed. The atmosphere is sex-positive. Young
or old, consenting people can be sexually intimate together. This system, which is based largely on the ancient communal adolescent
houses (such as with the Muria of India), has proven quite successful. Will the kibbutz system of bringing up children become more
common in the twenty-first century? Perhaps.

Tantra teaches that one does not own one's children, a hard
concept for any parent to accept, yet it is a fact that parents have
mostly a caretaking role. If we accept reincarnation as fact, we must
also accept that in a way, our children have chosen us.

We should try to be less attached to our children. Yes, we must
do our best to protect and educate them, surround them with love
and attention, reinforce the positive and direct away from the negative, practice what we preach, and try to always be a good friend.
But we should not try to dominate our children or mold them into
versions of our selves.

There are no easy answers as to what the future of sex, love,
marriage, and "family values" will be in the twenty-first century. A
lot will depend on leadership, on teachers, and on the amount of
positive dialogue that takes place within families.

There will obviously be a lot of changes, but provided there is
mutual respect and proper dialogue between men and women, our
sexual future will be spiritually empowered and culturally enriched.

Tantra and the New Spiritual Reality

Quoting an axion of Tantra, mythologist Joseph Campbell makes a
pertinent observation: "There is a well-known Tantric saying—'by
none but the godly may a god be worshipped.' " In the twenty-first
century, people will discover their godly nature. Those who examine
it closely will find it to be goddesslike—sensual, pleasure-loving, inspiring, compassionate, and spiritually uncompromising. This god-

dess/god within is the essence of Tantric truth and the prime positive hope for the future.

In the twenty-first century, Tantra will touch and bless those who are prepared to deal directly with the new spiritual reality. What do I mean by that? I mean the flowering of the phenomena that have been appearing in Western culture since the first seeds were planted at the beginning of the "Age of Aquarius," which is generally said to have commenced in January 1962.

Clues to the future are generally found from looking back into the past and exploring the possibilities within the present. The inevitable universal laws work, whether or not we believe in them. As individuals, we'd best grow up spiritually, authentically, and without limiting, outdated, and culturally biased superstitions. The time has come for us to complete what began in the sixties, to complete the truly democratic, radical, and loving journey of self-discovery, communication, and spiritual evolution.

What we can't do alone we must do together. Here again, Tantra holds the key. Tantra is all about communication, especially about communication between man and woman and between ourselves and the universe.

Nothing can stop the new spiritual reality from blooming. Nothing can stop men and women from discovering and experiencing spiritual sex and the new paradigm of proper human behavior. It will become universally established and will be cross-cultural, dynamic, and uncompromising.

So many things are changing. As we completely free ourselves from feelings of guilt and superstition, we'll give up blind allegiance to the jealous Judeo-Christian patriarchal God. Instead, we'll embrace and be embraced by the original Goddess and God, the divine "cosmic couple" of Tantra tradition, recognizing that their spiritual essence lives within each of us.

The Future of Tantra Is Like Woman's Best Orgasm

The future of Tantra is like a woman's best orgasm. Why? Because it is without limits. It embraces the beginnings and end of the universe and then it repeats itself. Like the best female orgasm, Tantra is a vast spiritual experience, expansive, oceanic, and filled with creative potential, vast and unlimited, wondrous and unpredictable.

Tantra teaches how to become master or mistress of our inner universe, how to be completely comfortable with whatever emotional, mental, or spiritual domain we find ourselves in.

I know of no better way to end this section than to refer to two quotes, the first from a Walt Whitman poem written more than a hundred years ago and the other from the *Hevajra Tantra*:

> Passage O soul to India!
> Eclaircise the myths Asiatic, the primitive fables.
> Not you alone proud truths of the world,
> Nor you alone ye facts of modern science,
> But myths and fables of old,
> Asia's Africa's fables,
> The far-darting beams of the spirit,
> The unloos'd dreams . . .

> There is no being that is not enlightened, if it but knows its own true nature.

9 TANTRA DATABASE

I am willing to answer questions by e-mail but i may not always have time to do so. I am neither embarrassed by the subject matter nor am i in search of virtual sex. I have no religious bias, but can discuss a multitude of historical and recent "sex religions" as well as non-religious tantra parallels like karezza.

—CATHERINE YRONWODE, from Web-page article
"The Biological Basis of Tantric Sex"

THIS TANTRA database contains material relevant to any deeper exploration of subjects covered in this book. It is by no means complete. Tantra is like the Internet—expanding exponentially, links everywhere, innovative, cross-cultural, knowing no boundaries, and changing day by day.

It is exciting for me to have been able to participate in the spread of Tantric knowledge. Thirty or more years ago, when I first started to seriously gather information on Tantra, information was hard to come by, but it is everywhere now. I offer this database as a starting point for those wishing to enter the world of Tantra on their own terms. Surf the Internet, read the books, check out the scene, and then ask yourself: "Isn't this truly a most exciting time? All the barriers are down. Initiation could be but a few clicks away!"

Tantra Related Web Sites on the Internet

The following are some home pages on the Internet of relevance to both traditional and contemporary Tantra and to topics covered in this book. Many of these pages have hyperlinks to other World Wide Web Sites. I have done my best to keep the universal resource locators (URL) site addresses current. However, should any of them not work (servers are frequently changed), enter the precise page title *as given*, into a search engine to find their latest URL. Enjoy!

TantraWorks™ **Home Page:** Created specifically for readers of this book.
http://www.tantraworks.com

Hindu Tantrik Home Page: An excellent Tantra site, from Mike Magee and associates, with many good pages and masses of reliable information, including graphics, translations of key texts, and lots of Tantra links.
http://www.hubcom.com/tantric/

International Journal of Tantric Studies: At Harvard University. An intellectual Tantric Journal with some informative articles.
http://www.shore.net/~india/ijts/

Church of Tantra Home Page: A large and glitzy Tantra and neo-Tantra site with details on sacred sex and Tantric publications, products and workshops, as well as good links to other related web sites.
http://www.Tantra.org/

Buddhism on the Net: A list of Dharma-related sites, including links to most Tibetan Buddhist centers representing all the major sects. A reliable resource for those interested in Tibetan Tantra.
http://www.manymedia.com/tibet/Buddhism.html

Global Hindu Electronic Network: The Hindu Universe: A very well constructed Web site with a wealth of information on Hinduism, India, and Asian spiritual traditions, with many good links.
http://hindunet.org
also at:
http://rbhatnagar.ececs.uc.edu:8080/alt_hindu/altH_1994.html

Indology Home Page: A good resource for students of Indology and Tantra, including a virtual archive of Indic texts, online dictionaries, digital art, electronic journals, etc.
http://www.ucl.ac.uk/~ucgadkw/indology.html

Developmental Techniques of Tantra/Sex Magic: A pagan Tantra guide from a workshop given by Frah. Geh. Mad at Lughnasad in

1995 and previously at a UC pagan studies group. Has some worth-while information.
http://www.greendome.org/archives/tantra/tantra.html

Amookos and the Natha Ganas: A fact sheet on Tantra, with information on how to connect with contemporary Tantra, and spiritual lineages.
http://www.compulink.co.uk/~mandrake/naths.htm

Kundalini Research Center: Nicely constructed artistic site with information on Kundalini, chakras, Tantra and other relevant topics.
http://aloha.net/~bpeay/kundalini/xindex.html

Kundalini Resource Center Home Page: Another Kundalini site, with some interesting information.
http://hmt.com/kundalini/index.html

Kundalini Research Foundation, Ltd: More on Kundalini.
http://www.renature.com/KRF/

"catherine yronwode's" Home Page: Spiritual sex subjects from a pioneer contributor of sacred sex on the Internet.
http://www.luckymojo.com/sacredsex.html

Guide to Tantric Sex: A site with good information, from Una Mac-Donoghue, including an article "Guidelines for a Tantric Ritual".
http://www.widemedia.com/fix/tantric.html/tantric.html

Tantra: Thoughts on Fantasy and its Relevance to Tantra: An informative article from Rose Dawn Scott, a pagan and Tantra savant.
http://www.telebyte.nl/krce/fantasy.html

Tantrism Overview: An article by Dinu Roman.
http://www.tantra.org/overview.htm

Tantra: The Path of Ecstasy: A page about "deeper states of love and ecstasy," from True L. Fellows.
http://www.aubergines.com/tantra/tantra.htm

Bindu: An on-line periodical on Yoga, Tantra, and meditation, published in Scandinavia.
http://inet.uni-cdk/~bindu/uk_bindu.htm

What Is Tantra: An article on the Tantric way of the Natha Siddha, by Sahajananda.
http://www.compnet.co.uk/perhome/jaga/tantra.htm

Dzogchen: Tibetan-style Tantra philosophy interpreted by Surya Das, a Westerner.
http://www.dzogchen.org/

New York Dharma Group: Home page for Tibetan Buddhist topics, including some good information on Buddhist Tantra.
http://www.fusebox.com/NYDG/nydg.html.

Popular Tantra: On the Buddha 10 Page from Tyagi. Copies of various articles relating to modern Tantra, including ''Divine Sexuality'' by David Ramsdale, ''What is Tantra'' by Charles and Caroline Muir, and ''Why Tara'' by Robert Frey.
http://www.dorje.com:8080/netstuff/dharma/buddha10

Tantra: The Art of Conscious Loving: The Charles and Caroline Muir home page.
http://www.resonate.com/places/articles/m-blend/tantra.htm

The Loving Center: Source for Information on Tantric Loving: A site promoting Tantra seminars, including ''Caring for the Corporate Couple,'' and a Tantra bibliography.
http://heartfire.com/tantric/loving.html

Tantra: The Lost Art of Fulfilling Sexuality: An article on sacred sex by Dave Hutchison.
http://www.online.com:80/~richardc/tsn/art005.html

E-sensuals Sacred Sex Catalog: A commercial site for Tantra books and products.
http://www.tantra.com/catalog.html

Dakinis: Sky Dancing Angels: Information on Dakinis and angels.
http://www.marigold.com/rt88/dakini.html

Sex and Spirit: Conversation with Swami Nostradamus Virato on His Work in Tantra: A transcript of an interview with Barbara Williams.
http://www.newfrontier.com/2/sexspir.htm

The Secrets of Sacred Sex: A commercial publication site.
http://www.aloha.net/~axiom/sacred.html

JBL Sacred Sex: A commercial site with information pertaining to Tantra.
http://www.jblstatue.com/sacredsex.html

World Art Erotica: Erotica with a Tantric theme, from Myles Kesten.
http://www.wae.org/

German Tantra Magazine Home Page: Based in Zurich, Switzerland.
http://ourworld.compuserve.com/homepages/TANTRA/

Maithuna: The site of an Italian Tantra Institute.
http://www.avt.krenet.it/tantra/tantra.htm

Tantra Resources in Croatia: A good multilingual site from Davor Stancic, a Tantra teacher from Croatia.
http://jayor.srce.hr/~dstancic/

Cyber Shrine: An artistic site with various Tantra-inspired imagery, especially from Maitreya Bowen.
http://www.rain.prg/~maisoui/shrine.html

The Island of Eros: Imaginative spiritual site about the sacred love mysteries at the Venusian Church, with temples, a university, a forum, and more.
http://www.venusian.org/venus_home.htm

The SPIRIT Web Page: Extensive site that includes information on reincarnation, meditation, Yoga, Theosophy and mysticism, plus glossaries and a neat search engine for spiritual subjects. Entry of Tantra into this search engine leads to other related pages, with topics such as Kundalini, Shaktipat, Kriyas and Siddha Yoga.
http://www.spiritweb.org/Spirit.html

Sahaja Yoga Home Page: A site on the teachings of Nirmala Devi, Kundalini, chakras, etc.
http://www.sahajayoga.org/more.htm

Meditation Information Network: A lot of information on transcendental meditation (TM).
http://minet.org/

The Integral Yoga Web Site: A site dedicated to the Sri Aurobindo, the Mother, the Aurobindo Ashram, etc.
http://www.webcom.com:80/~miraura/

Ramakrishna-Vivekananda Center of New York: An informative web site on these important Tantric teachers.
http://www.ramakrishna.org/

Self-Realization Fellowship: A good site from the organization founded by Paramahansa Yogananda, author of the important book *Autobiography of a Yogi.*
http://www.yogananda.srf.org/

Sri Vidya: An imaginative and informative traditional Hindu Tantra site.
http://www.frontiernet.net:80/kvenkat/SriVidya/index.html

Sri Sarada Mandir: Kali/Shiva: A virtual shrine to the goddess Kali with access to icons of Ganesha, Ramakrishna, Sarada Devi, Vivekananda, Kali Ma and Shiva.
http://www.scescape.com/saradama/mandir/temp5.html

The Kali Mandir: A virtual shrine to the goddess Kali in Laguna Beach, California. Put together by "a loosely-knit group of individuals from various spiritual and ethnic backgrounds who love God in various forms, especially in the form of Kali."
http://www.kalimandir.org/

Kali: Death of the Ego: A Kali ritual by Victoria and the Rainbow Connection.
http://hpproebster1.informatik.tumuenchen.de/Personen/rk/ txt/kali2.txt

Kali: A page with some relevant information on this Hindu goddess.
http://www.csulb.edu/~persepha/Kali.html

Mandala: Buddhist Tantric Diagrams: Details of mandala construction at the Nechung monastery in Tibet.
http://ccat.sas.upenn.edu/george/mandala.html

Asian Art Resource: Tantric information including Tibetan art, from Australia National University (ANU).

**http://coombs.anu.edu.au/WWWVL   Pages/TibPages/Art/
tibetart.html**

Asian Arts: A well-designed site with exhibits, including Tantric
subjects, mandalas, Tantric art, galleries, and articles.
http://www.webart.com/asianart/index.html

Mohan's Hindu Image Gallery: Images and relevant data.
http://www.geko.net.au/~mohan/images.html

Kalachakra: Data on Tibetan Tantra and Shambala
http://www.diamondway.org/stupa.htm

Kagyu Lineage: A site with information about the Tibetan Karma
Kagyu lineage of Tantric teachers.
http://www.maui.net:80/tsurphu/karmapa/kagyu_lineage.html

Nyingma Centers: An informative site from Lama Tarthang Tulku,
a Tibetan Buddhist Tantra teacher.
http://www.nyingma.org/

Lakshmi Divali: A page with topics like the Hindu goddess of preservation and prosperity and information on the Divali festival.
http://www.cascade.net/lakshmi.html

Aghor: A page from the Nine Gates Mystery School, founded by Gay
Luce, featuring topics such as Shiva and Baba Kinaram, a radical
Hindu Tantric teacher.
http://www.ninegates.com/Aghor2.html

The Gnostic Society in Norway: An index of Hinduism, resources,
including many good Tantra-related links.
http://home.sn.no/~noetic/hotlist/hindu.htm

Hinduism Today: An informative online publication with many fascinating articles on Hindu culture, put out by Satguru Subramani-
yaswami.
http://www.HinduismToday.kauai.hi.us/ashram/htoday.html

Engaged Buddhist Dharma Page: Excellent site with fine links to
sites covering a wide spectrum of philosophical, spiritual, social and
political issues.
http://www.maui.com/~lesslie/

Mind and Body: Links and articles with Yoga, TM, meditation, and related themes.
http://www.stud.unit.no:80/~olavb/mindbody.html

Mystical Crossroads Tantra Site: A commercial web page offering Tantra information together with books and Tantra products.
http://www.jersey.net:80/~mystical1/index2.htm

Isle of Avalon: A fun multi-dimensional neo-Tantra site based on chakras, with initiatory levels.
http://www.isleofavalon.co.uk/

Skydancing UK: A Tantra site from teachers of sacred sexuality.
http://www.rscom.com/seagreen/tantra/

Pagan Organisations: British Scarlet Tantric Pagan Center: Home page of a Tantra-related pagan group in England.
http://www.antipope.demon.co.uk/paganlink/organisations/bstpc.html

The Nepal Institute: Promoting the Tantric Way of Life: From Swami Virato and a Tantric Center in North Carolina.
http://www.newfrontier.com/nepal/

Tantric Knowledge: Methods of Perceiving the Unknown: Web site of the Tantra Tribe, featuring Tantric art, related links, and more.
http://www.accessone.com/~ttribe/

Eros: Michael Read's Tantric Tarot.
http://www.sun2001.com/eros.html

Trika Institute for Spiritual Development: An important site in both English and Romanian, featuring the teachings of Gregorian Bivolaru ("Greg"), articles on Tantra, a chat zone, and important Tantric dates.
http://lynx.neu.edu/home/httpd/c/cturcanu/trika

Yogi Bhajan Home Page: Information on this "White Tantra Yoga" teacher.
http://www.yogibhajan.com

Hi-Priestess Tantra: A largely encoded Tantra site with interesting graphics. Based in Kyoto, Japan.
http://www.hotline.co.jp:80/~hirahara/tantra.html

Mage-guide: The Mage's Guide to the Internet from Tyagi Naga-siva: A very complete guide to spirituality sites, including bulletin board systems (BBSs), Internet relay chat (IRC), multi-user dimensions (MUDs), file transfer protocols (FTPs), etc.
http://www.hollyfeld.org/magi/

Ceci Henningsson's Home Page: Spirituality, Paganism, and Tantra, with some excellent links.
http://www.lysator.liu.se/~ceci/

Shawn's occult and religious resources: Many, many links to relevant subjects, including home pages for alchemy, astrology, Buddhism, Christianity, Egyptology, paganism, Rosicrucianism, as well as to FTP sites, newsgroups, etc.
http://web1.andrew.cmu.edu/user/shawn/occult/

Magical Blend Magazine Online: A beautifully designed site with articles, excellent links, online horoscopes, etc.
http://www.eden.com/magical

Anders Magick Page: A well-researched site with topics such as Freemasonry, Golden Dawn, O.T.O and Thelema, Rosicrucians, neo-pagans, and more. Links to "pages related to magick, mysticism and similar matters."
http://www.nada.kth.se/~nv91-asa/magick.html

The Great Beast: Data on Aleister Crowley, with links to other related sites.
http://marlowe.wimsey.com/~rshand/streams/gnosis/beast.html

College of Thelema and Temple of Thelema: A site based in Los Angeles, with information on the teachings and philosophy of Thelema, Aleister Crowley, etc.
http://www.thelema.org/

Hermetic Order of the Golden Dawn Int'l: A stylish site with very good links to "magical" and other related sites.
http://www.cyberg8t.com/hogd/public_html/index.html

Ordo Templis Orientis Home Page: Devoted to information on the OTO.
http://www.crl.com/~thelema/oto.html

Gurdjieff Home Page: An informative site.
http://www.gurdjieff.org

Helena Petrovna Blavatsky: A page featuring a biography of Madame Blavatsky, founder of the Theosophical Society.
http://www.primenet.com/~wtmtn/HPB.HTML

Alan Watts Electronic University: Home page of a site with everything you need to know about the beat Zen teacher Alan Watts.
http://www.alanwatts.com/

Friends of Osho: A Rajneesh followers site, with information on publications, ashram life, their rules, and more.
http://earth.path.net:80/osho

The Ancient World Web: A site from Julia Hayden, with a mass of information and links to archaic culture, including mysticism, archaeology, and more.
http://atlantic.evsc.virginia.edu/julia/AW/meta.html

Ancient Civilizations: Information on archaic cultures.
http://www3.northstar.k12.ak.us:80/schools/awe/ancientciv.html

The WWWorld of Archaeology: Great information about classical and general archaeology.
http://www.he.net/~archaeol/wwwarky.html

Joseph Campbell Foundation's Web Site: All you need to know about Joseph Campbell, his life and works.
http://www.jcf.org/

Dr John Lilly's Home Page: Details on the life and work of John Lilly, one of the pioneers who wrote about the human biocomputer.
http://www.rain.org/~lili/DrJohnLilly/

Free Daism: The home page of the Daism organization, with a lot of information on Da Free John/Da Avabhasa (formerly Franklin Jones), the radical neo-Tantra guru.
http://www.adidam.org/

Surfing the Himalayas: Web site promoting the books of Frederick Lenz (Zen Master Rama)
http://www.himalaya.com/

The Goddess Home Page: A fun site dedicated to goddess culture.
http://clever.net/moonlight/mp/Goddess.html

The Goddess Page: Another worthwhile goddess page.
http://Venus.rdc.puc-rio.br/butthead/goddess.html

Temple of the Lady Home Page: A goddess-spirituality site.
http://www.nervecentre.com/Temple-of-the-Lady/

Yoni: Gateway to the Feminine: A well-designed and interesting female spirituality site in Australia with very good articles and links.
http://www.ion.com.au/yoni/

Spirited Women Online, the Sister Spirit Magazine: Spirituality and feminist links.
http://www.teleport.com/nonprofit/sister-spirit/
magazine.html

Wicca and Women's Spirituality: Information on Wicca and other goddess-centered religions.
http://www.io.com/~cortese/spirituality/wicca.html

The Covenant of the Goddess: Home page of a California based pagan organisation. Has some good links.
http://www.crc.ricoh.com/~rowan/COG/cog.html

Venus' Home Page: A fun site on goddess culture, including Aphrodite's Temple and useful links.
http://www.caw.org/deities/venus/index.html

Isis: the Black Virgin: A home page with extensive information on the goddess Isis in classical times, with links to other related informative sites.
http://marlowe.wimsey.com/~rshand/streams/scripts/
isis.html

The Lyceum of Isis of the Stars: Part of the *Fellowship of Isis*, "bringing awareness of the goddess in her many names and forms back into consciousness."
http://www.isis-of-the-stars.org

Ishtar, Lady of Heaven: Extensive information on the goddess Ishtar.
http://marlowe.wimsey.com/~rshand/streams/scripts/
ishtar.html

Stargate: The Real One: Doorways to the Past and Future: An imaginative and informative site from Mark Roberts, with data on the archaic matriarchy.
http://home.earthlink.net/~pleadesx/

Nine Gates Mystery School: from Dr. Gay Luce.
http://ninegates.com/

NilfhimR AzT: Interesting and highly imaginative neo-Tantra pagan site from an affiliate of the Adi Natha Sampradaya, with audio downloads, mantras, art, and links.
http://www.tornado.be/~clan

The Priestesses of Inanna: A page featuring an informative article by Anders Sandberg on this Sumerian goddess and her mythology.
http://www.student.nada.kth.se/~nv91-asa/Mage/inanna.html

Religions of Antique Civilizations: Goddess Worship in Old Europe: A site with a lot of data on goddess worship in ancient cultures, especially Marija Gimbutas's discoveries.
http://sorrel.humboldt.edu/~wh1/013.Ancient/Ancient.html

Diotima: Women and Gender in the Ancient World: A valuable resource of materials for the study of women and gender in the ancient world.
http://www.uky.edu/ArtsSciences/Classics/gender.html

Sarasvati-Sindhu Civilization (c.3000 BC): An excellent article on the Indus Valley Harappan culture.
http://www.ucl.ac.uk/~ucgadkw/indus.html

India Related Links: An important site from Srinivas Padmanabhuni, with tons of useful information on Hindu spiritual traditions, art, music, food, literature, astrology, news and travel.
http://ugweb.cs.ualberta.ca/srinivas/india1.html

Kayakalpa International: From Dr. Raam Pandey, with information about the Kaya Kalpa health system, products and services.
http://www.kayakalpa.com

Shanti Mandir: Home page of Swami Muktananda's successor, the new Nityananda.
http://www.shantimandir.com

Egyptology Resources: From Cambridge University. Articles and links to masses of good Egyptology resources.
http://www.newton.cam.ac.uk/egypt/

Pharaoh's Heart-Egyptology Page: Nicely put together, this site has links to other major Egyptology pages. Masses of information on ancient Egyptian culture, including art, spirituality, and mythology.
http://www.teleport.com/~ddonahue/phresour.html

The Gnosis Archive: A site with topics on Gnosticism, including a virtual library with many original Gnostic documents in English, such as those from Nag Hammadi.
http://www.webcom.com/~gnosis/

The Rosicrucian Home Page: Some relevant data.
http://www.cts.com/~rosfshp/

Mithraism: An informative site featuring details of the "Roman Empire's Final Pagan State Religion," from David Fingrut in Toronto, and including articles on the Persian Origins of Mithraism, Mithraic rites of initiation, etc.
http://www.1global.com/%7Ehermes3/mithras.htm

Alchemy Resources: A fascinating site with data on Chinese, Tibetan, Indian, Arabian, and European Alchemy.
http://www.maxinet.com/DHouchin/Html/Alchemy.htm

The Alchemy Virtual Library: Extensive information, with links.
http://www.colloquium.co.uk/alchemy/home.html
also at:
http://www.levity.com/alchemy/

Consolamentum: A page with the Cathar ritual of consolation, from Guy Wilson.
http://www.gnosis.org/gnosis/consolamentum.html

The Society for Human Sexuality: At the University of Washington. A very good database and sexuality library, with many links to sites covering virtually every aspect of human sexuality, including spiritual sex sites.
http://weber.u.washington.edu:80/~sfpse/

Libido: The Journal of Sex and Sensibility: An interesting online sexuality journal with good links.
http://www.indra.com/libido/

Paramour: Literary and Artistic Erotica: A sensual online journal with good articles.
http://www.paramour.com/paramour/

Regarding Sex: The Latest for Passionate People: An online magazine devoted to providing ''current and objective information about human sexuality to the Internet community.''
http://www.regsex.com/

AltSex: The main site on alternative sexuality with some interesting links to pages on polyamory, transgender issues and myriad other sexual arrangements.
http://www.altsex.org/

Reclaiming the Erotic: A forum on the erotic reality of today's world, with some worthwhile discussion on eroticism in Western culture.
http://www.rippleeffects.com/index.html

Journal of Buddhist Ethics: An important site for the serious student of Buddhism, with many useful links.
http://www.psu.edu/jbe/jbe.html

Welcome to Isis Plus: A site featuring the art and culture of women of the African diaspora, with good links.
http://www.netdiva.com/isislite

OrishaNet: The home page of the Yoruba African spiritual tradition, with many interesting links to related sites.
http://www.seanet.com/~efunmoyiwa/ochanet.html

***Face of the Gods*: *Art and Altars of Africa and the African Americas*:** A virtual African pagan shrine.
http://www.nando.net/prof/caribe/Gods.html

***A New Look at Juju*:** African spiritual beliefs. An informative article by Adu Kwabena-Essem.
http://www.kaiwan.com/~mcivr/juju.html

***The Voodoo Server*:** Home page, with good African and Caribbean spiritual culture links.
http://www4.nando.net/prof/caribe/voodoo.html

***Vodoun (or Voodoo) Information Pages*:** An extensive voodoo site.
http://www.vmedia.com/shannon/voodoo/voodoo.html

***Service of Mankind Church*:** Home page of the Essemian Sanctuary of the Darkside Goddess. A San Francisco-based site dedicated to goddess worship, centered on Tantra, with sexual role playing themes.
http://www.darkside-goddess.org/

***Sound Photosynthesis*:** A home page and audio video archive with information on psychedelics, shamanism, Timothy Leary, John Lilly, Terence McKenna, Marija Gimbutas, etc.
http://www.sound.photosynthesis/com/

***Island Web*:** A visionary site based around Aldous Huxley's ideas in the book *Island*, with many links, especially to psychedelic history and topics.
http://www.island.org/

***Body, Mind, Spirit Online Magazine*:** A valuable resource.
http://www.hinman.oro.net/~bmsweb/bmsmag,htm

***Links to Links to Links to Occult*:** Many links such as: sublimation of the ego, scientific explanations, music, visual arts, free thought, etc., covering just about every ''spirituality'' topic imaginable.
http://www.ism.net/cgi-bin/ogiwrap/~swd/rotate.pl

***New Age Journal On-Line*:** A good resource for New Age information.
http://www.newage.com/

ConsciousNet: An online New Age magazine with pertinent information, services and products, topics like meditation and astrology, and links to related sites.
http://www.consciousnet.com

Ex-cult Archive: An important site with data on many cults and links.
http://www.ex-cult.org/index.html

Links to Indigenous Peoples Resources: Masses of links on worldwide indigenous peoples and information, including information on art, music, museums and human rights resources.
http://www.acs.appstate.edu/~rq12560/aboriginal.html

Library of Congress: The ultimate research resource, now online.
http://ftp.loc.gov/

Use of search engines such as Excite, Altavista, Webcrawler, Yahoo!, Inktomi, DejaNews, etc., is the best way to find new Tantra and sacred sexuality sites and chat groups on the Internet. Many sites are hyperlinked, allowing ease of access to other locations carrying related data. Enter key words such as: Tantra, spiritual sex, sacred sexuality, Tantra goddess, Shiva, Shakti, Kundalini, Yoni, chakra, mandala, Magick, Pagan, Wicca, Inner, Secret, Spirituality, Samadhi, etc.

Use your imagination and be persistent!

CHRONOLOGY

People and Events Pertinent to Tantra, in a Historical Context

c. 2500 B.C.E. High point of the Indus Valley civilization. Famous archaeological finds, such as the Shiva seals, metal figures of dancing girls, and the wooden Tantra matriarch figure date from this period.

c. 2500 B.C.E. Stonehenge constructed in England.

c. 1700 B.C.E. Aryans invade India, introduce patriarchy and the Vedas, and push matriarchal tribal cultures into remote areas.

c. 624 B.C.E. Birth of Gautama, the Buddha, into a Hindu royal family who worshipped Shiva.

c. 578 B.C.E. Birth of Pythagoras, the Greek philosopher and mathematician who recognized the equality of women and men.

c. 544 B.C.E. Death of the Buddha.

c. 510 B.C.E. Death of Pythagoras.

c. 427 B.C.E. Birth of Plato, who taught that reincarnation is necessary for the development of consciousness.

c. 384 B.C.E. Birth of Aristotle, the Greek father of Western sexology.

c. 347 B.C.E. Death of Plato.

c. 322 B.C.E. Death of Aristotle.

c. 221 B.C.E.   Great Wall of China, 2,600 miles long, is built.

65 C.E.   Time of the first Buddhist Chinese king.

c. 105 C.E.   The Chinese invent paper.

391 C.E.   The Roman emperor Theodosius orders paganism outlawed in favor of Christianity.

c. 395 C.E.   The Mystery Temple of Eleusis, near Athens, is destroyed by the Visigoths.

c. 400 C.E.   The Hindu sage Vatsyayana writes the *Kama Sutra*, the first sexual how-to book.

439 C.E.   The Catholic church condemns all those who believe in reincarnation.

450 C.E.   Birth of Bodhidharma, founder of Zen meditation.

548 C.E.   Buddhism accepted by the Japanese Emperor Kimmei.

533 C.E.   The Ecumenical Council officially declares the doctrine of reincarnation incompatible with Christian belief.

570 C.E.   Birth of Mohammed, founder of Islam. In his lifetime, the Goddess images at Mecca are destroyed.

632 C.E.   Death of Mohammed.

712 C.E.   Moslems conquer much of present-day Pakistan.

c. 747 C.E.   Padmasambhava, Indian Tantric Siddha, visits Tibet, founds the Samye Monastery and establishes Tantric Buddhism there.

988 C.E.   Birth of Tilopa, Indian Tantric Siddha teacher.

1000   Vikings land in North America.

1008   Muslim invasions into India commence.

1010   Start of the exodus of Hindus from Rajasthan Europe, where they become known as the Romany people (gypsies). They introduce many Tantric concepts into European culture.

1012   Birth of Marpa the translator, in Tibet, the father of the Kargyudpa Tantric sect.

1016   Birth of Naropa, Indian Tantric Siddha, teacher of Marpa and founder of the Six Yogas.

1040   The Chinese introduce the compass and perfect the use of gunpowder.

1052	Birth of Milarepa, who became first a sorcerer and then the most illustrious follower of Marpa.
1079	Birth of Gampopa, prime teacher of the first Karmapa.
1100	The first Crusade. Catholics establish strongholds in the Middle East.
1110	Birth of the first Karmapa, supreme Tantric hierarch of the Tibetan Kargyudpa sect.
1135	Death of Milarepa, Yogi par excellence.
1205	The fourth Crusade. The Latin Christians seize Constantinople (now known as Istanbul).
1209	The massacre of Cathars begins, on orders from the Catholic Church.
1254	Birth of Marco Polo, the Venetian traveler who spent twenty years in the East and wrote about Yogis.
1260	The second Karmapa hierarch initiates the Chinese Mongol emperor Kublai Khan into the Tantric mysteries.
1271	Marco Polo visits India and China.
1357	Birth of Je Tsongkhapa, the Tibetan who established the Gelugpa sect of Lamaism.
1407	The fifth Karmapa hierarch initiates the Chinese Ming emperor Yung-lo into the Tantric mysteries.
1419	Death of Je Tsongkhapa.
1492	Christopher Columbus discovers the Americas.
1516	The Erasmus version of the New Testament of the Bible is produced, based on Greek manuscripts.
1543	Copernicus proposes that the Earth orbits the sun.
1610	Galileo invents the telescope.
1611	The authorized version of the Bible (the King James) is published, based on a sixteenth-century Greek text.
1619	First African slaves sold in the American colonies.
1642	Birth of Isaac Newton, alchemist and scientist.
1688	Birth of Emanuel Swedenborg, the Swedish scientist who proposed that spiritual reality can best be approached through communion with nature.

1712 Nicholas de Venette's book *Mysteries of Conjugal Love Reveal'd*, an early sexual how-to, is published.

1724 Birth of Immanuel Kant, who introduced transcendental doctrines and explored the metaphysics of philosophy.

1727 Death of Isaac Newton.

1747 The first Shaker manifestations in England.

1772 Death of Emanuel Swedenborg.

1774 Mother Ann Lee leads a small group of Shakers to America.

1789 Start of the French Revolution.

1793 Invention of the cotton gin.

1799 Napoleon's army discovers the Rosetta stone, which will become the key to reading Egyptian hieroglyphs.

1802 Birth of George Ripley, one of the founders of the transcendentalist movement in America.

1803 Birth of Ralph Emerson, one of the founders of the transcendentalist movement in America.

1804 Death of Immanuel Kant, the German philosopher.

1807 Abbé Dubois's book *Hindu Manners, Customs and Ceremonies* is published; it is the first account of Tantric sexual rites in a European language.

1810 Birth of Margaret Fuller, one of America's first feminists and an active member of the transcendentalist movement.

1811 Birth of John Noyes, founder of the Society of Perfectionists.

1814 The first steam locomotive is operational.

1817 Birth of Henry David Thoreau, a prominent transcendentalist.

1819 Birth of Walt Whitman, poet and transcendentalist.

1820 First Indian immigrants arrive in the United States.

1821 Birth of Richard Burton, adventurer and sexual anthropologist.

1824 Friederich Forberg's book *Manual of Classical Erotology* is published.

1824 Joseph Smith Jr., the founder of Mormonism, experiences his first vision.

1825	Birth of Paschal Beverly Randolph, the writer who helped introduce Tantra to America.
1826	Frances Wright establishes the Nashoba communal farm near Memphis, Tennessee, advocating free love and racial integration.
1829	The human egg is discovered by Western science.
1830	The *Book of Mormon* is published.
1831	Birth of H. P. (Madame) Blavatsky, writer and occultist.
1833	Birth of Alice Bunker Stockham, pioneer in obstetrics and promoter of women's rights.
1833	Slavery abolished in the British Commonwealth.
1836	Birth of Sri Ramakrishna.
1841	Brook Farm, a spiritual communal farm, is established in Massachusetts by the transcendentalists.
1841	Christian missionaries become established in Yoruba territory, present-day Nigeria. Local Orisa cults are discouraged.
1844	The death of Joseph Smith Jr. by assassination.
1846	John Noyes founds the Society of Perfectionists.
1848	The Fox sisters start to produce ''spirit rappings,'' creating interest in psychic phenomena and spiritualism in America.
1848	John Noyes and his followers found the Oneida Community in New York.
1850	Birth of Karl Kellner, founder of the Ordo Templis Orientis (OTO), a magical fraternity familiar with Tantra.
1852	Death of Frances Wright.
1855	Walt Whitman's epic poem, *Leaves of Grass*, first published.
1856	Birth of Sigmund Freud, the father of Freudian psychiatry.
1857	William Acton's *Functions and Disorders of the Reproductive Organs*, one of the first books in which sex is explicitly discussed, is published.
1859	Birth of Havelock Ellis, the father of modern sexology.
1859	Charles Darwin's book *The Origin of Species* is published.
1861	Start of the American Civil War.

1862	Death of Henry David Thoreau.
1862	Birth of Vivekananda, who will introduce Hinduism to America.
1863	American Emancipation Proclamation, freeing all slaves, is issued.
1865	Gregor Mendel discovers the basic laws of genetics.
1865	Birth of John Woodroffe, one of the first Westerners to penetrate into and publish on Hindu Tantra.
c. 1868	Birth of Rasputin, the Russian healer and mystic.
1870	Paschal Rudolph founds the Eulis Brotherhood in Boston.
1872	John Noyes's book *Male Continence* is published.
1873	Birth of Swami Ram Tirath, who influenced Tantra in America.
1873	Birth of Aurobindo Ghosh, scientist, writer, Tantric, and political activist.
1873	Birth of George Gurdjieff.
1873	The Comstock antiobscenity bill is passed by the U.S. Congress.
1873	The Theosophical Society is founded in New York.
1875	Death of Paschal Randolph.
1875	Birth of Peter Coon, later known as Pierre Bernard, the father of Tantra in America.
1875	Birth of Carl Jung, originator of Jungian psychiatry.
1875	Birth of Aleister Crowley.
1876	Invention of the telephone by Alexander Bell.
1877	Madame Blavatsky's *Isis Unveiled* is published.
1879	Thomas Edison develops the first commercial lightbulb.
1880	Death of George Ripley.
1881	The Revised Version of the New Testament of the Bible is published.
1882	Death of Ralph Waldo Emerson.
1882	The first electric power station is built.
1883	Richard Burton's translation of the *Kama Sutra* is published.
1884	Birth of Bronislaw Malinowski, anthropologist who studied matriarchal cultures.

1885	The Oliphants' book *Sympneumata*, featuring Tantric breathing techniques, is published.
1885	Richard Burton's translation of the *Ananga Ranga* is published.
1886	Death of John Noyes, founder of the Oneida Community.
1886	Death of Sri Ramakrishna, Hindu Tantric mystic.
1886	Karl Benz develops the first automobile.
1886–67	Madame Blavatsky's book *Secret Doctrines* is published.
1890	Death of Sir Richard Burton.
1891	Death of Helena Blavatsky, founder of the Theosophical Society.
1892	Death of Walt Whitman.
1893	The first Parliament of Religions opens in Chicago and Swami Vivekananda gives a moving address, promoting Hinduism.
1893	Birth of Paramahansa Yogananda, author and founder of the Self-Realization Fellowship.
1894	Birth of Aldous Huxley, writer and consciousness explorer.
1896	Alice Stockham's book *Karezza* is published.
1896	The American writer Mark Twain visits India.
1896	Birth of Anandamayi Ma, Bengali woman mystic.
1897	Swami Vivekananda's book *Raja Yoga* is published.
1897	Birth of Wilhelm Reich, discoverer of orgone energy.
1897	Havelock Ellis tries peyote for the first time.
1898	Aleister Crowley joins the Hermetic Order of the Golden Dawn.
1901	Birth of Margaret Mead, feminist anthropologist.
1902	Death of Swami Vivekananda.
1902	Birth of Verrier Elwin, anthropologist who studied India's tribal matriarchal cultures.
1904	Swami Ram Tirath visits America and interacts with various Americans who go on to found the Tantrik Order in America.
1904	Birth of Joseph Campbell, mythologist.

1905   Pierre Bernard establishes the Bacchante Academy in San Francisco, which is destroyed in the great earthquake of April 1906.

1906   The Tantrik Order in America is founded by Pierre Bernard and associates.

1906   Publication of *International Journal; Tantrik Order*, in St. Louis.

1906   Death of *Swami Ram Tirath*.

1907   Birth of Mircea Eliade, Romanian specialist on the history of religion.

1908   Birth of Muktananda.

1908   Birth of Theos Bernard, Tantric initiate and medical doctor.

1910   Pierre Bernard opens his Oriental Sanctum in New York.

1910   Aleister Crowley becomes a member of the OTO.

1912   Death of Alice Bunker Stockham.

1912   Anti-Indian racial riots on the West Coast of the United States; many Hindus are expelled.

1913   Rabindranath Tagore, the Bengali poet and artist, is awarded the Nobel prize for literature.

1914   The British Society for the Study of Sex is founded.

1914   Start of World War I.

1915   Birth of Alan Watts.

1915   James Frazer's book *The Golden Bough* is published.

1915   Birth of Ajit Mookerjee, museum curator, author, and promoter of Tantric art.

1916   First birth-control clinic opened in Brooklyn, New York.

1916   Death of Rasputin.

1917   The Bolsheviks take over Russia.

1918   End of World War I.

1918   Pierre Bernard opens the Braeburn Country Club in Upper Nyack, New York, and establishes a Tantric community there.

1918   English women gain the right to vote.

1919   The Institute of Sexual Science is founded in Berlin by Magnus Hirshfield.

1920	Pierre Bernard opens the Clarkstown Country Club in South Nyack, New York, and establishes a Tantric community there.
1920	American women gain the right to vote.
1920s	Radio broadcasting begins.
1921	Birth of Marija Gimbutas, archaeologist who studied the matriarchal cultures of old Europe.
1922	George Gurdjieff opens his Institute for the Harmonious Development of Man in Fontainbleau, France.
1922	Tutankhamun's intact tomb is discovered, causing surge of interest in ancient Egyptian spiritual beliefs.
1924	The ancient Indus Valley civilization discovered.
1928	Margaret Mead's book *Coming of Age in Samoa* is published.
1928	Birth of Albert Rudolph, later to become Swami Rudrananda.
1929	Bronislaw Malinowski's book *The Sexual Life of Savages* is published.
1931	Birth of Bhagwan ''Osho'' Rajneesh, founder of his own neo-Tantric cult.
1936	Theos Bernard visits Lhasa, Tibet.
1936	Death of Sir John Woodroffe.
1937	In Hollywood, Aldous Huxley and Gerald Heard study Hindu philosophy from Swami Prabhavananda.
1939	Theos Bernard's book *Heaven Lies Within Us* is published.
1939	W. Y. Evans-Wentz's book *The Tibetan Book of the Great Liberation* is published.
1939	Death of Havelock Ellis.
1939	Death of Sigmund Freud.
1939	Birth of Chögyam Trungpa, one of the first Tibetan High Lamas to teach Tantra in the West.
1939	Birth of Franklin Jones (Bubba Free John).
1939	Television broadcasting begins.
1939	Start of World War II.

1942   Wilhelm Reich's book *The Discovery of the Orgone: The Function of the Orgasm* is published.

1943   Albert Hofmann, a Swiss chemist, tries LSD, a substance he first synthesized in 1938, and has a "psychedelic" experience.

1945   The first nuclear device, the atom bomb, is exploded.

1945   End of World War II.

1945   Discovery of the Nag Hammadi library, a cache of early Coptic Christian manuscripts of "heretical" Gnostic type.

1947   Discovery of the Dead Sea Scrolls, early biblical manuscripts.

1947   Death of Aleister Crowley.

1947   Death of Theos Bernard, in Tibet.

1947   The Institute for Sexual Research is founded at the University of Indiana.

1947   Verrier Elwin's *The Muria and Their Ghotul* is published.

1948   Universal Declaration of Human Rights issued.

1948   Alfred Kinsey's book *Sexual Behavior in the Human Male* is published.

1949   Death of George Gurdjieff.

1952   Death of Paramahansa Yogananda.

1953   W. Y. Evans-Wentz's book *The Tibetan Book of the Dead* is published.

1953   Alfred Kinsey's book *Sexual Behavior in the Human Female* is published.

1953   Aldous Huxley takes mescaline for the first time. He describes it as "the most extraordinary and significant experience available to human beings this side of the Beatific Vision."

1953   William Burroughs, beat writer, tries ayahuasca, a South American Indian psychedelic, and tells the poet Allen Ginsberg about it.

1954   The first hydrogen bomb is exploded.

1954   Aldous Huxley's book *The Doors of Perception* is published.

1955   Valentina and Gordon Wasson try psilocybin "psychedelic" mushrooms in Mexico. They are the first Westerners to do so.

1955   Allen Ginsberg tries peyote for the first time and begins his epic beat poem, *Howl*.

1955	Aldous Huxley experiences LSD for the first time and is "spiritually over-whelmed."
1955	Death of Pierre Bernard, father of Tantra in America, on September 27, in New York.
1957	Death of Wilhelm Reich.
1957	Jack Kerouac's book *On the Road* is published.
1959	The Dalai Lama escapes Tibet and more than one hundred thousand Tibetans follow him to India.
1960	Timothy Leary tries psilocybin mushrooms in Mexico.
1960	Lama Govinda's book *Fundamentals of Tibetan Mysticism* is published.
1960–61	Birth-control pills first introduced commercially.
1961	Death of Swami Nityananda, teacher of Muktananda and others.
1961	Death of Carl Jung.
1961	Timothy Leary tries LSD for the first time and the following year becomes deeply involved in Tantric Buddhism.
1963	Timothy Leary, Richard Alpert, Ralph Metzner, and others found the International Foundation for Internal Freedom (IFIF), citing Tantra as one of the main topics relevant to members.
1964	The Civil Rights Act is passed by the U.S. Congress, prohibiting racial discrimination. All African Americans finally get the right to vote.
1964	Omar Garrison's book *Tantra: The Yoga of Sex* is published.
1964	The Beatles are initiated into transcendental meditation (TM) by Maharishi Mahesh Yogi.
1965	The U.S. Immigration and Naturalization Department cancels "racial qualifications" for immigrants wishing to become U.S. citizens.
1965	Agehananda Bharati's important book, *The Tantric Tradition*, is published.
1966	Timothy Leary and Ralph Metzner visit Lama Govinda and Dr. Bindu Joshi, in Almora, India. They investigate Tibetan Tantra and Hindu alchemy (*rasayana*).
1966	William Masters and Virginia Johnson's book *Human Sexual Response* is published.

1966   Ajit Mookerjee's important art book, *Tantra Art: Its Philosophy and Physics*, is published.

1968   Philip Rawson's book *Erotic Art of the East* is published and includes a Tantrism chapter.

1969   The first humans land on the moon.

1969   Yogi Bhajan arrives in the USA and establishes his 3HO organization.

1969   Nik Douglas's movie, *Tantra*, is released.

1970   Nik Douglas's book, *Tantra Yoga*, is published.

1970   *Chakra: A Journal of Tantra and Yoga*, edited by Nik Douglas, is published at the first World Conference on Scientific Yoga, held in New Delhi, India.

1971   Ajit Mookerjee's book *Tantra Asana: A Way of Self-realization* is published.

1972   The first major Tantra art exhibition, mainly featuring the Ajit Mookerjee collection, opens at London's Hayward Gallery.

1972   Death of Alan Watts, writer and Zen teacher.

1972   Alex Comfort's ground-breaking sexual how-to bestseller, *The Joy of Sex: A Gourmet Guide to Lovemaking*, is published.

1973   Death of Swami Rudrananda ("Rudi").

1973   Philip Rawson's book *Tantra: The Indian Cult of Ecstasy* is published.

1973   Philip Rawson's book *The Art of Tantra* is published.

1974   The sixteenth Karmapa hierarch visits Europe and North America.

1978   Death of Margaret Mead, anthropologist who studied matriarchal cultures.

1979   Nik Douglas and Penny Slinger's book, *Sexual Secrets: The Alchemy of Ecstasy*, is published.

1982   Death of Swami Muktananda.

1982   Death of Anandamayi Ma, the female Tantric adept.

1986   Death of Mircea Eliade.

1987   Death of Joseph Campbell, author and lecturer on world mythology and creator of the influential TV series *The Power of Myth*, with Bill Moyers.

1989   Death of Chögyam Trungpa.

1990   Death of Bhagwan Rajneesh.

1990   Death of Ajit Mookerjee.

1990   The Vatican condemns Yoga, Eastern meditation, and Oriental mysticism.

1990   The United Soviet Socialist Republic disintegrates, to be replaced by twelve democratic nations.

1991   First issue of *Tantra: The Magazine* is published.

1994   Death of Marija Gimbutas.

1996   Death of Timothy Leary.

1997   Death of Allen Ginsberg.

A Tibetan Thangka painting depicting the "Lord and Lady of Secrets," the central icon of the Guhyasamaja Tantra, seventeenth century.

I GIVE THANKS!

OM

I give thanks to the Creative Power; to the past, the present, and the future.

I give thanks to the Threefold Divine Aspects of Spiritual Reality and their Fivefold Manifestations.

I give thanks to those who have supported me; to my spiritual teachers, to Adefunke, to my family and children. I give thanks to all my mentors and friends.

I give thanks to the women that have touched my life positively, and to the men. I give thanks to the mothers and children. Thanks to those who have given me hope and much pleasure. I give thanks to the animals and to all the other creatures; to all living and growing things.

I give thanks to all of nature; to this world and to the heavens; to the elements and senses; to the seas and the stars; to the mountains, rivers, and beaches; to the hills and valleys; to the clouds and winds, the sun and moon; to the Fire and the Waters.

This book could not have been written without a lot of help from many people. I give thanks to all, who, knowingly or unknowingly, helped inspire this book and bring it to completion.

Special thanks to my literary agent, Deborah Schneider, and to Dan Slater at Pocket Books; to Jane Gelfman at Gelfman-Schneider Agency; Gina Centrello, Felice Javitz, Tom Spain, and Claire Zion at Pocket Books; Barbara Roberts at FPG; Valerie Kuscenko and Toinette Lippe at Knopf/Harmony Books; and special thanks to Andy Rosen, my illustrator. Thanks also to: Ian Alsop, Ian Baker, Dr. Viola Bernard, Bhaskar Bhattacharyya, Tom Binnie, Bill Breeze, Richard Brown, Adam Clayton, Mark Dyczkowski, Allen Ginsburg, John Giorno, Tej Hazarika, Michael and Suzie Heuman, Brian Kelly, Gene Kieffer, Paul Leake, Norman Luxembourg, Mike Magee, Howard Marks, Ajit Mookerjee,

Adrian Oradean, Raam Pandey, Daniel Reid, Steve Rhodes, Sheldon Rochlin, Dinu Roman, Richard Salmon, Leslie Shepard, Penny Slinger, John Snido, Gunther Spiesshofer, William Stablein, Loren Standlee, John Stevens, David Stiffler, Chip Suzuki, Robert Thurman, Roy Walford, Ganga White, Meryl White, Michael Winn, and others whose names I might have inadvertently overlooked. If you helped and I missed your name, sorry!

I give thanks to those special friends who were there for me when I needed them and those who gave good advice, or helped me directly, with research data, references, debate, and so on.

I give thanks to my publisher, to the distributors, the production and management departments, the copy editors, designers, salespersons and to all those who in any way helped to get this book produced and to its readers.

I give thanks to all who read this book with an open mind!

BIBLIOGRAPHY

Abbot, John. *The Keys of Power: A Study of Indian Ritual and Belief.* Secaucus, New Jersey: University Books, 1974.

Ackerman, Diane. *A Natural History of the Senses.* New York: Random House, 1990.

Afrika, O. Llaila. *African Holistic Health.* New York: A and B Books, 1989.

Agarwal, U. *Khajuraho: Sculptures and Their Significance.* Delhi, India: S. Chand, 1964.

Agrawala, Dr. Prithri K. *Early Indian Bronzes.* Varanasi: India: Prithivi Prakashan, 1977.

Agrawala, S. V. *The Glorification of the Great Goddess.* Varanasi: India: All-India Kashray Trust, 1963.

Agrawala, V. S. *Siva Mahadeva: The Great God.* Varanasi: India: Veda Academy, 1966.

Aivanhov, Omraam Mikhael. *Complete Works: Love and Sexuality* (Part II). Frejus: Editions Prosveta, 1978.

Al-Makhzoumi, Hussein. *The Fountains of Pleasure: Sexual Secrets from Ancient Araby.* London: Sphere Books, 1989.

Aldred, Caroline. *Divine Sex: The Tantric and Taoist Arts of Conscious Loving.* London: Carroll and Brown, 1996.

Allen, Marc. *Tantra for the West: Everyday Miracles and Other Steps for Transformation.* San Rafael, California: New World Library, 1992.

Allen, R. C. *A Mountain in Tibet.* London: Futura M, 1982.

Allgrove, George. *Love in the East.* London: Panther Books, 1964.

Anand, Margo. *The Art of Sexual Ecstasy: The Path of Sacred Sexuality for Western Lovers.* Los Angeles: Jeremy P. Tarcher, 1989.

Anand, Margo. *The Art of Sexual Magic.* New York: G. P. Putnam's Sons, 1995.

Anand, Mulk Raj. *Kama Kala: Some Notes on the Philosophical Basis of Hindu Erotic Sculpture.* Geneva: Nagel Publications, 1958.

Anand, Mulk Raj and Stella Kramrisch. *Homage to Khajuraho.* Bombay: Marg Publications, 1968.

Andrey, Robert. *African Genesis: A Personal Investigation into the Animal Origins and the Nature of Man.* New York: Delta Books, 1963.

Angus, S. *The Mystery Religions.* New York: Dover Publications, 1975.

Anuruddha, R. P. *An Introduction into Lamaism.* Calcutta: Deva Datta.

Apter, Andrew. *Black Critics and Kings: The Hermeneutics of Power in Yoruba Society.* Chicago: University of Chicago Press, 1992.

Archer, W. G. *The Hill of Flutes: Life, Love and Poetry in Tribal India.* London: W. G. Archer, 1974.

Ariès, Philippe and André Béjin. *Western Sexuality: Practice and Precept in Past and Present Times.* Oxford: Basil Blackwell, 1985.

Arundale, G. S. *Kundalini: An Occult Experience.* Madras, India: 1974.

Aryan, K. C. *The Little Goddesses (Matrikas).* Delhi, India: Rekha Prakashan, 1980.

Ashe, Geoffrey. *The Virgin.* London: Routledge and Kegan Paul, 1976.

Ashe, Geoffrey. *Dawn Behind the Dawn: A Search for the Earthly Paradise.* New York: John MaCrae/Henry Holt, 1992.

Austen, Hallie Inglehart. *The Heart of the Goddess: Art Myth and Meditations of the World's Sacred Feminine.* Berkeley: Wingbow Press, 1990.

Avalon, Arthur. *The Great Liberation: Mahanirvana Tantra.* Madras: Ganesh and Co., 1913.

Avalon, Arthur, ed. *Tantrik Texts: Kalivilasa Tantra.* London: Luzac and Co., 1917.

Avalon, Arthur. *Tantrik Texts.* Volume IX London: Luzac and Co., 1922.

Avalon, Arthur. *Tantraraja Tantra: A Short Analysis.* With a preface by Yogi Shuddhananda Bharati. Madras, India: Ganesh and Co., 1952.

Avalon, Arthur. *Kulacúdámani Nigama.* Madras, India: Ganesh and Co., 1956.

Avalon, Arthur. *The Greatness of Shiva.* Madras, India: Ganesh and Co., 1963.

Avalon, Arthur, trans. *Hymn to Kali (Karpuradi-Stotra).* Commentary by Swami Vimalananda. Madras, India: Ganesh and Co., 1965.

Avalon, Arthur and Sir John Woodroffe. *Wave of Bliss.* Madras, India: Ganesh and Co., 1961.

Avalon, Arthur and Ellen. *Hymns to the Goddess.* Madras, India: Ganesh and Co., 1964.

Baba, Pagal. *Temple of the Phallic King: The Mind of India.* New York: Simon & Schuster, 1973.

Bachland, G. *The Psychoanalysis of Fire.* London: Routledge and Kegan Paul, 1964.

Bagchi, P. C. *Studies in Tantras.* Calcutta: University of Calcutta Press, 1939.

Bagchi, P. C. *India and China.* New York: Philosophical Library, 1951.

Baigent, Michael, Richard Leigh, and Henry Lincoln. *The Holy Blood and The Holy Grail.* London: Jonathan Cape, 1982.

Ballantyne, J. R. and G. S. Deva. *Yoga Sutras of Patanjali.* Calcutta: Susil Gupta, 1960.

Bandyopadhyay, Pranab. *Mother Goddess Durga.* Calcutta: United Writers, 1993.

Banerjea, Akshaya. Kumar. *Philosophy of Gorakhnath.* With a preface by Gopinath Kaviraj. Gorakphur, India: Dig Vijai Nath Trust, 1962.

Banerjea, J. N. *Pauranic and Tantric Religion.* Calcutta: University of Calcutta, 1966.

Banerjee, S. C. *Tantra in Bengal.* Calcutta: Naya Prokash, 1978.

Banerjee, S. C. *A Brief History of Tantra Literature.* Calcutta: Naya Prokash, 1988.

Bardwick, Judith. *Psychology of Women: A Study of Bio-Cultural Conflicts.* New York: Harper and Row, 1971.

Barkhtar, L. *Sufi Expressions of the Mystic Quest.* London: Thames and Hudson, 1976.

Barre, W. *The Peyote Cult.* New York: Schocken Books, 1969.

Basu, Manoranjan. *Tantras: A General Study.* Calcutta: Shrimati Mira Basu, 1976.

Baudin, P. *Fetichism and Fetich Worshippers.* New York: Benzinger Bros., 1885.

Beane, Wendell Charles. *Myth, Cult and Symbols in Shakta Hinduism: A Study of the Indian Mother Goddess.* Leiden, The Netherlands: E. J. Brill, 1977.

Bedi, B. P. L. *The Art of the Temptress.* New Delhi, India: Pearl Books, 1968.

Ben Nahum, Pinhas. *The Turkish Art of Love.* New York: The Panurge Press, 1933.

Benko, Stephen. *Pagan Rome and the Early Christians.* Bloomington: Indiana University Press, 1984.

Bennett, John G. *Sex.* Sherborne: Coombe Springs Press, 1975.

Bernard, Theos. *Heaven Lies Within Us.* New York: Scribner's Sons, 1939.

Bernard, Theos. *Hatha Yoga.* London: Rider and Co., 1969.

Beyer, Stephen. *The Cult of Tara: Magic and Ritual in Tibet.* Berkeley: University of California Press, 1973.

Bhagavatapada, Sri Shankara. *Sri Lalita Trisati Bhasya.* Translated by Dr. Chaganti Murthy. Madras, India: Ganesh and Co., 1969.

Bhagwan, Das. *Tibetan Medicine With Special Reference to Yoga Sataka.* Delhi, India: Library of Tibetan Works and Archives, 1976.

Bharati, Agehananda. *The Ochre Robe.* Seattle: University of Washington Press, 1962.

Bharati, Agehananda. *The Tantric Tradition.* New York: Anchor Press/Doubleday, 1970.

Bharati, Agehananda. *The Light of the Center: Context and Pretext of Modern Mysticism.* Santa Barbara, California: Rose Erikson, 1976.

Bhattacharyya, B. *Saivism and the Phallic World* (in 2 volumes). Delhi, India: Oxford.

Bhattacharyya, B. *The World of Tantra.* New Delhi, India: Munshiram Manoharlal, 1988.

Bhattacharyya, Benoytosh. *Two Vajrayana Works.* Baroda, India: Gaekwad's Oriental Series, 1929.

Bhattacharyya, Benoytosh. *Guhya Samaja Tantra.* Baroda, India: Gaekwad's Oriental Series, 1931.

Bhattacharyya, Benoytosh. *Nispannayogavali of Mahapandita Abhyakara Gupta.* Baroda, India: Oriental Institute, 1949.

Bhattacharyya, Benoytosh. *An Introduction to Buddhist Esoterism.* Benares, India: 1964.

Bhattacharyya, Benoytosh, ed. *Sadhanamala.* Baroda, India: Orient Institute, 1968.

Bhattacharyya, Benoytosh. *The Indian Buddhist Iconography.* Calcutta: Firma K. L. Mukhopadhyay, 1968.

Bhattacharyya, Benoytosh. *Gem Therapy*. Calcutta: Firma K. L. Mukhopadhyay, 1971.

Bhattacharyya, Bhaskar with Nik Douglas and Penny Slinger. *The Path of the Mystic Lover: Baul Songs of Passion and Ecstasy*. Rochester, Vermont: Destiny Books, 1993.

Bhattacharyya, Narendra Nath. *Indian Puberty Rites*. Calcutta: 1968.

Bhattacharyya, Narendra. Nath. *History of Indian Erotic Literature*. Delhi, India: Munshiram Manoharlal, 1975.

Bhisagratna, Kaviraj, translator. *The Sushruta Samhita* (in 3 volumes). Varanasi, India: Chowkamba Sanskrit Series, 1963.

Biale, David. *Eros and the Jews: From Biblical Israel to Contemporary America*. New York: Basic Books/HarperCollins, 1992.

Bibby, Geoffrey. *Looking for Dilmun*. New York: Knopf, 1969.

Birks, Walter and R. A. Gilbert. *The Treasure of Montsegur: A Study of the Cathar Heresy and the Nature of the Cathar Secret*. London: Crucible/Aquarian Press, 1987.

Blavatsky, H. P. *The Secret Doctrine*. London: Theosophical Publishing, 1888.

Blavatsky, H. P. *An Abridgment of the Secret Doctrine*. London: Theosophical Publishing, 1966.

Blofeld, John. *The Tantric Mysticism of Tibet*. New York: E. P. Dutton, 1970.

Blofeld, John. *Mantras: Sacred Words of Power*. London: George Allen and Unwin, 1977.

Boardman, J. and E. La Rocca. *Eros in Greece*. New York: The Erotic Art Book Society.

Bolen, J. S. *The Heart of the Goddess*. Berkeley: Wingbow Press, 1990.

Boone, Sylvia Ardyn. *Radiance from the Waters: Ideals of Feminine Beauty in Mende Art*. New Haven: Yale University Press, 1986.

Bose, D. N. *Tantras: Their Philosophy and Occult Secrets*. Calcutta: 1965.

Bowness, Charles. *Romany Magic*. New York: Samuel Weiser, 1973.

Bradley, M. *Dawn Voyage: The Black African Discovery of America*. New York: A and B Books, 1992.

Brahamanda. *The Hathayoga Pradipika*. Madras, India: The Adyar Library and Research Centre, 1972.

Briggs, George W. *Gorakhnath and Kanphata Yogis*. Calcutta: 1958. Reprinted Delhi: Mutilal Banarsidass, 1973.

Brown, Richard. *Handbook of Planetary Gemology*. Hong Kong: McKinney International, 1990.

Brusendorff, Ove and Poul Henningsen. *A History of Eroticism*. New York: Lyle Stuart, 1963.

Bryk, Felix. *Dark Rapture: The Sex-Life of the African Negro*. Forest Hills, New York: Juno Books, 1944.

Bryk, Felix. *Voodoo-Eros: Ethnological Studies in the Sex-Life of the African Aborigines*. New York: United Book Guild, 1964.

Budge, Sir E. A. Wallis. *Egyptian Magic*. London: Routledge and Kegan Paul, 1989.

Bulka, Dr. Reuven P. *Sex in the Talmud*. New York: Peter Pauper Press, 1979.

Burton, Sir Richard. *The Perfumed Garden of the Shaykh Nefzawi.* London: Neville Spearman, 1963.

Burton, Sir Richard, translator. *The Perfumed Garden.* London: Luxor Press, 1970.

Burton, Sir Richard. *The Glory of the Perfumed Garden: The Missing Flowers.* London: Neville Spearman, 1975.

Burton, Sir Richard. *The Erotic Traveler.* Edited by Edward Leigh. New York: Barnes and Noble Books, 1993.

Burton, Sir Richard and F. F. Arbuthnot. *The Kama Sutra of Vatsyayana.* London: George Allen and Unwin, 1963.

Burton, Sir Richard with F. F. Arbuthnot and B. Jowett, translators. *The Ananga Ranga of Kalyana Malla and the Symposium of Plato.* London: Klimber Pocket Editions, 1963.

Burton, Richard with F. F. Arbuthnot, translators. Edited by John Muirhead. *The Kama Sutra of Vatsyayana.* Frogmore: Panther Books, 1967.

Burton, Sir Richard with F. F. Arbuthnot and Charles Fowkes, translators. *The Illustrated Kama Sutra: Ananga Ranga Perfumed Garden.* Rochester, Vermont: Park Street Press.

Butler, E. M. *The Myth of the Magus.* Cambridge: Cambridge University Press, 1993.

Calverton, V. F. and S. D. Schmalhausen. *Sex in Civilization.* London: George Allen and Unwin, 1929.

Campbell, Joseph. *The Masks of God: Oriental Mythology.* New York: Viking Press, 1970.

Campbell, Joseph. *The Way of the Animal Powers.* New York: Harper and Row, 1988.

Campbell, June. *Traveller in Space: In Search of Female Identity in Tibetan Buddhism.* New York: George Braziller, 1996.

Camphausen, Rufus C. *The Encyclopedia of Erotic Wisdom.* Rochester, Vermont: Inner Traditions, 1991.

Camphausen, Rufus C. *The Yoni: Sacred Symbol of Female Creative Power.* Rochester, Vermont: Inner Traditions, 1996.

Carden, M. L. *Oneida: Utopian Community to Modern Corporation.* Baltimore: Johns Hopkins University Press, 1969.

Carpenter, Edward. *Pagan and Christian Creeds.* New York: Harcourt Brace and Howe, 1920.

Carstairs, G. M. *The Twice Born.* London: Hogarth Press, 1957.

Cefalu, Richard F. ''Shakti in Abhinavagupta's Concept of Moksha.'' Doctoral dissertation. New York: Fordham University, 1973.

Chakravarti, C. *The Tantras: Studies on Their Religion and Literature.* Calcutta: Punthi Pustak, 1963.

Chakroborti, Haripada. *Pashupata Sutram.* Calcutta: Academic Publishers, 1970.

Chandra, Dr. Rai Govind. *Studies of Indus Valley Terracottas.* Varanasi, India: Bhartiya Publishing House, 1973.

Chandra, Moti. *The World of Courtesans.* Delhi, India: Vikas Publishing House, 1973.

Chang, Chen Chi and C. A. Muses. *Esoteric Teachings of the Tibetan Tantra*. Lausanne, Switzerland: Aurora Press, 1961.

Chang, Garma C.C. *Six Yogas of Naropa and Teaching of Mahamudra*. New York: University Press, 1963.

Chang, Garma C. C. *Teachings of Tibetan Yoga*. New York: University Books, 1963.

Chattopadhyaya, D. *Taranatha's History of Buddhism in India*. Calcutta: Indian Institute of Advanced Study, 1970.

Chattopadhyaya, Sudhakar. *Evolution of Hindu Sects*. New Delhi, India: Munshiram Manoharlal, 1970.

Chattopadhyaya, Sudhakar. *Reflections on the Tantras*. New Delhi, India: Motilal Banarsidass, 1978.

Chawdhri, L. R. *Practicals of Mantras Tantras*. New Delhi, India: Sagar Publications, 1985.

Chen, C. M. *Discriminations Between Buddhist and Hindu Tantras*. Kalimpong, India: Mani Printing Works, 1969.

Chesi, Gert. *Voodoo: Africa's Secret Power*. Austria, 1980.

Chew, Willa C. *The Goddess Faith: A Religion of the Mind*. Hicksville, New York: Exposition Press, 1977.

Chöpel, Gedün and Jeffrey Hopkins. *Tibetan Arts of Love*. Ithaca, New York: Snow Lion Publications, 1992.

Chopra, Deepak. *The Seven Spiritual Laws of Success*. New York: New World Library, 1994.

Claggett, Marshall. *Greek Science in Antiquity*. New York: Collier Books, 1955.

Clark, Grahame and Stuart Piggott. *Prehistoric Societies*. New York: Knopf, 1965.

Clarke, Sir Humphrey. *The Message of Milarepa: New Light upon the Tibetan Way*. London: John Murray, 1958.

Clow, Barbara Hand. *Liquid Light of Sex*. New York: Bear Books, 1991.

Colaabavala, F. D. *Tantra: The Erotic Cult*. New Delhi, India: Orient Paperbacks, 1976.

Cole, William. *Sex and Love in the Bible*. New York: Association Press, 1959.

Comfort, Alex. *The Koka Shastra and Other Medieval Indian Writings on Love*. London: George Allen and Unwin, 1964.

Comfort, Alex. *The Joy of Sex: A Gourmet Guide to Lovemaking*. New York: Simon and Schuster, 1972.

Comfort, Alex. *More Joy of Sex: A Lovemaking Companion to the Joy of Sex*. New York: Crown Publishers, 1973.

Comfort, Alex. *The New Joy of Sex: A Gourmet Guide to Lovemaking for the Nineties*. New York: Pocket Books, 1991.

Coon, Carlton S. *The Seven Caves*. New York: Knopf, 1957.

Coon, Carlton S. *The Origin of Races*. New York: Knopf, 1963.

Cooper, Emmanuel. *The Sexual Perspective*. London: Routledge and Kegan Paul, 1986.

Cowan, James C. *The Elements of the Aborigine Tradition*. London: Element Books, 1992.

Cozort, Daniel. *Highest Yoga Tantra*. New York: Snow Lion Publications, 1986.

Craze, Richard. *The Spiritual Traditions of Sex.* New York, Harmony Books, 1996.

Crenshaw, Teresa L. *The Alchemy of Love and Lust: Discovering Our Sex Hormones.* New York: G. P. Putnam's Sons, 1996.

Crowley, Aleister. *Eight Lectures on Yoga.* New York: New Falcon Publications, 1984.

Crowley, Aleister. *The Equinox.* Vol. III. New York: 93 Publishing, 1990.

Crowley, Aleister. *The Book of Wisdom or Folly.* New York: 93 Publishing, 1991.

Crowley, Aleister. *Magick: Book Four, Liber ABA.* Edited by Hymenaeus Beta. York Beach, Maine: Samuel Weiser, 1994.

Culling, Louis T. *A Manual of Sex Magick.* St. Paul, Minnesota: Llewellyn Publications, 1971.

Cumont, Franz. *Oriental Religions in Roman Paganism.* New York: Dover, 1956.

Cutner, H. A. *A Short History of Sex Worship.* London: Watts and Co., 1940.

Dalley, Stephanie. *Myths from Mesopotamia: Creation, The Flood, Gilgamesh and Others.* New York: Oxford University Press, 1989.

Daniélou, Alain. *Hindu Polytheism.* New York: Bollingen Foundation, 1964.

Daniélou, Alain. *Yoga: The Method of Re-Integration.* London: Johnson Publications, 1973.

Daniélou, Alain. *Shiva and Dionysus: The Omnipresent Gods of Transcendence and Ecstasy.* New York: Inner Traditions, 1984.

Daniélou, Alain. *While the Gods Play: Shaiva Oracles and Predictions on the Cycles of History and the Destiny of Mankind.* Rochester, Vermont: Inner Traditions, 1987.

Daniélou, Alain. *Yoga: Mastering the Secrets of Matter and the Universe.* Rochester, Vermont: Inner Traditions, 1991.

Daniélou, Alain. *The Complete Kama Sutra: The First Unabridged Modern Translation of the Classic Indian Text.* Rochester, Vermont: Park Street Press/Inner Traditions, 1994.

Danielsson, Bengt. *Love in the South Seas.* New York: Reynal and Company, 1956.

Dargyay, E. M. *The Rise of Esoteric Buddhism in Tibet.* Delhi, India: Motilal Banarsidass, 1977.

Das, H. C. *Tantricism: A Study of the Yogini Cult.* New Delhi, India: Sterling Publishers, 1981.

Dasgupta, Shashibhusan. *An Introduction to Tantric Buddhism.* Calcutta: University of Calcutta Press, 1950.

Dasgupta, Shashibhusan. *Obscure Religious Cults: As Background of Bengali Literature.* Calcutta: Firma K. L. Mukhopadhyay, 1946 and 1962.

Dass, Baba Hari and A. E. Kelly. *Sweeper to Saint: Stories of Holy India.* Sri Rama Publishing, 1980.

Datta, M. R. *The Secret Serpent.* Dacca, Bangladesh: 1913.

David-Neel, Alexander. *With Mystics and Magicians in Tibet.* London: 1931.

David-Neel, Alexander. *Secret Oral Teachings in Tibetan Buddhist Sects.* San Francisco: 1968.

David-Neel, Alexander. *Initiations and Initiates in Tibet.* London: Rider and Co., 1970.

Davis, Elizabeth Gould. *The First Sex*. New York: G. P. Putnam's Sons, 1971.

de Gourmont, Remy. *The Natural Philosophy of Love*. Translated and with introduction by Ezra Pound. London: Quartet Books, 1992.

Dehija, Vidya. *Yogini Cult and Temples: A Tantric Tradition*. New Delhi, India: National Museum, 1985.

Delaporte, L. *Mesopotamia: The Babylonian and Assyrian Civilization*. London: Routledge and Kegan Paul, 1925.

Delattre, Pierre. *Tales of the Dalai Lama*. California: Creature Art Books Company, 1971.

De Lubicz, Schwaller R. A. *Sacred Science: The King of Pharaonic Theocracy*. New York: Inner Traditions, 1982.

D'Emilio, John and Estelle Freedman. *Intimate Matters: A History of Sexuality in America*. New York: Harper and Row, 1988.

D'eon, C. *The Science of Regeneration or Sex Enlightenment*. California: Health Research Publications, 1968.

Deren, Maya. *The Voodoo Gods*. London: Thames and Hudson, 1953.

Derlon, Pierre. *Secrets of the Gypsies*. New York: Ballantine Books, 1977.

De Ropp, S. R. *Sex Energy: The Sexual Force in Man and Animals*. London: Corgi Books, 1972.

de Riencourt, Amaury. *Sex and Power in History: How the Difference Between the Sexes Has Shaped Our Destinies*. New York: David McKay, 1974.

De Rougemir, Denis. *The Myths of Love*. London: Faber.

Desai, Devangana. *Erotic Sculpture of India, A Socio-Cultural Study*. New Delhi, India: Tata McGraw-Hill Publishing, 1975.

De Smedt, Marc and David MacRae, translators. *The Kama Sutra: Erotic Figures in Indian Art*. New York: Crescent Books, 1980.

De, Sushil Kumar. *Ancient Indian Erotics and Erotic Literature*. Calcutta: 1959.

Deva, Krishna. *Sculptural Art of Khajuraho*. Delhi, India: Brijbasi, 1986.

De Venette, Nicholas. *The Mysteries of Conjugal Love Reveal'd*. Paris: Charles Carrington, 1906.

Devi, Kamala. *The Eastern Way of Love: Tantric Sex and Erotic Mysticism*. New York: Simon & Schuster, 1977.

Dewar, J. *The Unlocked Secret: Freemasonry Examined*. London: William Chubbier, 1966.

Dimmock, Edward. *The Thief of Love*. Chicago: University of Chicago Press, 1963.

Dimmock, Edward. *The Place of the Hidden Moon*. Chicago: University of Chicago Press, 1966.

Diop, Cheikh Anta. *The African Origin of Civilization: Myth or Reality*. Chicago: Lawrence Hill Books, 1974.

Diop, Cheikh Anta. *Civilization or Barbarism: An Authentic Anthropology*. Chicago: Lawrence Hill Books, 1991.

Doresse, Jean. *The Secret Books of the Egyptian Gnostics*. New York: Viking Press, 1960.

Dorje, Gyurme and Matthew Kapstein. *The Nyingma School of Tibetan Buddhism* (in 2 volumes). Boston: Wisdom Publications, 1991.

Douglas, Nik. *Tantra Yoga*. New Delhi, India: Munshiram Manoharlal, 1970.

Douglas, Nik. *Tibetan Tantric Charms and Amulets*. New York: Dover Publications, 1978.

Douglas, Nik. *The Art of Love*. Beverly Hills: Kreitman Gallery, 1979.

Douglas, Nik and Penny Slinger. *Mountain Ecstasy*. Paris and Rotterdam: Dragon's Dream Publications, 1978.

Douglas, Nik and Penny Slinger. *Sexual Secrets: The Alchemy of Ecstasy*. New York: Destiny Books, 1979.

Douglas, Nik and Penny Slinger. *The Secret Dakini Oracle*. New York: Destiny Books, 1979.

Douglas, Nik and Penny Slinger. *The Pillow Book: The Erotic Sentiment and the Paintings of India, Nepal, China and Japan*. New York: Destiny Books, 1981.

Douglas, Nik and Penny Slinger. *The Erotic Sentiment in the Painting of India and Nepal*. Rochester, Vermont: Park Street Press, 1989.

Douglas, Nik and Penny Slinger. *The Erotic Sentiment in the Painting of China and Japan*. Rochester, Vermont: Park Street Press, 1990.

Douglas, Nik and Meryl White. *Karmapa: The Black Hat Lama of Tibet*. London: Luzac and Company, 1976.

Douglas, Nik with Penny Slinger and Meryl White. *The Secret Dakini Oracle Deck: A Tantric Tarot*. New York: U.S. Games Systems, 1978.

Doumas, Christos. *Cycladic Art from the N. P. Goulandris Collection*. Houston: The Museum of Fine Art, 1981.

Dowman, Keith. *Tilopa's Mahamudra Instruction*. Kathmandu, Nepal: Diamond Snow Publication, 1978.

Dowman, Keith. *The Divine Madman: The Sublime Life and Songs of Drukpa Kunley*. Clearlake, California: Dawn Horse Press, 1980.

Dowman, Keith. *Sky Dancer: The Secret Life and Songs of the Lady Yeshe Tsogyal*. London: Routledge and Kegan Paul, 1984.

Dowman, Keith. *Masters of Mahamudra: Songs and Histories of the Eighty-Four Buddhist Siddhas*. New York: State University of New York Press, 1985.

Dowman, Keith. *Masters of Enchantment*. New York: Harper and Row, 1988.

Drewal, M. T. *Yoruba Ritual: Performers, Play, Agency*. Bloomington: Indiana University Press, 1992.

Droscher, Vitus B. *The Magic of the Senses: New Discoveries in Animal Perception*. London: Panther Books, 1971.

Dubois, Abbé J. A. *Hindu Manners, Customs and Ceremonies*. Translated by Beauchamp. London: 1936.

Durden-Smith, Jo and Diane deSimone. *Sex and the Brain*. New York: Warner Books, 1983.

Dyczkowski, Mark S. G. *The Doctrine of Vibration: An Analysis of the Doctrines and Practices of Kashmir Shaivism.* Albany: State University of New York Press, 1987.

Dyczkowski, Mark S. G. *The Canon of the Shaivagama and the Kubjika Tantras of the Western Kaula Tradition.* Albany: State University of New York Press, 1988.

Edwardes, Allen. *The Jewel in the Lotus: A Historical Survey of the Sexual Culture of the East.* New York: Julian Press, 1959.

Edwardes, Allen and R. E. L. Masters. *The Cradle of Erotica.* New York: Lancer Books, 1962.

Edwards, Gary and John Mason. *Black Gods: Orisa Studies in the New World.* Brooklyn: Yoruba Theological Archministry, 1985.

Eisler, Riane. *The Chalice and the Blade: Our History, Our Future.* San Francisco: Harper-Collins Publishers, 1987.

Eliade, Mircea. *Yoga: Immortality and Freedom.* New York: Bollingen/Pantheon, 1958.

Eliade, Mircea. *Shamanism, Archaic Techniques of Ecstasy.* London: Routledge and Kegan, 1964.

Eliade, Mircea. *Rites and Symbols of Initiation.* New York: Harper Torchbook, 1965.

Eliade, Mircea. *The Mysteries of Birth and Rebirth.* New York: Harper and Row, 1975.

Eliade, Mircea. *Autobiography: Journey East, Journey West.* Translated by Mac Ricketts. San Francisco: Harper and Row, 1981.

Eliade, Mircea and C. Lam Markmann, translator. *Patanjali and Yoga.* New York: Schocken Books, 1976.

Eliade, Mircea and W. R. Trask, translator. *Myth and Reality.* New York: Harper Colophon Books, 1975.

Elkin, A. P. *Aboriginal Men of High Degree.* Rochester, Vermont: Inner Traditions, 1994.

Eller, Cynthia. *Living in the Lap of the Goddess: The Feminist Spiritual Movement in America.* New York: Crossroad, 1993.

Ellis, Albert. *The Folklore of Sex.* New York: Charles Boni, 1951.

Ellis, Havelock. *Studies in the Psychology of Sex* (in 4 volumes). New York: Random House, 1936.

Ellis, Havelock. *Psychology of Sex: A Manual for Students.* New York: Emerson Books, 1944.

Elwin, Verrier. *The Banga.* London: Wyman and Sons, 1939.

Elwin, Verrier. *Muria: Murder and Suicide.* London: Oxford University Press, 1943.

Elwin, Verrier. *The Tribal Art of Middle India.* London: Oxford University Press, 1951.

Elwin, Verrier. *The Kingdom of the Young.* London: Oxford University Press, 1968.

Elwin, Verrier. *The Art of the North-East Frontier of India.* Itanagar, India: Pradesh, 1988.

Epega, Afolabi A. and John P. Neimark. *The Sacred Ifa Oracle.* San Francisco: Harper, 1995.

Estés, Clarissa Pinkola. *Women Who Run With the Wolves: Myths and Stories of the Wild Woman Archetype.* New York: Ballantine, 1992.

Evans, Arthur. *The God of Ecstasy: Sex-Roles and the Madness of Dionysas.* New York: St. Martin's Press, 1988.

Evans-Wentz, W. Y. *The Tibetan Book of the Dead.* London: Oxford University Press, 1927.

Evans-Wentz, W. Y. *The Tibetan Book of Great Liberation.* London: Oxford University Press, 1954.

Evans-Wentz, W. Y. *Tibetan Yoga and Secret Doctrines.* London: Oxford University Press, 1958.

Evola, Julius. *The Metaphysics of Sex.* New York: Inner Traditions, 1983.

Fagan, Brian M. *Men of the Earth: An Introduction to World Prehistory.* Boston: Little, Brown, 1974.

Fama, Chief. *Fundamentals of the Yoruba Religion (Orisa Worship).* San Bernardino, California: Ile Orunmila Communications, 1993.

Fantham, Elaine with Helen Foley, Pomeroy Kampen, and H. Alan Shapiro. *Women in the Classical World.* Oxford: Oxford University Press, 1994.

Farrell, Warren. *The Myth of Male Power.* New York: Berkeley Books, 1994.

Farrow, G. W. and I. Menon. *The Concealed Essence of the Hevajra Tantra.* Delhi, India: Motilal Banarsidass, 1992.

Ferguson, Marilyn. *The Aquarian Conspiracy: Personal and Social Transformation in the 1980's.* Los Angeles: J. P. Tarcher, 1980.

Feuerstein, Georg. *Holy Madness: The Shock Tactics and Radical Teachings of Crazy-Wise Adepts, Holy Fools, and Rascal Gurus.* New York: Paragon House, 1991.

Fielding, W. J. *Strange Customs of Courtship and Marriage.* New York: Perma Books, 1949.

Fields, Rich and Brian Catillo. *The Turquoise Bee: Love Songs of the Sixth Dalai Lama.* New York: HarperCollins, 1993.

Filliozat, J. *The Classical Doctrine of Indian Medicine: Its Origins and Its Greek Parallels.* Translated from the French by Dev Raj Chanana. Delhi, India: Munshiram Manoharlal, 1964.

Fiore, Silvestro. *Voices from the Clay: The Development of Assyro-Babylonian Literature.* Norman: University of Oklahoma Press, 1965.

Fiser, Ivo. *Indian Erotics of the Oldest Period.* Praha: Universita Karlova, 1966.

Fisher, Helen. *Anatomy of Love: The Natural History of Monogamy, Adultery and Divorce.* New York: W. W. Norton, 1992.

Ford, C. S. *Patterns of Sexual Behaviour.* New York: Harper and Bros., 1951.

Forsyth, Adrian. *A Natural History of Sex: The Ecology and Evolution of Sexual Behavior.* New York: Charles Scribner's, 1986.

Fortune, Dion. *Moon Magic.* London: Aquarian Press, 1956.

Foucault, Michel. *A History of Sexuality.* New York: Pantheon Books, 1978.

Fouce, P. and Denise Tomecko. *Shiva.* Bangkok: The Tantric Press, 1990.

Foucher, Max-Pol. *The Erotic Sculpture of India.* London: George Allen and Unwin, 1959.

Frawley, David. *Gods, Sages and Kings: Vedic Secrets of Ancient Civilization.* Salt Lake City: Passage Press, 1991.

Frawley, David. *Tantric Yoga and the Wisdom Goddesses.* Salt Lake City: Passage Press, 1994.

Frazer, J. G. *The Golden Bough: A Study in Magic and Religion* (in 12 volumes). London: Macmillan and Co., 1915.

Fremantle, Francesca and Chögyam Trungpa, translator. *The Tibetan Book of the Dead: The Great Liberation Through Hearing in the Bardo* (from the Tibetan). Berkeley: Shambala, 1975.

Frost, Gavin and Yvonne. *Tantric Yoga: The Royal Path to Raising Kundalini Power.* York Beach, Maine: Samuel Weiser, 1989.

Fulder, Stephen. *An End to Ageing? Remedies For Life Extension.* New York: Destiny Books, 1983.

Fuller, J. F. *Yoga: A Study of the Mystical Philosophy of the Brahmins and Buddhists.* London: Rider, 1923.

Fürer-Haimendorf, C. *The Naked Nagas.* Calcutta: Thacket, Spink and Co., 1946.

Furst, P. T. *Flesh of the Gods, the Ritual Use of Hallucinogens.* New York: Praeger Publishers, 1972.

Gadon, Elinor W. *The Once and Future Goddess: A Sweeping Visual Chronicle of the Sacred Female and Her Reemergence in the Cultural Mythology of Our Time.* New York: Harper and Row, 1989.

Garrison, Omar. *Tantra: The Yoga of Sex.* New York: Avon Books, 1964.

George, Christopher S. *The Candamaharosana Tantra, Chapters 1–8: A Critical Edition and English Translation.* Published doctoral dissertation. New Haven: American Oriental Series, 1974.

Getty, Adele. *Goddess: Mother of Living Nature.* London: Thames & Hudson, 1990.

Ghosh, D. P. *Kama Ratna: Indian Ideas of Feminine Beauty.* Delhi, India: 1973.

Ghurye, G. S. *Indian Sadhus.* Bombay: G. S. Ghurye, 1953.

Gichner, L. E. *Erotic Aspects of Hindu Sculpture.* Washington, D.C.: 1953.

Gies, Frances and Joseph. *Marriage and the Family in the Middle Ages.* New York: Harper and Row, 1987.

Gimbutas, Marija. *The Goddesses and Gods of Old Europe: Myths and Cult Images (6500–3500 B.C.).* Berkeley: University of California Press, 1982.

Gimbutas, Marija. *The Language of the Goddess.* San Francisco: HarperCollins, 1989.

Giri, Swami Hariharananda. *Kriya Yoga: The Scientific Process of Soul-Culture and the Essence of All Religions.* Calcutta: Kriya Yoga Ashram, 1989.

Giri, Swami Satyeswarananda. *Biography of A Yogi.* San Diego: The Sanskrit Classics, 1985.

Gold, E. J. and Cybele. *Tantric Sex.* Playa Del Rey: Peak Skill Publishing, 1988.

Goldberg, B. Z. *The Sacred Fire: The Story of Sex in Religion.* New York: University Books, 1958.

Goldenberg, Naomi. *The Changing of the Gods.* Boston: Beacon Press, 1979.

Goleman, Daniel. *The Meditative Mind.* Los Angeles: Jeremy P. Tarcher, 1988.

Goode, W. J. *Religion among the Primitives.* Chicago: Free Press, 1951.

Goodrich, Norma. *Priestesses.* New York: Harper Perennial, 1990.

Goswami, C. L. *Srimad Bhagawata Mahapurana.* Part I, Book 1–8. Gorakhpur, India: Gita Press, 1971.

Goswami, P. *The Springtime Bihu of Assam.* Gauhati, Assam, India: Shri Bichita Narayan Dutta, 1966.

Goudriaan, Teun, ed. *The Vinasikha Tantra.* Delhi, India: Motilal Banarsidass, 1985.

Goudriaan, Teun, ed. *Ritual and Speculation in Early Tantrism: Studies in Honor of André Padoux.* New York: State University of New York Press, 1992.

Govinda, Lama Anagarika. *Foundations of Tibetan Mysticism.* London: Rider and Company, 1960.

Grant, J. and K. Denys. *Many Lifetimes—Concerning Reincarnation and the Origin of Mental Illness.* London: Victor Gollancz, 1972.

Grant, Kenneth. *Cults of the Shadow.* New York: Samuel Weiser, 1976.

Grant, Michael. *Eros in Pompeii: The Secret Rooms of the National Museum of Naples.* New York: William Morrow, 1975.

Graves, Robert. *The White Goddess.* London: Faber and Faber, 1961.

Graves, Robert and Raphael Patai. *Hebrew Myths: The Book of Genesis.* New York: Doubleday Anchor Books, 1964.

Greer, Germaine. *The Female Eunuch.* New York: McGraw-Hill, 1970.

Gregersen, Edgar. *Sexual Practices: The Story of Human Sexuality.* London: Mitchell Beazley, 1982.

Grewal, R. Singh. *Kundalini: The Mother of the Universe.* Santa Barbara, California: Singh, 1930.

Grigson, Geoffrey. *The Goddess of Love: The Birth, Triumph, Death and Return of Aphrodite.* London: Constable, 1976.

Grof, Stanislav. *Beyond the Brain.* Albany: State University of New York Press, 1985.

Grosskurth, Phyllis. *Havelock Ellis: A Biography.* New York: Knopf, 1980.

Guenther, Herbert V. *The Jewel Ornament of Liberation.* London: Rider and Co., 1959.

Guenther, Herbert V. *The Life and Teaching of Naropa.* London: Clarendon Press, 1963.

Guenther, Herbert V., translator. *The Royal Song of Saraha: A Study in the History of Buddhist Thought.* Seattle: University of Washington Press, 1969.

Guenther, Herbert V. *Yuganaddha: The Tantric View of Life.* Calcutta: Chowkamba Publications, 1969.

Guenther, Herbert V., translator. *Gampopa's Jewel Ornament of Liberation.* (From the Tibetan.) London: Rider and Co., 1970.

Guenther, Herbert V. *Buddhist Philosophy: In Theory and Practice.* London: Penguin Books, 1974.

Guenther, Herbert V. and Chögyam Trungpa. *The Dawn of Tantra.* Berkeley: Shambhala, 1975.

Guirdham, Arthur. *The Cathars and Reincarnation.* Suffolk, England: Neville Spearman, 1970.

Guirdham, Arthur. *The Great Heresy: The History and Beliefs of the Cathars.* Jersey, Channel Islands (C.I.), England: Neville Spearman, 1977.

Gulabkunverba Society. *The Charaka Samhita* (in 6 volumes). Translated by a board of scholars. Jamnagar, India: Sri Gulabkunverba Ayurvedic Society, 1949.

Gupta, Sanjukta. *Lakshmi Tantra.* Leiden, The Netherlands: E. J. Brill, 1972.

Gupta, Sanjukta with Dirk Hoens and Teun Goudriaan. *Hindu Tantrism.* Leiden, The Netherlands: E. J. Brill, 1979.

Gupta, Sankar Sen. *Tree Symbol Worship in India: A New Survey of a Pattern of Folk-Religion.* Calcutta: Indian Publications, 1965.

Gupta, Shakti M. *Love of Hindu Gods and Sages.* Bombay: Allied Publishers, 1973.

Gurdjieff, George. *Meetings With Remarkable Men.* London: Routledge and Kegan, 1963.

Gurdijieff, George. *All and Everything.* New York: E. P. Dutton, 1969.

Gurumaraja, Rao B. K. *The Megalithic Culture in South India.* Mysore, India: Prasaranga, 1972.

Gyatso, Geshe Kelsang. *Clear Light of Bliss.* London: Wisdom Publication, 1982.

Gyatso, Geshe Kelsang. *Guide to Dakini Land: A Commentary to the Highest Yoga Tantra Practice of Vajrayogini.* London: Tharpa Publications, 1991.

Haich, Elisabeth. *Sexual Energy and Yoga.* New York: Aurora Press, 1982.

Hall, Manly. *The Secret Teachings of All Ages.* Los Angeles: 1973.

Harding, Elizabeth. *Kali: The Black Goddess of Dakshineshwar.* York Beach, Maine: Nicolas-Hays, 1993.

Harding, M. Esther. *The Way of All Women: A Psychological Interpretation.* New York: G. P. Putnam's Sons, 1970.

Harding, M. Esther. *Woman's Mysteries: Ancient and Modern.* New York: Harper and Row, 1976.

Harner, Michael J. *Hallucinogens and Shamanism.* London: Oxford University Press, 1973.

Harris, M. *Cows and Pigs, Wars and Witches: The Riddles of Culture.* London: Hutchinson, 1975.

Harrison, Michael. *The Roots of Witchcraft.* Secaucus, New Jersey: Citadel Press, 1974.

Harshe, R. G., translator and ed. *Satkarmasangraha.* Delhi, India: Yoga-Mamsa Praksana, 1970.

Hartsuker, D. *Sadhus: India's Mystic Holy Men.* Rochester, Vermont: Inner Traditions, 1993.

Hawkes, Jacquetta and Sir Leonard Woolley. *Prehistory and the Beginnings of Civilization.* New York: Harper and Row, 1963.

Hawkes, Jacquetta. *The World of the Past.* New York: Knopf, 1963.

Heilbrun, Carolyn G. *Toward a Recognition of Androgyny.* New York: Knopf, 1973.

Heinberg, Richard. *Memories and Visions of Paradise.* Los Angeles: Jeremy P. Tarcher, 1989.

Hindoo Kama Shastra Society, translators. *The Kama Sutra of Vatsyayana.* Benares, India: Kama Shastra Press, 1925.

Hixon, Lex. *Great Swan: Meetings With Ramakrishna.* Boston: Shambhala, 1993.

Hixon, Lex. *Mother of the Buddhas: Meditation on the Prajnaparamita Sutra.* Foreword by Robert Thurman. Wheaton, Illinois: Quest Books, 1993.

Hixon, Lex. *Mother of the Universe: Visions of the Goddess and Tantric Hymns of Enlightenment.* Wheaton, Illinois: Quest Books, 1994.

Hoffman, Helmut. *The Religions of Tibet.* London: George Allen and Unwin, 1961.

Hollingshead, Michael. *The Man Who Turned on the World.* London: Blond and Briggs, 1973.

Hopkins, Jeffrey. *Kalachakra Tantra Rite of Initiation.* Boston: Wisdom Publications, 1982.

Huet, Michel. *The Dance, Art and Ritual of Africa.* New York: Pantheon Books, 1978.

Hunt, Morton M. *The Natural History of Love.* New York: Knopf, 1959.

Huntington, Ellsworth. *Mainsprings of Civilization.* New York: Mentor, 1952.

Huxley, Francis. *The Way of the Sacred.* London: Aldus Books, 1974.

Hyatt, Christopher S. *Secrets of Western Tantra: The Sexuality of the Middle Path.* Las Vegas: Falcon Press/Golden Dawn Publications, 1989.

Idowu, Bolaji. E. *Olódùmarè: God in Yoruba Belief.* New York: A and B Books, 1994.

Isherwood, Christopher. *My Guru and His Disciple.* New York: Noonday Press/Farrar, Straus and Giroux, 1980.

Iverson, Jeffrey. *More Lives Than One?* London: Pan Books, 1976.

Jackson, John G. *Man, God and Civilization.* New York: Citadel Press/Carol Publishing Group, 1972.

Jacobs, Hans. *Western Psychotherapy and Hindu Sadhana.* London: George Allen and Unwin, 1961.

Jacobsen, Thorkild. *The Treasures of Darkness: A History of the Mesopotamian Religion.* New Haven: Yale University Press, 1976.

Jacobus, Dr. *Anthropology of the Sexual and Social Life of Strange Peoples of Four Continents.* New York: Falstaff Press, 1937.

Jacolliot, L. *Occult Science in India and Among the Ancients.* New York: University Press Books, 1971.

Jaggi, O. P. *Yogic and Tantric Medicine.* Delhi, India: Atma Ram and Sons, 1973.

Jattabhusan, Pandit Hemchandra. *Kamaratna Tantra.* Shillong, India: Assam Government Press, 1928.

Jayakar, Pupul. *The Earth Mother.* Foreword by Stella Kramrisch. New Delhi, India: Penguin Books, 1980.

Jhavery, Mohanlal. *Comparative and Critical Study of Mantrasastra.* Ahmedabad, India: Sarabhai Manilal Nawab, 1944.

John, Bubba Free. *Love of the Two-Armed Form.* Clearlake, California: The Dawn Horse Press, 1978.

Johnson, Buffie. *Lady of the Beasts: Ancient Images of the Goddess and Her Sacred Animals.* San Francisco: HarperCollins, 1990.

Johnson, R. and K. Moran. *The Sacred Mountain of Tibet: On Pilgrimage to Kailas.* Rochester, Vermont: Park Street Press, 1989.

Jonas, Hans. *The Gnostic Religion.* Boston: Beacon Press, 1963.

Jung, Carl G. *Psychology and Alchemy.* Princeton, New Jersey: Princeton University Press, 1953.

Jung, Carl G. *Psychology and Religion: West and East.* Princeton, New Jersey: Princeton University Press, 1958.

Jung, Carl G. *The Archetypes and the Collective Unconscious.* Princeton, New Jersey: Princeton University Press, 1959.

Jung, Carl G. *Psychological Reflections.* Selected by Jolande Jacobi. London: Routledge and Kegan Paul, 1971.

Jung, Carl G. *Man and His Symbols.* New York: Dell, 1964.

Jung, Emma. *Animus and Anima.* Zurich: Spring Publications, 1972.

Jwala. *Sacred Sex: Ecstastic Techniques for Empowering Relationships.* Ukiah: Inner Juice, 1993.

Jyotirmayananda and Lilian K. Donat. *Meditate the Tantric Yoga Way.* London: George Allen and Unwin, 1973.

Kakar, Sudhir. *Shamans Mystics and Doctors.* Chicago: The University of Chicago Press, 1982.

Kakati, Bani. *The Mother Goddess Kamakhya.* Gauhati; Assam, India: Lawyer's Books, 1967.

Kale, Arvind and Shanta. *Tantra: The Secret Power of Sex.* Bombay: Jaico Publishing, 1976.

Kannan, S. *Swara Chintamani: Divination by Breath.* Madras, India: Kannan Publications, 1967.

Karambelkar, V. W. *The Atharva-Veda and Ayur-Veda.* Nagpur, India: Usha Karambelkar, 1961.

Karanjia, R. K. *Kundalini Yoga: Reversing the Sex Energy, the 21st Century Mandate.* New York: Kundalini Research Foundation, 1977.

Kaviraj, Gopinath. *Aspects of Indian Thought.* Calcutta: University of Burdwan, 1966.

Kerényi, C. *Eleusis: Archetypal Image of Mother and Daughter.* New York: Schocken Books, 1977.

Khanna, Madhu. *Yantra: The Tantric Symbol of Cosmic Unity*. London: Thames and Hudson, 1979.

Khanna, Madhu and Ajit Mookerjee. *The Tantric Way*. London: Thames and Hudson, 1977.

Kiefer, Otto. *Sexual Life in Ancient Rome*. New York: Barnes and Noble, 1952.

Kieffer, Gene, ed. *Kundalini for the New Age: Selected Writings of Gopi Krishna*. London: Bantam Books, 1988.

King, Francis. *Sexuality, Magic and Perversion*. Secaucus, New Jersey: Citadel Press, 1974.

King, Francis. *The Western Tradition of Magic*. London: Thames and Hudson, 1975.

King, Francis. *Tantra: The Way of Action: A Practical Guide to Its Teachings and Techniques*. Rochester, Vermont: Destiny Books, 1990.

Kinsley, David. *The Sword and the Flute: Kali and Krishna, Dark Visions of the Terrible and the Sublime in Hindu Mythology*. Berkeley: University of California Press, 1975.

Kinsley, David. *The Goddess' Mirror: Visions of the Divine from East and West*. Ithaca: State University of New York, 1994.

Klein, Anne Carolyn. *Meeting the Great Bliss Queen: Buddhists, Feminists, and the Art of the Self*. Boston: Beacon Press, 1995.

Knight, Richard Payne. *A Discourse on the Worship of Priapus*. New York: University Books, 1974.

Koltuv, Barbara Black. *The Book of Lilith*. York Beach: Nicolas-Hays, 1986.

Kramer, Samuel Noah. *From the Tablets of Sumer*. Indian Hills: The Falcon's Wing Press, 1956.

Kramer, Samuel Noah. *The Sumerians: Their History, Culture and Character*. Chicago: The University of Chicago Press, 1963.

Kramer, Samuel Noah. *In the World of Sumer*. Detroit: Wayne State University Press, 1986.

Kramrisch, Stella. *Manifestations of Shiva*. Philadelphia: Museum of Art, 1981.

Kramrisch, Stella. *The Presence of Shiva*. Princeton, New Jersey: Princeton University Press, 1981.

Krishna, Gopi. *An Appeal to World Leaders Scientist and Scholars*. New York: NC Press, 1971.

Krishna, Gopi. *Kundalini: The Evolutionary Energy in Man*. London: Shambhala, 1971.

Krishna, Gopi. *Kundalini: Path to Higher Consciousness*. New Delhi, India: Orient Paperbacks, 1976.

Krishna, Gopi. *The Dawn of a New Science*. New Delhi, India: Kundalini Research and Publication Trust, 1978.

Krishna, Gopi. *Secrets of Kundalini in Panchastavi*. New Delhi, India: Kundalini Research and Publication Trust, 1978.

Krishna, Gopi. *The Secrets of Yoga*. Northamptonshire, England: Turnstone Press, 1981.

Krishnamurti, Y. G. and Chandrakanta Sharma. *Samudrika: The Hindu Art of Sex and Body Sign Predictions.* Delhi, India: 1971.

Kronhausen, Phyllis and Eberhard. *Erotic Art: A Survey of Erotic Fact and Fancy in the Fine Arts.* London: W. H. Allen, 1971.

Kunsang, Erik Pema, translator. *Dakini Teachings: Padmasambhava's Oral Instructions to Lady Tsogyal.* Boston: Shambhala, 1990.

Kuriansky, Dr. Judy. *Generation Sex: America's Hottest Sex Therapist Answers the Hottest Questions about Sex.* New York: HarperCollins, 1995.

Kuvalayananda, S. and Dr. S. A. Shukla. *Goraksashatakam.* With introduction, text, English translation. Bombay: Lonavla Publications, 1969.

Kvaerne, Per. *An Anthology of Buddhist Tantric Songs: A Study of the Caryagiti.* Bangkok: White Orchid Press, 1966.

Ladas, Alice Kahn, Beverly Whipple, and John D. Perry. *The G Spot and Other Recent Discoveries about Human Sexuality.* New York: Holt, Rinehart and Wisdom, 1982.

Laing, Lloyd and Jennifer. *Art of the Celts.* London: Thames and Hudson, 1992.

Lal, Kanwar. *Erotic Sculpture of India.* New York: Criterion Books, 1959.

Lal, Kanwar. *The Cult of Desire: An Interpretation of Erotic Sculpture of India.* New York: University Books, 1967.

Lal, Kanwar. *Erotic Sculpture of Khajuraho.* Delhi, India: Asia Press, 1970.

Lal, Kanwar. *Kanya and the Yogi.* Delhi, India: Arts and Letters, 1970.

Lal, Lakshmi. *Shiva: Eye of the Storm.* Bombay: IBH Publishers, 1992.

Lalita. *Choose Your Own Mantra.* New York: Bantam Books, 1978.

Latham, Ronald, translator. *Marco Polo: The Travels.* Harmondsworth, England: Penguin Books, 1958.

Law, B. Churn. *An Introduction to Buddhist Esoterism.* Varanasi, India: Chowkhamba Sanskrit Series, 1964.

Lawlor, Robert. *Voices of the First Day: Awakening in the Aboriginal Dreamtime.* Rochester, Vermont: Inner Traditions, 1991.

Lawson, E. Thomas. *Religions of Africa.* San Francisco: HarperCollins Publishers, 1985.

Leadbeater, C. W. *The Chakras.* London: 1972.

Leakey, Richard E. *Origins: What New Discoveries Reveal About Emergence of Our Species and Its Possible Future.* New York: E. P. Dutton, 1977.

Lee, Martin and Bruce Shlain. *Acid Dreams: The Complete Social History of LSD: The CIA, the Sixties, and Beyond.* New York: Grove Weidenfeld, 1985.

Leeson, Francis. *Kama Shilpa.* Bombay: Taraporevala, 1962.

Leigh, M. R. and Henry, L. *Holy Blood and Holy Grail.* London: Corgi Books, 1982.

Leroi-Gourhan, André. *The Hunters of Prehistory.* New York: Atheneum, 1989.

Lessing, Ferdinand D. and Alex Wayman. *Fundamentals of the Buddhist Tantras.* The Hague: Mouton, 1968.

Lessing, Ferdinand D. and Alex Wayman. *Introduction to the Buddhist Tantric Systems.* Delhi, India: Motilal Banarsidass, 1993.

Lewinsohn, Richard. *A History of Sexual Customs*. New York: Harper and Bros., 1958.

Lhalungpa, Lobsang, P. *The Life of Milarepa*. Boston: Shambhala, 1985.

Licht, Hans. *Sexual Life in Ancient Greece*. London: The Abbey Library, 1932.

Lilly, John. *The Human Biocomputer*. London: Abacus, 1974.

Lipski, Alexander. *Life and Teachings of Sri Anandamayi Ma*. Delhi, India: Motilal Banarsidass, 1977.

Lloyd, Seton. *The Art of the Ancient Near East*. New York: Frederick A. Praeger, 1961.

Longworth, T. Clifton. *The Worship of Love: A Study of Nature Worship throughout the World*. London: Torchstream Books, 1954.

Mackay, Ernest. *Early Indus Civilization*. New Delhi, India: Indological Book Corporation, 1976.

Mahadevan, T. M. P. *Ten Saints of India*. New Delhi, India: N. M. Kothari, 1961.

Majumdari, R. C. and A. D. Pusalker. *The Vedic Age: The History and Culture of the Indian People*. London: George Allen and Unwin, 1951.

Majupurias, T. C. and Indra. *Erotic Themes of Nepal*. Kathmandu, India: Craftsman/Devi, 1986.

Majupurias, T. C. and Indra. *Glories of Khajuraho*. Lashkar, India: Gupta/Craftsman, 1990.

Malandra, William W. *An Introduction to Ancient Iranian Religion*. Minneapolis: University of Minnesota Press, 1983.

Malinowski, Bronislav. *The Sexual Life of Savages: In North-Western Melanesia*. London: George Routledge and Sons, 1932.

Malinowski, Bronislav. *Sex, Culture and Myth*. London: Hart-Davis, 1963.

Malla, Kalayana. *Ananga Ranga Stage of the Bodiless One: The Hindu Art of Love*. New York: Medical Press of New York, 1964.

Mandel, Gabriele and Franco-Maria Ricci. *Tantra: Rites of Love*. New York: Rizzoli, 1979.

Mannering, Douglas. *The Art of the Kama Sutra*. New York: Shooting Star Press, 1994.

Mantegazza, Paolo. *Sexual Relations of Mankind*. Translated by Samuel Putnam. New York: Eugenics Publishing, 1935.

Marcade, Jean. *Eros Kalos: An Essay on Erotic Elements in Greek Art*. Geneva: Nagel, 1961.

Marcade, Jean. *Roma Armor: An Essay on Erotic Elements in Roman Art*. Geneva: Nagel, 1961.

Marr, G. S. *Sex in Religion: A Historical Survey*. London: George Allen and Unwin, 1963.

Marschack, Alexander. *The Roots of Civilization: The Cognitive Beginnings of Man's First Art, Symbol and Notation*. New York: McGraw-Hill, 1972.

Marwick, Max, ed. *Witchcraft and Sorcery*. London: Penguin Books, 1982.

Mason, John. *Four New World Yoruba Rituals*. Brooklyn: Yoruba Theological Archministry, 1985.

Massey, Gerald. *A Book of the Beginnings*. London: Williams and Norgate, 1881.

Massey, Gerald. *The Natural Genesis*. London: Williams and Norgate, 1883.

Masters, William and Virginia Johnson. *Human Sexual Response*. Boston: Little, Brown, 1966.

Masters, William, Virginia Johnson, and Robert Kolodny. *Masters and Johnson on Sex and Human Loving*. Boston: Little, Brown, 1986.

Mathers, E. P. *Eastern Love*. London: 1927.

Matory, J. Lorand. *Sex and the Empire That Is No More*. Minneapolis: University of Minnesota Press, 1944.

Matus, Thomas. *The Christian Use of Yoga: A Theoretical Study Based on a Comparison of the Mystical Experiences of Symeon the New Theologian and Some Tantric Sources*. Doctoral dissertation. New York: Fordham University, 1977.

May, Rollo. *Love and Will*. London: W. W. Norton and Company, 1969.

McGill, Ormond. *The Mysticism and Magic of India*. New York: A. S. Barnes, 1977.

McKenna, Terence. *The Archaic Revival: Speculations on Psychedelic Mushrooms, the Amazon, Virtual Reality, etc.* New York: Harper Collins, 1992.

McKenna, Terence. *Food of the Gods: The Search for the Original Tree of Knowledge*. New York: Bantam Doubleday Dell, 1993.

Mead. G. R. S. *Pistis Sophia*. London: John Watkins, 1921.

Mead, Margaret. *Coming of Age in Samoa*. New York: William Morrow, 1928.

Mead, Margaret. *From the South Seas: Studies of Adolescence and Sex in Primitive Societies*. New York: William Morrow, 1930.

Mead, Margaret. *Sex and Temperament in Three Primitive Societies*. New York: William Morrow, 1935.

Mead, Margaret. *Male and Female: A Study of Comparing Sexes in a Changing World*. New York: William Morrow, 1949.

Mehta, R. J. *Konarak: The Sun Temple of Love*. Bombay: 1971.

Mellaart, James. *Earliest Civilizations of the Near East*. London: Thames and Hudson, 1965.

Mellaart, James. *Catal Hüyük*. London: Thames and Hudson, 1967.

Mercer, Samuel A. B. *The Religion of Ancient Egypt*. London: Luzac and Co., 1949.

Meyer, Johan Jakob. *Sexual Life in Ancient India*. Delhi, India: Motilal Banarsidass, 1971.

Miller, Barbara S. *Exploring India's Sacred Art: Selected Writings of Stella Kramrisch*. Philadelphia: University of Pennsylvania Press, 1983.

Millet, Kate. *Sexual Politics*. New York, Doubleday, 1970.

Mishlove, Jeffrey. *The Roots of Consciousness: Psychic Liberation through History, Science and Experience*. New York: Random House, 1975.

Mishra, Rammurti. *Fundamentals of Yoga*. New York: Doubleday, 1974.

Mitter, Partha. *Much Maligned Monsters: History of European Reactions to Indian Art*. Oxford: Clarendon Press, 1977.

Moffett, Robert. *Tantric Sex*. New York: Berkley Medalion, 1974.

Mookerjee, Ajit. *Tantra Art: Its Philosophy and Physics.* New Delhi, India: Ravi Kumar, 1966.

Mookerjee, Ajit. *Tantra Asana: A Way to Self-Realization.* New Delhi, Ravi Kumar, 1971.

Mookerjee, Ajit. *Yoga Art.* London: Thames and Hudson, 1975.

Mookerjee, Ajit. *Kundalini: The Arousal of the Inner Energy.* New York: Destiny Books, 1982.

Mookerjee, Ajit. *Kali The Feminine Force.* London: Thames and Hudson, 1988.

Mookerjee, Ajit and Mulk Raj Anand. *Tantra Magic.* New Delhi, India: Arnold Heineman Publishers, 1977.

Mookerjee, Ajit and Madhu Khanna. *The Tantric Way: Art, Science, Ritual.* London: Thames and Hudson, 1977.

Morgenthaler, John and Dan Joy. *Better Sex Through Chemistry.* Petaluma, California: Smart Publications, 1994.

Moscati, Sabatino. *Ancient Semitic Civilizations.* London: Elek Books, 1957.

Mukherji, B. *Rasajalanidhi: An Indian Alchemy* (in 3 volumes). Benares, India: 1938.

Mukhopadhyaya, B. *Rasajalanidhi: The Ocean of Indian Chemistry and Alchemy* (in 5 volumes). Calcutta, 1926–28.

Mulin, G. H. and M. Richards, eds. *Meditation on the Lower Tantras.* Dharamsala, India: Library of Tibetan Works and Archives, 1983.

Muller-Ortega, Paul E. *The Triadic Heart of Shiva: Kaula Tantricism of Abhinavagupta in the Non-Dual Shaivism of Kashmir.* Albany: State University of New York Press, 1989.

Mumford, John. *Ecstasy through Tantra.* St. Paul, Minnesota: Llewellyn Publications, 1990.

Murchie, Guy. *The Seven Mysteries of Life: An Exploration in Science and Philosophy.* Boston: Houghton Mifflin, 1978.

Murphy, Paul E. *Triadic Mysticism: The Mystical Theology of the Shaivism of Kashmir.* Delhi, India: Motilal Banarsidass, 1986.

Murray, Margaret. *The Witch Cult in Western Europe.* London: Oxford University Press, 1921.

Murthy, Dr. C. S. *Sri Lalita Sahasranaman.* Madras, India: Ganesh and Co., 1962.

Muses, Charles A., ed. *Esoteric Teachings of the Tibetan Tantra.* London: Luzac and Co., 1961.

Nahum, Pinhas. D. *The Turkish Art of Love.* New York: The Panurge Press.

Narayanananda, Swami. *The Kundalini Shakti.* Rishikesh, India: 1950.

Nash, Elizabeth. *Plaisirs d'Amour: An Erotic Guide to the Senses.* San Francisco: HarperCollins, 1995.

Natarajan, B., translator. *Thirumandiram: A Classic of Yoga and Tantra* (in 3 volumes). Edited by M. Govindan. Montreal: Babaji's Kriya Yoga Publications, 1993.

Nath. R. G. *The Yogis of Bengal.* Calcultta: Mani Bhusan, 1909.

Natha, P. and Arthur Avalon. *Kama-Kala-Vilasa.* Madras, India: Ganesh and Co., 1961.

Nathan, Leonard, translator. *The Transport of Love.* Los Angeles: University of California Press, 1976.

Nathan, Leonard and Clinton Seely, translators. *Grace and Mercy in Her Wild Hair: Selected Poems to the Mother Goddess by Ramprasad Sen.* Boulder, Colorado: Great Eastern, 1982.

Nebesky-Wojkowitz, René de. *Oracles and Demons of Tibet: The Cult and Iconography of the Tibetan Protective Deities.* Introduction by Per Kvaerne. Graz, Austria: Akademische Druck, 1975.

Neimark, John P. *The Way of Orisa.* San Francisco: HarperSanFrancisco, 1993.

Neumann, Erich. *The Origins and History of Consciousness.* New York: Pantheon, 1954.

Neumann, Erich. *The Great Mother: An Analysis of the Archetype.* New York: Pantheon, 1955.

Newall, V. *The Encyclopedia of Witchcraft and Magic.* New York: Dial Press, 1974.

Nias, David and Glenn Wilson. *Love's Mysteries: The Secrets of Sexual Attraction.* London: Fontana Books, 1977.

Nikhilananda, Swami. *The Gospel of Sri Ramakrishna.* With a foreword by Aldous Huxley. New York: Ramakrishna/Vivekananda Center, 1942.

Nivedita, Sister. *Kali: The Mother.* Calcutta: Advaita Ashram, 1985.

O'Flaherty, Wendy Doniger. *Siva: The Erotic Ascetic.* Oxford University Press, London, 1973.

O'Flaherty, Wendy Doniger. *Asceticism and Eroticism in the Mythology of Shiva.* Delhi, India: Oxford University Press, 1975.

O'Flaherty, Wendy Doniger. *The Origin of Evil in Hindu Mythology.* Los Angeles: University of California, 1976.

O'Flaherty, Wendy Doniger. *Women, Androgynes and Other Mythical Beasts.* Chicago: University of Chicago Press, 1982.

Oates, Joan. *Babylon.* London: Thames and Hudson, 1979.

Obeyeskere, G. *Medusa's Hair, An Essay on Personal Symbols and Religious Experience.* Chicago: University of Chicago Press, 1981.

Ochs, Carol. *Behind the Sex of God.* Boston: Beacon Press, 1977.

Odier, Daniel. *Sculptures Tantriques du Népal.* Monaco: Editions du Rocher, 1970.

Olson, Carl, ed. *The Book of the Goddess: Past and Present.* New York: Crossroad, 1989.

Olson, Eleanor. *Tantric Buddhist Art.* New York: China House Gallery, 1974.

Oman, John Campbell. *The Mystics, Ascetics and Saints of India: A Study of Sadhuism, with an Account of the Yogis, Sanyasis, Bairagias, and Other Strange Hindu Sectarians.* London: Fisher Unwin, 1905.

Orage, A. R. *On Love: With Some Aphorisms and Other Essays.* London: The Janus Press, 1966.

Ornstein, R. E. *The Psychology of Consciousness.* New York: Viking Press, 1972.

Ouspensky, P. D. *A New Model of the Universe.* London: Routledge and Kegan Paul, 1931.

Ouspensky, P. D. *The Fourth Way: Based on the Teaching of G. I. Gurdjieff.* London: Routledge and Kegan Paul, 1957.

Ouspensky, P. D. *Tertium Organum: A Key to the Enigmas of the World.* London: Routledge and Kegan, 1965.

Ovid. *The Art of Love.* Translated by Rolfe Humphries. Bloomington: Indiana University Press, 1957.

Pagels, Elaine. *The Gnostic Gospels.* New York: Random House Vintage Books, 1979.

Pandit, M. P. *Thoughts of a Shakta.* Madras, India: Ganesh and Co., 1965.

Pandit, M. P. *Sri Aurobindo on The Tantra.* Pondicherry: Dipti Publications, 1967.

Pandit, M. P. *Kundalini Yoga.* Madras, India: Ganesh and Co., 1968.

Pandit, M. P. *Gems from the Tantras.* Madras, India: Ganesh and Co., 1969.

Paris, Ginette. *Pagan Meditations.* Dallas: Spring Publications, 1986.

Parrinder, Geoffrey. *Sex in the World's Religions.* New York: Oxford University Press, 1980.

Pathak, V. S. *History of Saiva Cults in Northern India.* Varanasi, India: Ram N. Varma, 1960.

Pauwels, L. and J. Bergier. *The Dawn of Magic.* London: Anthony Gibbs and Philips, 1963.

Pauwels, L. and J. Bergier. *Eternal Man.* Herts, England: Mayflower Books, 1974.

Payne, E. *The Shaktas: An Introduction and Comparative Study.* Calcutta: 1933.

Persuitte, David. *Joseph Smith and the Origins of the Book of Mormon.* Jefferson: McFarlane and Co., 1985.

Phillipson, D. W. *The Later Prehistory of Eastern and Southern Africa.* New York: Africana Publishing, 1977.

Piggott, Stuart. *Ancient Europe: From the Beginnings of Agriculture to Classical Antiquity: A Survey.* Chicago: Aldine Publishing, 1966.

Piggott, Stuart. *The Druids.* London: Thames and Hudson, 1989.

Possehl, Gregory L., ed. *Harappan Civilization: A Contemporary Perspective.* Warminster, England: Aris and Phillips, 1982.

Pott, Dr. P. H. *Yoga and Yantra: Their Interpretation and Their Significance for Indian Archeology.* The Hague: Martinus Nijhoff, 1966.

Pranavananda, Swami. *Exploration in Tibet.* Calcutta: University of Calcutta, 1950.

Pratyagatmananda, Swami. *Japasutram.* Madras, India: Ganesh and Co., 1961.

Pratyagatmananda, Swami. *The Metaphysics of Physics.* Madras, India: Ganesh and Co., 1964.

Pratyagatmananda, Swami. *Science and Sadhana.* Calcultta: Sri K. P. Maitra, 1966.

Pritchard, James B. *The Ancient Near East.* Princeton, New Jersey: Princeton University Press, 1958.

Priyanka, Benille and Anura Manatunga. *Studies in the Decipherment of the Harappan Script and Harappan Seals.* Colombo, Sri Lanka: Archaedocumentation Publishers, 1988.

Puharich, Andrija. *The Sacred Mushroom.* London: Victor Gollancz, 1959.

Puharich, Andrija. *Beyond Telepathy.* London: Dayton Longman and Todd, 1962.

Puharich, Andrija. *The Iceland Papers: Select Papers on Experimental and Theoretical Research on the Physics of Consciousness.* Ossining, N.Y.: Essentia Research Associates, 1979.

Qualls-Corbett, Nancy. *The Sacred Prostitute: Eternal Aspect of the Feminine.* Toronto: Inner City Books, 1988.

Rachewiltz, Boris de. *Eros Noir: Moeurs Sexuelles de L'Afrique de la Prehistoire à Nos Jours.* Milan: La Jeune Parque, 1963.

Raftery, Barry. *Pagan Celtic Ireland: The Enigma of the Irish Iron Age.* London: Thames and Hudson, 1994.

Raghavan, V. *Yantras or Mechanical Contrivances in Ancient India.* Bangalore, India: The Indian Institute of Culture, 1956.

Raglian, L. *The Temple and the House.* London: Routledge and Kegan Paul, 1964.

Rai, A. K. *Kundalini the Goddess.* Calcutta: 1908.

Rajneesh, Bhagwan (Osho). *Vigyan Bhairav Tantra: A Treatise to the Beyond.* Boulder, Colorado: Chidvilas, 1992.

Rajneesh, Bhagwan (Osho). *Tantra: The Supreme Understanding.* Boulder, Colorado: Chidvilas, 1993.

Rambach, P. *The Art of Japanese Tantrism.* Geneva: Edison A. S., 1979.

Ramsdale, David Alan and Ellen Jo Dorfman. *Sexual Energy Ecstasy: A Guide to the Ultimate Sexual Experience.* Playa Del Rey: Peak Skill Publishing, 1985.

Rao, Krishna M. V. N. *Indus Script Deciphered.* Delhi, India: Agam Kala Prakashan, 1982.

Raphael, A. *Goethe and the Philosophers Stone.* London: Routledge and Kegan Paul, 1965.

Rastogi, Navjivan. *The Krama Tantricism of Kashmir.* Delhi, India: Motilal Banarsidass, 1979.

Ravenscroft, Trevor. *The Spear of Destiny.* New York: Bantam Books, 1974.

Rawson, Philip. *Erotic Art of the East: The Sexual Theme in Oriental Painting and Sculpture.* New York: Prometheus Press, 1968.

Rawson, Philip. Introduction. *Tantra.* London: Arts Council of Great Britain, 1971.

Rawson, Philip. *Primitive Erotic Art.* New York: G. P. Putnam's Sons, 1973.

Rawson, Philip. *Tantra: The Indian Cult of Ecstasy.* London: Thames and Hudson, 1973.

Rawson, Philip. *The Art of Tantra.* London: Thames and Hudson, 1973.

Rawson, Philip. *Erotic Art of India.* London: Thames and Hudson, 1977.

Ray, Prafulla C. *History of Chemistry in Ancient and Medieval India.* Calcutta: Indian Chemical Society, 1956.

Ray, Tridibnath, translator. *Ananga Ranga of Kalyanamalla* (from the Sanskrit). Calcutta: 1944.

Reade, Julian. *Mesopotamia.* Cambridge: Harvard University Press, 1991.

Reden, V. C. *The Realm of the Great Goddess.* Englewood Cliffs, New Jersey: Prentice-Hall, 1962.

Reich, Ilse Ollendorff. *Wilhelm Reich: A Personal Biography.* New York: Avon/Discus Books, 1970.

Reich, Wilhelm. *The Function of the Orgasm: Sex-Economic Problems of Biological Energy.* Translated by Theodore Wolfe. London: Panther, 1968.

Reich, Wilhelm. *The Invasion of Compulsory Sex-Morality.* New York: Farrar, Straus and Giroux, 1971.

Reich, Wilhelm. *Ether, God and Devil/Cosmic Superimposition.* New York: Farrar, Straus and Giroux, 1973.

Reid, Daniel. *The Tao of Health, Sex and Longevity.* London: Simon & Schuster, 1989.

Rele, Vasant G. *Mysterious Kundalini.* Bombay: Taraporevala, 1927.

Rendel, Peter. *Introduction to the Chakras.* Wellingborough, England: The Aquarian Press, 1977.

Ricci, F. Maria and Gabriel Mandel. *Tantra Rites of Love.* New York: Rizzoli, 1979.

Rinpoche, Dudjom and Matthew Kapstein. *The Nyingma School of Tibetan Buddhism: Its Fundamentals and History* (in 2 volumes). Boston: Wisdom Publications, 1991.

Rivière, Jean Marquès. *Tantrik Yoga.* Wellingborough, England: The Aquarian Press, 1970.

Rivière, Jean Marquès. *Rituel de Magie Tantrique Hindoue: Yantra Chintamani.* Milan: Archè, 1976.

Rivlin, Robert and Karen Gravelle. *Deciphering the Senses.* New York: Simon & Schuster, 1984.

Roaf, Michael. *Cultural Atlas of Mesopotamia and the Ancient Near East.* New York: Equinox/Facts on File, 1990.

Robbins, Tom. *The Archaic Revival.* San Francisco: Harper, 1991.

Robie, W. F. *The Art of Love.* New York: The Eugenics Publishing Co., 1926

Ross, Anne and Don Robins. *The Life and Death of a Druid Prince.* New York: Simon & Schuster, 1989.

Roux, Georges. *Ancient Iraq.* Cleveland: World Publishing, 1964.

Roy, A. T. *Nervous System of the Ancient Hindus.* Hazaribagh, India: 1930.

Roy, Mira and B. V. Subbarayappa. *Rasarnavakalpa.* Delhi, India: Indian National Science Academy, 1976.

Rudrananda, (Rudi) Swami. *Spiritual Cannibalism.* New York: The Overlook Press, 1978.

Rudrappa, J. *Kashmir Shaivism.* Prasaranga, India: University of Mysore, 1969.

Runes, Dagobert. *Pictorial History of Philosophy.* New York: Philosophical Library, 1959.

Rustonji, N. *Verrier Elwin Philanthropologist Selected Writings.* Calcutta: North-Eastern Hill University Publications, 1989.

Ryder, Arthur W., translator. *The Panchatantra*. Calcutta: Jaico Publishing House, 1949.

Saggs, H. W. F. *The Greatness That Was Babylon*. London: Sidgwick and Jackson, 1988.

Saggs, H. W. F. *Civilizations before Greece and Rome*. New Haven, Connecticut: Yale University Press, 1989.

Sakthi, Sri. K. *Serpent Power*. Bangalore, India: Y. Subbaraya Sharma, 1971.

Saksena, S. K. *The Nature of Consciousness in Hindu Philosophy*. Benares, India: Chowkhamba, 1969.

Samdup, Lama Kazi Dawa. *Chakrasambhara Tantra*. Translation of selected chapters. London: Luzac and Co., 1910.

Sankalia, H. D. *Prehistoric Art in India*. Durham, North Carolina: Carolina Academic Press, 1978.

Sankarananda, Swami. *The Dictionary of Indian Hieroglyphs*. Calcutta: Abhedananda Academy of Culture, 1963.

Saradananda, Swami. *Sri Ramakrishna: The Great Master* (in 2 volumes). Mylapore, India: Sri Ramakrishna Math, 1991.

Saraswathi, Swami Ramanananda. *Tripura Rahasya or The Mystery Beyond the Trinity*. Tiruvannamalai: T. R. Venkataraman, 1980.

Saraswati, Swami Janakananda. *Yoga, Tantra and Meditation in Everyday Life*. London: Rider Books, 1975.

Saraswati, Swami Pratyagatmananda. *The Metaphysics of Physics: The Background of Modern Cosmological Conception in Vedic and Tantric Symbolism*. Madras, India: Ganesh and Co., 1964.

Saraswati, Swami Pratyagatmananda. *The Fundamental Unity of Human Races and Culture*. Garia, India: Saraswat Ashram, 1978.

Saraswati, Swami Pratyagatmananda and Sir John Woodroffe. *Sadhana for Self Realization*. Madras, India: Ganesh and Co., 1963.

Saraswati, Sunyata and Bodhi Avinasha. *Jewel in the Lotus: The Sexual Path to Higher Consciousness*. San Francisco: Kriya Jyoti Tantra Society, 1987.

Savramis, Demosthenes. *The Satanizing of Woman*. New York: Doubleday, 1974.

Schmidt, Toni. *The Eighty-Five Siddhas*. Stockholm: Stat Etnografiska Museum, 1958.

Scholem, Gershom G. *Zohar, The Book of Splendor, Basic Reading from the Kabbalah*. New York: Schocken, 1963.

Schroeder, L. and S. Ostrander. *Handbook of PSI Discoveries*. London: Sheila Ostrander, 1974.

Schultes, Richard E. *Hallucinogenic Plants*. New York: Golden Press.

Scott, George Ryley. *Far Eastern Sex Life*. London: Swan, 1949.

Scott, George Ryley. *Curious Customs of Sex and Marriage*. New York: Key Publishing, 1960.

Seligmann, Kurt. *The History of Magic*. New York: Pantheon Books, 1948.

Senet, André. *Man in Search of His Ancestors*. New York: McGraw-Hill, 1956.

Serrano, Miguel and F. MacShane, translator. *C. G. Jung and Hermann Hesse: A Record of Two Friendships*, New York: Schoken Books, 1970.

Seth, K. Nath. *Gods and Goddesses of India*. New Delhi, India: Diamond Pocket Books, 1990.

Seznec, J. *The Survival of the Pagan Gods*. New York: Pantheon, 1953.

Shah, Idries. *Oriental Magic*. London: Rider and Co., 1956.

Shankaranarayanan, S. *Glory of the Divine Mother Devi Mahatmyan*. Madras, India: Ganesh and Co., 1968.

Sharma. L. N. *Kashmir Shaivism*. Benares, India: Bharatiya Vidya, 1972.

Sharma, Pandit Shiv. *Yoga and Sex*. Bombay: B. I. Publications, 1973.

Sharma, Pushpendra Kumar. *Shakti Cult in Ancient India*. Varanasi, India: Bhartiya Publishing, 1974.

Sharma, Y. S. *Sri Kundalini Shakti: Serpent Power*. Bangalore, India: 1971.

Sharpe, Elizabeth. *The Secrets of the Kaula Circle: A Tale of Fictitious People Faithfully Recounting Strange Rites Still Practiced by this Cult*, together with *The Science of Breath* (a Hindu Tantric text translated). London: Luzac and Co., 1936.

Shastri, H. Prasad, translator. *The Avadhut Gita*. London: Shanti Sadan, 1989.

Shaw, Miranda. *Passionate Enlightenment: Women in Tantric Buddhism*. Princeton, New Jersey: Princeton University Press, 1994.

Sherfey, Mary-Jane. *The Nature and Evolution of Human Sexuality*. New York: Random House, 1972.

Shivananda, Swami. *Kundalini Yoga*. Sivanandanagar, India, 1968.

Short, Martin. *Inside the Brotherhood: Further Secrets of the Freemasons*. London: Harper-Collins, 1993.

Shukla, S. A. *The Goraksashatakam*. Translated from the Sanskrit. Bombay: Lonavla Publications, 1969.

Sierksma, Fokke. *Tibet's Terrifying Deities: Sex and Aggression in Religious Acculturation*. Vermont: Charles E. Tuttle, 1966.

Silburn, Lilian. *Kundalini, the Energy of the Depths*. Albany: State University of New York Press, 1988.

Simons, S. and M. D. Bial. *The Rabbi's Bible*. Behrman House, London, 1966.

Singer, Irving. *The Goals of Human Sexuality*. London: Wildwood House, 1973.

Singer, June. *Androgyny: Toward a New Theory of Sexuality*. New York: Anchor Press/Doubleday, 1976.

Singh, Lalan Prasad. *Tantra: Its Mystic and Scientific Basis*. New Delhi: India: Concept Publishing, 1976.

Sinha, A. K. *Science and Tantra Yoga*. Kurukshetra, India: Vishal Publications, 1981.

Sinha, India. *The Great Book of Tantra: Translations and Images from the Classic Indian Texts with Commentary*. Rochester, Vermont: Destiny Books, 1993.

Sinha, Jadunath. *Sakta Monism: The Cult of Shakti*. Calcutta: Sinha Publishing, 1966.

Sircar, D. C. *The Sakta Pithas*. Delhi, India: Indological Publishers and Booksellers, 1973.

Sircar, D. C. *The Sakti Cult and Tara*. Calcutta: University of Calcutta, 1967.

Skinner, B. F. *Walden Two*. New York: Macmillan, 1962.

Slater, Philip E. *The Glory of Hera: Greek Mythology and the Greek Family*. Boston: Beacon Press, 1968.

Smith, Anthony. *The Body*. New York: Walker and Company, 1968.

Smith, John Jr. *The Book of Mormon*. Salt Lake City, Utah: The Church of Christ of Latter-Day Saints, 1961.

Smith, Margaret, translator. *Readings from the Mystics of Islam*. London: Luzac and Co., 1972.

Snellgrove, David L. *The Hevajra Tantra: A Critical Study* (in 2 volumes). Translated from the Tibetan, with commentary. London: Oxford University Press, 1959.

Sobramania, S. V. and V. R. Madhavan. *Heritage of the Siddha Medicine*. Madras, India: Institute of Tamil Studies, 1983.

Sovatsky, Stuart. *Passions of Innocence: Tantric Celibacy and the Mysteries of Eros*. Rochester, Vermont: Inner Traditions, 1995.

Sperling, Harry and Maurice Simon, translator. *The Zohar* (in 5 volumes). London: The Secino Press, 1956.

Spink, M. Walter. *The Axis of Eros*. New York: Penguin Books, 1975.

Stablein, William. *The Mahakala Tantra: A Theory of Ritual Blessings and Tantric Medicine*. Doctoral dissertation. New York: Columbia University, 1976.

Stablein, William. *Mahakala the Neo-shaman: Master of the Ritual*. London: Hitchcock and Jones, 1976.

Stanton, Elizabeth. *The Original Feminist Attack on the Bible*. New York: Arno Press, 1974.

Starck, Marcia and Gynne Stern. *The Dark Goddess: Dancing with the Shadow*. Freedom, California: The Crossing Press, 1993.

Stein, Stephen J. *The Shaker Experience in America*. New Haven, Connecticut: Yale University Press, 1992.

Steiner, Rudolf. *Occult Science: An Outline*. London: Rudolf Steiner Press, 1962.

Stern, Bernnard. *The Scented Garden: Anthropology of Sex Life in the Levant*. New York: American Ethnological Press, 1934.

Stevens, Jay. *Storming Heaven: LSD and the American Dream*. London: Paladin/Grafton Books, 1989.

Stevens, John. *Lust for Enlightenment: Buddhism and Sex*. Boston: Shambhala, 1990.

Stone, Alexander. Lee. *The Power of a Symbol*. Chicago: Pascal Covici, 1925.

Stone, Merlin. *When God Was a Woman*. New York: Dial Press, 1976.

Stubbs, Kenneth Ray. *Women of the Light: The New Sacred Prostitute*. New York: Secret Garden Publishing, 1994.

Subramania, Aiyar A. V. *The Poetry and Philosophy of the Tamil Siddhars.* Tirunelveli, India: 1957.

Surieu, R. *An Essay on Love and the Representation of Erotic Themes in Ancient Iran.* Geneva: Nagel Publishers, 1967.

Suryanarayanamurthy, Dr. Chaganty. *Sri Lalita Sahasraranamam.* Madras, India: Ganesh and Co., 1962.

Svoboda, Robert E. *Aghora I: At the Left Hand of God.* Albuquerque: Brotherhood of Life, 1986.

Svoboda, Robert E. *Aghora II: Kundalini.* Albuquerque: Brotherhood of Life, 1993.

Szekely, Edmond Bordeaux. *The Essene Gospel of Peace.* San Diego: Academy of Creative Living, 1971.

Szekely, Edmond Bordeaux. *The Gospel of the Essenes.* London: C. W. Daniel, 1976.

Talese, Gay. *Thy Neighbor's Wife.* New York: Doubleday, 1980.

Tannahill, Reay. *Sex in History.* New York: Stein and Day, 1982.

Taranatha, Lama and B. Datta, translator. *Mystic Tales of Lama Taranatha.* Calcutta: Ramakrishna Vedanta Math, 1957.

Tart, C. T. *Altered States of Consciousness.* New York: John Wily and Son, 1969.

Tattabhusan, P. H., ed. *Kamaratna Tantra.* Gauhati, Assam, India: Government Press, 1928.

Taylor, G. Rattray. *Sex in History: The Story of Society's Changing Attitudes to Sex throughout the Ages.* New York: The Vanguard Press, 1954.

Tennant, F. R. *The Sources of the Doctrines of the Fall and Original Sin.* New York: Schocken, 1968.

Teubal, J. S. *The Lost Tradition of the Matriarchs.* New York: HarperCollins, 1990.

Thielicke, Helmut. *The Ethics of Sex.* Translated by John Doberstein. New York: Harper and Row, 1964.

Thirleby, Ashley. *Tantra: The Key to Sexual Power and Pleasure.* New York: Dell, 1978.

Thomas, P. *Kama Kalpa or The Hindu Ritual of Love.* Bombay: Taraporevala, 1959.

Thompson, H. and F. L. Griffith. *The Leyden Papyrus, An Egyptian Magical Book.* New York: Dover Publications, 1974.

Thorsten, Geraldine. *God Herself: The Feminine Roots of Astrology.* New York: Avon Books, 1981.

Thorwald, Jurgen. *Science and Secrets of Early Medicine.* Translated by Richard and Clara Winston. New York: Harcourt, Brace and World, 1962.

Trungpa, Chögyam. *Born in Tibet.* London: George Allen and Unwin, 1966.

Trungpa, Chögyam. *Meditation in Action.* Berkeley, California: Shambala, 1970.

Trungpa, Chögyam. *Mudra.* London: Shambala, 1972.

Trungpa, Chögyam, translator. *The Rain of Wisdom.* London: Shambala, 1980.

Tsogyal, Yeshe and Kenneth Douglas, translator. *The Life and Liberation of Padmasambhava.* Emeryville, California: Dharma Publishing, 1978.

Tucci, Guiseppe. *Rati Lila: An Interpretation of the Tantric Imagery of the Temples of Nepal.* Geneva: Nagel, 1969.

Ulanov, Ann Belford. *The Feminine in Jungian Psychology and in Christian Theology.* Evanston, Illinois: Northwestern University Press, 1971.

Unwin, J. D. *Sex and Culture.* London: Oxford University Press, 1934.

van Dam, E. *The Magic Life of Milarepa.* Boston: Shambala, 1991.

van Gulik, R. H. *Sexual Life in Ancient China: A Preliminary Survey of Chinese Sex and Society from 1500 BC to 1644 AD.* Leiden, The Netherlands: E. J. Brill, 1974.

van Kooij, K. R. *Worship of the Goddess According to the Kalikapurana.* Leiden, The Netherlands: E. J. Brill, 1972.

van Sertima, Ivan. *Egypt Revisited.* New Brunswick, Canada: Transaction Publishers, 1989.

van Sertima, Ivan. *Egypt: Child of Africa.* New Brunswick, Canada: Transaction Publishers, 1994.

Vasu, R. B. S. C., translator. *The Siva Samhita.* New Delhi, India: Munshiram Manoharlal, 1975.

Vasu, Sris C., translator. *The Gheranda Samhita.* London: Theosophical Publishing House, 1985.

Velan, A. S. *Siddhar's Science of Longevity and Kalpa Medicine of India.* Madras, India: Sakthi Nilayam, 1963.

Vetter, George B. *Magic and Religion.* New York: Philosophical Library, 1973.

Vira, Raghu and Shodo Taki. *A Dictionary of the Secret Tantric Syllabic Code: Daksinamurti Uddarakosa.* Lahore: 1938.

Vira, Raghu and Lokesh Chandra, eds. *Kálacakra—Tantra and Other Texts* (in 2 volumes). New Delhi, India: International Academy of Indian Culture, 1966.

Volin, Michael and Nancy Phelan. *Sex and Yoga.* London: 1967.

Volkman, G. *Thoreau on Man and Nature.* New York: Peter Pauper Press, 1960.

von Cles-Reden, Sibylle. *The Realm of the Great Goddess: The Story of the Megalith Builders.* Englewood Cliffs, New Jersey: Prentice-Hall, 1962.

Waddell, L. A. *Phoenician Origin of Britons, Scots and Anglo-Saxons.* London: Williams and Norgate, 1924.

Waddell, L. A. *The Makers of Civilization in Race and History.* London: Luzac and Co., 1929.

Waddell, L. A. *The British Edda.* London: Chapman and Hall, 1930.

Waite, Arthur Edward. *The Book of Ceremonial Magic.* New York: Bell, 1969.

Waldemar, Charles. *The Mystery of Sex.* Translated by Laura and Andrew Tilburg. New York: Lyle Stuart, 1960.

Walker, Barbara G. *The Woman's Encyclopedia of Myths and Secrets.* San Francisco: Harper, 1983.

Walker, Benjamin. *Sex and the Supernatural.* London: Macdonald, 1970.

Walker, K. *A Study of Gurdjieff's Teaching.* London: Jonathan Cape, 1957.

Wall, O. A. *Sex and Sex Worship (Phallic Worship)*. St. Louis: C. V. Mosby, 1922.

Wallace, Irving, Amy Irving, Sylvia Irving, and David Wallechinsky. *The Intimate Sex Lives of Famous People*. New York: Delacorte Press, 1981.

Warren, Frank Z. *Sexual Acupuncture*. New York: E. P. Dutton, 1978.

Wasson, R. Gordon, Carl A. P. Ruck, and Albert Hofmann. *The Road to Eleusis: Unveiling the Secret of the Mysteries*. New York: Harcourt Brace Jovanovich, 1978.

Wasson, R. Gordon. *The Wondrous Mushroom: Mycolatry in Mesopotamia*. New York: McGraw-Hill, 1980.

Wasson, R. Gordon. *Soma Divine Mushroom of Immortality*. New York: Harcourt Brace Jovanovich, 1973.

Watson, Lyall. *Supernature*. London: Hodder and Stoughton, 1973.

Watts, Alan. *Nature, Man and Woman: A New Approach to Sexual Experience*. London: Thames and Hudson, 1958.

Watts, Alan. *In My Own Way: An Autobiography*. New York: Random House Vintage Books, 1973.

Watts, Alan and Eliot Elisofon. *Erotic Spirituality: The Vision of Konarak*. New York: Collier Books, 1971.

Wayman, Alex. *The Buddhist Tantras: Light in Indo-Tibetan Esotericism*. London: Routledge and Kegan Paul, 1973.

Wayman, Alex. *Yoga of the Guhyasamaja Tantra*. Delhi, India: Motilal Banarsidass, 1977.

Wayman, Alex and Ferdinand Lessing. *Mkhas Drub Rje's Fundamentals of the Buddhist Tantra*. Paris: Mouton, 1968.

Wenke, Robert J. *Patterns in Prehistory: Humankind's First Three Million Years*. New York: Oxford University Press, 1984.

Westermarck, E. A. *The History of Human Marriage*. London: Macmillan, 1891.

Weyer, E. *Primitive Peoples Today*. London: Hamish Hamilton, 1959.

Wheatley, Dennis. *The Devil and All His Works*. New York: Hutchinson, 1971.

Wheeler, Sir Mortimer. *The Indus Civilization*. London: Book Club Associates, 1976.

White, John, ed. *Kundalini: Evolution and Enlightenment*. New York: Paragon Books, 1979.

Wickler, Wolfgang. *The Sexual Code: The Social Behavior of Animals and Men*. Translated by Francisca Garvie. New York: Doubleday Anchor, 1973.

Wilhelm, Richard, translator. *The Secret of the Golden Flower: A Chinese Book of Life*. New York: Harcourt Brace Jovanovich, 1965.

Wilson, Colin. *Rasputin and the Fall of the Romanovs*. London: Panther, 1964.

Wilson, Colin. *Sex Diary of a Metaphysician*. Berkeley: Ronin Publishing, 1988.

Wilson, Colin. *The Misfits: A Study of Sexual Outsiders*. London: Grafton Books, 1989.

Wilson, Colin. *Mysterious Powers, Spirits and Spirit Worlds*. London: Aldus Books, 1995.

Wilson, Edmund. *The Dead Sea Scrolls 1947–1969*. London: Collins, 1969.

Wilson, Robert Anton. *Cosmic Trigger: The Final Secret of the Illuminati.* New York: Pocket Books, 1977.

Wilson, Robert Anton. *Sex and Drugs.* Phoenix: Falcon Press, 1987.

Winternitz, M. *Notes on the Guhyasamaja Tantra and the Age of the Tantras.* Calcutta: IHQ, 1933.

Wolkenstein, Diane and Samuel Noah Kramer. *Innana: Queen of Heaven and Earth.* San Francisco: Harper and Row, 1983.

Wood, Clive. *Human Fertility: Threat and Promise.* New York: Funk and Wagnalls, 1966.

Woodroffe, Sir John. *The Garland of Letters (Vanamala).* Manipa, India: Manipa Power Press, 1922.

Woodroffe, Sir John. *Shakti and Shakta.* Madras, India: Ganesh and Co., 1929.

Woodroffe, Sir John. *The Serpent Power.* Madras, India: Ganesh and Co., 1931.

Woodroffe, Sir John. *Kamakalavilasa* (in English translation). Madras, India: Ganesh and Co., 1953.

Woodroffe, Sir John. *Introduction to Tantra Shastra.* Madras, India: Ganesh and Co., 1956.

Woodroffe, Sir John. *The World as Power.* Madras, India: Ganesh and Co., 1966.

Woodroffe, Sir John. *Hymns to the Goddess.* Madras, India: Ganesh and Co., 1973.

Woodroffe, Sir John and Muchyopahdyaya. *Mahamaya, the World as Power, Power as Consciousness.* Madras, India: Ganesh and Co., 1964.

Woolley, Sir Leonard. *Excavations at Ur.* New York: Thomas Y. Cromwell, 1965.

Yogananda, Swami. *Autobiography of A Yogi.* Los Angeles: Fellowship, 1946.

Young, Michael, ed. *Malinowski Among the Magi: The Natives of Mailu.* London: Routledge, 1988.

Young, Serinity, ed. *An Anthology of Sacred Texts By and About Women.* New York: Crossroad, 1993.

Young, Wayland. *Eros Denied: Sex in Western Society.* New York: Grove Press, 1964.

Zimmer, Heinrich. *Myths and Symbols in Indian Art and Civilization.* Edited by Joseph Campbell. New York: Bollingen Series/Pantheon/Random House, 1946.

Zvelebil, Kamil V. *The Poets of the Powers.* London: Rider and Co., 1973.

A Tibetan woodblock print depicting the "treasury charm" of the Cosmic
Father/Mother, with magical power phrases all around.